GENESIS:

Yesterday's Answers to Today's Problems

BRIAN YOUNG

ISBN 1-928765-01-7

Library of Congress Catalog Card Number: 99-70638

Any questions or comments may be directed to:

BRIAN YOUNG - CIA
Box 304
Plentywood, MT 59254

Other resources available through CIA:

For a free newsletter, *From the Beginning*, write to the address shown above. Also, CIA has many videos and books available that deal directly with the creation / evolution debate. For a more dynamic approach, contact Brian Young to speak personally at conferences, local churches, or for seminars today.

Printed by Maverick Publications
P.O. Box 5007 • Bend, Oregon 97708

GENESIS

INTRODUCTION

The author of Genesis is clearly God Himself as He inspired men to write His Words down (2 Timothy 3:16). Many commentators believe that Moses was the inspired author but used other inspired records that Adam and others had left behind. This is supported by the ten neatly divided accounts listed throughout the chapters. Each one begins by saying, "This is the account or written account of . . .." The word "account" in Hebrew is *towledah* and means "record of origins or family" and, therefore, may allude to historical records which Moses used. The first five accounts trace God's salvation for the people of the Flood era; the last five for the patriarchs. The accounts are as follows:

1. The account of heaven and earth - 2:4-4:26
2. The account of Adam - 5:1-6:8 (supported in Luke 3:36-38)
3. The account of Noah - 6:9-9:29
4. The account of the sons of Noah - 10:1-11:9
5. The account of Shem - 11:10-11:26
6. The account of Terah - 11:27-25:11 (longest)
7. The account of Ishmael - 25:12-25:18 (shortest)
8. The account of Isaac 25:19-25:34
9. The account of Esau - 36:1-37:1
10. The account of Jacob - 37:2-50:26

No other book is quoted more often then Genesis, especially in the New Testament times. Every New Testament author quotes it at least once, with Jesus Himself quoting it many times. Over 165 verses from Genesis are quoted in the New Testament, some being quoted more than once. Including verses alluded to, the total is over 200. Over 100 of these quotes are found in the first eleven chapters of Genesis substantiating their foundational importance. Jesus quotes from these eleven chapters at least six times.

It is very important to recognize the historical accuracy of this book and not view it as an allegory. This would mean Jesus himself mislead us in quoting it so often as true history. Archaeology supports that writing was around long before Moses and the above "accounts" support this as well. Therefore, there is no such thing as "prehistoric" because history was written down right from the beginning. In fact, the word Genesis means "origins." Genesis is a written record of our origins; the origin of sin, death, and many other doctrines of Christianity. In Matthew, Jesus is questioned about divorce by the Pharisees. Jesus answers them by referring them back to the origin of marriage in Genesis by stating, "Haven't you read, that at the beginning the Creator 'made them male and female,' and said, 'For this reason a man will leave his father and mother and be united to his wife, and the two will become one flesh'? So they are no longer two, but one. Therefore what God has joined together, let man not separate"

(Mat 19:4-6). Jesus gives historical accuracy to Adam and Eve and marriage. Christ said the two become one flesh. Wow! What does that mean for our marriages today? There is no "self" in a marriage because we are ONE. We shouldn't live together before marriage either because there is a spiritual meaning to marriage. Today many have the attitude that if we live and sleep together we are still two individuals. NO, you are ONE when the flesh is united in sexual relations. What does this say about divorce? Are you one after you divorce or a half? I don't want to undermine Christ's forgiveness, because you can be restored, but initially you are not one. This still doesn't make divorce right either. God hates divorce because, "what God has joined together, let man not separate." This is just one of many examples where the doctrines of Genesis apply so vividly to our lives today.

There are many connections to the books of Revelation and Genesis. People often read from Genesis to Jude, skipping Revelation. This is so unfortunate because to properly understand either, we need to see them in light of each other. The following are a few examples of these connections:

1. Division of light in Genesis (1:4) and no darkness in Revelation (21:25)
2. Division of land and sea in Genesis (1:10) and no sea in Revelation (21:1)
3. Sun and moon created in Genesis (1:16) but neither in Revelation (21:23)
4. The curse on man in Genesis (3:17) is lifted in Revelation (22:3)
5. Thorns in Genesis (3:18) but none in Revelation (21:4)
6. Garden is prepared for man in Genesis (2:8) but a city in Revelation (21:2)
7. River flows from tree of life in garden (2:10) from throne and tree in Revelation (22:1)
8. Gold in garden in Genesis (2:12) and city in Revelation (21:21)
9. Precious stones in garden (2:12) and in city (21:19)
10. God walks with man (Gen 3:8; Rev 21:3)
11. Man eats no meat in Genesis (3:18) and in Revelation (22:2)
12. Death begins in Genesis (3:19) but ends in Revelation (21:4)
13. Evil in Genesis (6:5) but none in Revelation (21:27)
14. Savior is promised in Genesis (3:15) and fulfilled completely in Revelation (5:9-10)
15. Man kept from tree of life in Genesis (3:24) but will have access in Revelation (22:14)
16. Satan free in Genesis (3:15) but destroyed in Revelation (20:10)
17. Man wears coats of skin in Genesis (3:21) but later robes of righteousness in Revelation (19:14)

Gen 1:1 In the beginning God created the heavens and the earth.

It has been said that this may be one of the most important verses for setting the proper foundation in Scripture. If people could only accept this verse, all the "isms" in the world have no ground to stand on. It refutes Atheism because God does exist as Creator and, therefore, evolutionism is also a fraud. The existence of only one God shows Polytheism false. In contrast to humanism, God is the ultimate reality. The list goes on and on, but the point is, God as Creator refutes so many false philosophies in existence today.

The word "God" is *"elohiym"* in Hebrew and is the plural form of a singular word showing God's triune existence. This is the first time it is used but will be seen over 2,000 times in the rest of the Bible.

The word for created is *"bara"* and is used specifically for God's creations. We will make this distinction as we continue through Genesis, but for now suffice it to say that man can only make things out of what God has already created.

Gen 1:2 Now the earth was formless and empty, darkness was over the surface of the deep, and the Spirit of God was hovering over the waters.

Here we see three problems that need to be solved. The earth is 1) formless, 2) empty, 3) dark. Each of these will be systematically solved as the creation days continue. What formless and empty are we cannot know, as it is beyond our realm of understanding. Just as the color green cannot be described to a man who has been blind from birth, eternity and formlessness are beyond our experiences and, therefore, unimaginable. How can water fit into a formless and empty world? Again, we cannot understand. All we know is that this is a Creation *ex nihilo,* or "Creation from nothing." Even an evolutionist must struggle with such thoughts, as one must accept by faith either eternal matter or eternal God.

There are other passages regarding this formless state. Proverbs shows that Christ was present in the world even before the earth took shape: "When there were no oceans, I was given birth, when there were no springs abounding with water; before the mountains were settled in place, before the hills, I was given birth, before He made the earth or its fields or any of the dust of the world. I was there when He set the heavens in place, when He marked out the horizon on the face of the deep" (Prov 8:24-27).

The Spirit of God shows the third person in the Trinity being present at Creation. Here He is "hovering" over the waters. The Hebrew word is *"rachaph"* and is only used three times in Scripture - Jer 23:9; Deut 32:11; Gen 1:2. The true meaning is to flutter or move back and forth. Therefore, the Spirit of God is fluttering over the waters. This back and forth movement shows an energizing quality bringing motion into a static and formless environment. There is one more passage which gives further insight into this "hovering" characteristic of the Spirit. The Greek equivalent of *"rachaph"* is *"phero"* and is used in 2 Peter 1:21 to show the Holy Spirit's energizing effect on believers. Therefore, the same energizing Spirit which brought energy to the world brings a Spirit led life to us.

Gen 1:3 And God said, "Let there be light," and there was light.

Here we find the second person of the Trinity, Christ Himself. Where? God said! Jesus is the Word of God and the Light of the world. We read in John, *"In the beginning* was the Word, and the Word was *with* God, and the

Word was God. He was with God in the beginning. *Through Him* all things were made; without Him nothing was made that has been made. In Him was life, and that life was the *light* of men. The *light* shines in the darkness, but the darkness has not understood it" (John 1:1-5). Another passage speaks of Christ as not only Creator from the beginning but also Sustainer: "He is the image of the invisible God, the *firstborn* over all creation. For by Him all things were created: things in heaven and on earth, visible and invisible, whether thrones or powers or rulers or authorities; *all things* were created by Him and for Him. He is before all things, and in Him all things *hold together*" (Col 1:15-17). In Hebrews it is written, "but in these last days He has *spoken* to us *by* His Son, whom he appointed heir of all things, and *through whom* He made the universe. The Son is the radiance of God's glory and the exact representation of His being, *sustaining* all things by His powerful word" (Heb 1:2-3). Therefore, we see all three parts of the Trinity in the first three verses of Genesis. Verse one shows the Father as the source of all things, verse two shows the Spirit as the Energizer of all things and verse three shows Christ (The Word) as Revealer and Sustainer of all things.

It is also important to note that we now have light. This solves one of the three problems mentioned in verse two, the problem of darkness. The question is, what is this light, because the sun has not been made and won't be for another three days? Some Christians try to make each day of creation vast time periods in order to account for millions of years needed for evolutionary philosophies, but if the sun isn't made until day four, how do plants get sunlight etc.? Clearly these days are 24 hours each. This light is Christ Himself. As we read earlier, "In Him was life, and that life was the *Light* of men. The *Light* shines in the darkness, but the darkness has not understood It" (John 1:5). Similarly, we read regarding the new city to come, "The city does not need the sun or the moon to shine on it, for the glory of God gives it light, and *the Lamb is its lamp*" (Rev 21:23). If Christ is the Word of God then Psalms says, "Your word is a lamp to my feet and a light for my path" (Psa 119:105).

Gen 1:4 God saw that the light was good, and he separated the light from the darkness. 1:5 God called the light "day," and the darkness he called "night." And there was evening, and there was morning--the first day.

Here God separated light from darkness. Why? Certainly part of the reason was to distinguish a 24 hour day (v. 5), but I think there may be more to this. To take this "light" a step further, 2 Corinthians 6:14 states, "What fellowship can light have with darkness?" This light may also symbolize truth, the opponent of evil. Note that the light was good but nothing is said of darkness. If the light is not the sun but the Son, then what is the darkness? Absence of Christ? If so, that is not good. Job refers to the morning light as instrumental in ridding the evils of darkness: "Have you ever given orders to the morning, or shown the dawn its place, that it might take the earth by the edges and shake the wicked out of it?" (Job 38:12-13). The light brings forth good, but darkness brings forth evil.

6

Furthering this line of thought, a man once told me that sin entered the world before Adam sinned and, therefore, evolution with its death and disease prior to man could be true because death was not a result of sin. First of all this false philosophy makes God a liar in passages such as Romans 6:23; 5:12; and 1 Corinthians 15:21, where death was clearly the punishment for sin. His reasoning for this belief was that Satan had already fallen before Adam or Eve had, as indicated by his tempting with the fruit. This is true, but Satan was not told "do not eat, or else." Further, Satan's fall is dealt with separately and differently than man's fall. Satan is to be crushed (Gen 3:15), while man was to simply die and have troubles and hardships. Also, man's sin was curable by Christ's death and he has heaven awaiting as a result. Satan, however, is doomed to everlasting torment and destruction, with no chance of salvation ever (Rev 20:10). Man was created for different purposes than angels and, therefore, man's sin had different consequences than the fall of angels. Now to the point at hand. Could the darkness represent the side of Satan's fall. . . or evil? The timeline suggests that it is possible that Satan had fallen by this time. We know that angels were created before the third day because Job says, "Where were you when I laid the earth's foundation? Tell me, if you understand. Who marked off its dimensions? Surely you know! Who stretched a measuring line across it? On what were its footings set, or who laid its cornerstone-- while the morning stars sang together and all the angels shouted for joy?" (Job 38:4-7). The angels were in existence and shouted for joy when the foundation of the earth was laid. Therefore, perhaps they were created here on the first day to be "ministering spirits sent to serve those who will inherit salvation" (Hebrews 1:14). If this is true, Satan and 1/3 of the angels may have fallen almost immediately after their creation; thus darkness being separated from light. This can only be a hypothetical conclusion, as Scripture is not clear on this, but it does seem plausible. One other possibility is that Satan fell sometime after the sixth day before man fell into sin. The Bible does not say how long after Adam and Eve were in the garden that they fell into sin (I'm sure it wasn't long). One possible argument against this idea is that the tree of the knowledge of good and evil may have been put in the garden along with the vegetation on day three of creation and, therefore, knowledge of evil was present. Either way, day one concluded with the first night.

Gen 1:6 And God said, "Let there be an expanse between the waters to separate water from water." 1:7 So God made the expanse and separated the water under the expanse from the water above it. And it was so. 1:8 God called the expanse "sky." And there was evening, and there was morning--the second day.

Now comes the separation of water to begin solving the problem of formlessness in verse two. Water was separated from water on a vertical scale and the "expanse" was what resulted. This expanse is sometimes translated as "firmament," but the Hebrew is "*raqiya*." There are many different ideas as to what this firmament was, but the Bible only says one thing; it was water above. We also know that it was commonly accepted that there were three heavens.

Isaiah writes, "The stars of heaven (*shamayim*) and their constellations will not show their light. The rising sun will be darkened and the moon will not give its light" (Isa 13:10). Yet *shamayim* appears in 419 other verses. Using another word, Ezekiel noted, "Spread out above the heads of the living creatures was what looked like an expanse (*raqiya*), sparkling like ice, and awesome" (Ezek 1:22). *Raqiya* is only found in 16 other verses, one of which uses both *raqiya* and *shamayim*: "A psalm of David. The heavens (*shamayim*) declare the glory of God; the skies (*raqiya*) proclaim the work of his hands" (Psa 19:1). Finally, in Matthew and in 281 other places, "Blessed are those who are persecuted because of righteousness, for theirs is the kingdom of heaven (*ouranos*)" (Mat 5:10). *Ouranos* clearly seems to be God's eternal kingdom and is not the "expanse." Though in some cases *raqiya* and *shamayim* are used interchangeably, sometimes they are differentiated, as in Psa 19:1, and, therefore, many scholars believe there are two other heavens (3 total).

The Jews believed there were three heavens: sky or cloud filled area, star filled area, God's area. Consider the following: "I know a man in Christ who fourteen years ago was caught up to the *third* heaven (*ouranos*). Whether it was in the body or out of the body I do not know--God knows" (2 Cor 12:2); "But will God really dwell on earth? The heavens, even *the highest* heaven, cannot contain You. How much less this temple I have built!" (1 Kings 8:27).

More food for thought comes from Josephus, who wrote concerning this expanse or firmament, "on the second day, He placed the heaven over the whole world, and separated it from the other parts; and He determined it should stand by itself. He also placed a crystalline [firmament] round it, and put it together in a manner agreeable to the earth" (Antiquities of Josephus, 1(30) pg. 29). Not only does Josephus refer to heaven having separate parts, but also as crystalline. Some scholars say that *raqiya* means to spread out and flatten some type of metal or crystalline material. We saw in Ezekiel 1:22 that the expanse sparkled like ice. The question posed is, was the firmament water, ice, vapor, what? The answer is simply that we don't know. The important thing is that it was water in some state. Although, even being water above, there was no rain until the day of Noah's Flood. Genesis 2:5 tells us that instead of rain, artesian wells watered the whole earth.

It is also important to note that many scholars have pointed out that the firmament may have kept a tropical climate world-wide and provided for superior living conditions on earth. This would explain many questions as to how people lived 900 plus years prior to the Flood, how the fossil record shows such large animals like dragonflies with five foot wingspans and cockroaches a foot long. (For greater detail see the chapter on The Very Good Pre-Flood World in, Doubts About Creation? Not After This!).

Gen 1:9 And God said, "Let the water under the sky be gathered to one place, and let dry ground appear." And it was so. 1:10 God called the dry ground "land," and the gathered waters he called "seas." And God saw that it was good.

Continuing to solve the problem of formlessness, we now see a horizontal separation of the water left below the expanse. The water was gathered to ONE place and dry ground (singular) formed. This may give support for Pangea, the one super continent proposed by science. It is possible that at the time of Noah's Flood this Pangea was split into the continents we see today. The seas were probably not as salty as they are today, and at this point nothing lived in them until day five.

The presence of liquid water on earth is unique to all the planets. Why? Because without it life could not exist, because the temperature would be too high. Water absorbs great amounts of heat, allowing life to flourish. God created the world with us in mind.

Gen 1:11 Then God said, "Let the land produce vegetation: seed-bearing plants and trees on the land that bear fruit with seed in it, according to their various kinds." And it was so. 1:12 The land produced vegetation: plants bearing seed according to their kinds and trees bearing fruit with seed in it according to their kinds. And God saw that it was good. 1:13 And there was evening, and there was morning--the third day.

The problem of emptiness was taken care of when the land produced mature vegetation. Again we see evidence against millions of years and the long day theory that some use to try to fit science into the Bible, rather than fitting the Bible into science. As of yet the sun was not created, yet plants were abundant. If each day was a long period of time, these plants would die without the sun.

In addition, I believe the earth was created with the appearance of age. If one counted the rings on a tree (which is already bearing fruit in verse 12), it would probably have appeared many years old, even though it was just created. God created an earth fully functional from the beginning, with Adam walking and talking, trees that bore fruit, and rocks already formed.

Gen 1:14 And God said, "Let there be lights in the expanse of the sky to separate the day from the night, and let them serve as signs to mark seasons and days and years, 1:15 and let them be lights in the expanse of the sky to give light on the earth." And it was so. 1:16 God made two great lights--the greater light to govern the day and the lesser light to govern the night. He also made the stars. 1:17 God set them in the expanse of the sky to give light on the earth, 1:18 to govern the day and the night, and to separate light from darkness. And God saw that it was good. 1:19 And there was evening, and there was morning--the fourth day.

The sun was finally created, even though it is not called the sun, but rather a greater light. Today we are told that the sun is a star. I am not so sure of that. Verse 16 says He also made the stars, distinguishing between them and the sun. We also read, "The sun has one kind of splendor, the moon another and the stars another; and star differs from star in splendor" (1 Cor 15:41). If one inch represented one million miles the sun would be 93 inches away. By comparison, the nearest star (the best we can guess from science today) would be almost 400 miles away using the same one inch equals 1 million miles. When we know so little about the sun, I suspect we know almost nothing about the stars. What an awesome God we serve!

The role of these lights is to separate day from night, marking our 24 hour day. Also, they are to serve as signs and to mark seasons, days, and years. As far back as time, the sun and moon have been used to track days, months and years. Some still use them to know when the best time to plant would be, as well. Perhaps most important, however, are the "signs" that they serve. We must be careful not to go too far with this, as astrologers do. As always, the devil likes to take Scripture and twist it into something else. We are warned, "Do not learn the ways of the nations or be terrified by signs in the sky, though the nations are terrified by them" (Jer 10:2). On the other hand, the heavenly bodies have been, and will be, signs of important religious events. It was a star that resided over the baby Jesus in Bethlehem. Concerning the end, "there will be great earthquakes, famines and pestilences in various places, and fearful events and great signs from heaven" (Luke 21:11). Other signs of the end show that the moon will turn blood red, the sun will not give its light (Mat 24:29-30) and the stars will fall from the sky (Rev 6:13). See also Rev 13:13-14. Clearly the purposes of the sun, moon and stars have not been completed.

It is also important to see God's ultimate purpose with the sun, to make life possible for his special creation, mankind. If the sun were any closer or further, life would not be possible for our present physical bodies, as we would either burn up or freeze.

Gen 1:20 And God said, "Let the water teem with living creatures, and let birds fly above the earth across the expanse of the sky." 1:21 So God created the great creatures of the sea and every living and moving thing with which the water teems, according to their kinds, and every winged bird according to its kind. And God saw that it was good. 1:22 God blessed them and said, "Be fruitful and increase in number and fill the water in the seas, and let the birds increase on the earth." 1:23 And there was evening, and there was morning--the fifth day.

Now we see an important turn in the creation week. The formed land, air and water had to be filled with living creatures. There are two ways to divide the creation week. The first three days created foundational matter and the next three filled each of those creations, with day one corresponding with day four, day two with day five and day three with day six. The second division simply has the first four days being material matter while the next two focus on living things and the last being a day of rest. This corresponds with the four/three splits seen in the book of Revelation, where there is a different focus or message after the fourth seal, trumpet, bowl etc. (See commentary on Revelation for further detail).

Day 1- Light-   Day 4- (fills light) sun, moon, stars
Day 2- Firmament   Day 5- (fills firmament)
    Blue Sky-   Birds in sky
    Blue Water-   Fish in sea
Day 3- Land & Vegetation-   Day 6- (fills land) man & animals

OPTION TWO

Day 1- Light   Day 5- Living birds and fish
Day 2- Firmament   Day 6- Living man and animals
Day 3- Land and vegetation
Day 4- Heavenly bodies   (Day 5,6 have *nephesh*, or life)

In either case, these verses filled the firmament with living creatures. This was clearly the first time anything living had been created. Verse 21 shows God created (*bara*) life from nothing. As said earlier, man can only make things from what God has already created, and here something new is created. Life is new! God gave the animals a *nephesh,* which is also translated as "soul." Therefore animals do have souls (*nephesh*). Before one gets too excited, this does not put animals and humans on the same scale. First of all, God personally breathed man's *nephesh* into him by His Spirit. While we have a soul, we also have a spirit. In many cases these words are used interchangeably, but at times separated, as in Hebrews where we read, "For the word of God is living and active. Sharper than any double-edged sword, it penetrates even to dividing soul and spirit" (Heb 4:12). The importance of this will be discussed later, but for now take note that we were made in God's image, a trinity; body, soul and spirit. Animals on the other hand have only *nephesh* and body. Does that mean animals will go to heaven? Nobody knows, even Solomon: "Who knows if the spirit of man rises upward and if the spirit of the animal goes down into the earth?" (Eccl 3:21).

Another important word in these verses is *tanniyn* (v. 21) or as here, "great creatures." The same word appears over a dozen times in the rest of Scripture and is translated as "dragon." Therefore, God created great dragons, distinguished with the word "great" showing them to have been a special creation and setting them apart from the other animals of the sea. Many believe that some of these may have been the sea dwelling dinosaurs we find in the fossil record. Dinosaurs and dragons certainly bear the same descriptions. See also Job 40:15ff and Job 41, where dinosaurs or dragons are described in great detail.

Verse 22 tells of God's command for the birds and sea creatures to be fruitful and multiply. This seems to be a natural command for a new beginning. Compare this to His command immediately after Noah's Flood (Gen 9:1-7).

One final note to conclude this fifth day or 120th hour. According to evolution, marine animals evolved first, followed by plants and birds. Here in Genesis we see plants came first, while birds and sea creatures came at the same time, only a day later. Surely one cannot combine evolution with Scripture.

Gen 1:24 And God said, "Let the land produce living creatures according to their kinds: livestock, creatures that move along the ground, and wild animals, each according to its kind." And it was so. 1:25 God made the wild animals according to their kinds, the livestock according to their kinds, and all the creatures that move along the ground according to their kinds. And God saw that it was good.

Day six is filled the dry land that was created on day three with land animals of all kinds. Note in verse 25 that God "made" (*asaph*) the animals, he did not create (*bara*) them. God had already created the dirt (v.9) and *nephesh* (v.21) of which animals were made. He now simply used the materials already in existence. We see this pattern throughout the creation week. In verse six God said, "let there be" and it became. Then in verse seven it states, "so God made." The word "so" can imply that it was already done. Again in verse 14, God says "let there be lights" and in verse 16 God "made two great lights." Here also, verse 24 is "let there be" and in verse 25 they are made. We see that in chapter one God only created in verse one (heavens and earth), verse 21 (life or living creature) and verse 27 (man). This also shows a unique creation in man with God's image; something animals do not have.

Gen 1:26 Then God said, "Let us make man in our image, in our likeness, and let them rule over the fish of the sea and the birds of the air, over the livestock, over all the earth, and over all the creatures that move along the ground." 1:27 So God created man in his own image, in the image of God he created him; male and female he created them.

Note that man is first "made" (v.26) and then "created (v.27)." It is as if the physical body and the life (*nephesh*) which were already in existence, were made. Then something new was created in man. Many believe it was the personal Spirit of God that was put in man; hence God's image. As mentioned, we became a trinity of body, soul and spirit (*ruwach*). John writes, "God is spirit, and His worshipers must worship in spirit and in truth" (John 4:24). However, the *nephesh* (soul) is the life and the life is in the blood, as we read in Lev 17:11: "For the life of a creature is in the blood." (See also Gen 9:4). Therefore, when death comes the body and *nephesh* are gone, yet the spirit will live on. Many passages refer to both soul and spirit going to heaven; perhaps because the spirit gives new life to man's soul. In any case, man has been created with a special relationship and image that animals clearly do not have. Another interesting passage which shows God's making of our spirit reads, "This is the Word of the Lord. . .who forms the spirit of man within him" (Zech 12:1). One possible way to view the soul and spirit is that the soul is in relationship to God's creation and the spirit is in relationship to God as Creator.

The words "*our* image" (v. 26) also shows that God is a triune God of Father, Son and Holy Spirit.

Part of man's role is to rule over the other living creatures and the earth. This shows that we are not on the same level as animals and, therefore, should not treat the dolphins or any other animal like humans. That is not to say we should kill animals for no reason, but to kill an animal is not like killing a human being. We have dominion over plants, animals, and land. Certainly we are not equals, as the new age religion and even the courts may suggest.

Another special role is alluded to in making one male and one female. Of the animals, many couples were made, but of man, only one. This should cause a special relationship between man's union. We read in Mal 2:15, "Has not the LORD made them one? In flesh and spirit they are His. And why one? Because He was seeking godly offspring. So guard yourself in your spirit, and do not break faith with the wife of your youth."

Gen 1:28 God blessed them and said to them, "Be fruitful and increase in number; fill the earth and subdue it. Rule over the fish of the sea and the birds of the air and over every living creature that moves on the ground." 1:29 Then God said, "I give you every seed-bearing plant on the face of the whole earth and every tree that has fruit with seed in it. They will be yours for food. 1:30 And to all the beasts of the earth and all the birds of the air and all the creatures that move on the ground--everything that has the breath of life in it--I give every green plant for food." And it was so. 1:31 God saw all that he had made, and it was very good. And there was evening, and there was morning--the sixth day.

Again we see a special blessing given to man and the command to be fruitful and multiply, just as after the Flood (Gen 9:1-7). Today we are worried about overpopulating the earth and taking drastic (sinful) steps to assure this does not happen with aids such as sterilents, abortion etc. Besides the fact that all the world's population could fit into the state of Iowa, God has promised he would meet our needs. The real problem is not overpopulation, it is greed. Man won't spread out and move away from the cities for financial reasons. (See article on Population Crunch in Doubts About Creation? Not After This!) Also the command to subdue both animals and land was given, showing our hierarchical position in creation and opposing the pagan theories of evolution, which put us on the same scale.

Verses 29-30 show that both man and animals were created vegetarians. Even the ferocious T-rex would have eaten only plants. This all changes after Noah's Flood, however: "Everything that lives and moves will be food for you. Just as I gave you the green plants, I *now* give you everything" (Gen 9:3). Before the fall into sin, death was not in the world and, therefore, nothing living could die and be eaten. After the fall, however, some were used for sacrifices (Gen 4:4), as there was a distinction made between clean and unclean animals (Gen 7:2). Perhaps some of the violent men that were destroyed in the Flood also killed animals to eat. All we know is that permission was not granted to eat meat until after the Flood.

The new heaven and earth will also exhibit these first eating habits, as there will be no predators: "The wolf will live with the lamb, the leopard will lie down with the goat, the calf and the lion and the yearling together; and a little child will lead them. The cow will feed with the bear, their young will lie down together, and the lion will eat *straw* like the ox. The infant will play near the hole of the cobra, and the young child put his hand into the viper's nest" (Isa 11:6-8). We also read in Hosea, "In that day I will make a covenant for them with the beasts of the field and the birds of the air and the creatures that move along the ground. Bow and sword and battle I will abolish from the land, so that all may lie down in safety" (Hosea 2:18). Also in the New Jerusalem we see, "On each side of the river stood the tree of life, bearing twelve crops of fruit, yielding its fruit every month. And the leaves of the tree are for the healing of the nations" (Rev 22:2).

God looked at all He had made and it was VERY good. Except day two where nothing is said, all other days were just "good." The sixth day was set apart in this way perhaps because death and sin had not yet come into the world. The devil had *perhaps* fallen already, but his fall did not bring about death as did man's (Rom 5:12; 6:23).

Gen 2:1 Thus the heavens and the earth were completed in all their vast array. 2:2 By the seventh day God had finished the work he had been doing; so on the seventh day he rested from all his work. 2:3 And God blessed the seventh day and made it holy, because on it he rested from all the work of creating that he had done.

Chapter two would have been better started at verse four, but chapter breaks were not put into the Bible by man until the 13th century by the Archbishop of Canterbury, Stephen Langton.

All that is in the "vast array" of the universe has now been made, with the focus and climax being man. As mentioned in the comments for 1:4, support for extraterrestrial life has no foundation or purpose (not to mention illogical because of death and its curse).

It only took six days for everything in the universe to exist, not millions of years. Contrary to popular belief, there is much scientific evidence to support this quick creation. Radio-halos in granite suggest that this foundational rock formed within a hundredth of a second, backing the "Christian Big Bang" theory, "God said and bang it was." Much more evidence can be seen in, Doubts About Creation? Not After This!

Key words to these verses are "completed," "finished," "rested," and "had done." They are all past tense, showing God's creation was finished on day six. Some believe God is still creating, but these verses do not support that. God is certainly involved in sustaining and perhaps changing things that are now already in existence (therefore He is not still resting, either). As Solomon stated, "There is nothing new under the sun. Is there anything of which one can say, 'Look! This is something new'? It was here already, long ago; it was here before our time" (Eccl 1:9-10).

Verse three gives a special blessing for the Sabbath and is a good reminder for us all. We too should rest on the Sabbath and dedicate this day to our Lord, making it holy. Too often we use Sunday as another day of work to catch up on our busy lives. We must be careful not to make this a law issue (thou shalt rest on Sunday) but rather because God rested, we will too. Scientifically, a day of rest has been proven to be good for our bodies, and I know God knew this as well. Have you ever wondered why God took so long to create the world? Why six days? We find the answer in Exodus: "Remember the Sabbath day by keeping it holy. Six days you shall labor and do all your work, but the seventh day is a Sabbath to the LORD your God. On it you shall not do any work. . ... For in six days the LORD made the heavens and the earth, the sea, and all that is in them, but He rested on the seventh day. Therefore the LORD blessed the Sabbath day and made it holy" (Exo 20:8-11). Therefore, God made the creation week as a model for us to follow. Just as God worked six days and rested one, we too shall work six days and rest one. Isn't it interesting that ever since the creation of the world the institution of the "week" has never changed. It has always been seven days because God made it and man cannot change it. We read again in Exodus, "The Israelites are to observe the Sabbath, celebrating it for the generations to come as a lasting covenant. It will be a sign between me and the Israelites *forever*, for in six days the LORD made the heavens and the earth, and on the seventh day He abstained from work and rested" (Exo 31:16-17).

Gen 2:4 This is the account of the heavens and the earth when they were created.

Chapter two has often been used as evidence that the Bible contradicts itself because details differ from chapter one. As we continue you will see that this is not true, but rather the purpose or focus of chapter two is different from that of chapter one. Chapter two simply gives more information about the creation week, with its focus on the purpose of creation - man. As mentioned in the introduction, this is the beginning of the inspired account that Adam probably wrote and which Moses uses to compile Genesis.

When the LORD God made the earth and the heavens--Gen 2:5 and no shrub of the field had yet appeared on the earth and no plant of the field had yet sprung up, for the LORD God had not sent rain on the earth and there was no man to work the ground, 2:6 but streams came up from the earth and watered the whole surface of the ground-- 2:7 the LORD God formed the man from the dust of the ground and breathed into his nostrils the breath of life, and the man became a living being.

An interesting change in word usage begins here with "LORD God," or *Jehovah Elohim*. Anytime the word LORD appears in capital letters it is *Jehovah* in the Hebrew. We have moved now to a personal God, man's God. This points to the focus of chapter two being man and his relationship with God and the creation. Chapter one was more impersonally focused on God's relationship with His creation.

No rain had fallen on the earth which caused no plants or shrubs, but God took care of this problem, not by bringing rain, but by artesian wells that sprang forth from the ground. The first rain fall probably was at the time of Noah's Flood. It is possible that the firmament created on day two allowed for this environment.

God also provided man to work the ground once the water was available. Just as dirt consists of nitrogen, oxygen and calcium, we too are made of these materials. So what separates us from dirt? God *personally* breathed the breath of life (*neshamah*), our spirit and soul into us and we became a living being (*nephesh*). See 1 Cor 15:45-47.

Gen 2:8 Now the LORD God had planted a garden in the east, in Eden; and there he put the man he had formed. 2:9 And the LORD God made all kinds of trees grow out of the ground--trees that were pleasing to the eye and good for food. In the middle of the garden were the tree of life and the tree of the knowledge of good and evil.

Adam was put in the Garden of Eden in the east. This suggests Adam was made outside of the garden, since he had to be put there. Eden being in the east is significant in that this direction was used for Christ's coming. The star of Bethlehem was seen in the east (Matt 2:9), and Christ will come again in the east. Also significant is that Eden foreshadowed heaven, where man will reside again along with the tree of life, but with no tree of the knowledge of good and evil. (Rev 2:7; 22:2 22:14). Also, as we will see in Genesis 3:24, man was driven out of Eden but will have access to heaven through Christ.

The tree of life must have been taken out of Eden (if not the whole garden) sometime prior to Noah's Flood, as it is seen again in heaven (Rev 22:2). How this tree grants life we cannot know. The tree of the knowledge of good and evil is not in heaven, because in heaven we will know no evil. This is important because even in the garden evil did reside in this tree and in Satan himself. But Adam was *able not to sin*. After the curse however, Adam was *not able not to sin*. In heaven we will *not be able to sin,* as evil is destroyed forever and Satan is thrown into the Abyss along with his angels.

Gen 2:10 A river watering the garden flowed from Eden; from there it was separated into four headwaters. 2:11 The name of the first is the Pishon; it winds through the entire land of Havilah, where there is gold. 2:12 (The gold of that land is good; aromatic resin and onyx are also there.) 2:13 The name of the second river is the Gihon; it winds through the entire land of Cush. 2:14 The name of the third river is the Tigris; it runs along the east side of Asshur. And the fourth river is the Euphrates.

A river flowed from the garden, and a river will flow from the throne of God (Rev 22:1) in heaven with the tree of life standing on both sides. The river here in Eden must have been rather large, because four others come from it - Gihon, Tigris, Pishon, Euphrates. These must have been destroyed by the Flood, and certain rivers formed after the Flood were given the same names. Some try to pinpoint the Garden of Eden today based on the Tigris and Euphrates, but this cannot be accurate, as the world of Adam's day was completely destroyed.

Havilah had gold and other precious stones as will heaven (Rev 21:11; 21:19). This land must have been impressive enough for the sons of Noah to later name their descendants Havilah (Gen 10:7;10:29).

Verse ten states, a river "flowed," showing it to be past tense. It is possible (but not necessary) that this account was written by Adam after the fall, as he looked back.

Gen 2:15 The LORD God took the man and put him in the Garden of Eden to work it and take care of it. 2:16 And the LORD God commanded the man, "You are free to eat from any tree in the garden; 2:17 but you must not eat from the tree of the knowledge of good and evil, for when you eat of it you will surely die."

Something that has always fascinated me is that Adam was put in the garden to work. Initially, his work must have been mostly harvesting, because there were no weeds or thorns until after the fall. Work would have been very enjoyable at this point, but after the curse we read, "By the sweat of your brow you will eat your food" (Gen 3:19). If one has been out of work for a while, he knows it is not the best thing to be idle; even in paradise. In fact, Rev 22:3 shows that in heaven we will be serving the Lord. Some view this as a downside to heaven. It won't be (if you see it this way maybe you won't need to worry about it either), as true service to God in the spirit will be the most exciting and fulfilling thing one ever does. We also read in John, "'What must we do to do the works God requires?' Jesus answered, 'The work of God is this: to believe in the One He has sent'" (John 6:28-29).

Man was given permission to eat from all trees except the tree of the knowledge of good and evil. To eat of this tree meant sure death. Some say that since Adam lived to be 930 years old, the Bible lies. No! He did die spiritually and also death began physically. The Hebrew literally reads, "dying thou shalt die." This tree is not found in heaven because NO evil can be found there. This is an important distinction between what paradise was and what it will be. Nobody should desire to understand evil; to do so means you must die, for nothing evil can enter the gates of heaven. Already in the first two chapters we are beginning to understand why sin brought death and why death is not something that just happens, as evolutionists would like to believe (they say dinosaurs died before humans lived and, therefore, death did not come about as a result of man's fall).

Many wonder why the first paradise even had the option of knowing evil. Why did God put this tree here? Martin Luther points out that God wanted man to move from a created innocence to a conscious holiness. God created us with a free will, not only for our benefit but also for His. To have something worship you because you programmed it to do so brings no satisfaction. However, to have something worship you because it wants to out of love brings great satisfaction. God wanted man to consciously choose not to eat of this tree in submission to, and out of love for Him.

Gen 2:18 The LORD God said, "It is not good for the man to be alone. I will make a helper suitable for him." 2:19 Now the LORD God had formed out of the ground all the beasts of the field and all the birds of the air. He brought them to the man to see what he would name them; and

whatever the man called each living creature, that was its name. 2:20 So the man gave names to all the livestock, the birds of the air and all the beasts of the field. But for Adam no suitable helper was found. 2:21 So the LORD God caused the man to fall into a deep sleep; and while he was sleeping, he took one of the man's ribs and closed up the place with flesh. 2:22 Then the LORD God made a woman from the rib he had taken out of the man, and he brought her to the man.

So far there has been no mention of animals being created, but man is already formed. Now verse 19 states that animals were made from the ground. Some say this contradicts chapter one because animals were made first. Again, the point of chapter two is not to present a chronological order of creation but to show how creation fits into the purpose of man. Verse 19 does show that they *had* been formed- past tense.

This section opens with God stating that man should not be alone. Some say that God failed in His first attempt to find a mate for Adam with the animals, but this is ludicrous; God does not fail, nor did He ever intend for man to be united with animals. Keep in mind that the animals were made first and, therefore, God did not make man and then began making animals to try and find Adam's helper.

The fact that Adam named all these animals and remembered them the next day is remarkable. I believe Adam used 100% of his brain compared to the 10-15% science is telling us we use today. Some compare this to idiot savants who sometimes cannot write or speak but have amazing abilities in other areas. For example, one savant could give the answer to a math question faster than a calculator, even though the answer was a 28 digit number. Some scientists are suggesting that they are using 100% of *that area* of the brain. If this is so, one can only imagine what it must have been like to have the entire brain operating at 100%.

Another important thing about this task is what Adam would gain from naming these animals. In Biblical times, names were not given because they sounded nice but because they fit the quality or character of that person. Therefore, Adam must have examined these animals very thoroughly to understand them before naming them. Since God made these animals, in a sense Adam was beginning to understand God and His qualities through His creations. We read in Romans, "For since the creation of the world God's invisible qualities--His eternal power and divine nature--have been clearly seen, being understood from what has been made" (Rom 1:20). In addition to knowing God, the naming of these animals by man shows man's dominion over them, not equality with them.

Out of all these animals, Adam must have noted that there were pairs, males and females. Perhaps he felt alone. To remedy this, God put him in a deep sleep for what we would call surgery. Though most Bibles read that Adam's rib was removed the actual Hebrew word is "*tsela*" and means "side." Only here is this word translated as rib. Therefore, perhaps part of Adam's side was removed, consisting of flesh, bone and blood. This may also be why verse 23 says Eve was "bone of my bones and flesh of my flesh." Therefore, there was indeed bone, but also flesh. By the way, because of verses 21-22, some have said that women have one less rib than men do, but this is untrue.

Gen 2:23 The man said, "This is now bone of my bones and flesh of my flesh; she shall be called 'woman, ' for she was taken out of man." 2:24 For this reason a man will leave his father and mother and be united to his wife, and they will become one flesh. 2:25 The man and his wife were both naked, and they felt no shame.

With woman being made out of the flesh and bone of man, the two became one flesh (See also 1 Timothy 2:13; 1 Corinthians 11:8). Not only does this happen because of the physical uniting of the bone and flesh, but also because of the spiritual uniting with Adam and Eve as marriage partners. This all started when no suitable mate was found for Adam. Further evidence of this is found in the New Testament when Jesus is questioned about divorce, the breaking apart of marriage. Jesus answered His critics by saying, "'Haven't you read,' He replied, 'that at the beginning the Creator made them male and female, and said, for this reason a man will leave his father and mother and be united to his wife, and the two *will become* one flesh? So they are no longer two, but one. Therefore what God has joined together, let man not separate'" (Mat 19:4-6). Clearly Adam and Eve were perceived as married at the beginning. More importantly today, however, when any man and woman sleep together, they too are united as one flesh. When people get divorced, do they become half a person? Through the forgiveness of Christ we can be made whole again, but that still doesn't make divorce right.

Why did God choose to make the man and woman one? Scripture answers that question: "Has not the LORD made them one? In flesh and spirit they are His. And why one? *Because He was seeking godly offspring.* So guard yourself in your spirit, and do not break faith with the wife of your youth. I hate divorce, says the LORD God of Israel" (Mal 2:15-16). God joined a husband and wife together because He wants us to procreate. One of the first commands He gave Adam in 1:28 was to fill the earth. Again after the Flood they are told to be fruitful, multiply, and increase in number (:1-7). It is ironic that today we are being told by the secular world to stop multiplying because of the overpopulation myth. Many households believe children are too expensive or they will take too much of their time. According to what we just read, what does God want us to do?

Another important reason for this type of union is to represent our union with Christ. Just as Adam and Eve became one by the sharing of flesh and blood, we are "one in Christ" (Gal 3:28) through communion. Jesus stated, "Whoever eats My flesh and drinks My blood remains in Me, and I in him" (John 6:56). We also read in Ephesians, "For we are members of His body" (Eph 5:30).

Note also that Adam and Eve were joined together as one, not Adam and Steve. God made one man and one woman to compliment each other. Jesus went back to Genesis (Mat 19:4) to answer His critics by using the creation account as the foundation, or standard, for the rules of marriage. Just as the first time a new vocabulary word is made it establishes a definition, the first marriage sets the meaning for all marriages to come. God intended at the beginning for a male/female relationship. Why has the world changed this? Because of sin. Paul wrote, "Although they claimed to be wise, they became fools and exchanged the glory of the immortal God for images made to look like mortal man and birds and animals and reptiles. Therefore God gave them over in the sinful desires of their hearts to sexual impurity for the degrading of their bodies with one another. They exchanged the truth of God for a lie, and worshipped and served created things rather than the Creator--who is forever praised. Amen. Because of this, *God gave them over to* shameful lusts. Even their women exchanged natural relations for unnatural ones. In the same way the men also abandoned natural relations with women and were inflamed with lust for one another. Men committed indecent acts with other men, and received in themselves the due penalty for their perversion" (Rom 1:22-27). When men rejected God as Creator and followed their own passions, *God gave them over to* these shameful things.

Verse 25 shows that no sin had entered the human world at this point because Adam and Eve could look at each other in the perfect relationship in which they were created. This will all change in the next chapter.

Gen 3:1 Now the serpent was more crafty than any of the wild animals the LORD God had made. He said to the woman, "Did God really say, 'You must not eat from any tree in the garden'?"

Chapter three gives us the truth about the problems of the world today. Evolution suggests sin is and always has been natural, but Scripture clearly says otherwise. Here we see why sin and death came about.

The serpent is clearly Satan and is introduced for the first time (See Rev 12:9; 20:2). He is crafty but doomed to destruction as a result of his previous fall. Scripture describes Satan as being a cherub (chief angel), proud and beautiful, but he tried to be like God and was cast out of heaven along with a third of the angels who followed him. We read, "How you have fallen from heaven, O morning star, son of the dawn! You have been cast down to the earth, you who once laid low the nations! You said in your heart, "I will ascend to heaven; I will raise my throne above the stars of God; I will sit enthroned on the mount of assembly, on the utmost heights of the sacred mountain. I will ascend above the tops of the clouds; I will make myself like the Most High. But you are brought down to the grave, to the depths of the pit" (Isa 14:12-15). Also, "You were the model of perfection, full of wisdom and perfect in beauty. You were in Eden, the garden of God; every precious stone adorned you: ruby, topaz and emerald, chrysolite, onyx and jasper, sapphire, turquoise and beryl. Your settings and mountings were made of gold; on the day you were created they were prepared. You were anointed as a guardian cherub, for so I ordained you. You were on the holy mount of God; you walked among the fiery stones. You were blameless in your ways from the day you were created till wickedness was found in you. Through your widespread trade you were filled with violence, and you sinned. So I drove you in disgrace from the mount of God, and I expelled you, O guardian cherub, from among the fiery stones. Your heart became proud on account of your beauty, and you corrupted your wisdom because of your splendor. So I threw you to the earth" (Ezek 28:12-17) See also, Rev 12:4-9; Matt 25:41; Luke 10:18.

If Satan was so beautiful why is he called a serpent? First of all, the serpent wasn't anything like what we have today. This one spoke (no surprise to Eve) and apparently could walk since this privilege was taken away (3:14). However, we also see that Satan many times was able to possess other physical bodies (Matt 4:24; 8:16; 8:28; 8:33; 9:32; 9:33), so perhaps the snake was simply demon possessed. We simply can't say if the animals all talked or if it was simply by the spirit within them. Balaam's donkey spoke (Num 22:28) and even this didn't seem to surprise Balaam. It probably did surprise him, but Scripture didn't record it, as it isn't necessary for the lesson to be learned. Perhaps it is the same here with Eve. Maybe, Eve had not been around the animals yet, and this was her first contact with a serpent. Physically animals are incapable of speech no matter how much we try to communicate sometimes. There is absolutely no connection between animal and human language, but perhaps this was changed after the curse. It really doesn't matter for the lesson to be learned here either. The point is, Satan did use the serpent to tempt Eve.

And what a lesson can be learned from these verses. Satan proudly asserted, "Did God *really* say that?" These few words are the basis for almost all sins today. As soon as we begin to *doubt* God's Word, authority, and His power, we open ourselves up to the deception of Satan. Today, the doubt or wavering doctrines of creation have been the first step in the destruction of our society. First we doubt if God created, then if God is really God, or did He really rise from the dead, or did Jonah really get swallowed by a great fish, or is there really a hell, or are we really one in marriage, or is homosexuality really that bad, or is divorce always bad, or is pornography wrong if you don't abuse it; or is sin really the cause of death, or was Noah's Flood really mountain covering, and on and on and on. Trust in God's Word as truth. Paul writes, "They exchanged the truth of God for a lie" (Rom 1:25) and, "Now we know that God's judgment against those who do such things is based on truth" (Rom 2:2).

When we doubt God's Word we doubt Christ. For John 1:1 shows that the Word was made flesh in Christ. God's Word is Christ. We must not doubt Scripture because it is the Word which saves.

Gen 3:2 The woman said to the serpent, "We may eat fruit from the trees in the garden, 3:3 but God did say, 'You must not eat fruit from the tree that is in the middle of the garden, and you must not touch it, or you will die.'"

Eve's answer wasn't exactly what God said earlier in 2:17, because God did not say (at least from what Scripture shows) that they must not touch the tree. The consequence is right on the nose however: "you will die." One can conclude from this that God wants us far away from evil. We are not to even *touch* it. One example that comes to mind is the wigi board. So many have fallen today, simply by experimenting with what appears to simply be a game. Stay completely clear of evil.

Gen 3:4 "You will not surely die," the serpent said to the woman. 3:5 "For God knows that when you eat of it your eyes will be opened, and you will be like God, knowing good and evil."

I find it ironic that we often laugh at people who fall for the same joke time after time. Satan must think we are hilarious. For thousands of years he has been using the same temptation and we continue to fall for it. New Age, Mormonism and many other false religions say that you too can be like God. There is always a different twist to find the "divinity within," whether through meditation, hypnosis, belonging to a certain group, or simply evolving, but the bottom line is the same and the result is eternal damnation.

Having taught school children, I find it interesting that so often when one gets into trouble, he wants to drag others down with him. The same can be seen with Satan. We saw earlier that Satan said, "I will ascend to heaven; I will raise my throne above the stars of God. . . I will make myself like the Most High" (Is 14:12-14). He is using the same temptation on us that he himself fell into. Yet we still have not learned from this lesson that Scripture clearly warns us of. Satan doesn't blatantly invite us to sin, rather he promises happiness and added excitement to our lives. John writes concerning Satan, "He was a murderer from the beginning, not holding to the truth, for there is no truth in him. When he lies, he speaks his native language, for he is a liar and the father of lies" (John 8:44). Paul also warns, "I am afraid that just as Eve was deceived by the serpent's cunning, your minds may somehow be led astray from your sincere and pure devotion to Christ" (2 Cor 11:3). For this reason we will know Scripture, so that Satan can not deceive us through the twisting of God's Word.

Just as children often do, Satan simply changes parts or leaves bits of information out to make a story untruthful. In the New Testament, Satan attempted to trick Christ (as if this were possible) by quoting Scripture. In Matthew 4:6 Satan is quoted as saying, "If you are the Son of God throw yourself down. For it is written: 'He will command His angels concerning You, and they will lift You up in their hands, so that You will not strike Your foot against a stone.'" Satan quoted Psalms 91:11 which states, "He will command His angels concerning You to guard You in all Your ways; they will lift You up in their hands, so that You will not strike Your foot against a stone." Did you catch Satan's deception? He left out some very important words: "to guard You *in all Your ways.*" This is why it is so important to study Scripture and not follow everyone who quotes the Bible. Satan almost always uses mostly truth and corrupts just a little at a time, making it all wrong. We will not compromise God's Word.

Back to Satan's deception of Eve. Eve should have known right away when Satan called God a liar when he said, "you *will not* die." Then the devil went to his usual subtle approach and didn't tell Eve the whole truth. Eating of the tree of the knowledge of good and evil would indeed make us like God, knowing both good and evil, but is knowing evil something we desire? Certainly not. Be on guard and as Paul states, "Take up the shield of faith, with which you can extinguish all the flaming arrows of the evil one" (Eph 6:16).

Gen 3:6 When the woman saw that the fruit of the tree was good for food and pleasing to the eye, and also desirable for gaining wisdom, she took some and ate it. She also gave some to her husband, who was with her, and he ate it. 3:7 Then the eyes of both of them were opened, and they realized they were naked; so they sewed fig leaves together and made coverings for themselves.

The fact that Eve appeared to be seeing this fruit for the first time suggests that the fall took place very soon after creation. This along with the fact that they had no children yet, because it seems Adam and Eve would have obeyed God's command to "fill the earth" right away.

I find one of the most interesting passages in Scripture deals with overcoming selfish desires. Peter writes, "he who has suffered in his body is done with sin" (1 Pet 4:1). What a deep truth. When one can surrender his all to God, he is done with sin. Think of how many sins we fall into as a result of our concern for self. Whether it be hunger, escape from pain, being tired, lazy, sexual desires needing fulfillment, or need of attention, it all comes back to me, me, me. When one can surrender all these aspects of our life to God, allowing ourselves to suffer hunger or lack of sleep, etc., it keeps our focus on God and, in a sense, we are done with sin. Obviously we don't ever stop sinning because of our sinful nature, but we certainly lead a sanctified life through the Spirit of God and the forgiveness of Christ. I have found fasting to be such a blessing to help me be aware of self. The first time I fasted I was surprised at how many times my attention was directed toward self. The blessings came when each time those desires of self appeared, I immediately directed my thoughts to God and looked to Him for comfort rather than to food, etc. It made me realize how many fleshly desires take our focus off Christ. But suffering allows us to redirect our thoughts to God for deliverance. If you have not set aside a day for prayer and fasting, I would encourage you to do so, not as an experiment or for personal health, but as a day dedicated to the Lord. I believe you will see what I am talking about.

The point of all this is seen with Eve's desire to fulfill self. She saw the tree was good for food and thereby would satisfy her physical appetite. She also saw that it was pleasant to the eyes and, therefore, appealed to her senses and emotions. Finally, her mind and spirit were being satisfied with the tree's ability to grant wisdom and intellectual growth. These three desires encompass almost all sins known to man. Look at what Scripture states, "For everything in the world--the *cravings of sinful man*, the *lust of his eyes* and the *boasting of what he has and does*--comes not from the Father but from the world" (1 John 2:16). Henry Morris's book The Genesis Record (highly recommended) also points out that Satan's temptation of Christ followed this same theme. First Christ was tempted with bread (physical appetite), then He was shown the many kingdoms from a high point (emotions and senses), and finally, He was told to prove His divinity and authority by having His angels rescue Him (pride) (Luke 4:1-12). In a sense, Christ showed here that He had overcome ALL sin.

23

Next, Eve got Adam to eat of the tree as well. This is partly why the woman has the submissive (not unequal) role. We read in Timothy, "I do not permit a woman to teach or to have authority over a man; she must be silent. For Adam was formed first, then Eve. And *Adam was not the one deceived*; it was the *woman who was deceived* and became a sinner" (1 Tim 2:12-14). This does not make Adam free of guilt, as he too ate of the tree, and "For as in Adam all die, so in Christ all will be made alive" (1 Cor 15:22; See also Rom 5:15).

The first result of their sin was the awareness of shame and nakedness. No longer did they have control of their sexual desires and they could not look at one another in the same pure way. We are told that if a man even lusts after a woman he commits adultery. This is also why it is important especially for a woman, to dress decently and be fully covered today. If not, because of man's weaknesses and sinful nature, he may fall into sin as a result of the woman not covering herself. Paul writes, "Do not cause anyone to stumble" (1 Cor 10:32). To do so is a sin and, therefore, if a woman causes a man to sin by her clothing, she also sins. These fig leaves certainly did not do the job Adam and Eve had hoped they would.

Gen 3:8 Then the man and his wife heard the sound of the LORD God as he was walking in the garden in the cool of the day, and they hid from the LORD God among the trees of the garden. 3:9 But the LORD God called to the man, "Where are you?" 3:10 He answered, "I heard you in the garden, and I was afraid because I was naked; so I hid."

Immediately after hearing the LORD coming, Adam and Eve hid themselves from God. This is exactly what sin makes us do today. When we do something wrong we almost always try to hide it, keep it to ourselves, rather than going to God in repentance or confession. Fear is what usually motivates this action and is also seen here in verse ten. Now Adam and Eve knew evil, just as the serpent had said, but knowing fear was something they could have done without. What a strange and terrible emotion this must have been to experience for the first time, especially after having complete peace prior to this.

God was walking in the garden, apparently not something foreign to Adam and Eve. What a joy that must have been. Out of all the curses that came upon man as a result of sin, this must have been the thing they missed most. We do have the promise of future walks with God; however, ""Now the dwelling of God is with men, and He will live with them. They will be His people, and God Himself will be with them and be their God" (Rev 21:3).

Both Adam and Eve experienced shame from their nakedness before God. Strangely enough, this was a good thing. Without shame there would have been no hope of forgiveness. Shame shows the attitude of repentance that was within their now pounding hearts. Also, this fear and shame should have produced hope in salvation and forgiveness. John writes, "I counsel you to buy from me gold refined in the fire, so you can become rich; and white clothes to wear, so you can cover your shameful nakedness" (Rev 3:18). White clothes will be given to us to wear one day, for we read, "Fine linen, bright and clean, was given her to wear" (Fine linen stands for the righteous acts of the saints) (Rev 19:8). In this day, there will be no more fear or shame.

> **Gen 3:11 And he said, "Who told you that you were naked? Have you eaten from the tree that I commanded you not to eat from?" 3:12 The man said, "The woman you put here with me--she gave me some fruit from the tree, and I ate it." 3:13 Then the LORD God said to the woman, "What is this you have done?" The woman said, "The serpent deceived me, and I ate."**

Once sin entered the world it came in full force. Rather than answering God with a simple and honest, "yes," Adam pointed fingers and tried to pass blame on to Eve. In a sense, she was to blame (1 Tim 2:12-14) but Adam was not innocent in this matter either.

Adam's answer did cause God to turn to Eve, who also tried to put blame on someone else, the serpent. We often hear this argument today when people say, "the devil made me do it." It doesn't work now, nor did it work for Eve. The devil doesn't make us do things. We decide what we do, who we follow and what side of the fence we will be on. When judgment day comes, there will be no excuses.

Another point is that Adam and Eve were both so concerned with the act of eating the fruit, but what God was really concerned with was the act of disobedience. God commanded them not to do something and they did it anyway.

> **Gen 3:14 So the LORD God said to the serpent, "Because you have done this, "Cursed are you above all the livestock and all the wild animals! You will crawl on your belly and you will eat dust all the days of your life. 3:15 And I will put enmity between you and the woman, and between your offspring and hers; he will crush your head, and you will strike his heel."**

Eve's pointing of the finger also worked for the time being. The serpent was dealt with first, since he was the one who started everything, as indicated by "because you have done this." Verse 16 addresses the woman next, as she was the second person involved. Finally, man was affected in verse 17, since he was the last to disobey God.

The serpent was cursed above all the other animals and was doomed to crawl on its belly and have no legs. The real purpose was to shame the serpent and bring it to its lowly position.

Verse 15 is perhaps one of the most important verses in Genesis, as it sets the foundation and scope for the rest of Scripture. Right in the middle of all this cursing and gloom is the Gospel message. At this point the serpent must have felt somewhat successful, since he deceived the woman into following him; however, it was through this woman that Christ would come and ultimately crush satan's head. The seed of the serpent is none other than Satan while the seed of the woman is Christ. Evolution tries to get rid of a literal curse because then there is no need of a literal Savior. Here, however, it is promised that Christ would deliver man and destroy the devil through His death on the cross, the very thing that the curse brings about (death) is what cures our sin. How ironic. In a literal sense the enmity between the serpent and woman can still be seen today in the hatred that most people have toward snakes.

Gen 3:16 To the woman he said, "I will greatly increase your pains in childbearing; with pain you will give birth to children. Your desire will be for your husband, and he will rule over you."

Part of the woman's curse was the pain that all women have today when giving birth. As always, God provides a relief even in this curse, however. "A woman giving birth to a child has pain because her time has come; but when her baby is born she forgets the anguish because of her joy that a child is born into the world" (John 16:21). What joy can be found in such suffering. Often times the bitterness makes the moment that much more sweet. We read in Romans, "We know that the whole creation has been groaning as in the pains of childbirth right up to the present time" (Rom 8:22) awaiting its deliverance. The entire creation has been subjected to this frustration in order to direct our focus back to the Fall of man. From the Fall we are brought to the hope in Christ, who will bring the final deliverance from death, pain, and suffering. We also read, "But women will be saved through childbearing" (1 Tim 2:15). It was through the woman that offspring would come, and the ultimate offspring is Christ who saves us all.

Another part of the woman's curse was that she was put in the submissive role to her husband. Today we see the woman fighting this role of submission, and I believe this is predicted here. The word for "desire" (*teshuwqah*) is also translated as "to devour or control." Thus, in context we clearly see that the woman would try to control her husband but he would rule over her. If women were to simply have desire for their husbands, what kind of curse is that? Clearly the meaning is that women would want control. The well know Promise Keepers have taken much criticism from groups like NOW (National Organization for Women) for trying to stand on Biblical principles by having their wives be submissive while they themselves take the headship role properly in love. Groups such as NOW clearly display the woman's desire for power and control, control that God does not want them to have. The following are a few verses showing how women are to live. The number of verses speaks not only of its importance but perhaps to the vast rejection of this role.

1. "Wives, in the same way be submissive to your husbands. . . Your beauty should not come from outward adornment, such as braided hair and the wearing of gold jewelry and fine clothes. Instead, it should be that of your inner self, the unfading beauty of a gentle and quiet spirit, which is of great worth in God's sight. For this is the way the holy women of the past who put their hope in God used to make themselves beautiful. They were submissive to their own husbands" (1 Pet 3:1-5).

2. "Wives, submit to your husbands as to the Lord. For the husband is the head of the wife as Christ is the head of the church" (Eph 5:22-23).
3. "Then they can train the younger women to love their husbands and children, to be self-controlled and pure, to be busy at home, to be kind, and to be subject to their husbands, so that no one will malign the word of God" (Titus 2:4-5).
4. "I also want women to dress modestly, with decency and propriety, not with braided hair or gold or pearls or expensive clothes, but with good deeds, appropriate for women who profess to worship God. A woman should learn in quietness and full submission. I do not permit a woman to teach or to have authority over a man; she must be silent. For Adam was formed first, then Eve. And Adam was not the one deceived; it was the woman who was deceived and became a sinner" (1 Tim 2:9-14).
5. "Wives, submit to your husbands, as is fitting in the Lord. Husbands, love your wives and do not be harsh with them" (Col 3:18-19).
6. "In the same way, their wives are to be women worthy of respect, not malicious talkers but temperate and trustworthy in everything" (1 Tim 3:11).
7. "So I counsel younger widows to marry, to have children, to manage their homes and to give the enemy no opportunity for slander" (1 Tim 5:14).

Unfortunately, the male has left his responsibility and has often treated the wife unfairly and not out of love. If we both follow the roles God has ordained for a marriage, what a beautiful marriage it will be.

Gen 3:17 To Adam he said, "Because you listened to your wife and ate from the tree about which I commanded you, 'You must not eat of it,' Cursed is the ground because of you; through painful toil you will eat of it all the days of your life. 3:18 It will produce thorns and thistles for you, and you will eat the plants of the field. 3:19 By the sweat of your brow you will eat your food until you return to the ground, since from it you were taken; for dust you are and to dust you will return."

Adam finally got his. The reason was because Adam "listened to his wife." This is not to say that men are not to listen, but in spiritual cases (of which man is to be the head) Adam should never have been submissive. He left his role of headship and let the wife take charge of his spiritual well being by trying to gain wisdom.

When we examine the curse we see that it corresponds to the entire creation. Not only are the animals (verse 14) and humans cursed, (verses 16-19) but the physical universe is also subjected to frustration (Rom 8:22). Here the ground was cursed, causing it to produce thorns and other weeds, making Adam work for his food. No longer would it be simply harvesting, now it would take the sweat of his brow to bring in food. This process would be lifelong and then he would die, returning to that from which he was made-- dust. Though once Adam was to rule over and control the ground, now it would control him.

An interesting parallel can be made with the curse and Christ. We read, "Christ redeemed us from the curse of the law by becoming a curse for us" (Gal

3:13). We just read how, as a result of eating from the tree, Adam was cursed with pain, thorns, sweat and death. Christ himself hung on a tree (Gal 3:13) taking us back to the Fall. He suffered pain (Heb 5:7; Ps 22), wore a crown of thorns (Mark 15:17), sweat blood (Luke 22:44), and died for us, but more than that, He rose from the dead. He indeed became the very curse of man in order to redeem us from this curse through His death and resurrection, so that there would be no more pain (Rev 21:4; 22:3). Praise God! It is true that the price of the curse has been paid, but it will not be completely delivered until the end of the world (2 Peter 3:10). We read, "But in keeping with His promise we are looking forward to a new heaven and a new earth, the home of righteousness" (2 Pet 3:13; see also Rev 21:1; 20:11).

These verses also show a common law of science that was set in motion, the Second law of Thermodynamics. This law states that all things in the universe are in a state of decay. Not only does this go against the theory of evolution where things are increasing in complexity, it also is a reminder that this world will someday end and either heaven or hell awaits. After the curse plants began to wither and die, animals and humans began to age, with diseases and suffering to boot. The stars began to burn out, the earth began to erode along with many of its qualities (electromagnetic field etc.). Scientifically this has been seen first hand, giving support to what the Bible already states: "He also says, 'In the beginning, O Lord, You laid the foundations of the earth, and the heavens are the work of Your hands. They will perish, but You remain; they will all wear out like a garment'" (Heb 1:10-11); and "All men are like grass, and all their glory is like the flowers of the field; the grass withers and the flowers fall, but the Word of the Lord stands forever" (1 Pet 1:24-25).

How these changes took place nobody knows. Perhaps there were many genetic changes, or maybe God simply withdrew His sustaining power. If the serpent was changed physically, there is no reason to suspect the other animals could not have been changed also. Perhaps the spider was given the ability to make a web, which has the function of death. We don't know and it really doesn't matter, as the point is, what once was is not but shall be again, through the death and resurrection of Christ Jesus, our Lord!

Gen 3:20 Adam named his wife Eve, because she would become the mother of all the living. 3:21 The LORD God made garments of skin for Adam and his wife and clothed them. 3:22 And the LORD God said, "The man has now become like one of us, knowing good and evil. He must not be allowed to reach out his hand and take also from the tree of life and eat, and live forever." 3:23 So the LORD God banished him from the Garden of Eden to work the ground from which he had been taken.

Adam named his wife Eve, meaning "lifegiver." This shows Adam's faith in God's promise to bring a Savior through her.

God then proceeded to kill the first animal as a blood sacrifice to cover the sin of Adam and Eve with its skin. Since this was the first death in the world, this must have been a sobering experience for Adam and Eve to realize that they themselves brought death by their sin. Though Scripture does not say it, it is very possible that the animal killed was a lamb to symbolize the Lamb to come, whose blood would be shed on the cross to cover the sins of the whole world. John writes, "The next day John saw Jesus coming toward him and said, 'Look, the Lamb of God, who takes away the sin of the world'" (John 1:29).

No longer did Adam and Eve have access to the tree of life to live forever. Though this was part of the curse, a blessing went along with this. With man not living in his flesh forever, evil will not remain forever either. All evil will be cast into everlasting darkness when the present world ends (Rev 20-22). To assure that man could not go to the tree of life, they were expelled from the garden.

Gen 3:24 After he drove the man out, he placed on the east side of the Garden of Eden cherubim and a flaming sword flashing back and forth to guard the way to the tree of life.

It must have been difficult for Adam and Eve to be standing outside the garden looking in and knowing they could not go back. Apparently, the garden would be a reminder of their sin for some time. If it was destroyed before or during Noah's Flood we do not know. However, as mentioned earlier, whenever it was removed from this earth the tree of life went to heaven, as we will see it again. (Revelation 2:7; 22:2; 22:14).

The garden was guarded by cherubim, apparently some of the highest ranking angels. These amazing creatures are described in great detail in Ezekiel 1:4-28; 10:1-22, and Revelation 4:5-8. As we discussed earlier, Satan himself was a cherub before falling (Ezekiel 28:14).

Another significance of these cherub is that they seem to always be in God's presence. David wrote, "Hear us, O Shepherd of Israel, You who lead Joseph like a flock; You who sit enthroned between the cherubim" (Ps 80:1; see also Ps 18:10; 99:1). This may mean that God remained in the garden from time to time or maybe stayed by the tree of life. In Exodus we see that the cherub were engraved over the Ark of the covenant showing God's presence wherever the Ark was (Exodus 25:17-22). We read, "There, above the cover between the two cherubim that are over the Ark of the Testimony, I will meet with you and give you all My commands for the Israelites" (Exo 25:22). This "mercy seat," as it was called, was kept in the most holy place of the Temple where the priests entered once a year on the day of atonement. On this day the priest would sprinkle blood (foreshadowing Christ's blood to come) on the Ark to purify or forgive the people of all their sins (Heb 9:7-28; Lev 16).

Gen 4:1 Adam lay with his wife Eve, and she became pregnant and gave birth to Cain. She said, "With the help of the LORD I have brought forth a man." 4:2 Later she gave birth to his brother Abel. Now Abel kept flocks, and Cain worked the soil. 4:3 In the course of time Cain brought some of the fruits of the soil as an offering to the LORD. 4:4 But Abel brought fat portions from some of the firstborn of his flock. The LORD

looked with favor on Abel and his offering, 4:5 but on Cain and his offering he did not look with favor. So Cain was very angry, and his face was downcast.

When Cain was born, Eve cried out, "With the help of the LORD I have brought forth a man." Martin Luther and others have translated this as possibly being, "I have brought forth a man, the Lord." The name Cain means "gotten," and many allude to "gotten the Savior." Understanding the context, that Eve was just told that her offspring would crush Satan's head and thus bring salvation, she may have thought Cain was going to bring that salvation. Even if this is true, I know this thought did not last long, as Cain would be known as the wicked one for generations to come: "Do not be like Cain, who belonged to the evil one and murdered his brother" (1 John 3:12).

Abel, another of Eve's children was a contrast to Cain, in that he was "righteous" (Matt 23:35) and is in the Great Hall of Faith (Heb 11:4). Abel means, "vanity" or "empty." Perhaps at this time Eve was realizing the extent of the curse upon all of creation. Adam and Eve do have other children (5:4) but we are not told when or how many. In order to follow the line of Christ, Cain and Abel are all that are needed.

Permission was not given to eat meat until after the Flood and, therefore, the purpose of Abel's flocks must have been for clothing and sacrifice. We know that sacrifices must have taken place from verse four and the fact that Noah knew how to go about sacrificing animals after he got out of the ark. The purpose and details of these sacrifices are not given, but they must have been different from that of the Levitical priesthood. These sacrifices would have also served as a constant reminder of the first sacrifice God gave to cover the sins of Adam and Eve with clothing of animal skins. Cain's farming abilities were useful for food as well as for offerings.

Why Cain's sacrifice was not acceptable we are not told, but we can be sure that it was not the sacrifice itself, but rather the attitude of the heart while he offered it. The same can be true of us today when we tithe. God wants us to give from the heart, not out of obligation. The blessings that come from a giving heart are tremendous. We read in Malachi, "Bring the whole tithe into the storehouse, that there may be food in My house. Test Me in this, says the LORD Almighty, and see if I will not throw open the floodgates of heaven and pour out so much blessing that you will not have room enough for it" (Mal 3:10).

Instead of realizing his heart was not with his offering, Cain got angry with envy at his brother. We must remember that one cannot please God without faith (Heb 11:6) or by living in the sinful nature (Rom 8:8). "Everything that does not come from faith is sin" (Rom 14:23).

How old were Cain and Abel at this time? We don't know for sure but they had to have been under 130 years old according to 5:3 which states that Adam was 130 when Seth was born. Seth replaced Abel.

Gen 4:6 Then the LORD said to Cain, "Why are you angry? Why is your face downcast? 4:7 If you do what is right, will you not be accepted? But if you do not do what is right, sin is crouching at your door;

it desires to have you, but you must master it." 4:8 Now Cain said to his brother Abel, "Let's go out to the field." And while they were in the field, Cain attacked his brother Abel and killed him.

The Lord immediately asked Cain why he was so sad and points out that it was his sin, not his brother's. It was almost as if God gave Cain one last warning not to do what he was contemplating. Cain didn't listen, however, and let evil master him rather than he mastering evil. Cain knew what he was going to do all along as he invited Able out to the killing field. Therefore, this was not a quick lapse of judgment, but a heart defiled with sin.

Gen 4:9 Then the LORD said to Cain, "Where is your brother Abel?" "I don't know," he replied. "Am I my brother's keeper?" 4:10 The LORD said, "What have you done? Listen! Your brother's blood cries out to me from the ground. 4:11 Now you are under a curse and driven from the ground, which opened its mouth to receive your brother's blood from your hand. 4:12 When you work the ground, it will no longer yield its crops for you. You will be a restless wanderer on the earth."

Without waiting, God came to Cain (Cain didn't go to God) asking where Abel was. Unlike Adam and Eve at their fall, Cain's response showed an unrepentant and guilt free conscience, as he seemed to disrespectfully reply, "Am I my brother's keeper?" Not only was he rude, but he was a liar and a child of the devil, the serpent's offspring, "You belong to your father, the devil, and you want to carry out your father's desire. He was a murderer from the beginning, not holding to the truth, for there is no truth in him. When he lies, he speaks his native language, for he is a liar and the father of lies" (John 8:44). God wanted Cain to confess, giving him every opportunity, but Cain would not.

Without a willing heart of repentance the LORD showed no mercy and exposed Cain's murder. He was driven out of the Land and thus out of God's presence, just as all the wicked will be (2 Thess 1:9). Cain's end was not a happy one. The crops that he once harvested and offered to God would no longer be, and he would be restless, always unhappy and empty. Rest can only come from Christ, "Come to me, all you who are weary and burdened, and I will give you rest" (Matt 11:28). As for Cain however, "It would have been better for them not to have known the way of righteousness, than to have known it and then to turn their backs on the sacred command that was passed on to them" (2 Pet 2:21).

Gen 4:13 Cain said to the LORD, "My punishment is more than I can bear. 4:14 Today you are driving me from the land, and I will be hidden from your presence; I will be a restless wanderer on the earth, and whoever finds me will kill me." 4:15 But the LORD said to him, "Not so; if anyone kills Cain, he will suffer vengeance seven times over." Then the LORD put a mark on Cain so that no one who found him would kill him. 4:16 So Cain went out from the Lord's presence and lived in the land of Nod, east of Eden.

Cain thought his punishment was too much. A repentant heart would probably feel this punishment was well deserved and fitting, but Cain still was only worried about himself. The fact that Cain was worried about his life suggests violence was not a new thing on the earth at this time. As Henry Morris points out in his book, The Genesis Record, if each family was having six children (probably low for this time period based on family records of Genesis 5) and lived only 400 years (low compared to ages given), there would have been about 120,000 men on earth in the first 800 years of Cain's life. Therefore, Cain may have had a legitimate concern. However, based upon 5:3 it seems only a few thousand people (at most) would have been on the earth at this time, since the killing of Abel had to be within the first 130 years of Adam's life if Seth's birth replaced Abel.

God, however, put a sign on Cain to protect him. We do not know what this sign was, but it served to preserve Cain's life. Anyone who attempted to kill Cain would suffer vengeance seven times over. Again, we don't know what type of vengeance this was, but capital punishment doesn't seem to come about until Genesis 9:6, after the Flood.

Cain left the presence of God and went to the land of Nod, which means "wandering" and was fitting for the punishment of Cain in verse 14.

Gen 4:17 Cain lay with his wife, and she became pregnant and gave birth to Enoch. Cain was then building a city, and he named it after his son Enoch. 4:18 To Enoch was born Irad, and Irad was the father of Mehujael, and Mehujael was the father of Methushael, and Methushael was the father of Lamech. 4:19 Lamech married two women, one named Adah and the other Zillah. 4:20 Adah gave birth to Jabal; he was the father of those who live in tents and raise livestock. 4:21 His brother's name was Jubal; he was the father of all who play the harp and flute. 4:22 Zillah also had a son, Tubal-Cain, who forged all kinds of tools out of bronze and iron. Tubal-Cain's sister was Naamah.

Where did Cain get his wife? He married his sister. This was not a bad thing at this time in history, as it is not made illegal until the book of Leviticus. Perhaps this was because Adam and Eve were created genetically perfect and, therefore, there was no danger in incest. However, as genetic defects came about (rapidly after the Flood destroyed the radiation protecting firmament) incest became physically dangerous, as offspring could become mentally retarded.

Cain built a city, perhaps as he tried not to be a wanderer as it was said he would be. The word "was" may imply he never finished it or left it to his son Enoch.

Enoch's descendants were Irad, Mehujael, Methushael, and Lamech. This line is probably traced simply to show you the way to Lamech, a proud and ungodly man who gives rise to the Caananites. Lamech married two women and thus went against God's plan of one man and one woman, ushering in polygamy. Adah means "ornament" and Zillah means "shade." These names suggest beauty and, therefore, it is possible that Lamech was also only interested in outward beauty, not the beauty of the heart (1 Pet 3:3-4).

From Adah came Jabal, meaning "wanderer," and he made tents and had cattle. Tents allowed him to "wander" from place to place. His brother, Jubal (sound), was musically talented in both stringed and unstringed instruments.

From Zillah, Tubal-Cain was skilled in metallurgy for tools which would have aided in agricultural and architectural development. His sister, Naamah (pleasant), must have been a pretty young lady.

These above verses are remarkable in that they go against the theories proposed by evolution. According to secular beliefs, cities, agriculture, animal domestication, music and metallurgy were developed hundreds of thousands of years apart, and certainly not by the first men. Here however, we see that all these requirements of civilized societies were given by God to the earliest people.

Gen 4:23 Lamech said to his wives, "Adah and Zillah, listen to me; wives of Lamech, hear my words. I have killed a man for wounding me, a young man for injuring me. 4:24 If Cain is avenged seven times, then Lamech seventy-seven times."

Lamech's poem gives insight into the growing spiritual depravity in the earth. Lamech boasted that if Cain was protected by God, Lamech would also be protected, but even more so. The 77 times is contrasted in Matthew where we read, "'Lord, how many times shall I forgive my brother when he sins against me? Up to seven times?' Jesus answered, 'I tell you, not seven times, but seventy-seven times'" (Mat 18:21-22). Not only did Lamech think highly of himself, but he also showed his lack of concern for God's care of providence. The world's inventions and accomplishments had their effect on the minds of man. Rather than acknowledging God as the giver of all things, man saw himself as the designer behind the design.

Gen 4:25 Adam lay with his wife again, and she gave birth to a son and named him Seth, saying, "God has granted me another child in place of Abel, since Cain killed him." 4:26 Seth also had a son, and he named him Enosh. At that time men began to call on the name of the LORD.

Now we turn from the boasting of sinful men (Cain's descendants) back to Adam and the line of God fearing men. God replaced Abel with Seth, meaning "appointed" or "substituted." It is through Seth that the promised Messiah will begin to be traced.

Seth had Enosh, meaning "mortal frailty," showing the awareness of man's need of God. It was during his day that men began to call on the name of the Lord. We read in Exodus, "I appeared to Abraham, to Isaac and to Jacob as God Almighty, but by My name the LORD I did not make Myself known to them" (Exo 6:3). Some say this contradicts verse 26 here in chapter four. However, the Hebrew text lacks punctuation, and this problem can be solved by simply putting a question mark at the end of Exodus 6:3, making it a rhetorical question with an obvious answer of "yes."

Calling on the name of the Lord was so important in preserving the righteous seed of the woman. The following verses explain this importance: "Therefore God exalted Him to the highest place and gave Him the name that is above every name, that at the name of Jesus every knee should bow, in heaven and on earth and under the earth, and every tongue confess that Jesus Christ is Lord, to the glory of God the Father (Phil 2:9-11); and, "Everyone who calls on the name of the Lord will be saved" (Rom 10:13 see also Joel 2:32; Acts 2:21).

One can't help but wonder what emotional suffering went on with Adam and Eve as they watched so many of their family turn away from God. The curse must have had a very personal and deep meaning for them. One thing is sure however, their prayer life must have flourished as a result.

Gen 5:1 This is the written account of Adam's line. When God created man, he made him in the likeness of God. 5:2 He created them male and female and blessed them. And when they were created, he called them "man."

From here on out in Scripture, the Sethite branch is traced and we leave the Cainite branch behind. Some names are the same, but the people are certainly different.

Not only did we have music, metallurgy, agriculture and so on, but we also had a written language, as verse one states. We mentioned earlier that this may suggest Moses used previously compiled written and inspired records to write Genesis. Here we have a written record of the first Adam, but in the beginning of the New Testament we see a written record of Christ, the second Adam (Matt 1:1). We read in the letter to Corinth, "The first man Adam became a living being; the last Adam, a life-giving spirit" (1 Cor 15:45).

We go back once again to see that God created man (1:27; 2:7). Chapter one showed the whole creation, with man simply being a part of it. Chapter two showed man as the focus of that creation, and now chapter five is showing man's lineage and decline. In verse one we see that Adam was made in God's image. Jumping ahead a bit, verse three shows that Adam's son Seth however, was born in Adam's image. After sin entered the world, we lost the complete holiness and righteousness of Adam. Today, through Christ, we have that righteousness and holiness, but it is still under different circumstances than what Adam experienced. Paul writes, "Therefore, just as sin entered the world through one man, and death through sin, and in this way death came to all men, because all sinned-- for before the law was given, sin was in the world. But sin is not taken into account when there is no law. Nevertheless, death reigned from the time of Adam to the time of Moses, even over those who did not sin by breaking a command, as did Adam, who was a pattern of the one to come" (Rom 5:12-14). Death came to all men because of one man's sin, and we are, therefore, in the image of the one sinful man. The verses following continue to show how, through Christ's death, we have been made righteous.

Note that God created male and female and called them both "man."
The last couple of decades has shown woman's attempt to rid this idea. No
longer can we say, "God loves all men" but, rather, to be politically correct we
must say, "God loves all men and women." In God's eyes, an unnecessary use
of extra words.

**Gen 5:3 When Adam had lived 130 years, he had a son in his own
likeness, in his own image; and he named him Seth. 5:4 After Seth was
born, Adam lived 800 years and had other sons and daughters. 5:5
Altogether, Adam lived 930 years, and then he died. 5:6 When Seth had
lived 105 years, he became the father of Enosh. 5:7 And after he became
the father of Enosh, Seth lived 807 years and had other sons and daughters.
5:8 Altogether, Seth lived 912 years, and then he died. 5:9 When Enosh
had lived 90 years, he became the father of Kenan. 5:10 And after he
became the father of Kenan, Enosh lived 815 years and had other sons and
daughters. 5:11 Altogether, Enosh lived 905 years, and then he died. 5:12
When Kenan had lived 70 years, he became the father of Mahalalel. 5:13
And after he became the father of Mahalalel, Kenan lived 840 years and
had other sons and daughters. 5:14 Altogether, Kenan lived 910 years, and
then he died. 5:15 When Mahalalel had lived 65 years, he became the
father of Jared. 5:16 And after he became the father of Jared, Mahalalel
lived 830 years and had other sons and daughters. 5:17 Altogether,
Mahalalel lived 895 years, and then he died. 5:18 When Jared had lived
162 years, he became the father of Enoch. 5:19 And after he became the
father of Enoch, Jared lived 800 years and had other sons and daughters.
5:20 Altogether, Jared lived 962 years, and then he died.**

These lists of names in Scripture are not always the most exciting of the
Bible's content. However, the names listed are of utmost importance. Not only
do they show man's decline in longevity, (to be discussed further after Noah) but
most importantly it traces the line of Christ. The promised Messiah would come
from the seed of Eve and, as prophesied, from the line of David. Thus, in order
to prove Christ as the Messiah, it was important to prove His lineage to the Jews.
This is why Matthew began his book with a genealogy. He was saying, "before
we begin, let me explain from Scripture that this man, Christ, is the Messiah."
Not only is this important in proving Christ the Messiah but also in disproving
anyone else. Today, all the Jewish records of genealogy have been destroyed
and, therefore, no one can come saying he is the Messiah and be able to prove it.
I don't think it was simply an accident that the records beyond Christ have been
lost.

Another importance in names is that they give a general time frame in
earth's history. From these lists we know about when Noah's Flood was, when
Christ came, and about how old the earth is. The main intent of the names is to
show Christ's lineage, but they do indeed show the earth to be young, as well.
Many claim there are gaps in the genealogies. Even if this were so, the earth
could be no more than about 15,000 years old. If there are no gaps, the earth is
only about 6,000 years old. Further historical support for these names without

gaps comes from 1 Chronicles 1:1-4 and Luke 3:36-38, where they are listed again. The famous Ussher chronology gave a date for Abraham's birth at 2056 B.C. (1,948 years after creation). Another man, Edwin R. Theile, expanded upon Ussher's study and has placed Abraham's birth at 2167 B.C. The latter has become widely accepted today. According to Theile then, the Flood would be about 2459 B.C. and the Babel dispersion about 2358 B.C., assuming no gaps of course.

Without gaps, Shem was living simultaneously with Abraham, in fact, Shem would outlive Abraham by 35 years since he died 502 years after the Flood. Noah also lived 350 years post-Flood enabling Abraham and he to become acquainted.

Chapter five will go through a list of ten patriarchs from Adam to Noah. Based upon the ages of these men when they died and when they had children, the date of the Flood must have been about 1656 years after Creation. The following will show what year they must have died: Adam -930; Seth- 1042; Enos -1140; Cainan -1235; Mahalaleel -1290; Zared -1422; Enoch (never died, but was taken to heaven alive in 987); Methuselah -1656 (when the Flood came); Lamech -1651; Noah -2006.

Gen 5:21 When Enoch had lived 65 years, he became the father of Methuselah. 5:22 And after he became the father of Methuselah, Enoch walked with God 300 years and had other sons and daughters. 5:23 Altogether, Enoch lived 365 years. 5:24 Enoch walked with God; then he was no more, because God took him away. 5:25 When Methuselah had lived 187 years, he became the father of Lamech. 5:26 And after he became the father of Lamech, Methuselah lived 782 years and had other sons and daughters. 5:27 Altogether, Methuselah lived 969 years, and then he died.

Some have claimed that because of the great ages listed, only months were counted, not years. This is not true and is clearly shown here with Enoch being 65 years old when he fathered Methuselah. If these were months, then he had a child at just over five years old. There are good reasons why man lived longer prior to the Flood, but we will discuss this after the Flood.

Enoch was the seventh from Adam in Seth's line and was a faithful man. In contrast, Lamech was seventh from Adam in Cain's line and was evil.

Enoch was the first of two men who would be taken to heaven alive (Enoch in the Sethite branch, not the Enoch of the Cainite branch in 4:17). Elijah was the second (2 Kings 2:11). Some believe that it will be Enoch and Elijah who will return as the two witnesses in Revelation 11. It is clear that Elijah will return (Malachi 4:5-6; Matthew 17:11), but no clear reference is made for Enoch. It is interesting that Elijah prophesied midway between Abraham and Christ, while Enoch prophesied midway between Adam and Abraham. Others say that it isn't Enoch, but rather Moses, who will return, since the miracles performed by the two witnesses fit both their ministries and that they were the ones who appeared at the Transfiguration of Christ in Matthew 17. Although only Elijah and Enoch never experienced death, the devil argued over the body of Moses (Jude 9) and the Lord personally handled his body (Deut

34:5-6). On the other hand, Hebrews 9:27 says all men must die but once, so Enoch and Elijah would fit this requirement. Anyway, it is very likely that the two witnesses in Revelation 11 are Elijah and either Moses or Enoch.

Enoch is mentioned in the Great Hall of Faith in Hebrews 11. We read, "By faith Enoch was taken from this life, so that he did not experience death; he could not be found, because God had taken him away. For before he was taken, he was commended as one who pleased God" (Heb 11:5). Enoch must have been a remarkable man to be blessed with such an experience. Where did Enoch go? To God in heaven. We, too, have a place prepared for us: "In My Father's house are many rooms; if it were not so, I would have told you. I am going there to prepare a place for you. And if I go and prepare a place for you, I will come back and take you to be with Me that you also may be where I am" (John 14:2-3).

Regarding Methuselah, at 969 he was the oldest man who ever lived. Some have said that his name could be rendered as "When he dies, it shall be sent." This is possible, but not a necessary translation. It would be significant, as Methuselah died the year of the Flood. This means one of two things. Methuselah either died in the Flood as a result of wickedness, or he died in the year of the Flood, but before it came. If the above meaning of his name is correct, then his life served as a time frame for the sending of the Flood. The fact that he was so old would also show God's patience with mankind, for it was during Methuselah's lifetime that it was said, "God waited patiently in the days of Noah while the ark was being built" (1 Peter 3:20).

Gen 5:28 When Lamech had lived 182 years, he had a son. 5:29 He named him Noah and said, "He will comfort us in the labor and painful toil of our hands caused by the ground the LORD has cursed." 5:30 After Noah was born, Lamech lived 595 years and had other sons and daughters. 5:31 Altogether, Lamech lived 777 years, and then he died. 5:32 After Noah was 500 years old, he became the father of Shem, Ham and Japheth.

This Lamech is not the same one we read about in 4:23 who was the son of Methushael and the father of Jubal and Jabal. This Lamech was in the line of Seth, the Godly offspring of Adam. His son was given the name Noah, which means "rest." Lamech, therefore, may have received divine revelation from God in the naming of Noah. If this is true, Lamech could be called one of the earliest prophets, and he prophesied here, "He will comfort us in the labor and painful toil of our hands caused by the ground the LORD has cursed." This prophecy shows that the curse was still very near in their minds. Adam must have shared what his experience in the garden was like, and Methuselah also would have passed this information along. Also, as mentioned earlier, it is very possible that the garden was still there but not accessible. Either way, the curse is very real. Another aspect of Noah's name meaning "rest" is that it is through him that line of Christ is followed and, therefore, in a way, true rest will come through him, the father of all post-Flood people.

As with Adam and others, it is said that Lamech had other sons and daughters and, therefore, Noah had brothers and sisters who must have perished in the Flood. Noah has only three sons listed here, and it is highly probable to assume that he, too, had "other sons and daughters" who also perished, since he is 500 years old before Shem, Ham and Japheth are born. Noah must have had other children before his 500th birthday. We often think of Noah being safe and full of joy in the ark; however, this must have been a day of great sadness as many of his own family were left behind.

One major purpose of Genesis is to trace the line of Christ. Shem is mentioned here because it is from his line that Christ will come. The rest of the world's population would come from either the line of Ham or Japheth.

Gen 6:1 When men began to increase in number on the earth and daughters were born to them, 6:2 the sons of God saw that the daughters of men were beautiful, and they married any of them they chose. 6:3 Then the LORD said, "My Spirit will not contend with man forever, for he is mortal ; his days will be a hundred and twenty years."

Chapter six continues to give reasons for the destruction of the pre-Flood world. As mentioned earlier, based on an average age of 400 years and an average number of children being six (probably more in this era) , the population at this time could have been at least 7 billion people.

Verse two begins a very interesting line of thought regarding man's wickedness. It states that the "sons of God" were marrying the "daughters of men." This has often been interpreted as Godly men marrying ungodly women. There is no question that this type of union should not take place, as Paul states, "Do not be yoked together with unbelievers. For what do righteousness and wickedness have in common? Or what fellowship can light have with darkness?" (2 Cor 6:14). Regarding remarriage, Paul writes, "if her husband dies, she is free to marry anyone she wishes, but he must belong to the Lord" (1 Cor 7:39). Therefore, this interpretation is fitting; however, another possibility remains.

The term "sons of God" is *ben elohiym* and is used five other times in Scripture, three being in the book of Job and two in Genesis. The two in Genesis can be found in reference to Isaac (Gen 21:4; 22:8). In Job something completely different is meant. We read, "One day the angels came to present themselves before the LORD, and Satan also came with them" (Job 1:6). The word "angels" in this verse is really *ben elohiym* and is translated as "sons of God" in other translations of the Bible. The point being, however, the term *ben elohiym* is referring to angels here. Note that they also appear to be fallen angels, since Satan came with them. In Job 2:1 almost the same thing is stated, with Satan again accompanying them. Another verse states, "the morning stars sang together and all the angels shouted for joy" (Job 38:7). The "angels" here are also the "sons of God;" in other translations and is *ben elohiym* in the Hebrew. The only difference is that here they are good angels. Another form of *ben elohiym* is *bar elahh* and is used only in Daniel 3:25, where it is also translated as "sons of God" and refers to an angel. *Ben el,* or "sons of the Almighty," is another form of this word which is only found in Psalm 29:1 and 89:6 and, again, means angels. We read, "For who in the skies above can compare with the LORD? Who is like the LORD among the *heavenly beings*? Here *ben el* is translated as "heavenly beings" (Psalm 89:6).

Therefore, according to the original language, it seems most probable that *ben elohiym* in Genesis 6:2 should also be translated as evil angels. In the Septuagint (Greek translation), many ancient Jewish writers and Josephus also have interpreted this verse as being angels. Josephus wrote, "for many angels of God [joined] with women, and begat sons that proved unjust, and despisers of all that was good, on account of confidence they had in their own strength; for the tradition is that these men did what resembled the acts of those whom the Grecians call giants." The footnote states, "This notion, that the fallen angels were, in some sense, the fathers of the old giants was the constant opinion of antiquity" (Antiquities 3:1:73). It seems that Augustine and Chrysostom were the first to translate this verse as merely Godly people. The very fact that these are "sons of God" must be interpreted as either spiritual "sons" or physical "sons" of God. The fact that so much of the world was wicked would suggest the spiritual sons of God would be few. The only true physical sons of God were Adam (Luke 3:38) and the angels (whether fallen or not Ps 148:2-5; 104:4; Col 1:16). Another factor involved, which will soon be discussed, is that their offspring were giants. With the uniting of so many mixed marriages today, why does the same thing not happen?

I am not saying that angels slept with human beings. Scripture states that angels do not marry: "At the resurrection people will neither marry nor be given in marriage; they will be like the angels in heaven" (Mat 22:30). However, the possibility that demon possessed human beings slept with other human beings is an option that needs to be explored. Although demon possession today is often thought of as myth or simply existent in only rare cases, Scripture and experience suggests otherwise. We do see that in many New Testament cases demon possession caused physical changes to take place. Some suffered from seizures that threatened their physical well being (Matt 17:15); others were thrown down on the ground (Luke 4:35); some gave men strength to break chains (Luke 8:29); some kept men from speaking (Luke 11:14); and others possessed animals and led them to their death (Mat 8:31). It is not unreasonable, therefore, that in the days of Noah demon possession could have caused physical changes to take place, making "giants."

Today, there is probably much more demon possession going on than we realize. We have the idea that once someone is possessed their eyes should glow and they should foam at the mouth. However, the devil is much more clever than this and uses deception, disguising himself as an angel of light (2 Cor 11:14). Many people have slowly but surely gone insane as a result of demon possession. Carl Jung and Sigmund Freud were two such men. Jung especially began by talking to the dead, much like many people do today in seeking their "spirit guides." At first the demons must be summoned but later they appear without being called. Eventually they become such a problem, one goes insane. Shirley McClain and others have been teaching to find the divinity within and, often times, spirit guides (demons) are helpful in pointing out such wisdom. The point being, demon possession can come in many forms; the subtle searching for wisdom can perhaps be the most dangerous temptation. Eve fell into it.

Along the same line, we have already discussed the fact that once one marries the two become ONE. "Do you not know that he who unites himself with a prostitute is one with her in body? For it is said, 'The two will become one flesh'" (1 Cor 6:16). Whether demon possessed or not, when the sons of God married the daughters of men, the result was a union of two opposing spirits. Romans states, "Those who live according to the sinful nature have their minds set on what that nature desires; but those who live in accordance with the Spirit have their minds set on what the Spirit desires" (Rom 8:5). The result in either case is wickedness.

The result of this was that God gave man 120 years. What does this mean? There are two possible interpretations. It is most probable that God was going to give man 120 years to repent, and if they did not, the Flood would come. We read in Genesis 15:16 that God gave the Amorites time to repent before their destruction, "for the sin of the Amorites has not yet reached its full measure." Likewise the sin of the pre-Flood people may not have reached its full measure. This means that Noah would also have had about 120 years to build the ark. Also, at the time of this message, Shem, Ham and Japheth had not yet been born and, therefore, Methuselah and Noah had a big job in preaching God's Word. In the New Testament, Noah is called a preacher of righteousness (2 Peter 2:5). And we sometimes think we are a minority!

The other possibility is that man would now only live up to 120 years. This does not seem to be a good interpretation, as people lived over 120 years of age for a short time after the Flood.

Gen 6:4 The Nephilim were on the earth in those days--and also afterward--when the sons of God went to the daughters of men and had children by them. They were the heroes of old, men of renown.

The word Nephilim means "giants" and is translated as such in the King James. Regarding giants, Numbers 13:33 states, "We saw the Nephilim [giants] there (the descendants of Anak come from the Nephilim). We seemed like grasshoppers in our own eyes, and we looked the same to them." Goliath was over nine feet tall (1 Sam 17:4). All of these people were ungodly men. Also, in the fossil record we have found human remains that are very large, and cities built on a scale for giants have also been seen. We already discussed above how demon possession has and could produce physical changes such as these.

Gen 6:5 The LORD saw how great man's wickedness on the earth had become, and that every inclination of the thoughts of his heart was only evil all the time.

God saw that the earth was filled with wickedness and that all their time was spent thinking about evil. I think a key to understanding this is "all the time." Luke 17:26-30 predicts, "As it was in the days of Noah, so shall it be also in the days of the Son of man. They did eat, they drank, they married wives, they were given in marriage, until the day that Noah entered into the ark, and the Flood came, and destroyed them all. Likewise also as it was in the days of Lot;

they did eat, they drank, they bought, they sold, they planted, they builded; but the same day that Lot went out of Sodom it rained fire and brimstone from heaven, and destroyed them all. Even thus shall it be in the day when the Son of man is revealed."

If you think the way I do, then images of violence and sexual immorality entered the mind when these verses were read. Sodom was inundated with the practice of homosexuality, and yet today we see the same thing occurring in our society. Is this what the passage really said? Take a closer look; nothing was said about violence, lawlessness or sexual perverseness; rather Luke refers to the heart of man, where the interests and joys of life have replaced the commitment we should have to God out of love for Christ. With "time saving" inventions like the microwave, fast food, cars, and computers, one would think we would have time to give our Lord praise, worship and meditation upon His Living Word. Instead, we have picked up more needless projects and vacations to fill up our time; hence, "eat, sleep and go fishing;" or perhaps as Scripture reveals, "while they are saying, 'Peace and safety!' then destruction will come upon them suddenly like birth pangs upon a woman with child; and they shall not escape" (I Thess. 5:3).

Let's go back to Luke and examine the things people are spending their time on: eating, drinking (he did not say drunkenness), marrying, buying, selling, planting and building. None of these were bad practices, but good. Hebrews 13:4 states, "marriage is honorable," and I Cor. 7:28 says, "if thou marry, thou hast not sinned." In addition, a virtuous wife is said to "considereth a field and buyeth it: with fruit of her hands she planteth a vineyard" (Prov. 31:16). Why does God tell us that we will be doing "good," worthwhile things before the Lord returns? Clearly it is a warning for us to pay attention, listen and commit our lives to the Great Commission (Matt 28:19), rather than become absorbed with our own interests. In Noah's day everyone was so busy eating, drinking , marrying and socializing with friends that they did not take time to listen to the preaching of Noah. This is the same reason the prophet Jeremiah wrote, "wherefore say My people...we will come no more to Thee... My people have forgotten Me days without number... Yet thou sayest...I am innocent" (Jer. 2:31). People had become so involved with business and personal affairs that they "forgot" to seek the Lord day after day (days without number). Yet Luke reminds us," thus shall it be."

Consider, also, the parable of the wedding banquet in Luke 14:16-24. Upon the call to come eat with our Lord, "they all with one consent began to make excuse" --excuses which were good, legitimate uses of time, yet time was put before commitment to God. The first man replied, "I have bought a piece of ground, and I must needs go and see it: I pray thee have me excused" (v. 18). The second man bought five yoke of oxen and desired to test them out, so he too asked, "I pray thee have me excused" (v.19). Finally, the third said, "I married a wife, and therefore I cannot come" (v.20). What was the grave sin of these men? They put land, oxen and marriage before fellowship with Christ. Again we hear Luke's prophetic warning, "as it was in the days of Noah, so shall it be," when we eat, drink, marry, buy and sell until our heart's content, but woe to the man who does not give his time to God. Take heed to the fate of these three men in this parable, for God says, "I say unto you, that none of those men which were bidden shall taste of My supper" (Luke 14:24).

Scripture reminds us that God is "Father of all who is over all and through all and in all" (Eph 4:6). God is "all in all." We often prioritize our lives putting God first, family second, job third etc., but for God to be all in all He must be first, second and third. God deserves all of our time, for "lo I am with you always," says Christ. In today's society, however, many Christians are professing their faith, yet their lives and commitment show faith to be lacking. "Even so faith, if it has no works, is dead, being by itself" (Jam 2:17). Revelation begins by going through seven churches which, many commentators agree, speak not only about specific churches of the past but also represent ascending time periods of history, with the last church (Laodicea) reflecting the attitude of society today. Two things need to be mentioned here. First, each church and time frame receives an attribute of Christ which fits the time and circumstances each church is going through. It is no coincidence that the attribute chosen for the last church is Christ as Creator; a reminder for us today when this is so widely denied (Rev 3:14). Secondly, the attitude of society is "lukewarm." John writes, "I know your deeds, that you are neither cold nor hot. I wish you were either one or the other! So, because you are lukewarm- neither hot nor cold- I am about to spit you out of My mouth. You say 'I am rich; I have acquired wealth and do not need a thing.' But you do not realize that you are wretched, pitiful, poor, blind and naked" (Rev. 3:15-17). Indeed, today many Christians are lukewarm, having the appearance of faith, but yet they are dead spiritually. Even Christ points this out when he warned, "Many will say to Me on that day, 'Lord, Lord, did we not prophesy in Your name, and in Your name cast out demons, and in Your name perform many miracles?' And then I will declare to them, 'I never knew you'" (Matt. 7:22-23). Indeed, these were good, worthwhile things, but they were done without faith and perhaps in pursuit of personal dreams and interests. Perhaps even more so, these people did not surrender their entire being to the Spirit. The only way we can overcome carnal desires is to let "Thine will be done, not our will." When selfish interests and personal issues interfere with our spiritual life, ask yourself: Is this His will? Will this benefit the kingdom? Our families? Our spirit?

The Bible warns against putting our interests first. Unfortunately, for many, occasional business transactions, vacation, extra sleep and football games get in the way of our Sunday worship (and perhaps daily worship), yet the Bible warns us "consider how to stimulate one another to love and good deeds, not forsaking our own assembling together, as is the habit of some, but encouraging one another; and all the more, as you see the day drawing near" (Hebrews 10:24-25).

Clearly, anything not done in faith is sin and evil (Rom 14:23). The people of Noah's day did not take time for God.

Gen 6:6 The LORD was grieved that he had made man on the earth, and his heart was filled with pain. 6:7 So the LORD said, "I will wipe mankind, whom I have created, from the face of the earth--men and animals, and creatures that move along the ground, and birds of the air--for

I am grieved that I have made them." 6:8 But Noah found favor in the eyes of the LORD.

God grieved over man's sin and was filled with pain because man had left the presence of God. We must be careful not to think that God wished he had never made man. Our finite minds cannot comprehend God's knowledge and justice. God never repents of anything He does, and He already knows the outcome of His decisions. However, God can be disappointed with man's rejection of Him through free will. For, "Those controlled by the sinful nature cannot please God" (Rom 8:8; see also 1 Thess 4:1; Heb 11:6). We are even warned, "do not grieve the Holy Spirit of God, with whom you were sealed for the day of redemption" (Eph 4:30).

As a result of man's wickedness, God promised to wipe them and the animals off the face of the earth. Why the animals? They, too, live in a sinful environment cursed by God. Noah's Flood served as a type of purification of man, animals and land. Today, baptism makes us children belonging to God. Noah's Flood served as a Baptism for all on earth, making them God's personal possession, and ridding all sin from the earth. Peter writes, "God waited patiently in the days of Noah while the ark was being built. In it only a few people, eight in all, were saved through water, and this water symbolizes baptism that now saves you also--not the removal of dirt from the body but the pledge of a good conscience toward God. It saves you by the resurrection of Jesus Christ" (1 Pet 3:20-21).

Regarding wiping things from the face of earth, some believe that since everything perished in the watery Flood, that may be why we read in the book of Revelation, "The sea gave up the dead that were in it, and death and Hades gave up the dead that were in them" (Rev 20:13). We also see that many of the evil spirits in Scripture either come out of or go into water.

Noah found favor in God's eyes, however. Noah was a preacher of righteousness (2 Peter 2:5) who found favor in God's eyes. The word "favor" can also mean grace. It is significant that Noah received grace, showing God's mercy upon those who call upon Him. "Everyone who calls on the name of the Lord will be saved" (Rom 10:13).

Gen 6:9 This is the account of Noah. Noah was a righteous man, blameless among the people of his time, and he walked with God. 6:10 Noah had three sons: Shem, Ham and Japheth. 6:11 Now the earth was corrupt in God's sight and was full of violence. 6:12 God saw how corrupt the earth had become, for all the people on earth had corrupted their ways. 6:13 So God said to Noah, "I am going to put an end to all people, for the earth is filled with violence because of them. I am surely going to destroy both them and the earth.

Noah is the only man outside of Enoch (Gen 5:22) of whom Scripture says, "walked with God." Indeed he was a righteous man and a preacher of righteousness (2 Peter 2:5); he had holy fear and was an heir of righteousness (Heb 11:7); considered among the three most righteous men along with Job and

Daniel (Eze 14:14); and was in the line of Christ (I Chr 1:4; Luke 3:36). Despite his righteousness, however, Noah could only save seven others in his family, while the rest perished.

The account of Noah also shows that God's ultimate deliverance (Christ) would not come from the Flood itself but from the line of Noah.

In verse 13, God told Noah that all people would die. Verse 7 indicates animals would also be destroyed. The fact that God was going to destroy both the people and the earth also suggests this. Some try to say that this was a local flood that destroyed only the people and some animals. However, here it is clearly said that the earth would be destroyed. We also read in 2 Peter that people would one day deny a world Flood: "But they deliberately forget that long ago by God's Word the heavens existed and the earth was formed out of water and by water. By these waters also the world of that time was deluged and destroyed" (2 Pet 3:5-6).

Gen 6:14 So make yourself an ark of cypress wood; make rooms in it and coat it with pitch inside and out. 6:15 This is how you are to build it: The ark is to be 450 feet long, 75 feet wide and 45 feet high. 6:16 Make a roof for it and finish the ark to within 18 inches of the top. Put a door in the side of the ark and make lower, middle and upper decks.

God's means of rescue for Noah was an ark. He gave Noah the instructions of how to construct it. It was to be 300 cubits long, 50 cubits wide and 30 cubits high. The cubit was anywhere from 18-24 inches and, therefore, the translation here in the NIV can vary a bit. However, using the most common cubit of about 18 inches, the above measurements are given. This means that it could very easily be bigger than what we have here.

The shape of the boat is nothing like what most pictures portray. It is actually described as being a long, rectangular box with another rectangular ridge running along the top of it for windows. We must remember that this was not a sailing vessel but a floating one. Battleships have been constructed using these dimensions and shape, and they proved to be some of the most stable and reliable boats ever built.

As far as capacity goes, using the lower end of the cubit, the ark would hold about 1,400,000 cubic feet of material. That is about the same as 522 railroad box cars. With each box car holding 240 sheep, about 125,000 sheep-size animals could go on the ark. This is especially adequate when we realize that even the average size of the dinosaurs is that of a sheep to a chicken, according to evolutionists. With about 18,000 *kinds* of animals estimated, two of every kind would be 36,000. Double this to allow for extinct species and you would have 72,000. Add 3,000 more for clean animals and only 60% of the ark's capacity would be filled.

The ark was to have three stories, each filled with individual pens or rooms. It was to be made of gopher wood, which we do not know about today. Some think that gopher wood was not a type but a process, much like particle board is today. It really makes no difference for our purposes here.

44

There was to be but one door of entrance into the ark. This door may have represented Christ, the only door to salvation. In order to escape judgment, one must enter through the door. Christ also says He is the door (John 10:7-9). Along the same lines, the ark was covered in pitch. We do not know what this pitch is, but the word itself means to "cover." It is also the word used for "atonement" and, thus, just as the ark was covered in pitch, we have received a covering or atonement through the blood of Christ. The word for ark is *tebah* meaning simply "a box." The same word is used to describe the "ark" that Moses was put in to float on the river in Egypt (Exodus 2:3). This "ark" was also covered in pitch. Other than with Moses, this is the only time this word is used.

Bill Cosby used to make jokes regarding what people must have thought about Noah building such a ridiculous thing in his backyard. Without rain (Gen 2:5) people must have made fun and ridiculed him while he only preached righteousness back to them (2 Peter 2:5). Despite the unknown, Noah kept the faith. It appears that, through this faith, God then showed him what was to come, "By faith Noah, when warned about things *not yet seen*, [like rain] in holy fear built an ark to save his family" (Heb 11:7).

Gen 6:17 I am going to bring floodwaters on the earth to destroy all life under the heavens, every creature that has the breath of life in it. Everything on earth will perish. 6:18 But I will establish My covenant with you, and you will enter the ark--you and your sons and your wife and your sons' wives with you. 6:19 You are to bring into the ark two of all living creatures, male and female, to keep them alive with you. 6:20 Two of every kind of bird, of every kind of animal and of every kind of creature that moves along the ground will come to you to be kept alive. 6:21 You are to take every kind of food that is to be eaten and store it away as food for you and for them." 6:22 Noah did everything just as God commanded him.

God again says that He will bring a Flood. The word for flood is "*mabbuwl*" and is used ONLY for Noah's Flood. Even in the New Testament, Noah's Flood receives a special word to distinguish it from other floods (*kataklusmos*; Mat 24:38-39; Luke 17:27; 2 Pet 2:5). Therefore, anyone who tries to say that Noah's Flood was only a local one has no merit. This Flood was so unique that it received its own word, "deluge."

Everything with the breath of life (*ruach*) would perish, along with everything else on land. Some of the sea creatures would survive in the water, however. God also says that He will (future tense) establish His covenant with them. This is the first time this word is used, and it will be given when they get off the ark (9:9ff.). Note that it is God's covenant, not man's. This covenant will be given and will depend solely on God, not on any effort of man.

Only eight people would enter through the doors of salvation (1 Peter 3:20).

We have already discussed the size of the ark and how many animals were estimated to be taken. Two of every kind but seven of every clean animal. The extra clean animals were taken to be sacrificed to God after they got off the ark (8:20). The two of every kind were simply to fill the earth. It is also important to realize that "kind" is a very broad term. This means only two dog kinds and two cat kinds, etc., needed to go on the ark, not two great danes, two pinchers, two blood hounds, two foxes, etc.

Verse 20 shows that these animals came to the ark. Noah did not have to go looking for them. He was also to take supplies along. Some have claimed that these animals would eat much more than there was room for, however, this could be answered by the fact that many animals would go into a state of hibernation under cold and unstable situations.

The chapter ends saying that Noah did everything God commanded him. We see this again in 7:5; 7:9 and 7:16.

Gen 7:1 The LORD then said to Noah, "Go into the ark, you and your whole family, because I have found you righteous in this generation. 7:2 Take with you seven of every kind of clean animal, a male and its mate, and two of every kind of unclean animal, a male and its mate, 7:3 and also seven of every kind of bird, male and female, to keep their various kinds alive throughout the earth. 7:4 Seven days from now I will send rain on the earth for forty days and forty nights, and I will wipe from the face of the earth every living creature I have made."

The NIV translates verse one as, "Go into the ark." However, the KJV has a more accurate translation which says, "Come into the ark." The fact that the LORD said, "come" means that the LORD was going with them. All the scientific speculation in the world cannot compare to this one simple fact: God was with those on the ark. We often have a tendency to try to explain everything away; however, with the God who created the universe, anything is possible, whether understood or not.

God then gave the specifics as to how many animals were to go into the ark. Seven clean animals left some for sacrificing (8:20), and the rest were for filling the earth. What distinguished clean and unclean animals has not yet been said in Scripture. Noah must have known from God's prior instructions or from this being passed down from Adam. Perhaps God made this distinction when the sacrifices began way back in the days of Cain and Abel (4:4). It is not until Leviticus 11 that we are given this distinction. The word, "throughout" in verse three shows that the animals were not going to stay in one location but would go to all parts of the earth, just as we see today. Perhaps this was one reason why God put the fear of man in animals after they disembarked; to run away (9:2).

Seven days were given to get everything ready. The 120 years given to repent had now been completed, with no others being saved. Right after the doors were closed on the seventh day (7:13), rain fell on the earth for the first time in history (2:5) and it didn't just fall, but it poured. The period of 40 days and nights was also symbolic for a time of testing. Jesus was tempted for 40 days (Mat 4:2); Moses was on Mount Sinai for 40 days (Ex 24:18; 34:28); those sent to spy out the promised land immediately after the exodus went for 40 days (Num 13:25); Israel wandered in the desert for 40 years (Num 14:34); Goliath taunted the Israelites for 40 days (1 Sam 17:16); Elijah, in a time of trouble, traveled 40 days to reach Horeb (1 Kings 19:8); and Jesus came back after his crucifixion to give "convincing proofs" for 40 days (Acts 1:3).

The fact that it rained forty days and nights also suggests a source of rainwater unknown today. Most scholars attribute this to the "firmament" which was created when God vertically separated water from water. This firmament may have collapsed, not only providing rain but also to alter the earth's environment completely, as will be discussed later.

The fact that "every creature" God had made was wiped from the face of the earth also shows it's a global covering, not a large local flood, as some have tried to say in order to buy into the philosophy of evolution.

Gen 7:5 And Noah did all that the LORD commanded him.

See note on 6:22.

Gen 7:6 Noah was six hundred years old when the floodwaters came on the earth. 7:7 And Noah and his sons and his wife and his sons' wives entered the ark to escape the waters of the flood. 7:8 Pairs of clean and unclean animals, of birds and of all creatures that move along the ground, 7:9 male and female, came to Noah and entered the ark, as God had commanded Noah. 7:10 And after the seven days the floodwaters came on the earth.

Noah was 600 years old when the Flood came. The fact that his age is given lends to the assurance that this is a historical narrative, not a myth. Only eight people went on the ark to escape the Flood waters. Pairs of animals came to Noah and were taken into the ark to assure continued breeding. This whole process took all of seven days and when the last animal boarded the rain began to fall. One can only imagine what was going through Noah's mind at this point.

Gen 7:11 In the six hundredth year of Noah's life, on the seventeenth day of the second month--on that day all the springs of the great deep burst forth, and the floodgates of the heavens were opened. 7:12 And rain fell on the earth forty days and forty nights. 7:13 On that very day Noah and his sons, Shem, Ham and Japheth, together with his wife and the wives of his three sons, entered the ark.

Again Noah's age is mentioned to be sure there is no mistake and to emphasize the historical importance of this event. Even more accurate than Noah's age is the month and day of the Flood. We cannot be sure what day this would be for us, since different calendars were in use and very little is known about pre-Flood dating. We will discuss this further in 8:4, but there is good reason to believe that the second month here refers not to the Jewish religious calendar but to a calendar based upon the creation of the world. That being the case, the Flood would have occurred in late November or December. However, the most important fact dealing with this date is that it shows the length of time by which the waters covered the earth.

Whatever day this was, it marked a day of great upheaval as the springs of the great deep burst forth. We saw in 2:5 that no rain was upon the earth, so streams came up from the ground and watered the whole face of the earth. It appears that these streams or artesian wells broke open, causing water to shoot out or "burst" from below. Though one can never be sure exactly how all these events took place, it would seem that once the earth cracked the heavy plates pushed down upon the waters of the deep, causing them to shoot skyward into the firmament. As these cracks continued, one would also expect much volcanic activity along with severe earthquakes. The dust and gases being put into the atmosphere, along with the water shooting high into the air, could have served as a means of penetrating the firmament and bringing it down as rain for 40 days and nights. Simply put, however, God called the waters upon the earth; *how* is not important. It does appear that the breaking forth of the subterranean waters was the initial act that got the ball rolling.

Taking this one step further, this whole process is also a great explanation of how and why the ice-age may have taken place. The warmer waters prior to the Flood would have became even warmer as the volcanic activity grew. This would have caused greater evaporation, but with colder climates caused by gases in the volcanoes, the moisture would have came down as snow in some places. As we have seen in recent history, Krakatoa caused the year without summer, and thus, we would expect a few summerless years after the Flood as things began to stabilize. Snow would come down and not go away in the summer, causing it to build up into what we know as the ice-age. Interesting references to ice have been noted in Job, which is believed to have been written soon after the Flood (Job 6:16; 37:10; 38:29).

On the same day the last animals got into the ark, the purification and baptism of God's creation began. We read from Peter, "when God waited patiently in the days of Noah while the ark was being built. In it only a few people, eight in all, were saved through water, and this water symbolizes baptism that now saves you also" (1 Pet 3:20-21).

Gen 7:14 They had with them every wild animal according to its kind, all livestock according to their kinds, every creature that moves along the ground according to its kind and every bird according to its kind, everything with wings. 7:15 Pairs of all creatures that have the breath of life in them came to Noah and entered the ark. 7:16 The animals going in were male and female of every living thing, as God had commanded Noah. Then the LORD shut him in.

The repetition continues to drive home the importance of this literal event. Two of all kinds of animals came to the ark. If this was merely a local flood only regional animals would have come.

The door of the ark was then shut by the LORD. This shows Gods providence and care for His redeemed. The LORD shut Noah, his family, and the animals into a box of atonement. There was nothing that they could do on their own to save themselves, they were in complete submission to God and looked only to Him for deliverance.

48

Gen 7:17 For forty days the Flood kept coming on the earth, and as the waters increased they lifted the ark high above the earth. 7:18 The waters rose and increased greatly on the earth, and the ark floated on the surface of the water. 7:19 They rose greatly on the earth, and all the high mountains under the entire heavens were covered. 7:20 The waters rose and covered the mountains to a depth of more than twenty feet.

Here again we have important verses showing the extent of this global Flood. As mentioned earlier, raining for 40 days and nights is not of realistic proportions today. The water was deep enough to raise a boat the size of the ark high ABOVE the earth, even 20 feet over the highest mountain. This clearly is not a local flood, but rather a global catastrophe that left the billions of fossils found today, with many of them being found high on mountain tops.

We have good reason to believe that prior to the Flood the mountains were not as high as they are now, nor were the valleys as deep. This also explains how the earth could be easily covered with water. If one would level out the earth today, there would be enough water to cover the earth well above a mile high. One reference which may allude to the mountains being raised and the valleys being lowered is Psalm 104 which reads, "But at Your rebuke the waters fled, at the sound of Your thunder they took to flight; they flowed over the mountains, they went down into the valleys, to the place you assigned for them. You set a boundary they cannot cross; never again will they cover the earth" (Psa 104:7-9). The RSV translates it as, "the mountains were raised and the valleys were lowered." Again, how the Flood waters covered the earth is not important, the fact that they did is what counts. Evolutionists must eliminate a global flood for their theories to stand; therefore, man will go to great lengths to avoid accepting a world-wide, mountain covering deluge. I believe Scripture predicted that the day would come when men would deny the historical accuracy of this event. Peter says that in the "last days" people will, "deliberately forget that long ago by God's word the heavens existed and the earth was formed out of water and by water. By these waters also the world of that time was deluged and destroyed" (2 Pet 3:3-6). I don't believe that God could have been any more plain about the global extent of the Flood, yet people feel the need to deny God's power and wisdom.

Gen 7:21 Every living thing that moved on the earth perished-- birds, livestock, wild animals, all the creatures that swarm over the earth, and all mankind. 7:22 Everything on dry land that had the breath of life in its nostrils died. 7:23 Every living thing on the face of the earth was wiped out; men and animals and the creatures that move along the ground and the birds of the air were wiped from the earth. Only Noah was left, and those with him in the ark. 7:24 The waters flooded the earth for a hundred and fifty days.

Once more the global aspect of the Flood is shown with "every" living thing perished, even the birds and wild animals. If this was merely local, why couldn't at least some of the birds have been able to fly to dry land. Verse 22 shows everything on dry land died. Therefore, many sea creatures would have survived, yet many also perished. The result was billions of dead fish fossils around the world, not just in local areas.

In addition to living, breathing life, verse 23 states every living "thing" also died. The word "thing" is *yequwm,* meaning "substance" and, therefore, would refer to plant life as well.

Those trying to discredit Scripture (as if it could be done) often say that verse 24 contradicts the 40 days and nights in 7:12. First of all, it rained for 40 days and nights and nothing is said of how long the water from the deep continued to come up. Secondly, it is most probable that the waters continued to rise for 40 days and then began to recede for the next 110 days until the ark actually touched the highest mountain (See 8:3). According to verse 20, this means the waters decreased 20 feet in those 110 days. In addition, no flood ever know to man outside of this one has lasted even close to 150 days.

Gen 8:1 But God remembered Noah and all the wild animals and the livestock that were with him in the ark, and he sent a wind over the earth, and the waters receded. 8:2 Now the springs of the deep and the floodgates of the heavens had been closed, and the rain had stopped falling from the sky. 8:3 The water receded steadily from the earth. At the end of the hundred and fifty days the water had gone down,

That God "remembered" Noah and those in the ark does not suggest that He forgot about them for a while; rather, the Hebrew indicates that He simply began "to do something for their sake." In order for the Flood to stop and the waters to recede God used a "wind," closed up the windows of heaven and the deep; and perhaps, as we said earlier, He raised the mountains and lowered the valleys (See note on 7:19). In these verses, however, the wind drying the land and the waters stopping are the two forces put into effect.

The "wind" is *ruach* in the Hebrew and is also translated as "spirit." One must use the context to decide which meaning is to be used. In this case either translation could be true. A true wind may have helped dry the waters up or the energizing Spirit of God may have supernaturally aided the waters in receding.

The rain from the windows of heaven had already been shut (after the first 40 days) and the fountains of the great deep had also been closed. Therefore, no more water was coming upon the land and the waters could recede, finally bringing the waters down 20 feet after the first 110 days.

Gen 8:4 and on the seventeenth day of the seventh month the ark came to rest on the mountains of Ararat.

Careful note was given to explain that the ark landed on Ararat on "the seventeenth day of the seventh month" (Genesis 8:4). Henry Morris gives a possible explanation for this detail as being a topological reference to Christ's deliverance. Dr. Morris writes, "The Lord Jesus Christ rose from the dead also on 'the seventeenth day of the second month.' The seventh month of the Jewish civil year (and this is probably the calendar used here in Genesis 7 and 8) later was made the first month of the religious year, and the Passover was set for the fourteenth day of that month (Exodus 12:2). Christ, our Passover (I Corinthians 5:7), was slain on that day, but then rose three days later, on the seventeenth day of the seventh month of the civil calendar" (Morris, Genesis Record, p.209). As Noah was delivered from the bondage of the ark, we too have been delivered from the bondage of sin.

The 17th day of the 7th month is the 17th of Nisan on the Jewish Calendar, corresponding to our April 17th. Also, *deliverance* first came on the 17th of Nisan through the ark of Noah. However, a **second** deliverance came on the same day (17th of Nisan) years later, at the parting of the Red Sea. About this time, the Passover was first instituted as the 14th of Nisan, where God said, "And this day shall be unto you for a memorial; and ye shall keep it a feast to the LORD *throughout your generations*; ye shall keep it a feast by an ordinance *for ever*" (Exodus 12:14). The Israelites left Egypt the following day (15th of Nisan) and camped that evening at Succoth. On the 16th of Nisan they traveled again as far as Ethan, and finally, on the 17th of Nisan, they reached Migdol and the Red Sea (Num 33:1-8).

Before the Exodus, a **third** deliverance on the 17th of Nisan was the entrance into Egypt. We know this event because Scripture tells us that the above exodus occurred on the exact day 430 years earlier when the Israelites entered Egypt through Jacob's family. We read, "Now the sojourning of the children of Israel, who dwelt in Egypt, *was* four hundred and thirty years. And it came to pass at the end of the four hundred and thirty years, even the *selfsame day* it came to pass, that all the hosts of the LORD went out from the land of Egypt" (Exodus 12:40-41).

Also a **fourth** deliverance occurs on this same day about 40 years later, after the Israelites wandered in the desert before being allowed to take the promised land. After crossing the Jordan, the Passover was celebrated (always on the 14th of Nisan). On the 15th day, "And they did eat of the old corn of the land on the morrow after the Passover, unleavened cakes, and parched *corn* in the selfsame day" (Joshua 5:11). On the 16th day, "the manna ceased on the morrow after they had eaten of the old corn of the land; neither had the children of Israel manna any more; but they did eat of the fruit of the land of Canaan that year" (Joshua 5:12). That now brings us to the 17th day of Nisan again, where Joshua went to check out the walls of Jericho and saw a man with a drawn sword. Joshua asks him if he is a friend or an enemy, whereupon this "man" replied, "Nay, but as captain of the host of the Lord am I now come" (Joshua 5:13). Joshua then received detailed instructions of how to conquer Jericho. Jericho itself did not fall until seven days later, due to the seven days of marching around the city walls, but one can say that the same day the angel gave Joshua those instructions was the same day in which Jericho was doomed to fall.

A **fifth** deliverance on this day occurs about 800 years after the entrance into the promised land. After the period of the judges, (Saul, David and Solomon), the kingdom was divided and a series of evil kings ruled Israel, causing worship in God's Temple to cease. One of the last evil kings, Ahaz, was replaced by his son Hezekiah, a righteous man who cleansed the Temple and restored worship there. 2 Chronicles 29:1-28 gives us the chronological events climaxing on the 17th day of Nisan. Here we see that on the 16th day of Nisan the cleansing of the temple is complete. Worship and sacrifice then begins on the 17th of Nisan, a most important day in Jewish and Christian history, for their salvation is again restored.

Yet a **sixth** deliverance occurred on this notable day. The book of Esther contains a story about the entire Jewish race being nearly wiped out by Haman, who was under king Xerxes command. Through a long process of Godly intervention, the Jews again are saved on the 17th day of Nisan. Haman had tricked King Xerxes into signing an edict to kill all of the Jews. Esther 3:12 tells us that this signing took place on the 13th of the first month, that being the month of Nisan. Immediately after Esther heard of this decree, she had the entire Jewish community fast and pray for three days. When finished on the 16th day of Nisan, (Esther 5:1) Esther went to the king and invited him and Haman to a banquet the following day, the 17th of Nisan. At this banquet Haman's evil tricks were exposed. He was executed by the king and the Jews had been delivered once again.

As mentioned at the beginning of this section, by far the most important of all the events that took place on the 17th of Nisan was the resurrection of Christ. A **seventh** deliverance, for all mankind. Christ was crucified on the 14th of Nisan, the day the Passover began. After remaining in the grave for three days, Christ rose from the dead on the 17th. If one calculates the odds of so many important events occurring on any given day, the result is 1 in 783,864,876,960,000,000. From this alone it is clear that God controls the world and He watches over His people. Isn't it wonderful to have a personal relationship with such a loving and powerful God who has promised heavenly dwellings for all who follow Him? Certainly, nothing stands in the way of this promise, not even Satan himself.

Gen 8:5 The waters continued to recede until the tenth month, and on the first day of the tenth month the tops of the mountains became visible. 8:6 After forty days Noah opened the window he had made in the ark 8:7 and sent out a raven, and it kept flying back and forth until the water had dried up from the earth. 8:8 Then he sent out a dove to see if the water had receded from the surface of the ground. 8:9 But the dove could find no place to set its feet because there was water over all the surface of the earth; so it returned to Noah in the ark. He reached out his hand and took the dove and brought it back to himself in the ark. 8:10 He waited seven more days and again sent out the dove from the ark. 8:11 When the dove returned to him in the evening, there in its beak was a freshly plucked olive leaf! Then Noah knew that the water had receded from the earth. 8:12 He waited seven more days and sent the dove out again, but this time it did not return to him. 8:13 By the first day of the first month of Noah's six hundred and first year, the water had dried up from the earth. Noah then

removed the covering from the ark and saw that the surface of the ground was dry. **8:14** By the twenty-seventh day of the second month the earth was completely dry.

Today, Mount Ararat is about 17,000 feet in elevation, and thus, if the mountains had already been raised, nearly 17,000 feet of water still had to be removed. This would have been an additional seven months added to the five that had already passed. After the ark landed on Ararat, Noah waited two and a half months before the tops of the other mountains could be seen above the water. He waited another 40 days to send out a raven, which did not return but kept flying back and forth. He also sent out a dove which returned, since there was no dry ground yet. It has been suggested that the raven did not return because it is a scavenger and would not hesitate to land in shallow water, but the dove will not land unless there is dry ground.

Seven days after the dove returned, he sent it out again, and this time it did not return until the evening, carrying an olive leaf showing vegetation was beginning to grow and dry land appearing. Seven more days went by before he sent out the dove, but this time it did not return.

All in all, Noah, his family and the animals resided in the ark for 371 days. It was 29 more days (first day of the first month in verse 13) before Noah opened the top covering to see dry ground for himself. God still did not let them come out of the ark because there must have still been a fair amount of water nearby. Therefore Noah remained another 57 days in the ark before God invited him out.

When Noah stepped off the ark he must have felt very strange, as the whole world had changed completely. A flood of this magnitude did not simply make things wet, it laid down thousands of feet of sediment and volcanic rock. It formed canyons, rivers, lakes, and mountains. It left a barren and desolate landscape unfamiliar to anyone seeing the pre-Flood world.

Gen 8:15 Then God said to Noah, 8:16 "Come out of the ark, you and your wife and your sons and their wives. 8:17 Bring out every kind of living creature that is with you--the birds, the animals, and all the creatures that move along the ground--so they can multiply on the earth and be fruitful and increase in number upon it." 8:18 So Noah came out, together with his sons and his wife and his sons' wives. 8:19 All the animals and all the creatures that move along the ground and all the birds--everything that moves on the earth--came out of the ark, one kind after another.

Note that Noah did not leave the ark until God told him to. The animals were also let out immediately, in order to multiply and fill the earth. Once off the ark, the animals spread throughout the world, possibly using land bridges, later exposed due to the ice-age. This ice-age could have been caused by colder climates as a result of the many expected volcanoes exploding gases into the atmosphere. Some animals must have found it difficult to adjust to such climates, and I suspect some may have become extinct as a result.

Many critics have claimed that the earth would be unable to support animals and that they would not be able to breed fast enough to survive. However, Mount St. Helens has shown otherwise, as elk and many other animals thrived in a very short time after the area's devastation. Many animals bred more quickly due to less competition and lack of predators, and perhaps also due to an apparent hormonal change which took place. What scientists said would take hundreds of years to restore came back in less than ten years.

Gen 8:20 Then Noah built an altar to the LORD and, taking some of all the clean animals and clean birds, he sacrificed burnt offerings on it. 8:21 The LORD smelled the pleasing aroma and said in his heart: "Never again will I curse the ground because of man, even though every inclination of his heart is evil from childhood. And never again will I destroy all living creatures, as I have done. 8:22 "As long as the earth endures, seedtime and harvest, cold and heat, summer and winter, day and night will never cease."

The first thing Noah did after he left the ark was to build an altar of sacrifice for the LORD. What great faith Noah showed in giving God thanks and praise for his deliverance, rather than complaining about the loss of such a beautiful world or fearing what to do next. Instead, he took some of ALL the clean animals and birds to offer up to the LORD. With so few animals left on the earth, this showed great faith that God would restore these animals by making the few that remained, flourish. Interestingly enough, a short distance down Mount Ararat many remains which appear to be types of altars have been found, along with stones engraved with eight Sumerian crosses; the oldest crosses known to man.

The LORD was pleased with this sacrifice and promised never again to curse the ground or the animals on account of man's wickedness. Note nothing is said of man, because a day is coming when man will be judged according to what his faith has produced (2 Cor 5:10; Rev 22:12; Rom 2:6), for just as a tree is judged by its fruit (Mat 12:33), so too a man's faith is judged by what he does.

Verse 22 is interesting because as long as the earth endures, there will be seasons, days and nights. However, a day is coming when the earth will no longer endure, but is replaced by a new earth. Consider the following: "Behold, I will create new heavens and a new earth. The former things will not be remembered, nor will they come to mind" (Isa 65:17); "As the new heavens and the new earth that I make will endure before me, declares the LORD, so will your name and descendants endure" (Isa 66:22); "But in keeping with His promise we are looking forward to a new heaven and a new earth, the home of righteousness" (2 Pet 3:13); and "Then I saw a new heaven and a new earth, for the first heaven and the first earth had passed away, and there was no longer any sea" (Rev 21:1). When this new earth comes there will be no cold, heat, winter, or night (Rev 21:25; 22:5), even though there is no sun (Rev 21:23). In our lives we need never fear that there will be no food, warmth or sun, because God has promised His care for us. We now wait for the day these things are not needed anymore.

The curse that came upon the earth (Gen 3:14-19) was first seen in Genesis. The promise never to make such an encompassing curse again is seen here in verse 21. This does not mean the curse was removed, but that no additional curses would ever take place. We read in Romans that the current curse still is very real: "The creation waits in eager expectation for the sons of God to be revealed. For the creation was subjected to frustration, not by its own choice, but by the will of the one who subjected it, in hope that the creation itself will be liberated from its bondage to decay and brought into the glorious freedom of the children of God. We know that the whole creation has been groaning as in the pains of childbirth right up to the present time" (Rom 8:19-22). The curse on man is also seen, in that "the wages of sin is death, but the gift of God is eternal life in Christ Jesus our Lord" (Rom 6:23); and "Therefore, just as sin entered the world through one man, and death through sin, and in this way death came to all men, because all sinned--" (Rom 5:12). The joy is that in Revelation, the close of Genesis, the curse is no more for "No longer will there be any curse. The throne of God and of the Lamb will be in the city, and His servants will serve Him" (Rev 22:3). There will be no more curse because, "Christ redeemed us from the curse of the law by becoming a curse for us" (Gal 3:13).

Gen 9:1 Then God blessed Noah and his sons, saying to them, "Be fruitful and increase in number and fill the earth. 9:2 The fear and dread of you will fall upon all the beasts of the earth and all the birds of the air, upon every creature that moves along the ground, and upon all the fish of the sea; they are given into your hands.

It's as if we were starting all over again, except this time with Noah and his family in a not so perfect world. Just as Adam was blessed and told, "Be fruitful and increase in number; fill the earth and subdue it" (Gen 1:28), so also Noah was commanded to do the same. Noah was not told to subdue the earth here, though he was still to control it, as suggested in the fact that he was allowed to subdue animals for food. One difference in this not so perfect world was that the animals were no longer tame. In Adam's day, the animals must have been very friendly and seemed almost as pets. Now, however, God put the fear of man into the animals so they would run away and spread out. Also, now that man was given permission to eat them, the animals were given the sense to get away.

One may ask, "What about the domesticated animals; were they afraid of man?" To a point, yes. Even today, there are what one could consider wild domesticated animals. However, one must also note that fear would come upon beasts, birds and creatures that move along the ground. In 7:14 it mentions the animals that were on the ark were wild animals, creatures that moved along the ground, birds, and livestock. The fact that livestock is left out of verse two may also imply that fear was not something genetically coded into these domestic animals; at least not in the same sense as other creatures on earth today.

The fact that the animals were given into man's hands and that he was also allowed to eat them (v. 3) reiterates our superior status to animals. We are not simply higher up on the evolutionary ladder, we were created above the animals as God's special creation.

Gen 9:3 Everything that lives and moves will be food for you. Just as I gave you the green plants, I now give you everything. 9:4 "But you must not eat meat that has its lifeblood still in it. 9:5 And for your lifeblood I will surely demand an accounting. I will demand an accounting from every animal. And from each man, too, I will demand an accounting for the life of his fellow man. 9:6 "Whoever sheds the blood of man, by man shall his blood be shed; for in the image of God has God made man.

In Genesis 1:29-30 we see that man was created to be a vegetarian. Now, however, God added meat to our diet, with a few restrictions. Though today we are able to eat any kind of meat (Acts 10:10-11:7); at this point Noah was only allowed to eat clean animals.

Not only this, but any meat that was eaten must not have had the lifeblood in it (Lev 17:12). Blood is a very important substance as, scientifically and Biblically speaking, it indeed appears to be where life resides. Leviticus gives us further insight into why blood was not to be eaten: "For the life of a creature is in the blood, and I have given it to you to make atonement for yourselves on the altar; it is the blood that makes atonement for one's life" (Lev 17:11). In other words, if the blood makes atonement for our life and the blood is life, it was the life of the animals that made atonement for our lives under the old covenant law. The animal's blood (life) covered our sinfulness and made atonement for us. This also foreshadowed the ultimate sacrifice to come: "Nor did He [Jesus] enter heaven to offer Himself again and again, the way the high priest enters the Most Holy Place every year with blood [life] that is not his own. Then Christ would have had to suffer many times since the creation of the world. But now He has appeared once for all at the end of the ages to do away with sin by the sacrifice of Himself. Just as man is destined to die once, and after that to face judgment, so Christ was sacrificed once to take away the sins of many people; and He will appear a second time, not to bear sin, but to bring salvation to those who are waiting for Him" (Heb 9:25-28). Christ's blood (life) was shed once for all (Rom 6:10) to cover our sins permanently, so that the life of animals was no longer needed to preserve our lives.

We see how Satan attempts to distort God's Word today, and in the past. Scripture states that the life is in the blood. The word for life is *nephesh,* which is "soul." Therefore, our soul is in blood or our soul is life. Many following the ways of evil have put into practice in the various rituals the drinking of blood, in hopes that the life or characteristics of that blood would be incorporated into one's own. We see here that this is clearly sinful and a tool of the devil.

There is one more interesting point dealing with eating meat with blood in it. We often say that the Old Testament laws are not necessary for us today, since we live under the New Covenant of Christ. Indeed, we need not follow these laws for salvation (although we will follow them anyway out of love and devotion); however, what we just read in Genesis is not from the Levitical law which was, in a sense, revoked by the resurrection of Christ. When the Gentiles in the New Testament were being brought into the church this is what was required of them: "It is my judgment, therefore, that we should not make it difficult for the Gentiles who are turning to God. Instead we should write to them, telling them to abstain from food polluted by idols, from sexual immorality, from the meat of strangled animals and from blood" (Acts 15:19-20; also Acts 21:25). Even in the New Testament era we would do well to abstain from the lifeblood, just as it was stated to Noah.

Let us examine the Acts 15 passage in more depth. The Gentile believers were to abstain from four things: 1) food sacrificed to idols 2) sexual immorality 3) strangled animals 4) blood. All four of these have a common bond, that being all of them deal with unity or "oneness" with someone or something. First, food sacrificed to idols would be like having communion with false gods. When a sacrifice to Baal or any other god was done, the food was then eaten and you partook of a communion meal with that god. When we think about it, Christ was a "food" sacrificed to the true God. Today we still celebrate this and participate in this ritual in our communion practice. When eating the "bread of life" we take in Christ's flesh and blood into our bodies, becoming one. We read in John, "Whoever eats My flesh and drinks My blood has eternal life, and I will raise him up at the last day. For My flesh is **real food** and My blood is **real drink**. Whoever eats My flesh and drinks My blood **remains in Me, and I in him**. Just as the living Father sent Me and I live because of the Father, so the one who feeds on Me will live because of Me. This is the Bread that came down from heaven. Your forefathers ate manna and died, but he who feeds on **this Bread** will live forever" (John 6:54-58). To have this kind of "fellowship" with anything or anyone but Christ would be a grave error.

Second, sexual immorality would also go against the oneness reserved only for Christ. "I am jealous for you with a godly jealousy. I promised you to one Husband, to Christ, so that I might present you as a pure virgin to Him" (2 Cor 11:2). This is why we see the parable of the wedding banquet in Matthew 22 and the final fulfillment of this parable in Revelation: "For the wedding of the Lamb has come, and His bride has made herself ready. Fine linen, bright and clean, was given her to wear. (Fine linen stands for the righteous acts of the saints.)" (Rev 19:7-8). The Scriptures make it clear that to have sexual relations with someone means to become ONE with them since, "the two became one flesh" (Matt 19:5). We also see this truth in Corinthians where we read, "Do you not know that your bodies are members of Christ Himself? Shall I then take the members of Christ and **unite them** with a prostitute? Never! Do you not know that he who unites himself with a prostitute **is one with her in body**? For it is said, 'The two will become one flesh.' But he who unites himself with the Lord **is one with Him** in spirit. Flee from sexual immorality. **All other sins a man commits are outside his body**, but he who sins sexually sins against his own body. Do you not know that your body is a temple of the Holy Spirit, who is **in you**, whom you have received from God? You are not your own" (1 Cor 6:15-19). Therefore, sexual immorality compromises our unity in Christ just as food sacrificed to idols did.

Third, not eating meat with blood in it and abstaining from strangled animals are one and the same. An animal that is strangled does not have all of its blood drained properly and, therefore, to eat of this animal would be to eat of its blood. As discussed above, the life is in the blood and, therefore, you are partaking of the *nephesh* of someone or something other than Christ. This is why Christ's blood is reserved for us. In communion His blood or *nephesh* (soul) is taken in, and unity takes place. As seen earlier, "Whoever eats My flesh and drinks My blood remains in Me, and I in him" (John 6:56; see also I Cor 11:27). Therefore, all of these commands to the Gentile church deal with the compromising of oneness in Christ. We are to be one with only One.

We must remember that these commands were given to Noah before the Levitical law was instituted. Noah was given permission to eat meat, and so is the New Testament church (Rom 14; 1 Tim 4:3-4; Acts 10:15). Also, the act of capital punishment was laid out here in verse six and this, too, is accepted in the New Testament church (Acts 25:11; Rom 13:4). This is not to say that capital punishment is always the answer, because in many New and Old Testament examples God forgave men of their sins and did not kill them. The attitude of the heart needs to be measured and true repentance must exist.

Not only was man going to be held accountable for his actions, but so were animals, as stated in verse five. We read in Exodus, "If a bull gores a man or a woman to death, the bull must be stoned to death" (Ex 21:28). Similarly today, often when dogs bite or bears attack, the animals are killed, and righteously so.

What we see happening in these verses is the establishment of the first government. Perhaps prior to the Flood no formal governmental regulations were put into effect and, thus, evil became rampant without any accountability to one another. We did see boastful threats as with Lamech (4:24), but these punishments were based on avenging one another. Indeed, these men were held accountable to God, but not to any form of written code.

This began to change with the Noahic covenant and was later added upon in the Levitical laws. Although the Levitical laws do not apply to us today (although some are still good rules to follow), the Noahic laws seem to still be in effect as they came under a covenant somewhat unknown. We read in Hebrews, "Jesus, who went before us, has entered on our behalf. He has become a high priest forever, in the order of Melchizedek" (Heb 6:20). Melchizedek was a priest in the time of Abraham of whom we know little. It is said that he was "without father or mother, without genealogy, without beginning of days or end of life, like the Son of God he remains a priest forever" (Heb 7:3). It is as if those from the time of Noah to Abraham lived in a period of grace, not salvation by law as those under the Levitical priesthood. They were, " in the order of Melchizedek, not in the order of Aaron" (Heb 7:11). Perhaps that is why we read of Abraham, "If, in fact, Abraham was justified by works, he had something to boast about--but not before God. What does the Scripture say? 'Abraham believed God, and it was credited to him as righteousness.' Now when a man works, his wages are not credited to him as a gift, but as an obligation. However, to the man who does not work but trusts God who justifies the wicked, his faith is credited as righteousness" (Rom 4:2-5). Also, "We have been saying that

Abraham's faith was credited to him as righteousness. Under what circumstances was it credited? Was it after he was circumcised, or before? It was not after, but before! And he received the sign of circumcision, a seal of the righteousness that he had by faith while he was still uncircumcised" (Rom 4:9-11). And, "The words 'it was credited to him' were written not for him alone, but also for us, to whom God will credit righteousness--for us who believe in Him who raised Jesus our Lord from the dead" (Rom 4:23-24). Therefore, Adam and Noah were saved through faith in God and in Christ as the coming Messiah, just as we too are saved through faith. Therefore, the Noahic commands given here are also meaningful in our lives today.

Gen 9:7 As for you, be fruitful and increase in number; multiply on the earth and increase upon it." 9:8 Then God said to Noah and to his sons with him: 9:9 "I now establish my covenant with you and with your descendants after you 9:10 and with every living creature that was with you--the birds, the livestock and all the wild animals, all those that came out of the ark with you--every living creature on earth. 9:11 I establish my covenant with you: Never again will all life be cut off by the waters of a flood; never again will there be a flood to destroy the earth."

With the current population today, the command to increase in number has certainly been obeyed. From eight people we now have over five plus billion people on the earth. The only problem is, people are not trusting God to take care of their needs (Rom 8:32; Phil 4:19; Mat 7:7). Many nations are looking for new ways of population control and praising abortion as one of these means. We are being falsely told that the earth cannot supply enough food or water for such masses. However, this is clearly not true, as all the world's population could fit in the state of Iowa alone and yet be no more crowded than Tokyo. Granted, I don't want to live like those in Tokyo, but there certainly is a lot more land in the world than simply Iowa. The real problem is greed! People swarm to live in cities because that is where the big money is and, therefore, the cities are overpopulated because people are not spreading out.

God made a covenant with all animals and people to come, that He would never again send a flood to destroy the earth. The fact that this promise was given again shows the global aspect of the Flood. If this was not a world-wide flood, then God did not keep His promise because we have seen large scale flooding today, but clearly not of Biblical proportions where it destroyed the earth and cut off ALL life.

Just because a flood will not destroy the earth does not mean the earth will remain forever. A day is coming when the earth will be destroyed forever and a new earth put in its place (Rev 21:1; 2 Pet 3:13; Isa 65:17: 66:22).

Gen 9:12 And God said, "This is the sign of the covenant I am making between me and you and every living creature with you, a covenant for all generations to come: 9:13 I have set my rainbow in the clouds, and it will be the sign of the covenant between me and the earth. 9:14 Whenever I bring clouds over the earth and the rainbow appears in the

clouds, 9:15 I will remember my covenant between me and you and all living creatures of every kind. Never again will the waters become a flood to destroy all life. 9:16 Whenever the rainbow appears in the clouds, I will see it and remember the everlasting covenant between God and all living creatures of every kind on the earth." 9:17 So God said to Noah, "This is the sign of the covenant I have established between me and all life on the earth."

We now receive more details regarding this "covenant." This promise on God's part, not man's, is repeated over and over in 6:18; 7:9,11,12,13,15,16 and 17. To remind man of God's promise a permanent "sign" was put in the sky, a rainbow. Even though today the rainbow comes and goes without so much as a thought of Noah's Flood, God has not forgotten His promise. We would do well to give thanks and praise to God everytime we see a beautiful rainbow. The fact that the rainbow is not seen until after the Flood shows again that there was no rain until the Flood, as seen also in 2:5. Once rain came upon the earth, the rainbow was seen.

In addition to the promise of God, His very presence should come to mind when viewing a rainbow. The rainbow is only seen three other times outside of these verses in Genesis. All three show the rainbow to be in God's presence; thus, it need not show in the sky for God to think about His promise. In Ezekiel 1:28 we see the rainbow around God's throne: "Like the appearance of a rainbow in the clouds on a rainy day, so was the radiance around Him. This was the appearance of the likeness of the glory of the LORD." In Revelation 4:3 we again see the rainbow at God's throne: "And the one who sat there had the appearance of jasper and carnelian. A rainbow, resembling an emerald, encircled the throne." And, finally, in Revelation 10:1 when the Lord returns He is accompanied by the rainbow: "Then I saw another mighty angel coming down from heaven. He was robed in a cloud, with a rainbow above His head." Even though God is coming to judge the world, the rainbow shows it will not be by water.

Gen 9:18 The sons of Noah who came out of the ark were Shem, Ham and Japheth. (Ham was the father of Canaan.) 9:19 These were the three sons of Noah, and from them came the people who were scattered over the earth.

The entire world today has come from one of these three men, Shem, Ham and Japheth. Much wasted time and energy has been spent trying to figure out man's human ancestry back to apes. Genetically speaking, science has proven that man has come from ONE distant relative, and they have even named her Eve. Though these scientists reject the Biblical story of Adam and Eve, they believe that at one time the first living creature evolved and led down to us today. Scripture clearly teaches that man has come from Adam and started again with the sons of Noah (Acts 17:26; Gen 10:32).

Ham was the father of Canaan. This was probably mentioned to show that Ham was the father of those who would fight against the Israelites and their right for the promised land. The upcoming actions of Ham clearly show how his descendants could be so evil.

Gen 9:20 Noah, a man of the soil, proceeded to plant a vineyard. 9:21 When he drank some of its wine, he became drunk and lay uncovered inside his tent. 9:22 Ham, the father of Canaan, saw his father's nakedness and told his two brothers outside. 9:23 But Shem and Japheth took a garment and laid it across their shoulders; then they walked in backward and covered their father's nakedness. Their faces were turned the other way so that they would not see their father's nakedness.

Noah planted a vineyard shortly after the Flood and drank some of its wine. The fact that he became drunk may show a time of weakness, or perhaps a hard lesson learned under a new environment. Some have suggested that the pre-Flood conditions allowed one to drink more wine with less effects. The Flood may have left a world with perhaps less oxygen and air pressure, the wine had more of an effect than what Noah was used to. Even so, Noah had to have felt himself become less aware and, therefore, was at a time of weakness. One of the most beautiful truths in Scripture is that even the most Godly of men, could only live by the grace of God. We are all sinful by nature and are in need of Christ's forgiveness.

The pre-Flood society had to have had adverse effects upon Noah and his children. While Noah lay in his tent, drunk and naked, Ham happened to come along. Upon seeing his father, Ham went out and told his two brothers "with delight" as the Hebrew implies. It appears that Ham fell into one of two sins. The word "saw" in verse 22 means to "gaze upon" and could imply homosexual lusts. Indeed, this was probably not a foreign idea to the violent and ungodly pre-Flood world. However, Ham apparently did not follow this crowd, as indicated by his deliverance on the ark. Another possible interpretation is that Ham was simply making fun of his father's weakness in an attempt to feel better about himself.

It is also interesting that, once again, it is mentioned that Ham was the father of Canaan, hence the Canaanites. Stating this fact again shows Cain's changing attitude toward God. Canaan became a wicked nation because their father, Ham, was a wicked example.

A more proper example was set by the two brothers who covered Noah's nakedness and shielded their eyes from seeing this sinful display.

Gen 9:24 When Noah awoke from his wine and found out what his youngest son had done to him, 9:25 he said, "Cursed be Canaan! The lowest of slaves will he be to his brothers."

When Noah woke up and found out what Ham had done, curses were pronounced. Just as from the fall of Adam the curse resulted, so also from the fall of Ham, curses followed. Apparently, Ham's brothers must have either gotten Ham to confess or they told on him. The earlier mentioned idea that Ham gazed upon his father with homosexual lust may be somewhat supported, in that

Noah found out what his son "had done to him." If this interpretation is correct, perhaps nothing had to be said.

Canaan, Ham's son, was to be the lowest of slaves. The word "slave" can also be translated as "steward." From what we know of Canaan's history, he or his descendants were never completely enslaved by either of the brothers or their descendants, suggesting that "steward" may be a better translation. Some have attempted to say that the black slaves were descendants of Ham, but this has no Biblical or historical backing.

Henry Morris points out some interesting clues into understanding the Canaan curse in his book, The Genesis Record. He points out that as man is made up of the triune - physical body, soul and spirit - so men follow one of these aspects of their being. Men either follow physical pleasures, intellectual appetites, or spiritual submission. The descendants of Ham appear to be the Egyptians and Sumerians, Chinese, Japanese, Phoenicians, Hittites, Canaanites, and the American Indians. All were interested in the physical world, yielding many inventions, warriors and laborers. Morris points out that while they invented many things, the Japhethites and Semites later took them over and developed them for their service to mankind; thus the Hamites were stewards.

Some believe that the Gibeonites having been subjected to Joshua was a fulfillment of being the "lowest of slaves." (See Joshua 9:27; 16:10; Judges 1:28-35; 1 Kings 9:20-21).

A parallel between Adam and Noah is pointed out by Morris. Both Adam and Noah were commanded to fill the earth and have authority over it; both were ancestors of all men; both sinned by eating of the fruit (Noah's wine); both became naked as a result of their sin; both were covered by someone else; both received curses which affected all of mankind; both receive a blessing that affects all of mankind - the prophecy of a coming Savior.

Gen 9:26 He also said, "Blessed be the LORD, the God of Shem! May Canaan be the slave of Shem. 9:27 May God extend the territory of Japheth ; may Japheth live in the tents of Shem, and may Canaan be his slave." 9:28 After the flood Noah lived 350 years. 9:29 Altogether, Noah lived 950 years, and then he died.

Along with the curse of Ham came the blessing of his two brothers. Shem appeared to take a more spiritual route in life, and thus it is said, "Blessed be the LORD, the God of Shem!" It was through the line of Shem that our blessed LORD, Jesus Christ, would come. The apparent descendants of Shem are the Jews and Moslems, showing their theological focus on life. (This will be discussed in greater detail in the coming chapter.)

As for Japheth, he was to be enlarged. The word "extend" may allude not to a physical land size but rather to intellectual extension. The Japheth line seems to produce the Greeks, Romans, European and American peoples. Thus those from Shem have had a focus on science and philosophy, based upon the technology of the Caananites.

Noah lived 350 years after the Flood. The longevity of man greatly decreased from now on due to the changed environment caused by the Flood.

Since Noah lived 950 years total, that meant Abraham would have been about 58 years old when Noah died (Gen 11).

Gen 10:1 This is the account of Shem, Ham and Japheth, Noah's sons, who themselves had sons after the Flood. 10:2 The sons of Japheth: Gomer, Magog, Madai, Javan, Tubal, Meshech and Tiras. 10:3 The sons of Gomer: Ashkenaz, Riphath and Togarmah. 10:4 The sons of Javan: Elishah, Tarshish, the Kittim and the Rodanim. 10:5 (From these the maritime peoples spread out into their territories by their clans within their nations, each with its own language.)

The genealogical record seen in this chapter has been said to be one of the most historically accurate records ever. Many of the names of these men and their cities have been identified in archaeology, giving further support for Biblical inerrancy.

We will rely heavily upon the interpretation given by Henry Morris as he has done a tremendous amount of valuable research in this area.

Here begins the account of Noah's sons after the Flood, beginning with Japheth. There may be good reason to believe that Shem had written this account, as he is the one who is in the line of Christ. Also, he lived 502 years after the Flood (Gen 11:10-11) and lived through the entire time discussed in the Table of Nations. Yet another interesting clue comes from the fact that Shem's descendants are traced to the sixth generation, while Japheth and Ham are traced only to the third generation. Some have suggested that this may mean Shem had lost contact with his brothers at the dispersion at the Tower of Babel.

The accounts below are based upon the most reliable information available. While some names are uncertain, based upon historical records and ancient literature it is not unreasonable to trace these names to the present nations today.

Japheth was the oldest of Noah's sons and his line is traced first. Although only the names of his sons are listed, it is not unreasonable to assume there were also many daughters included with all the descendants in these records. The names of Japheth's sons are all names that can be seen in the Indo-European past. Henry Morris again writes, "The name of Japheth himself, for example, is found in the literature as Iapetos, the legendary father of the Greeks, and Iyapeti, the reputed ancestor of the Aryans in India. The first son, Gomer, is generally identified (by Herodotus, Plutarch, and other ancient writers) with the district of Cimmeria, north of the Black Sea, a name surviving to the present in the form Crimea" (Record, p. 247). Josephus also recorded that the sons of Gomer were called the Galatians or Gauls; previously called Gomerites. The Gomerites migrated towards France and Spain. For many years France was called Gaul and even to this day northwest Spain is called Galicia.

Another of Japheth's sons was Magog. Josephus wrote that Magog gave way to the Scythians who began near the Black Sea. Morris further explains, "Magog is commonly associated in the Bible with two other sons of Japheth - Meshech and Tubal (especially Ezekiel 38:2). Meshech clearly is preserved in the name Muskovi (the former name of Russia) and Moscow. In fact, today a section of the Meschera Lowland is still known as Meshech. Tubal is known in the Assyrian monuments as the Tibareni, and probably has been preserved in the modern Russian city of Tobolsk. Tiglath-pileser I, king of Assyria (1100 B.C.), said that the descendants of Tubal were called Tabali. Josephus also recorded their names as the Thobelites, who were later called the Iberians. In the days of Josephus, the Iberian land was what we know as the former Soviet state of Georgia. In fact, the capital of this Soviet state is still called Tbilisi. In Ezekiel 38:2 the descendants of Tubal are associated with "Rosh," a name from which modern "Russia" was derived. Generally speaking, therefore, these three sons of Japheth -- Magog, Meshech, Tubal -- can be considered the progenitors of the modern Russian peoples" (Record, p 248).

Madai, the third in the line of Japheth, was the ancestor of the Medes in Persia, as believed by almost all scholars. It was probably through Madai that the Aryan people descended. They later went into India and lead us down to the "Indian" nations.

Javan's name, the fourth in the list of Japheth, comes from the word Ionia, which was the same name given to Greece. Sometimes "Ionia" is translated as "Greece" and at other times the same word is translated as "Javan." Thus Javan along with Japheth are considered to be the fathers of the Greeks.

The names of Javan's sons also give further evidence leading back to the Greeks. Elishah is taken from the word "Hellas," which also originated in Greece as "Hellespont" and "Hellenists." Even the *Iliad* talked about the Eilesian people. Also, the Amarna tablets told of the Alasian people, who apparently came from Cyprus.

Another of Javan's sons was Tarshish, who has been connected with Tartessos in Spain and Carthage of North Africa. As Morris points out, "Both of these, however, were Phoenician cities and the Phoenicians were Canaanites. It is possible that the descendants of Tarshish may have been early settlers of Spain and North Africa, but that the Phoenicians were later more prominent in their development" (Record, p. 248).

Dodanim may be the same name as Rodanim in 1 Chronicles 1:7. His name may lead to the area of Dardanelles and Rhodes.

Tiras, the last of Japheth's sons, is traced to the Etruscans of Italy by Josephus. They were called the Thirasians for some time until the Greeks changed their names to the Thracians. Thrace has been known to be what is now Yugoslavia. Even *the World Book Encyclopedia* states, "The people of Thrace were savage Indo-Europeans, who liked warfare and looting" (1968).

The names of Gomer's sons (names, not actually his sons) also can be identified in history. Ashkenaz has been related to Germany by the Jews because Ashkenaz is the Hebrew word for Germany. In fact, even today the Jews in Germany are referred to as Ashkenazi. Togarmah is thought to be the ancestor of the Armenians, and the Armenian traditions also support this belief. Since ancient Armenia went into Turkey, Togarmah may also have some connection with Turkey and Turkestan, but this is uncertain.

Keep in mind also that the Japhethites, as discussed earlier, seem to have been motivated by the intellectual (soul), pursuing philosophy and the sciences. For whatever reason, five of Japheth's son's were not listed. We do know that the names of those that God intended us to remember are here.

Verse five suggests that this account was written after the scattering at the Tower of Babel.

Gen 10:6 The sons of Ham: Cush, Mizraim, Put and Canaan. 10:7 The sons of Cush: Seba, Havilah, Sabtah, Raamah and Sabteca. The sons of Raamah: Sheba and Dedan. 10:8 Cush was the father of Nimrod, who grew to be a mighty warrior on the earth. 10:9 He was a mighty hunter before the LORD; that is why it is said, "Like Nimrod, a mighty hunter before the LORD." 10:10 The first centers of his kingdom were Babylon, Erech, Akkad and Calneh, in Shinar. 10:11 From that land he went to Assyria, where he built Nineveh, Rehoboth Ir, Calah 10:12 and Resen, which is between Nineveh and Calah; that is the great city.

The sons of Ham were Cush, Mizraim, Put and Canaan. To start with, Cush is the same as "Ethiopia" and is often translated as such in the Scriptures. According to the Amarna tablets, Ethiopia is called "Kashi."

Mizraim appears to lead down to the Egyptians and is so called in Scripture as well. In Psalm 105:23 it is said that Egypt is the land of Ham. This may mean Ham's descendants, or that Ham followed his son to Egypt. Out of the hundreds of times the word "Egypt" appears in Scripture, all but one are translated as Mizraim.

Put and Libya are one and the same in the Bible. Josephus, as well, has confirmed Put as the area of Libya today.

Now we begin with five sons of Cush: Seba, Havilah, Sabtah, and Raamah. Seba leads down to Sudan or the Sabeans. This name is seen in Isaiah 45:14 and is heard in Arabia and Africa. Josephus pinpointed "Saba" as "Meroe," which is in upper Egypt.

Havilah, Sabtah, Raamah, and Sabtechah all stem from Arabia and may explain the ancient city of Sabatah found there. Do not confuse the Havilah here with the son of Joktan in Genesis 10:29. Sheba and Dedan, Raamah's sons, are the only ones listed of Cush's immediate family.

Cush was also the father of Nimrod. Nimrod is an interesting name, meaning "let us rebel." The fact that Cush gave his son this name may give insight into Cush's heart. Nimrod became a mighty warrior and gathered a great following. He built many cities and started the kingdom of Babel. The reference to him having been a "mighty hunter before the LORD" really means he was a "mighty hunter against the LORD." It is very possible that Nimrod first gained fame from killing some of the larger animals we see in the fossil record that roamed freely after the Flood. However, he probably gained his followers more from his warrior skills. The Jerusalem Targum states this of Nimrod: "He was powerful in hunting and in wickedness before the Lord, for he was a hunter of the sons of men, and he said to them, 'Depart from the judgment of the Lord, and adhere to the judgment of Nimrod!' Therefore it is said: 'As Nimrod the strong one, strong in hunting, and in wickedness before the Lord.'" (Record, p. 252).

As mentioned, Nimrod probably was the king and leader of those who built the great Tower of Babel in Genesis 11. Using Babel as his center, Nimrod built surrounding cities such as Erech, Akkad, and Calneh, which is in Shinar. Erech (Uruk) is a city about 100 miles southeast of Babylon and, interestingly enough, is the home of the legendary Gilgamesh, the hero in the Babylonian flood story. Archaeological digs have revealed ancient writings that pre-date Abraham. Akkad was just north of Babylon and became the Akkadian empire, otherwise known as the Sumerian empire. We do not know where Calneh was located, aside from the fact that it was in Shinar. It is possible that this is "Sumer," which in Daniel 1:2 is a reference to Babylon.

From the upper end of the Euphrates (Babylon), Nimrod went to the upper end of the Tigris (Assyria). Nineveh was about 200 miles north of Babylon and became the capital of Assyria. One can see its greatness in the book of Jonah. According to Diodorus, a Greek historian, Nineveh had walls 100 feet tall with a circumference from seven to eight miles. Outside the walls were suburbs with a 60 mile circumference. Truly it was a great city in any day. Later, the Semites would conquer both Assyria and Babylon, but the Hamites built them both. As for Rehoboth and Resen, nothing has yet been found of these two cities. Although Resen is suppose to be between Nineveh and Calah. Calah was located about 20 miles south of Nineveh on the Tigris. In fact, it is called "Nimrud," after Nimrod.

Gen 10:13 Mizraim was the father of the Ludites, Anamites, Lehabites, Naphtuhites, 10:14 Pathrusites, Casluhites (from whom the Philistines came) and Caphtorites. 10:15 Canaan was the father of Sidon his firstborn, and of the Hittites, 10:16 Jebusites, Amorites, Girgashites, 10:17 Hivites, Arkites, Sinites, 10:18 Arvadites, Zemarites and Hamathites. Later the Canaanite clans scattered 10:19 and the borders of Canaan reached from Sidon toward Gerar as far as Gaza, and then toward Sodom, Gomorrah, Admah and Zeboiim, as far as Lasha. 10:20 These are the sons of Ham by their clans and languages, in their territories and nations.

Mizraim was the one responsible for first settling Egypt. Nothing is really known about the Ludites, Anamites, Lehabites or Naphtuhites. The Pathrusites and Caphtorites are both associated with the Philistines; the Pathrusites here in verse 15 and the Caphtorites in Amos 9:7 and Jeremiah 47:4.

Canaan, Ham's youngest son, had eleven children, with his oldest son Sidon leading to the Phoenicians. The Hittites were around from the time of Abraham (Gen 15:19-21) all the way up into the reign of Solomon (2 Chronicles 1:17). It is probable that the Hittites were in some way related to the Mongoloids, as both have been known for similar achievements, including smelting, and horse breeding. The Hittites centered in Asia Minor and lived among Canaan from around 1800 B.C. to 1200 B.C.. The Jebusites lived in Jerusalem early on (Joshua 15:63) and in fact, Jerusalem was called Jebus for part of Israel's history (Judges 19:10-11; 1 Chronicles 11:4). The ground on which Solomon will build the Temple is purchased from the Jebusites. The

Amorites were one of the largest tribes of the Canaanite clans and were sometimes referred to as representing all the clans (Genesis 15:16). The Girgashites are unknown, other than their name being frequently mentioned in Scripture (Gen 10:16; 15:21; Duet 7:1; Josh 3:10; 24:11; 1 Chron 1:14; Neh 9:8). The Hivites are also prevalent throughout the Bible and have been shown in many archaeological digs ranging from Sidon to Jerusalem. The Arkites may come from Arka in Syria. The Sinites are interesting in that "Sin" has been carried down for centuries. A prominent Assyrian god was named Sin, along with another son of Canaan. In archaeological finds near Ur, "Sin" was said to have made, "laws and justice." It is also significant that today the Chinese are referred to using the prefix "Sino" (Sino-Japanese War or, as in the study of Chinese history, Sinology). The Arvadites settled in Arvad, which was a port city for the Phoenicians, and the Zemarites about six miles south of Arvad. The Hamathites came from Hamath, a Syrian city also mentioned in Scripture over 37 times.

Regarding the above, Morris writes, "The evidence is tenuous, but of all the names in the Table of Nations, it does seem that two sons of Canaan, Heth (Hittites-Khittai-Cathay) and Sin (Sinites-Sinim-China), are the most likely to have become ancestors of the Oriental peoples.. . . It is reasonable to conclude that the Mongoloid peoples (and, therefore, also the American Indians) have come mostly from the Hamitic line." (Record, p 256).

The Canaanite line is the only one mentioned that was scattered. This may suggest that they spread out more than any other line, perhaps taking them north and east into Asia and later into North and South Africa by the Bering Sea land bridge (possibly existed during ice-age). The area described in verses 19-20 is not overly large, but it's from here that they spread out.

Verse 20 clearly shows that this account was written after the Tower of Babel since the Hamite clan has already been divided by languages. From these groups of common languages nations were established.

Again, the Hamites were motivated by physical pleasures (body), whereas the Japhethites were motivated by the mind (soul). Next we will examine the Shemites, who have a religious focus (spirit).

Gen 10:21 Sons were also born to Shem, whose older brother was Japheth; Shem was the ancestor of all the sons of Eber. 10:22 The sons of Shem: Elam, Asshur, Arphaxad, Lud and Aram. 10:23 The sons of Aram: Uz, Hul, Gether and Meshech. 10:24 Arphaxad was the father of Shelah, and Shelah the father of Eber.

It is from the line of Shem that Christ would come. Perhaps that is why Shem's line was traced to the fifth generation, whereas Ham was traced only to the third and Japheth to the second generation. We see here, and earlier, that Japheth was the oldest son of Noah (9:6) and Shem the youngest.

Shem was the ancestor of Eber. Eber was a well known clan and may be where the "Hebrew" people come from. Some archaeological records note the "Habiru," may refer to the people of Eber.

Five of Shem's sons are listed. Elam was the father of a well known people called the Elamites. We see them both in Scripture (Acts 2:9) and history. The city of Susa, or Shushan, was the Elamite capital, and it is believed that these people later joined forces with the Medes to form the Persian empire. Keep in mind that the Medes descended from Madai, the son of Japheth.

Asshur seems to have formed the Assyrian culture, but Nimrod (from the line of Ham) took over Asshur; thus, the Assyrian nation stemmed from both Asshur and Nimrod.

Arphaxad was in the direct line to Abraham and Christ (Luke 3:34-36). He was born to Shem when Shem was 100 years old (Gen 11:10) and, outside of his genealogy, little is know about him. His descendants seem to be the Chaldeans according to the Nuzi Tablets. In any case, this shows Scripture's divine attention to names for the important purpose of tracing the Messiah.

Josephus records that Lud leads to the Lydians of Asia Minor. The Lydians were famous archers, according to Isaiah 66:19.

Aram was responsible for the Arameans, otherwise called the Syrians. Perhaps what these people are most noted for was their Aramaic language, which infiltrated much of the ancient world. Parts of Daniel and Ezra are written in Aramaic; it was spoken by many at the time of Christ, but today only one family line in Israel continues to speak this language.

All of Aram's sons are unknown, except for Uz who apparently settled in the land where Job would live (Job 1:1; Jer 25:20).

Only one of Arphaxad's sons was listed, probably to simply continue the real purpose in these names - to trace the genealogy of Christ. We see again in Luke 3:34-35 that Shelah and Eber both are listed in the line of Christ.

Gen 10:25 Two sons were born to Eber: One was named Peleg, because in his time the earth was divided; his brother was named Joktan.

Entire books have been written in response to this one verse: "And unto Eber were born two sons: the name of one was Peleg; for in his days was the earth divided." This is the only place in all of the Table of Nations that a son's name was given along with its meaning. Therefore, it must have some significance. Some interpret this division of people at the Tower of Babel as political, not a physical land separation. Further examination pinpoints the time of Peleg in relation to the Tower of Babel. Assuming there are no gaps in the genealogies around this time, Peleg would have been the great-great-great-great grandson of Noah and lived to be 239, according to the Massoretic text, or 339 years in the LXX text. This also means, according to the Massoretic text, that Noah would still have been living at the time of Abram. This interpretation, however, is strongly rejected by those who believe gaps occur in the genealogies. Dr. Erich Von Fange writes concerning these possible gaps, "Some students of the Bible believe that the scattering of the people at Babel is the Peleg event. If this is so, we have another good argument for a long period of time between the Flood and Abram. Traditional chronology had Noah, Shem, and other forefathers of Peleg living through the lifetime of Peleg. How could the division then be linked to Peleg when much more prominent patriarchs were living at the time. The only reasonable conclusion is that 'begat' is used in an ancestral manner here. Thus Peleg must have been a distant descendant of those named as his father and other forefathers. This is supported also by the fact that a sharp drop in life span occurred between the time of Eber and the time of Peleg. There is further support for extending the period of time between the Flood and Abram. At the time of Babel the people were still unified geographically. . . .All this is in sharp contrast to Abram's day when there were already long established kingdoms, such as Egypt" (Von Fange, pp. 291-292).

In a similar fashion, it is also proposed that the division at the time of Peleg in Genesis 10:25 was a physical land separation. Genesis 10:4-5 records, "The sons of Javan were Elishah, Tarshish, Kittim, and Dodanim. From these the coastland peoples of the Gentiles were separated into their lands, everyone according to his language, according to his families, into their nations." These verses obviously are talking about the Tower of Babel because of the separation of people and languages; however, Peleg is not mentioned until verse 25, twenty verses later, where the earth is divided. If the Tower of Babel and Peleg were at the same time, why would they be listed so far apart in the genealogical record? Therefore, an alternate view states that at the time of Babel there was a political and language division and once these people were sufficiently spread out, God divided the land physically to keep them separated (Von Fange, p. 293). I believe it is also important to note that the two Hebrew words used for division in verses 5 and 25 are different, suggesting a possible difference in usage. However, some reject this as evidence, saying that they possess the same meaning and usage and thus describe the same event. In the one case, it is a linguistic division; in the other, a geographical division caused by the linguistical changes.

One more problem is how the land was divided; by actual splitting of continents or simply by the meltdown of glaciers covering the once existing land bridges, a scientific possibility. Both divisions could be possible, making it just a matter of timing. If the continents split near the end of the Flood and provided a reservoir for the water, then the energies needed for such an event are apparent. Meanwhile the ice-age would have exposed land bridges which would allow people to separate at the time of Babel. (Note: The sin at the tower of Babel was direct disobedience to God's command to spread out and fill the earth. The people were building a city out of sun dried bricks, something used for permanent settlements.) Later, at the time of Peleg near the end of the ice-age, snow melted rapidly as the geological evidence suggests, and the separation was completed. Therefore, perhaps the separation in Peleg's day was simply "finishing the job" and making sure that once the people were separated by language they did not return.

Gen 10:26 Joktan was the father of Almodad, Sheleph, Hazarmaveth, Jerah, 10:27 Hadoram, Uzal, Diklah, 10:28 Obal, Abimael, Sheba, 10:29 Ophir, Havilah and Jobab. All these were sons of Joktan. 10:30 The region where they lived stretched from Mesha toward Sephar, in the eastern hill country. 10:31 These are the sons of Shem by their clans and languages, in their territories and nations. 10:32 These are the clans of

Noah's sons, according to their lines of descent, within their nations. From these the nations spread out over the earth after the flood.

Joktan was Peleg's brother and thirteen of Joktan's sons are listed here. Most of the names are unknown, but it seems that most settled in Arabia. However, Ophir has been known for its abundance of gold (1 Kings 9:28; 10:11; 22:48; Job 22:24; 28:16; Psalm 45:9; Isaiah 13:12).

Verse 31 again recaps the division of these people by languages after the Tower of Babel.

Verse 32 states that the names in chapter ten are all the clans of Noah and thus the clans of the world at this time. It is significant that 70 nations are listed in Noah's clan. Why? Perhaps due to the symbolic meaning of completeness or, perhaps, to foreshadow things to come. We know that when all of Israel entered Egypt there were 70 people in all. (Gen 46:27). We also see that there are 70 weeks (Dan 9:24); 70 elders (Num 11:16;25); 70 members of the Sanhedrin in the New Testament era; 70 year captivity in Babylon (Jer 25:12); the temple of Jesus' day was destroyed in 70 AD; 70 scholars translated the Greek Old Testament (Septuagint); and perhaps most fascinating, the number 70 appears 71 times in Scripture in 70 verses.

We close this chapter with the words of Moses, as he remarked about the number of the sons of Israel: "Remember the days of old; consider the generations long past. Ask your father and he will tell you, your elders, and they will explain to you. When the Most High gave the nations their inheritance, when He divided all mankind, He set up boundaries for the peoples according to the number of the sons of Israel (Deu 32:7-8).

Gen 11:1 Now the whole world had one language and a common speech. 11:2 As men moved eastward, they found a plain in Shinar and settled there.

Today there are more than five thousand languages, and all stem from this one common language. Nobody knows for sure what this language was, but it is very possible it was a Semitic language such as Hebrew. Some reasons to suggest this include the fact that the pre-Flood names all have meanings in the Hebrew language (and its cognate languages). Also, it is reasonable to assume that Shem would not have participated in this settlement and, therefore, perhaps his native tongue was not changed. It is also interesting to note that, although we have many languages stemming from this one event, all these languages are somewhat interconnected; yet, animal communication has no link with human communication.

The plain of Shinar is essentially Babylon and was set southeast of Ararat by the Tigris and Euphrates River. The fact that the Tigris and Euphrates were positioned here suggests that the people saw some similarities between this area and the pre-Flood paradise and the original Tigris and Euphrates (2:14). From here, the people and nations of the world were scattered, taking with them knowledge and common experiences to all parts of the world. This is clearly why there are so many legends of dinosaurs in over 250 countries today. It also explains why almost every nation has a "legend" of a huge flood which destroyed all the world except one family. Everyone at the Tower of Babel knew about the Flood and took this knowledge with them, sharing it with their children and grandchildren. This common origin shows why paganism can be traced back to Babylon, why the ancient gods of Greece, Rome, Egypt and India have roots in Babylon. This may be why John writes, "This title was written on her forehead: MYSTERY BABYLON THE GREAT, THE MOTHER OF PROSTITUTES AND OF THE ABOMINATIONS OF THE EARTH" (Rev 17:5). Babylon was the "mother" of abominations and the world has continued to welcome her with open arms.

Gen 11:3 They said to each other, "Come, let's make bricks and bake them thoroughly." They used brick instead of stone, and tar for mortar. 11:4 Then they said, "Come, let us build ourselves a city, with a tower that reaches to the heavens, so that we may make a name for ourselves and not be scattered over the face of the whole earth."

The fact that these people were making baked bricks indicated a permanent settlement was in mind. Although stones could have been used, they were not all that plentiful in the plain of Shinar. Perhaps this is why even today archaeology has uncovered kiln-baked bricks in the Babylonian area. The tar which was used is also a common ingredient found in Babylon today. Making a permanent city was going against God's directive to "fill the earth" after Noah left the ark. Instead, man wanted to centralize authority and remain together, rather than "be scattered."

It is possible that Nimrod, the founder of this project, desired to be the "king" of the world. In order for this to occur, the people needed to remain together and he needed the people to turn to him for help, rather than to God. The means of achieving this goal was to "make a name for ourselves" and building "a tower that reached to the heavens." By "making a name" they were ensured to stick together, and this appealed also to the pride, which dwells in our sinful nature. However, in order for this project to be successful, Nimrod knew there had to be a religious twist; hence, build a tower. The word "reaches" is not in the original text and, unfortunately, gives a wrong meaning in verse four. The actual text reads, "with a tower unto heaven." This does not mean Nimrod was trying to build a tower high enough to escape the waters of another flood, as commonly believed. If this were the case, the city would not have been in the plain of Shinar. Secondly, Nimrod was intelligent enough to realize this would not have been possible; especially with a tower of bricks which could not be stacked up high enough without being crushed. The true meaning of the tower was to be a dedication to the heavens and perhaps aided in worshipping the stars. Historically and according to the text, this is the best interpretation. The Babylonians were well known for their astrology and creation worship. As mentioned, it is from Babylon that our pagan deities have their roots. Creation worship was the religious twist needed to unite the people together into one body of support.

Gen 11:5 But the LORD came down to see the city and the tower that the men were building. 11:6 The LORD said, "If as one people speaking the same language they have begun to do this, then nothing they plan to do will be impossible for them. 11:7 Come, let us go down and confuse their language so they will not understand each other." 11:8 So the LORD scattered them from there over all the earth, and they stopped building the city. 11:9 That is why it was called Babel --because there the LORD confused the language of the whole world. From there the LORD scattered them over the face of the whole earth.

One can see that it wasn't the tower that disturbed God, but the unity and congregating into one place that was against God's command. United together, they looked to one another to solve problems instead of turning to God. They had the boastful attitude that there was nothing they couldn't do. We would do well to think about this in our own lives, since today we also have the attitude that there is nothing we cannot do. Also, we again have reunited ourselves with the world with the aid of airplanes, computers etc. Do we look to God to help with our problems or do we arrogantly look to take these problems on ourselves? We read in Psalms: "The kings of the earth take their stand and the rulers gather together against the LORD and against His Anointed One" (Psalm 2:2). Today our government has restricted God from being presented in our schools, but be assured, God will not lose this battle.

In verse seven we again see a reference to the Trinity in "let us" go down. The Holy Trinity then proceeded to confuse the language of the people into many languages, so that they could not work together so proudly. Even though their communication was hindered, their minds were of the same thought, "They plot injustice and say, 'We have devised a perfect plan!' Surely the mind and heart of man are cunning. But God will shoot them with arrows; suddenly they will be struck down." (Psa 64:6-7).

The final result of this confusion was that people scattered throughout the earth and what God had commanded earlier would now happen. Science tries to teach us that man slowly evolved both physically and socially. However, Babel gives good reason why we see the, so called, "stone age" people. Once people began to scatter, small groups would have no need for mass agriculture, metallurgy etc. Hunting and gathering would be sufficient. Also, many probably kept on the move until finally reaching a desirable place. As they traveled and first became settled, quickly made, disposable, stone tools would have been very useful. As time went on, the smaller groups may have been taken over by the larger, more advanced societies, leaving what appear to be evolving social skills in the strata layers. This also explains why it appears that civilizations seemed to have appeared about the same time all over the world.

This separation of people also explains the many races today, as well. When small, interbreeding groups are isolated from the mass population, certain genes become dominant, resulting in dominant physical characteristics. At this time in history, interbreeding would not be harmful as it is today, because the gene pool had not deteriorated to the level we see today. Keep in mind that Adam and Eve were created genetically perfect, and it wasn't until after the fall that these genes began to mutate. After Noah's Flood it is likely that there was much more solar radiation, causing the genetic deterioration to take place even faster. By the time we read Leviticus, the gene pool had reached a dangerous point, which is why God then commands this practice to stop (Lev 18:6-14).

A day is coming, however, when our language will again be united, "Then will I purify the lips of the peoples, that all of them may call on the name of the LORD and serve him" (Zep 3:9).

It will now be about 200 years before we continue this progressive story, as nothing is said about this time of resettlement in Scripture.

Gen 11:10 This is the account of Shem. Two years after the Flood, when Shem was 100 years old, he became the father of Arphaxad. 11:11 And after he became the father of Arphaxad, Shem lived 500 years and had other sons and daughters. 11:12 When Arphaxad had lived 35 years, he became the father of Shelah. 11:13 And after he became the father of Shelah, Arphaxad lived 403 years and had other sons and daughters. 11:14 When Shelah had lived 30 years, he became the father of Eber. 11:15 And after he became the father of Eber, Shelah lived 403 years and had other sons and daughters. 11:16 When Eber had lived 34 years, he became the father of Peleg. 11:17 And after he became the father of Peleg, Eber lived 430 years and had other sons and daughters.

It now appears that the account of Shem is over and we have a brief note left, perhaps by Terah. It seems these verses are simply recorded to make the connection between Terah and Shem. In tracing these names we see an obvious decline in longevity, as Noah lived 950 years, Shem 600, Arphaxad 438, Shelah 433, Eber 464, Peleg 239 (v. 18), Reu 239, Serug 230, and Nahor, who lived 148 years. Something happened after the Flood that caused man's lifespan to drop drastically. It is most probable that this decline was caused by more solar radiation resulting when the previous firmament (which acted as a filter) had collapsed. Also, evidence suggests that at one time there was more oxygen and air pressure, which is essentially a hyperbaric chamber, where we see amazing biological benefits today. Add this to the fact that the gene pool was becoming more imperfect, the electromagnetic field was declining and there were harsher climates and living conditions after the Flood, one can easily see how longevity decreased.

Another point of interest is that in Luke's genealogy (3:36) he added the name Cainan between Arphaxad and Shelah. This name was not seen here, or in the records of 1 Chronicles 1:18 and Genesis 10:24. Since this name is found only in the Septuagint text (Greek translation of the Old Testament), it is possible that this was a scribal error in Luke, or as I am more inclined to believe, we don't have all the information. It is also worth mentioning that this name does not appear in the older Septuagint texts.

There is much question regarding the number of people at the time of Babel, since many do not think there would have been enough people so soon after the Flood. According to these verses, Peleg was 101 years after the Flood and this is probably the time of Babel, since in his day "the earth was divided"

(Gen 10:25). It is possible that this was from actual confusion of the languages, or perhaps God separated the continents after Babel in order to keep the people from returning again. In either case, about 100 years was all it took for those at Babel to unite after the Flood. Between Shem, Ham and Japheth there are 16 named sons, not including their other unnamed children. Henry Morris points out, "Thus the first generation after the Flood had at least 32 people, an increase of 533% over their original six parents. Assuming this proportion remained the same (and this is a conservative assumption), then the second generation had 171 people and the third 912, making a total of at least 1,120 mature adults at the time of the Dispersion at Babel. . . .Furthermore, it is quite possible that each family had many more children than the numbers calculated above. A growth rate of only 8% annually would produce a population of nine thousand in only one hundred years" (Record, p. 283). Clearly there were adequate numbers of people to construct such a tower and leave us such a record today.

Gen 11:18 When Peleg had lived 30 years, he became the father of Reu. 11:19 And after he became the father of Reu, Peleg lived 209 years and had other sons and daughters. 11:20 When Reu had lived 32 years, he became the father of Serug. 11:21 And after he became the father of Serug, Reu lived 207 years and had other sons and daughters. 11:22 When Serug had lived 30 years, he became the father of Nahor. 11:23 And after he became the father of Nahor, Serug lived 200 years and had other sons and daughters. 11:24 When Nahor had lived 29 years, he became the father of Terah. 11:25 And after he became the father of Terah, Nahor lived 119 years and had other sons and daughters. 11:26 After Terah had lived 70 years, he became the father of Abram, Nahor and Haran.

There are about 222 years listed from the time of the Flood to the birth of Terah. Some believe there are gaps in these genealogies and feel this would take care of the contradiction in Biblical dates versus secular science. However, even with gaps, not nearly enough time is made up for the millions of years needed to fit evolutionary thinking.

These names then bring us up to Abram, the one through whom God's chosen people would come.

Gen 11:27 This is the account of Terah. Terah became the father of Abram, Nahor and Haran. And Haran became the father of Lot. 11:28 While his father Terah was still alive, Haran died in Ur of the Chaldeans, in the land of his birth. 11:29 Abram and Nahor both married. The name of Abram's wife was Sarai, and the name of Nahor's wife was Milcah; she was the daughter of Haran, the father of both Milcah and Iscah. 11:30 Now Sarai was barren; she had no children. 11:31 Terah took his son Abram, his grandson Lot son of Haran, and his daughter-in-law Sarai, the wife of his son Abram, and together they set out from Ur of the Chaldeans to go to Canaan. But when they came to Haran, they settled there. 11:32 Terah lived 205 years, and he died in Haran.

Verse 27 begins the next "account" tracing the line of Terah. Haran's daughter Milcah became Nahor's wife (she was his niece). Haran's son Lot was later taken under the wing of Abram after Haran's death.

It is interesting that Sarai is said to have been barren here. This is perhaps to show that Abram would have no children while he lived at Ur or Mesopotamia, as the promised child had to be born in the promised land.

After Abram married Sarai (his half sister- Gen 20:12) and Haran apparently died, Terah took Abram, Sarai, and Lot out of Ur to the city of Haran. Nahor stayed behind with Milcah for unknown reasons, but may have moved later to the city of Nahor near Haran (Gen 22:20-24; 24:10; 27:43; 28:2; 29:4). Their original intent was to go into the yet to be promised land of Canaan, but for some reason they stopped before they arrived there. The city of Ur has been recognized by archaeology as a city full of wickedness and idolatry. It rests on the lower end of the Euphrates valley in the Persian Gulf and may have once been a great seaport. This great city was very advanced and even contained a large library, showing intellectual pursuits. Perhaps this is one reason Terah left Ur. Some believe that God may have called Terah to go to Canaan and he disobeyed by stopping in Haran (600 miles northwest of Ur), but there is no Biblical evidence of this. Others have suggested that Haran may have been a city started by Lot's father, Haran, and this encouraged their stopping; however, the Hebrew name of the town Haran is spelled differently than the name of Abraham's brother. The city of Haran still remains today, and at the time of Terah it was an important trade route of Canaan and Syria. It may have met the needs of the aging Terah who was weary from traveling. In any case, Terah settled here and died at the age of 205.

In Acts 7:4 Stephen records that Abram left Haran when his father died. There is good reason to believe that this meant the spiritual death of Terah, not a physical one. First, if Abram was Terah's oldest son (which seems most likely in the order of names given) then Terah was only 145 years old when Abram left Haran, not 205. (Genesis 12:4 says Abram was 75 when he left Haran). Second, we do know that Terah was an ungodly man as Joshua writes, "This is what the LORD, the God of Israel, says: 'Long ago your forefathers, including Terah the father of Abraham and Nahor, lived beyond the River and worshipped other gods'" (Joshua 24:2; see also 14-15). Therefore, it is easy to see how Terah could have been viewed spiritually dead in Acts 7:4. Further support for this theory comes from Matthew, where Jesus said, "Follow me, and let the dead bury their own dead" (Matt 8:22). It seems most probable that the idolatries in Haran and Ur had a negative effect on Terah and, therefore, the Lord said to Abram, "Leave your country, your people and your father's household and go to the land I will show you" (Gen 12:1). In obeying God, Abram became the father of many nations (Rom 4:18).

Gen 12:1 The LORD had said to Abram, "Leave your country, your people and your father's household and go to the land I will show you. 12:2 I will make you into a great nation and I will bless you; I will make your name great, and you will be a blessing. 12:3 I will bless those who

bless you, and whoever curses you I will curse; and all peoples on earth will be blessed through you."

We left Abram in Haran in verse 31 of chapter 11. Apparently, God had already called Abram and Terah out of Ur to go to Canaan (Acts 7:2-3), but for whatever reason, they stopped at Haran. Therefore, God again affirmed His desire for Abram to leave and settle in Canaan, the promised land. It is here that God began to make His chosen nation, stemming from Abram. Not only did Abram have many offspring, but his name was to be remembered forever. Those who blessed Abram were to be blessed through their faith in Christ (who comes from Abram). Abram was also protected from harm by divine power, as those who went against him were cursed. The ultimate blessing which came through Abram was obviously Christ and our faith in Him. Thus we see a seven-fold blessing was given: 1) great nation, 2) be blessed, 3) make his name great, 4) he will be a blessing, 5) bless those who bless you, 6) curse those who curse you, and 7) all people blessed through you. We see the promise of all people being blessed through Abraham quoted in Acts 3:25 in reference to the Jewish believers and again in Galatians 3:8 in reference to the Gentile believers.

Abraham's name is used over 230 times in Scripture, showing what a blessing he is. We read in Matthew, "I say to you that many will come from the east and the west, and will take their places at the feast with Abraham, Isaac and Jacob in the kingdom of heaven" (Mat 8:11). Paul writes, "And He is also the father of the circumcised who not only are circumcised but who also walk in the footsteps of the faith that our father Abraham had before he was circumcised" (Rom 4:12). Abraham serves as a model for us who believe by faith that Christ rose from the dead: "Abraham believed God, and it was credited to him as righteousness" (Rom 4:3).

Gen 12:4 So Abram left, as the LORD had told him; and Lot went with him. Abram was seventy-five years old when he set out from Haran. 12:5 He took his wife Sarai, his nephew Lot, all the possessions they had accumulated and the people they had acquired in Haran, and they set out for the land of Canaan, and they arrived there. 12:6 Abram traveled through the land as far as the site of the great tree of Moreh at Shechem. At that time the Canaanites were in the land. 12:7 The LORD appeared to Abram and said, "To your offspring I will give this land." So he built an altar there to the LORD, who had appeared to him. 12:8 From there he went on toward the hills east of Bethel and pitched his tent, with Bethel on the west and Ai on the east. There he built an altar to the LORD and called on the name of the LORD. 12:9 Then Abram set out and continued toward the Negev.

What faith it must have taken to pick up and leave at the age of 75 on a 400 mile journey. What physical condition Abram was in we do not know, but we can be sure it was better than those of 75 today, as the aging process was still slower than it is today. The author of Hebrews records, "By faith Abraham, when called to go to a place he would later receive as his inheritance, obeyed and went, even though he did not know where he was going" (Heb 11:8). Lot accompanied Abram's family, as Abram became somewhat of a second father to him after his real father (Haran) died. Unfortunately, Lot did not display the same faith as Abram; nonetheless he remained a righteous man (2 Pet 2:8).

Once they reached Shechem, the Lord made a covenant promising the land of Canaan to his descendants forever, even though at this time it was not even Abram's. In thanks and praise, Abram built an altar to the Lord so that this covenant would always be remembered. An interesting fact to note is that here we see the first theophany, or actual appearance of God, to someone else. Verse seven states that the LORD appeared to Abram. We know that this was not an appearance of God in His full glory, as noone could see God and live. However, as almost all commentators would agree, this was Christ Himself who appeared. John records that, "grace and truth came through Jesus Christ. No one has ever seen God, but God the One and Only, who is at the Father's side, has made Him known" (John 1:17-18). The "Him" is Christ. We see other evidence suggesting that this is Christ in later appearances of the "Angel of the Lord." In Genesis 18, three "visitors came to Abraham" and we see that two were angels (19:1) while one was the LORD Himself (Gen 18:10, 13, 17).

Shechem is a land with much history, as it is here that Jacob will become a stench to the Shechemites because Levi and Simeon revenge their sister's rape (Gen 34). It is also here that Joseph will be sold as a slave.

From Shechem the group traveled about 35 miles further south to Bethel, where Abram again built an altar to the LORD. Bethel will be a very important town in the history of Israel. In Scripture, only Jerusalem is mentioned more often (See Gen 28:10-22; 35:1-8; 1 Ki 12:26-29). No covenant was given, nor did the LORD appear, so why was the altar built at Bethel? The text says that he called on the name of the LORD. Immediately afterward, Abram continued to the Negev. This may mean that Abram looked to God for guidance in his travels. Should he stop or continue on? Where did he go? It appears God told him to go to the Negev, where he again had his faith tested (this will be discussed in verse ten). Also, once he reached the Negev he had passed through all of Canaan and, therefore, had seen the promised land.

Gen 12:10 Now there was a famine in the land, and Abram went down to Egypt to live there for a while because the famine was severe. 12:11 As he was about to enter Egypt, he said to his wife Sarai, "I know what a beautiful woman you are. 12:12 When the Egyptians see you, they will say, 'This is his wife.' Then they will kill me but will let you live. 12:13 Say you are my sister, so that I will be treated well for your sake and my life will be spared because of you." 12:14 When Abram came to Egypt, the Egyptians saw that she was a very beautiful woman. 12:15 And when Pharaoh's officials saw her, they praised her to Pharaoh, and she was taken into his palace. 12:16 He treated Abram well for her sake, and Abram acquired sheep and cattle, male and female donkeys, menservants and maidservants, and camels.

As just mentioned, Abram's faith was tested again. We have seen how Abram put his full trust in God to take him wherever God wanted him to be, while Abram himself did not know where that was (Heb 11:8). What must Abram have thought when the land God brought him to suffered from a famine, as we see in verse ten? Though God wanted him to trust that He would provide, it seems that Abram took things into his own hands and decided to go to Egypt without seeking God's guidance. It may be that this was a weak period in Abram's life, a time when things weren't going as well as he wished. As much as these times are trying, they try our faith and refine it. Abram's faith was about to be refined.

Once in Egypt, Abram showed even less faith in God's protection. Even though God had promised protection and blessing, Abram didn't put his full trust in this promise YET! The Egyptians were an immoral culture, tracing back to the line of Ham. Noting their cruelty, Abram decided to have Sarai pretend to be only a sister and not a wife. Abram didn't lie, as Sarai was his half sister (Gen 20:12), but what God wanted was Abram to trust in His promises and protection no matter what. Abram should have known that his life would not have been taken, because God promised him offspring and blessings.

The fact that Sarai was still so attractive, at a minimum of 65 years old but probably over 70, also shows the aging factor was not yet what we see today. When Pharaoh saw her beauty she was taken into the palace where she was to be prepared to become his wife. Meanwhile, Abram was treated well. But even though Sarai had not married Pharaoh, he must have had some fear of what would happen to her. This would have never been a problem had he simply trusted the LORD.

Historically, Egypt at this time was a great empire. Most scholars suggest that this could not have taken place any later than the 12th dynasty of Egypt. The pyramids are believed to have been built somewhere around the fourth dynasty and, therefore, Abraham may have seen them himself. This fits well with the theory that the pyramids were built shortly after the Babel dispersion and that the first pyramid was the largest and better one, since technology and intelligence were high. The smaller pyramids were built later as the skills declined.

Gen 12:17 But the LORD inflicted serious diseases on Pharaoh and his household because of Abram's wife Sarai. 12:18 So Pharaoh summoned Abram. "What have you done to me?" he said. "Why didn't you tell me she was your wife? 12:19 Why did you say, 'She is my sister,' so that I took her to be my wife? Now then, here is your wife. Take her and go!" 12:20 Then Pharaoh gave orders about Abram to his men, and they sent him on his way, with his wife and everything he had.

Now the LORD stepped in to show Abram that He could be trusted and rebuked him for his lack of faith. Once Pharaoh was inflicted with some sort of disease, he somehow knew it was a result of Abram and Sarai, so he summoned them. Pharaoh admonished them and gave Sarai back to Abram, probably in disgust not only of them, but also toward a God who had such followers.

Though Pharaoh feared the LORD, he did not accept Him as the One and Only God.

God indeed was faithful to His promises and assured that nothing happened to either Abram or Sarai. Sarai never laid with another man, to ensure that the promised offspring would be of the seed of Abraham. Despite Abram's lack of faith in God, God poured out blessings upon them as they left Egypt with more than what they came with.

Gen 13:1 So Abram went up from Egypt to the Negev, with his wife and everything he had, and Lot went with him. 13:2 Abram had become very wealthy in livestock and in silver and gold. 13:3 From the Negev he went from place to place until he came to Bethel, to the place between Bethel and Ai where his tent had been earlier 13:4 and where he had first built an altar. There Abram called on the name of the LORD.

Abram returned to the Negev, along with all the blessings the LORD poured out upon him. From the Negev he continued to Bethel, where he had previously built an altar to the LORD when he looked for guidance after first moving to Canaan (Gen 12:8). Perhaps Abram made this religious tour to make amends for his lack of faith in Egypt.

Gen 13:5 Now Lot, who was moving about with Abram, also had flocks and herds and tents. 13:6 But the land could not support them while they stayed together, for their possessions were so great that they were not able to stay together. 13:7 And quarreling arose between Abram's herdsmen and the herdsmen of Lot. The Canaanites and Perizzites were also living in the land at that time. 13:8 So Abram said to Lot, "Let's not have any quarreling between you and me, or between your herdsmen and mine, for we are brothers. 13:9 Is not the whole land before you? Let's part company. If you go to the left, I'll go to the right; if you go to the right, I'll go to the left." 13:10 Lot looked up and saw that the whole plain of the Jordan was well watered, like the garden of the LORD, like the land of Egypt, toward Zoar. (This was before the LORD destroyed Sodom and Gomorrah.) 13:11 So Lot chose for himself the whole plain of the Jordan and set out toward the east. The two men parted company: 13:12 Abram lived in the land of Canaan, while Lot lived among the cities of the plain and pitched his tents near Sodom. 13:13 Now the men of Sodom were wicked and were sinning greatly against the LORD.

God had blessed Abram and Lot so extensively that the land no longer supported them as one family. Besides, the herdsmen argued among each other, causing further problems. Why the arguing occurred we are not told, but with our sinful nature as it is, it is likely that the abundance of material blessings may have caused the quarrels.

Abram learned a valuable lesson in Egypt and let Lot choose where he wanted to live, while Abram trusted that the LORD would provide no matter where he went. Lot seemed to not have the same faith or consideration and chose the Jordan plain, which was apparently much more beautiful than it ever has been in our history. It is likened to the garden of Eden and Egypt near Zoar. Lot, having recently come from Egypt, probably missed this abundant and carefree environment.

Today, however, the Jordan plain is fertile near the river itself, but possesses nothing as described here. The reason is given in verse ten, where it says this was *before* Sodom and Gomorrah were destroyed. Since the destruction of this entire area, things have never been the same. One need only take a drive along the Dead Sea to see this complete devastation.

Abram lived in the land of Canaan and was blessed profusely, while Lot left and pitched his tents *near* Sodom. This again shows Lot's lack of spirituality, as he was swayed by greed looking down at the fertile valley. Not only this, but the people of Sodom were very sinful, yet Lot began living near the city and presumably entered from time to time. In his visits, he began to fall into the worldly trap of material possessions and carnal desires. As we will see, soon afterward Lot moved into the city itself (Gen 14:12). Once living in the city, his life began to take on the city's attitudes, as he later sat in the gates of Sodom (Gen 19:1) where business transactions and important people met. Whether Lot simply fell into a time of temptation or was weak in faith, he is recorded in history as a righteous man (2 Pet 2:8). We would do well to learn from this lesson. Just as Adam and Eve were not even to touch the tree of evil, we should also stay as far away from evil as possible.

Gen 13:14 The LORD said to Abram after Lot had parted from him, "Lift up your eyes from where you are and look north and south, east and west. 13:15 All the land that you see I will give to you and your offspring forever. 13:16 I will make your offspring like the dust of the earth, so that if anyone could count the dust, then your offspring could be counted. 13:17 Go, walk through the length and breadth of the land, for I am giving it to you." 13:18 So Abram moved his tents and went to live near the great trees of Mamre at Hebron, where he built an altar to the LORD.

God now told Abram to look in all directions and showed him the land which was going to be given to him and all his offspring. Though Abram would never actually own this land himself, his descendants would. Currently Israel owns the land, but throughout most of history his descendants have not possessed it. Therefore, God is not finished with this land. Ultimately, this promise will be fulfilled spiritually in the new heaven and new earth of Revelation 21.

Abram's offspring were to be like the dust of the earth in number. Over and over in Scripture we see that Abram is the father of all believers. We read, "Against all hope, Abraham in hope believed and so became the father of many nations, just as it had been said to him, 'So shall your offspring be'" (Rom 4:18) and "Therefore, the promise comes by faith, so that it may be by grace and may be guaranteed to all Abraham's offspring--not only to those who are of the law but also to those who are of the faith of Abraham. He is the father of us all" (Rom 4:16). We ourselves are also Abraham's offspring, even if we are not

Jews, for, "It is not the natural children who are God's children, but it is the children of the promise who are regarded as Abraham's offspring" (Rom 9:8) and "If you belong to Christ, then you are Abraham's seed, and heirs according to the promise" (Gal 3:29). Therefore, it is not difficult to see how Abraham's offspring could be like the dust of the earth or the sand of the sea. However, may Israel be warned, "Isaiah cries out concerning Israel: 'Though the number of the Israelites be like the sand by the sea, only the remnant will be saved. For the Lord will carry out his sentence on earth with speed and finality'" (Rom 9:27-28).

Abram was told to walk through the land that had been given to him and his offspring. Though he walked through some of it in Genesis 12:6-8 when he moved there, he was now told to go in all directions to see what a blessing he had received.

After this, Abram went to Mamre at Hebron. Mamre was named for the Amorite ally of Abraham (Gen 14:13) who lived there earlier. The fact that it was in Hebron suggests this was written after the fact, because at this point Hebron had not yet been built, according to Numbers 13:22. It was here that Abram built another important altar to the LORD, and Abram remained here for a long time.

Gen 14:1 At this time Amraphel king of Shinar, Arioch king of Ellasar, Kedorlaomer king of Elam and Tidal king of Goiim 14:2 went to war against Bera king of Sodom, Birsha king of Gomorrah, Shinab king of Admah, Shemeber king of Zeboiim, and the king of Bela (that is, Zoar). 14:3 All these latter kings joined forces in the Valley of Siddim (the Salt Sea). 14:4 For twelve years they had been subject to Kedorlaomer, but in the thirteenth year they rebelled. 14:5 In the fourteenth year, Kedorlaomer and the kings allied with him went out and defeated the Rephaites in Ashteroth Karnaim, the Zuzites in Ham, the Emites in Shaveh Kiriathaim 14:6 and the Horites in the hill country of Seir, as far as El Paran near the desert. 14:7 Then they turned back and went to En Mishpat (that is, Kadesh), and they conquered the whole territory of the Amalekites, as well as the Amorites who were living in Hazazon Tamar. 14:8 Then the king of Sodom, the king of Gomorrah, the king of Admah, the king of Zeboiim and the king of Bela (that is, Zoar) marched out and drew up their battle lines in the Valley of Siddim 14:9 against Kedorlaomer king of Elam, Tidal king of Goiim, Amraphel king of Shinar and Arioch king of Ellasar--four kings against five. 14:10 Now the Valley of Siddim was full of tar pits, and when the kings of Sodom and Gomorrah fled, some of the men fell into them and the rest fled to the hills. 14:11 The four kings seized all the goods of Sodom and Gomorrah and all their food; then they went away. 14:12 They also carried off Abram's nephew Lot and his possessions, since he was living in Sodom.

For 12 years the kings of this area paid tribute to the kings of Shinar (Babylon); Ellasar (Southern Babylon), Elam (Persia), and Goiim (Northeast Babylon). In the 13th year they decided enough was enough and rebelled, causing these kings to come and attack under the leadership of Kedorlaomer (v. 4-5). This was the first battle in Scripture and probably took place around 2100 B.C., according to archeological and historical records.

The kings gathered for battle in the Valley of Siddim, or the Salt Sea area (probably the Dead Sea). The first people to be attacked were the Rephaites, whose name means "strong ones;" the Zuzites, who are probably the same as the Zamzummites in Deuteronomy 2:20 who were "giants;" the Emites, whose name means "terrible ones," are found in Deuteronomy 2:10 as being giants as well; and the Horites, who were later destroyed by Esau's descendants (Deut 2:21,22).

With these kings captured, the north, east, and west ends of the Salt Sea were secured, so then the invasion turned back to Kadesh and attacked the Amalekites and Amorites. It is significant that the sons of Anak were mentioned, because they also seem to be of large size. When first viewing the promised land, Israel was afraid to enter because of the large men who lived there: "We saw the Nephilim there (the descendants of Anak come from the Nephilim). We seemed like grasshoppers in our own eyes, and we looked the same to them" (Num 13:33). As a result of their fear and lack of trust in God, Israel was forced to wander in the desert for 40 years. In any case, almost all of these kings in the Jordan valley have names which imply great size and strength.

The four invading kings went against the five Jordanian kings and won the battle. Many men fell into the numerous tar pits which were in this area at the time, while others fled to the surrounding hills which were full of caves. Sometimes lumps of asphalt can be seen floating on the southern end of the Dead Sea today.

What seems to be a side note is one of the main points in the story. Lot was captured and taken prisoner because he lived in Sodom. Once he was only near the city, but sin lured him into its dreadful grip.

The En Mishpat mentioned in verse seven means "spring of justice." It is called Meribah Kadesh, meaning "quarreling at Kadesh" in Deuteronomy 32:51 and Numbers 27:14. Later it will be called Kadesh Barnea in Numbers 32:8 where the twelve spies were sent out to view the promised land.

Gen 14:13 One who had escaped came and reported this to Abram the Hebrew. Now Abram was living near the great trees of Mamre the Amorite, a brother of Eshcol and Aner, all of whom were allied with Abram. 14:14 When Abram heard that his relative had been taken captive, he called out the 318 trained men born in his household and went in pursuit as far as Dan. 14:15 During the night Abram divided his men to attack them and he routed them, pursuing them as far as Hobah, north of Damascus. 14:16 He recovered all the goods and brought back his relative Lot and his possessions, together with the women and the other people. 14:17 After Abram returned from defeating Kedorlaomer and the kings allied with him, the king of Sodom came out to meet him in the Valley of Shaveh (that is, the King's Valley).

One man escaped the battle and ran to tell Abram of the attack and Lot's capture. Abram gathered 318 men from his household, and perhaps some Amorite men, and pursued the four kings. With God's help they were successful and returned not only Lot, but also the spoils. With only 318 men, one can be sure this battle was divinely fought, just as Gideon's battle in Judges 6:7 and 8:10.

This is the first time the word Hebrew is used, and it is applied to Abram. The origin of this word is unknown, although it may come from Eber, the great-grandson of Shem.

After defeating the four kings, Abram returned to the King's Valley where Bera (v. 2), King of Sodom, came to meet Abram. No doubt Abram was well received among these people.

Gen 14:18 Then Melchizedek king of Salem brought out bread and wine. He was priest of God Most High, 14:19 and he blessed Abram, saying, "Blessed be Abram by God Most High, Creator of heaven and earth. 14:20 And blessed be God Most High, who delivered your enemies into your hand." Then Abram gave him a tenth of everything.

Melchizedek is one of the most fascinating characters in all of Scripture. His name appears only here, in Psalm 110:4 and in various places in Hebrews. Let us examine who this man is based on what little Scripture does say. Due to the length, we will omit some of the verses, but it is strongly recommended that one read Hebrews 7 in its entirety. We read in part, Heb 7:1, "This Melchizedek was king of Salem and priest of God Most High. Salem is a shortened term for Jerusalem, meaning peace (Ps 76:2; Heb 7:2). He met Abraham returning from the defeat of the kings and blessed him, and Abraham gave him a tenth of everything. First, his name means "king of righteousness;" also, "king of Salem" means "*king of peace.*" *Without father or mother*, without genealogy, *without beginning of days or end of life, like the Son of God* he remains a priest forever. Just think how great he was: Even the patriarch Abraham gave him a tenth of the plunder! Now the law requires the descendants of Levi who become priests to collect a tenth from the people. . . This man, however, did not trace his descent from Levi, yet he collected a tenth from Abraham and blessed him who had the promises. . . *the lesser person is blessed by the greater*" (Hebrews 7:1-10). Here is a man without father or mother, beginning or end, greater than Abraham, and is a priest forever. Just as Christ was the prince of peace, Melchizedek is the "king of peace." Jesus was a priest in the order of Melchizedek (Heb 5:6,10; 6:20; Ps 110:4); an order of grace rather than law. It is no wonder that many believe that Melchizedek was Christ himself.

A few things are left unsettled. How did such a righteous priest live in such a godless land? How did he get to be a priest when Scripture makes no mention of a priesthood, let alone one that is greater than the Aaronic priesthood? How did he become a priest without genealogy when this was a requirement of the priesthood, at least the Aaronic priesthood?

Most people believe that Melchizedek was a real man who simply typified Christ. This may well be. However, based upon what is seen in Hebrews, the most likely interpretation is that he was God incarnate as a man in the double role of king and priest.

It is fascinating to think that this type of priesthood, one that Christ Himself would be like, existed in Old Testament times. We discussed earlier how Noah made sacrifices after he left the ark. How he knew sacrificial procedures, we were not told. We also saw how he was under certain laws, such as not eating meat with blood in it, just as we are today, even under the new covenant (See comments on 9:3). Those who lived prior to the establishing of the Levitical priesthood seem to have been under a type of new covenant where faith in God was righteousness. We see in Romans, "Abraham believed God, and it was credited to him as righteousness" (Rom 4:3). Abraham was righteous before the law was given. During the Levitical priesthood, things depended upon works and sacrifices. Christ replaced that priesthood with a new one, one in the order of Melchizedek. One must be careful in saying the Old Testament is only law with no Gospel.

Also note the message Melchizedek preaches. He pronounced God as the Most High and Creator of the universe, a message that is important for a world filled with evolutionary philosophies and a culture worshipping the creation rather than the Creator.

Gen 14:21 The king of Sodom said to Abram, "Give me the people and keep the goods for yourself." 14:22 But Abram said to the king of Sodom, "I have raised my hand to the LORD, God Most High, Creator of heaven and earth, and have taken an oath 14:23 that I will accept nothing belonging to you, not even a thread or the thong of a sandal, so that you will never be able to say, 'I made Abram rich.' 14:24 I will accept nothing but what my men have eaten and the share that belongs to the men who went with me--to Aner, Eshcol and Mamre. Let them have their share."

The king of Sodom was very thankful for Abram's help and only wanted his townsmen back, offering all the spoils to Abram (note that Lot returned to Sodom, having not learned his lesson yet). Abram responded by accepting nothing, because of his faith that the LORD would provide and follow through on His promises. I find this to be an extraordinary witness for us today. Abram would not take money from the world because he wanted the world to know that God provides. Abram called God the Most High and Creator of the universe, as did Melchizedek. Recognizing God as Creator and Most High, Abram showed that if God could create a universe, He could surely fulfill His promises in ways we never imagined.

This leaves us with a question. Should churches today be willing to accept money from outside sources? Many would say, "If we don't we will never make it." It is indeed a challenge and a faith walk to turn our backs on financial gifts, but do we want the world to say, "we made this church?" Something to think about.

Gen 15:1 After this, the word of the LORD came to Abram in a vision: "Do not be afraid, Abram. I am your shield, your very great reward." 15:2 But Abram said, "O Sovereign LORD, what can you give me since I remain childless and the one who will inherit my estate is Eliezer of Damascus?" 15:3 And Abram said, "You have given me no children; so a servant in my household will be my heir."

Sometime after Abram's show of faith, the LORD appeared to Abram in a vision, reassuring Abram that He would indeed reward him, not because of Abram's faithfulness but because of God's promise. Previously we saw God appear in theophanies, or God incarnate. Here we see a vision which was received while awake, whereas a dream comes when asleep. Verse one says the "Word" of the Lord came to Abram in a vision. What is the Word? Christ Himself, "In the beginning was the Word, and the Word was with God, and the Word was God" (John 1:1). Later, verse 14 of John states, "The Word was made flesh."

God can always be trusted, for "The LORD is faithful to all His promises and loving toward all He has made" (Ps 145:13). God says, "*I* am your shield and *reward*." This is the first of the "I am's" in Scripture and points to God incarnate in Christ. In John, Christ claimed to be the "I am" when He said, "I tell you the truth, before Abraham was born, I am!" (John 8:58). This caused a big scene, because the Pharisees knew that only God could be the "I am." When Moses asked who to say sent him, "God said to Moses, 'I AM WHO I AM. This is what you are to say to the Israelites: 'I AM has sent me to you'" (Exo 3:14). The Jews, knowing this verse well, thought Christ was blaspheming the name of God, not realizing that Jesus was God.

Abram was now looking for the promise he was given to be fulfilled. God said, "I am your reward." This was important because Abram was looking for his seed or offspring. God would surely provide this in Isaac, but this wasn't the true fulfillment of the promise, Christ was. Christ was the ultimate reward given to Abraham through his line. We read in Paul's letter to the Galatians, "The promises were spoken to Abraham and to his seed. The Scripture does not say 'and to seeds,' meaning many people, but 'and to your seed,' meaning one person, who is Christ" (Gal 3:16).

Without understanding, Abram answered the LORD in his vision by showing lack of faith again. Just as we do in our lives, Abram showed signs of strength and weakness from day to day. This shows how important it is to daily put off the old Adam. Abram was concerned that since he had not had a child of his own, his servant would receive his inheritance, as was the custom when there were no children.

Gen 15:4 Then the word of the LORD came to him: "This man will not be your heir, but a son coming from your own body will be your heir." 15:5 He took him outside and said, "Look up at the heavens and count the stars--if indeed you can count them." Then he said to him, "So shall your offspring be." 15:6 Abram believed the LORD, and he credited it to him as righteousness. 15:7 He also said to him, "I am the LORD, who

brought you out of Ur of the Chaldeans to give you this land to take possession of it."

God assured Abram that his servant would not be the heir of the promise, rather a son from his own body. To make the promise even more outstanding, Abram was taken outside to look at all the stars as a frame of reference to the number of offspring he would have. Due to less air pollution Abram probably saw many more stars than we can see today with our naked eye. However, with telescopes we see that the number of stars is mind boggling, as is the number of Abram's offspring.

Abram believed God and it was credited to him as righteousness. This verse shows such an important aspect of spirituality that it is quoted three times in the New Testament (Rom 4:3; Gal 3:6; Jam 2:23). It is faith that makes us righteous, not the act of doing things for God. Naturally, because of faith, good works will be produced, but good works by themselves are of no value. We read in James, "But someone will say, 'You have faith; I have deeds.' Show me your faith without deeds, and I will show you my faith by what I do" (James 2:18). One must also be careful in saying that simply believing in Christ will get you to heaven, for the next verse states, "You believe that there is one God. Good! Even the demons believe that--and shudder" (James 2:19). There is a big difference between knowing God exists and actually accepting Him as your Savior.

God also told Abram that this land would be his possession and it would be inhabited by the offspring he was just promised.

Gen 15:8 But Abram said, "O Sovereign LORD, how can I know that I will gain possession of it?" 15:9 So the LORD said to him, "Bring me a heifer, a goat and a ram, each three years old, along with a dove and a young pigeon." 15:10 Abram brought all these to him, cut them in two and arranged the halves opposite each other; the birds, however, he did not cut in half 15:11 Then birds of prey came down on the carcasses, but Abram drove them away.

Abram asked God how he would know that this promise would come true. The LORD proceeded to describe what today would be the signing of a contract. Five acceptable sacrificial animals were chosen to be cut in half from head to tail (except the birds). Each half was then laid opposite the other with a trench going down between the halves. The tradition was that each party concerned in the contract would take off his sandals and walk through the trench, which was filled with blood. This symbolized that if the contract was broken, the same fate which overtook these animals would come upon that person. The real importance of this contract is coming up in verses 12-21, but for now simply understand the formality of this agreement.

The birds of prey may symbolize Satan's helpers. This contract is an everlasting covenant with Abram and his offspring. Understanding that the true offspring alluded to is Christ (Gal 3:16) Satan will do all he can to thwart God's plan. In Leviticus birds of prey are considered to be detestable. We see the same imagery used in the parable of the sower, where birds (Satan) try to destroy the seed which is sowed. In Revelation 19:17-21 it is the birds who will gorge themselves on the flesh of the evil inhabitants of the earth.

Gen 15:12 As the sun was setting, Abram fell into a deep sleep, and a thick and dreadful darkness came over him. 15:13 Then the LORD said to him, "Know for certain that your descendants will be strangers in a country not their own, and they will be enslaved and mistreated four hundred years. 15:14 But I will punish the nation they serve as slaves, and afterward they will come out with great possessions. 15:15 You, however, will go to your fathers in peace and be buried at a good old age. 15:16 In the fourth generation your descendants will come back here, for the sin of the Amorites has not yet reached its full measure." 15:17 When the sun had set and darkness had fallen, a smoking firepot with a blazing torch appeared and passed between the pieces. 15:18 On that day the LORD made a covenant with Abram and said, "To your descendants I give this land, from the river of Egypt to the great river, the Euphrates-- 15:19 the land of the Kenites, Kenizzites, Kadmonites, 15:20 Hittites, Perizzites, Rephaites, 15:21 Amorites, Canaanites, Girgashites and Jebusites."

As the sunset came, Abram fell into a deep sleep. God revealed that his descendants would be foreigners and enslaved for 400 years. This naturally was referring to the Egyptian bondage. Some believe this was a round figure, since it was actually 430 years that they were in Egypt according to Exodus 12:40, which says, "Now the length of time the Israelite people lived in Egypt was 430 years. At the end of the 430 years, to the very day, all the Lord's divisions left Egypt." However, this does not say they were slaves the entire 430 years. It is more likely that it took 30 years from the time Jacob entered Egypt when Joseph called him to the time the new Egyptian dynasty (Ex 1:8) came to be and enslaved the Israelites. Thus 400 years later they left Egypt.

The Egyptians were indeed punished, as most were killed in the Red Sea while others suffered from the plagues of Moses. Even Pharaoh's officials said, "How long will this man be a snare to us? Let the people go, so that they may worship the LORD their God. Do you not yet realize that Egypt is ruined?" (Ex 10:7). Upon leaving Egypt, the Israelites were also given many spoils by the Egyptians, furthering the total devastation of this country.

Though Abram's descendants would suffer greatly, he was assured that he would die at a good old age and in peace (fulfilled in 25:8). His descendants had to wait to receive their inheritance until the sin of the Amorites reached its full measure. God is indeed patient, not wanting anyone to suffer. Just as God gave the pre-Flood inhabitants 120 years to repent (Gen 6:3), he gave the Amorites over 400 years to change; knowing, however, that they would not. It has been said that God's love is what saves us. This is not true, as God loves all mankind but not all are saved. It is God's grace and mercy that we sinners need. That mercy comes through faith in Him.

Now the meat of the covenant appears in verse 17. Note that God, in a blazing torch, passed through the trench of blood when it was dark. (Other references showing blazing torches or smoke symbolizing God's presence can be found in Exodus 3:2; 14:24; 19:18; 1 Kings 18:38 and Acts 2:3-4). Abram himself never walked through. Why? Because this is God's covenant with us, not our covenant with God. There is nothing man can do to change this promise, it will come no matter what we do. This can be likened to Baptism, which is a covenant making children of the world into children of God. Baptism has nothing to do on our part, or with what frame of mind we are in. Baptism is God's promise to us, not our promise to God. What a beautiful picture of God's love and faithfulness. Even in the darkest moments in our lives, God's promise is always there for us. It is a free gift that one can only accept.

Verse 18 is fulfilled in Joshua 1:2-9 and 21:43.

The *entire* land from the Egypt River to the Euphrates was only possessed by Israel for a short time during the reign of Solomon (1 Kings 8:65) and maybe under Jeroboam II (2 Kings 14:25). Therefore, this again indicates a future, permanent fulfillment of this promise.

Gen 16:1 Now Sarai, Abram's wife, had borne him no children. But she had an Egyptian maidservant named Hagar; 16:2 so she said to Abram, "The LORD has kept me from having children. Go, sleep with my maidservant; perhaps I can build a family through her." Abram agreed to what Sarai said. 16:3 So after Abram had been living in Canaan ten years, Sarai his wife took her Egyptian maidservant Hagar and gave her to her husband to be his wife. 16:4 He slept with Hagar, and she conceived. When she knew she was pregnant, she began to despise her mistress.

Sometime later Sarai and Abram got tired of waiting. As a result, they felt that maybe God could use a little help since Abram was already 85 years old and Sarai was 75 (See 12:4; and 16:16). They took matters into their own hands, but this time it was Sarai who decided to give her husband to another woman.

The custom of this day was that if your spouse was unable to have children, a servant could have children for the first wife. The child of the servant would legally belong to the first wife. Therefore, Abram reasoned that this could easily be how God had intended his offspring to come.

Hagar was not the means God had intended, but He blessed this union anyway. God wanted Abram and Sarai to trust Him no matter what and, therefore, He was waiting until it seemed impossible for Sarai to bear children.

Even though Abram fell into a polygamous marriage, the LORD blessed him; however, troubles did arise as a result of this sin. As soon as Hagar found out she was pregnant, Sarai became extremely jealous.

Gen 16:5 Then Sarai said to Abram, "You are responsible for the wrong I am suffering. I put my servant in your arms, and now that she knows she is pregnant, she despises me. May the LORD judge between you and me." 16:6 "Your servant is in your hands," Abram said. "Do with her whatever you think best." Then Sarai mistreated Hagar; so she fled from her. 16:7 The angel of the LORD found Hagar near a spring in the desert; it was the spring that is beside the road to Shur. 16:8 And he said, "Hagar,

**servant of Sarai, where have you come from, and where are you going?"
"I'm running away from my mistress Sarai," she answered. 16:9 Then the
angel of the LORD told her, "Go back to your mistress and submit to her."
16:10 The angel added, "I will so increase your descendants that they will
be too numerous to count."**

Even though it was Sarai's idea to give Hagar to Abram, she blamed
him for her troubles. She claimed that Hagar despised her yet Sarai despised
Hagar. It is said that God will always take responsibility for the consequences of
our obedience, but who takes responsibility for the consequences of our
disobedience? Sarai now found out the answer to that question the hard way.

Abram told Sarai that Hagar was her servant and, therefore, she could
do what she wished to her. It was unfortunate that Abram allowed his wife to
make such sinful decisions in the state of mind that she was in. Sarai mistreated
Hagar to the point that Hagar had to flee.

Hagar appears to have been going back to Egypt, her real home. Once
she left, an angel of the LORD appeared to Hagar in the desert and told her to
return to Sarai. This again was God incarnate, not simply an angel, as we see
from verse 13. Hagar was obedient to this command. Just as Abram's offspring
would multiply greatly through Isaac, so through Ishmael many descendants
would come (Gen 25:13-16). However, those from the line of Ishmael would
not be under God's covenant promise.

**Gen 16:11 The angel of the LORD also said to her: "You are now
with child and you will have a son. You shall name him Ishmael, for the
LORD has heard of your misery. Gen 16:12 He will be a wild donkey of a
man; his hand will be against everyone and everyone's hand against him,
and he will live in hostility toward all his brothers." 16:13 She gave this
name to the LORD who spoke to her: "You are the God who sees me," for
she said, "I have now seen the One who sees me." 16:14 That is why the
well was called Beer Lahai Roi ; it is still there, between Kadesh and Bered.
16:15 So Hagar bore Abram a son, and Abram gave the name Ishmael to
the son she had borne. 16:16 Abram was eighty-six years old when Hagar
bore him Ishmael.**

Along with the promise of many descendants, Hagar received
information about the baby within her womb. It didn't seem to be a message of
great joy. God told her to name the boy Ishmael, meaning "the Lord hears."
Ishmael would be a wild donkey (Job 24:5; Hos 8:9) and would live in hostility
toward his brothers, especially Isaac, from whom Israel would come. Right up
to the present we see that Ishmael (Arabs) and Isaac (Israel) have great animosity
toward one another.

Hagar seemed to develop a more personal relationship with God here
and gave Him the name El Roi, or "the God who sees." This was a strong
contrast to the gods of Egypt, with whom she was familiar.

Abram must have had great joy seeing Hagar return, as it was indeed
his son in her womb. At the age of 86 Abram received his first child.

Gen 17:1 When Abram was ninety-nine years old, the LORD appeared to him and said, "I am God Almighty ; walk before me and be blameless. **17:2** I will confirm my covenant between me and you and will greatly increase your numbers." **17:3** Abram fell facedown, and God said to him **17:4** "As for me, this is my covenant with you: You will be the father of many nations. **17:5** No longer will you be called Abram ; your name will be Abraham, for I have made you a father of many nations. **17:6** I will make you very fruitful; I will make nations of you, and kings will come from you. **17:7** I will establish my covenant as an everlasting covenant between me and you and your descendants after you for the generations to come, to be your God and the God of your descendants after you. **17:8** The whole land of Canaan, where you are now an alien, I will give as an everlasting possession to you and your descendants after you; and I will be their God."

As we discussed in the end of chapter 15, God made a covenant with Abram, not Abram with God. This is reiterated in the fact that God will use the word "covenant" thirteen times in this chapter alone. Nine of these times He calls it "My covenant," three times He calls it an "everlasting covenant," and only once "a covenant between Me and you."

Thirteen years had passed since Ishmael had been born, and Abram still had no other children. The time had now come for the covenant to be confirmed and the true offspring of Abraham to come. As a sign of this confirmation, Abram was now to be called Abraham, because he would be the father of many nations as he was told earlier. In addition to the name change of Abram, God now also revealed Himself as *El Shaddai*, or God Almighty. Names are of utmost importance, as they give insight into characters and purpose.

The true meaning of this "everlasting covenant" is that God will be the God of us all forever. The land that was previously promised was again promised to all of Abraham's descendants, and God will be with them.

Gen 17:9 Then God said to Abraham, "As for you, you must keep my covenant, you and your descendants after you for the generations to come. **17:10** This is my covenant with you and your descendants after you, the covenant you are to keep: Every male among you shall be circumcised. **17:11** You are to undergo circumcision, and it will be the sign of the covenant between me and you. **17:12** For the generations to come every male among you who is eight days old must be circumcised, including those born in your household or bought with money from a foreigner--those who are not your offspring. **17:13** Whether born in your household or bought with your money, they must be circumcised. My covenant in your flesh is to be an everlasting covenant. **17:14** Any uncircumcised male, who has not been circumcised in the flesh, will be cut off from his people; he has broken my covenant."

As a sign of this *everlasting* covenant for Abraham and his descendants, all males were to be circumcised. God may have had sanitary and health reasons for this command, but there no doubt was more to it. Henry Morris explains, "The male sexual organ is the remarkable, divinely created vehicle for the transmission of this seed from one generation to another. The circumcision (cutting around) of this channel would thus picture its complete enclosure within God's protective and productive will. Furthermore, it was primarily a sign only to the individual concerned . . .. The cutting of the foreskin spoke of a surgical removal, a complete separation, from the sins of the flesh. . . such sins largely centered in the misuse of the male organ in adultery, fornication and sodomy" (Record, p. 333-334).

It is also significant that this is an *everlasting* covenant. Today we no longer view this as the sign of the covenant because we have a new covenant with God. In the Old Testament, every male at eight days old (babies) were circumcised. This, however, was not what brought salvation; it was merely a sign of the promise of salvation. These babies were not aware of any faith or conscious of any covenant, yet God was aware, and the sign of circumcision was for them also. Paul writes, "The one who is not circumcised physically and yet obeys the law will condemn you who, even though you have the written code and circumcision, are a lawbreaker. A man is not a Jew if he is only one outwardly, nor is circumcision merely outward and physical. No, a man is a Jew if he is one inwardly; and circumcision is circumcision of the heart, by the Spirit, not by the written code. Such a man's praise is not from men, but from God" (Rom 2:27-29). Also referring to Abraham, "And he received the sign of circumcision, a seal of the righteousness that he had by faith while he was still uncircumcised" (Rom 4:11). Abraham was righteous *before* this *sign* was administered.

The Arabs (Ishmael's descendants) still practice circumcision today, but not as a sign of the covenant, rather a sign of manhood at the age of 13.

Today, baptism has replaced circumcision as a sign of God's new covenant with us through Christ. Circumcision was a sign of the Messiah to come. Baptism a sign of the second coming. We see in Colossians, "In Him [Christ] you were also circumcised, in the putting off of the sinful nature, not with a circumcision done by the hands of men but with the *circumcision done by Christ*, having been buried with him in *baptism*" (Col 2:11-12). We also see in Ephesians 2:11-13 that, though we as Gentiles have been called the uncircumcised, we have been brought near to God through the blood of Christ. Thus baptism is God's covenant with us, not our covenant with God, and it replaces the act of circumcision.

Failure to take upon this sign of the covenant meant being cut off from the covenant. We see later that Moses was almost killed because his son had not been circumcised (Ex 4:25). One must not take this sign lightly.

Gen 17:15 God also said to Abraham, "As for Sarai your wife, you are no longer to call her Sarai; her name will be Sarah. 17:16 I will bless her and will surely give you a son by her. I will bless her so that she will be the mother of nations; kings of peoples will come from her." 17:17 Abraham fell facedown; he laughed and said to himself, "Will a son be born

to a man a hundred years old? Will Sarah bear a child at the age of ninety?" 17:18 And Abraham said to God, "If only Ishmael might live under your blessing!" 17:19 Then God said, "Yes, but your wife Sarah will bear you a son, and you will call him Isaac. I will establish my covenant with him as an everlasting covenant for his descendants after him. 17:20 And as for Ishmael, I have heard you: I will surely bless him; I will make him fruitful and will greatly increase his numbers. He will be the father of twelve rulers, and I will make him into a great nation. 17:21 But my covenant I will establish with Isaac, whom Sarah will bear to you by this time next year." 17:22 When he had finished speaking with Abraham, God went up from him. 17:23 On that very day Abraham took his son Ishmael and all those born in his household or bought with his money, every male in his household, and circumcised them, as God told him. 17:24 Abraham was ninety-nine years old when he was circumcised, 17:25 and his son Ishmael was thirteen; 17:26 Abraham and his son Ishmael were both circumcised on that same day. 17:27 And every male in Abraham's household, including those born in his household or bought from a foreigner, was circumcised with him.

Sarai also received a new name of Sarah, meaning "princess," as she would be the mother of kings (v. 16). Upon hearing that Sarah would have a baby at 90 years of age, Abraham laughed. Some believe this was the laughter of joy and amazement, rather than doubt. This may be true, but taking into consideration that Abraham asked "if only Ishmael might live under your blessing," it may mean that even Abraham was not fully convinced at first. As with us today, our initial response usually comes from the flesh, followed by a better, spiritual one.

God's answer to Abraham with regard to Ishmael's blessing was that he would indeed be blessed, but he was not to be under the everlasting covenant. Ishmael would be the father of 12 great nations, which are later listed in Genesis 25:12-16.

God seemed to have gone up to heaven and Abraham was left to circumcise his entire household, including Ishmael and the foreigners. Even though Ishmael was not under the covenant, he was circumcised, for as long as he remained under the roof of Abraham he was under the covenant, in a sense. However, later Ishmael left the protection of Abraham and the covenant to begin his own nation, where the prophecy of his hostility would continue.

Gen 18:1 The LORD appeared to Abraham near the great trees of Mamre while he was sitting at the entrance to his tent in the heat of the day. 18:2 Abraham looked up and saw three men standing nearby. When he saw them, he hurried from the entrance of his tent to meet them and bowed low to the ground. 18:3 He said, "If I have found favor in your eyes, my lord, do not pass your servant by. 18:4 Let a little water be brought, and then you may all wash your feet and rest under this tree. 18:5 Let me get you something to eat, so you can be refreshed and then go on your way-- now that you have come to your servant." "Very well," they answered, "do

as you say." 18:6 So Abraham hurried into the tent to Sarah. "Quick," he said, "get three seahs of fine flour and knead it and bake some bread." 18:7 Then he ran to the herd and selected a choice, tender calf and gave it to a servant, who hurried to prepare it. 18:8 He then brought some curds and milk and the calf that had been prepared, and set these before them. While they ate, he stood near them under a tree.

The LORD appeared to Abraham again in a preincarnate state, along with two angels. Verse one is simply a narrative explaining what happened from God's view, while verse two describes Abraham's story. Mamre again was the place Abraham moved to in 13:18 and had remained ever since. When Abraham saw these "three men" (who seem to have just appeared) he went out to invite them in. Unlike today, during this time the custom was to invite strangers into your home. Some believe Abraham apparently did not know it was the LORD at this point, based upon the fact that he called them "my lord," which can sometimes refer to magistrates. However, other lines allude to the fact that he may have known these were angels and the LORD. It seems that Abraham went above and beyond the call of hospitality. He "hurried" to meet them, "bowed low," called himself a "servant," "hurried" to get Sarah and prepare food. These words suggest not only reverence, but an attitude of excitement or urgency. Perhaps Abraham was praying at the entrance of his tent and felt this was an answer to his prayers. One can only guess. The point being, Abraham knew he had important guests.

The guests accepted Abraham's offer to stay for a meal and rest. Sarah baked bread and a servant prepared a tender calf.

Gen 18:9 "Where is your wife Sarah?" they asked him. "There, in the tent," he said. 18:10 Then the LORD said, "I will surely return to you about this time next year, and Sarah your wife will have a son." Now Sarah was listening at the entrance to the tent, which was behind him. 18:11 Abraham and Sarah were already old and well advanced in years, and Sarah was past the age of childbearing. 18:12 So Sarah laughed to herself as she thought, "After I am worn out and my master is old, will I now have this pleasure?" 18:13 Then the LORD said to Abraham, "Why did Sarah laugh and say, 'Will I really have a child, now that I am old?' 18:14 Is anything too hard for the LORD? I will return to you at the appointed time next year and Sarah will have a son." 18:15 Sarah was afraid, so she lied and said, "I did not laugh." But he said, "Yes, you did laugh."

Sarah remained in the tent nearby and listened in on the conversation, but was not seen by Abraham. The LORD again promised that Sarah would have a child one year from now. Upon hearing this Sarah laughed with doubt, since she was 90 years old. The LORD asked Abraham why Sarah laughed as Sarah, out of fear, denied doing it. Without any more said, the LORD convicted her with a quick response, "Yes, you did laugh." We cannot hide our sins from God.

At this point, Sarah and Abraham must have known that these men were at least angels. Sarah must have had great fear knowing she had just tried to lie to God Himself. The book of Hebrews gives us a rather interesting warning, "Do not forget to entertain strangers, for by so doing some people have entertained angels without knowing it" (Hebrews 13:2).

Gen 18:16 When the men got up to leave, they looked down toward Sodom, and Abraham walked along with them to see them on their way. 18:17 Then the LORD said, "Shall I hide from Abraham what I am about to do? 18:18 Abraham will surely become a great and powerful nation, and all nations on earth will be blessed through him. 18:19 For I have chosen him, so that he will direct his children and his household after him to keep the way of the LORD by doing what is right and just, so that the LORD will bring about for Abraham what He has promised him." 18:20 Then the LORD said, "The outcry against Sodom and Gomorrah is so great and their sin so grievous 18:21 that I will go down and see if what they have done is as bad as the outcry that has reached me. If not, I will know." 18:22 The men turned away and went toward Sodom, but Abraham remained standing before the LORD.

When the two men got up they looked down and headed toward Sodom with Abraham following. God asked whether He should hide what He was about to do. No doubt, this was not a question looking for an answer, rather a question making a statement. Abraham must have known in his heart what was going on, since he knew the wickedness of the cities below, as seen in verses 23ff.

The LORD proceeded to explain why Abraham must be filled in on the judgment of these cities. Abraham would become a powerful nation and thus, he needed to be able to preach and witness to this nation. If Abraham did not know what really happened to Sodom and Gomorrah, some would have tried to call it an act of nature. But Abraham was to "direct his children and household after him to keep the way of the LORD by doing what is right and just." Sodom was to serve as a warning for us, and Abraham no doubt used the plain below as a visual lesson for his children. We read that fathers are to teach their children and to "bring them up in the training and instruction of the Lord" (Eph 6:4).

God told Abraham that the outcry *against* Sodom and Gomorrah was great and, therefore, He had to go down to see what was going on. We saw once before that when God "came down" to see what was being done at Babel, He intervened to change matters completely. Note also that it was never said that God was going to destroy the city, but Abraham seemed to know. While the two angels left to go down into the city, Abraham and the LORD remained for a most amazing prayer.

Gen 18:23 Then Abraham approached him and said: "Will You sweep away the righteous with the wicked? 18:24 What if there are fifty righteous people in the city? Will You really sweep it away and not spare the place for the sake of the fifty righteous people in it? 18:25 Far be it from You to do such a thing--to kill the righteous with the wicked, treating

the righteous and the wicked alike. Far be it from You! Will not the Judge of all the earth do right?" 18:26 The LORD said, "If I find fifty righteous people in the city of Sodom, I will spare the whole place for their sake." 18:27 Then Abraham spoke up again: "Now that I have been so bold as to speak to the Lord, though I am nothing but dust and ashes, 18:28 what if the number of the righteous is five less than fifty? Will You destroy the whole city because of five people?" "If I find forty-five there," he said, "I will not destroy it." 18:29 Once again he spoke to him, "What if only forty are found there?" He said, "For the sake of forty, I will not do it. 18:30 Then he said, "May the Lord not be angry, but let me speak. What if only thirty can be found there?" He answered, "I will not do it if I find thirty there." 18:31 Abraham said, "Now that I have been so bold as to speak to the Lord, what if only twenty can be found there?" He said, "For the sake of twenty, I will not destroy it." 18:32 Then he said, "May the Lord not be angry, but let me speak just once more. What if only ten can be found there?" He answered, "For the sake of ten, I will not destroy it." 18:33 When the LORD had finished speaking with Abraham, He left, and Abraham returned home.

Abraham approached God (as we should) and asked if the city would be destroyed if there were but only 50 righteous people in the city. This prayer continued from 50 to 45, to 40, to 30, to 20, to 10. Abraham may have felt fairly comfortable that ten righteous people could be found, especially since there were five cities of the plain to be destroyed. In addition, Lot himself had ten in his family with he and his wife, two sons (Gen 19:12), four daughters (Gen 19:8,14), two sons-in-law (Gen 19:8).

Abraham may have been surprised to see only four people who were righteous in the entire plain. Though Lot himself was considered righteous, he must have struggled with giving up earthly pleasures, or else he would not have stayed in such a place. He no doubt wrestled with the wickedness therein, but maybe did not set himself apart enough to do much witnessing. We read in 2 Peter, "He rescued Lot, a righteous man, who was distressed by the filthy lives of lawless men (for that righteous man, living among them day after day, was tormented in his righteous soul by the lawless deeds he saw and heard)--" (2 Pet 2:7-8). We ourselves are often frustrated with the wickedness of this present world, but look to someone else to change things. Others like to "ride the fence," wanting to keep one foot in the world and another in church. God, however, would have us jump onto the side of the fence which blocks worldly cares and corruption.

It is interesting, as well, that God was willing to spare the cities for the sake of only ten righteous people. One cannot help but wonder what percentage of the righteous in the United States are keeping this country from certain destruction. God warns us, "Make sure there is no man or woman, clan or tribe among you today whose heart turns away from the LORD our God to go and worship the gods of those nations; make sure there is no root among you that produces such bitter poison. . . .[he] thinks, 'I will be safe, even though I persist in going my own way.' This will bring disaster on the watered land as well as the dry. The LORD will never be willing to forgive him; His wrath and zeal will burn against that man. All the curses written in this book will fall upon him, and the LORD will blot out his name from under heaven. . . Your children who follow you in later generations . . .will see the calamities that have fallen on the land . . . The whole land will be a burning waste of salt and sulfur--nothing planted, nothing sprouting, no vegetation growing on it. It will be like the destruction of Sodom and Gomorrah, Admah and Zeboiim, which the LORD overthrew in fierce anger. . .. All the nations will ask: 'Why has the LORD done this to this land? Why this fierce, burning anger?' And the answer will be: 'It is because this people abandoned the covenant of the LORD, the God of their fathers'" (Deu 29:18-25).

Gen 19:1 The two angels arrived at Sodom in the evening, and Lot was sitting in the gateway of the city. When he saw them, he got up to meet them and bowed down with his face to the ground. 19:2 "My lords," he said, "please turn aside to your servant's house. You can wash your feet and spend the night and then go on your way early in the morning." "No," they answered, "we will spend the night in the square." 19:3 But he insisted so strongly that they did go with him and entered his house. He prepared a meal for them, baking bread without yeast, and they ate. 19:4 Before they had gone to bed, all the men from every part of the city of Sodom--both young and old--surrounded the house. 19:5 They called to Lot, "Where are the men who came to you tonight? Bring them out to us so that we can have sex with them." 19:6 Lot went outside to meet them and shut the door behind him 19:7 and said, "No, my friends. Don't do this wicked thing. 19:8 Look, I have two daughters who have never slept with a man. Let me bring them out to you, and you can do what you like with them. But don't do anything to these men, for they have come under the protection of my roof." 19:9 "Get out of our way," they replied. And they said, "This fellow came here as an alien, and now he wants to play the judge! We'll treat you worse than them." They kept bringing pressure on Lot and moved forward to break down the door. 19:10 But the men inside reached out and pulled Lot back into the house and shut the door. 19:11 Then they struck the men who were at the door of the house, young and old, with blindness so that they could not find the door.

After the two angels left Abraham, they went down to Sodom that evening when Lot was sitting in the gate of the city. The fact that Lot was sitting in the gateway may suggest that he was some kind of official in Sodom, as this is where many important people took care of business. However, since it was evening and judging by the response he received from the townsmen in verse nine, it is also possible that this was simply part of Lot's daily routine, not a job. It seems unlikely that such an outcast would be of much importance in such a wicked city. In any case, Lot bowed down before them (out of respect, not worship) and invited them to his house to stay.

The angels declined Lot's offer, only to have him insist so fervently that they later accepted. We know that during this time hospitality was of the utmost importance; however, Lot's reaction to the angels spending the night in the town square is even excessive for this era. This leads us to believe that Lot knew what commonly happened to visitors of Sodom, and he may have stayed in the gate to spare travelers from this wickedness.

Once Lot brought them to his home, he cooked a dinner and made bread without yeast. Two things stand out in this statement. First, Lot did the cooking, and second, the bread was unleavened (without yeast). Why Lot's wife did not make a meal is unknown. Perhaps she was not pleased with Lot bringing guests home all the time. We simply don't know. Regarding the bread without yeast, yeast is often used in Scripture to symbolize evil. Appropriately, this is the first time we see bread made in such a manner, and the next time it appears is at the Passover meal (Exodus 12:15). Not only were the Israelites to make bread without yeast, but they were even to rid their house of yeast. Unleavened bread thus symbolized speed (the Exodus was fast) and purity, just as it symbolized here with Lot. We also see grain offerings were to be pure, without yeast (Lev 2:4,5,11), as were thank offerings (Lev 7:12-13). Jesus himself said, "Be on your guard against the yeast of the Pharisees and Sadducees" (Matt 16:6). Thus, Lot's unleavened bread showed purity and speed in the judgment soon to take place.

Before the men went to bed, ALL the townsmen, both young and old, came pounding at the door, demanding that Lot bring the two visitors out so that they could have sex with them. This shows the great wickedness of this city, and we would do well to learn from this event, since our society is beginning to go down the same path. Lot stepped out and shut the door behind him to plead with the townsmen to not do such a wicked thing. These visitors had come to the protection of Lot's home, and Lot was going to assure proper hospitality. It is strange that he went as far as to offer his two virgin daughters as replacements. It is possible that Lot knew this was not what interested them, and perhaps they would see his sincerity and leave. If so, it is still a drastic plea. There is no indication that the visitors are known as angels, yet Lot still offers his daughters. If Lot knew these men were angels, it could be that he was putting a spiritual matter above an earthly one, although, "If anyone does not provide for his relatives, and especially for his immediate family, he has denied the faith and is worse than an unbeliever" (1 Tim 5:8). With Lot being a righteous man (2 Pet 2:7), it is most likely that we do not have all the story, nor enough understanding of the customs of the time to pass judgment on this apparent sin.

As mentioned, all the men in the town came out to rape these other men. There is no question in context or original language that the sin of Sodom was homosexuality. Many in the homosexual movement today try to claim that the sin of Sodom was not sexual perverseness, but inhospitality. One need not explain this in great detail to realize that this statement is only an attempt to justify and relieve a guilty conscience that comes as a result of their sin. Paul writes, "they show that the requirements of the law are written on their hearts, their consciences also bearing witness, and their thoughts now accusing, now even defending them" (Rom 2:15).

Why did this city become so evil in the sin of homosexuality? The same reason our society does today. Not because they are born that way (another attempt to justify a guilty conscience), but rather as Scripture explains, "For since the creation of the world God's invisible qualities--His eternal power and divine nature--have been clearly seen, being understood from what has been made, so that men are without excuse. For although they knew God, they neither glorified Him as God nor gave thanks to Him, but their thinking became futile and their foolish hearts were darkened. Although they claimed to be wise, they became fools and exchanged the glory of the immortal God for images made to look like mortal man and birds and animals and reptiles. *Therefore* God *gave them over* in the sinful desires of their hearts to sexual impurity for the degrading of their bodies with one another. . ... *Because of this*, God *gave them over* to shameful lusts. Even their women exchanged natural relations for unnatural ones. In the same way the men also abandoned natural relations with women and were inflamed with lust for one another. Men committed indecent acts with other men, and received in themselves the *due penalty for their perversion*" (Rom 1:20-27). In a time when God is being rejected as Creator and the creation is being praised and worshipped, is it any wonder that our society has become so sexually perverse?

Lot's attempt to appease the mob failed and they even threatened to mistreat Lot, a foreigner himself, if he did not cooperate. If Lot did not know his guests were angels he was about to find out, as they would rescue him. They opened the door, pulled Lot inside and struck the men outside with blindness. This type of blindness may not be one of sight but rather confusion. The word used here for blindness is only used one other time in Scripture, where the Syrian army was struck with a blindness of the mind to save Elisha's life (2 Kings 6:18ff). Therefore, it is possible that the men outside Lot's door forgot why they were standing at his door and were dazed. This explains how Lot was able to leave his house in verse 14. Either way, they could not find Lot's door even though it was right in front of them, and God delivered Lot.

Gen 19:12 The two men said to Lot, "Do you have anyone else here--sons-in-law, sons or daughters, or anyone else in the city who belongs to you? Get them out of here, 19:13 because we are going to destroy this place. The outcry to the LORD against its people is so great that he has sent us to destroy it." 19:14 So Lot went out and spoke to his sons-in-law, who were pledged to marry his daughters. He said, "Hurry and get out of this place, because the LORD is about to destroy the city!" But his sons-in-law thought he was joking. 19:15 With the coming of dawn, the angels urged Lot, saying, "Hurry! Take your wife and your two daughters who are here, or you will be swept away when the city is punished." 19:16 When he hesitated, the men grasped his hand and the hands of his wife and of his two daughters and led them safely out of the city, for the LORD was merciful to them 19:17 As soon as they had brought them out, one of them said, "Flee for your lives! Don't look back, and don't stop anywhere in the plain! Flee to the mountains or you will be swept away!" 19:18 But Lot said to them, "No, my lords, please! 19:19 Your servant has found favor in your eyes, and you have shown great kindness to me in sparing my life. But I can't flee to the mountains; this disaster will overtake me, and I'll die. 19:20 Look,

here is a town near enough to run to, and it is small. Let me flee to it--it is very small, isn't it? Then my life will be spared." 19:21 He said to him, "Very well, I will grant this request too; I will not overthrow the town you speak of. 19:22 But flee there quickly, because I cannot do anything until you reach it." (That is why the town was called Zoar.) 19:23 By the time Lot reached Zoar, the sun had risen over the land.

The angels proceeded to warn Lot of the coming destruction and instructed him to leave with his family. As lot went to gather his family, his sons-in-law did not believe him. This gives us an indication that Lot's daughters had not chosen their future husbands well. It appears time was running out, as Lot again was instructed to hurry out of town with his two daughters and wife. This whole section leaves us with a sense of indecisiveness and confusion. Lot must have pleaded with his sons-in-law and others, but they simply would not listen. Lot wanted more time, going back and forth trying to figure out what to do. Finally, the angels had to grab Lot, his wife and daughters by the hand to lead them to safety. Why? Because the LORD was merciful. This is important, because if it wasn't for Christ's mercy upon us, we would perish just as Sodom. The LORD knew that Lot was hanging on to his worldly cares and wasn't getting off the middle of the fence to follow God completely, yet He was merciful. This type of grace is seen in Corinthians where we see that many will squeeze into heaven by faith in Christ, despite their errors. We read: "By the grace God has given me, I laid a foundation as an expert builder, and someone else is building on it. But each one should be careful how he builds. For no one can lay any foundation other than the one already laid, which is Jesus Christ. If any man builds on this foundation using gold, silver, costly stones, wood, hay or straw, his work will be shown for what it is, because the Day will bring it to light. It will be revealed with fire, and the fire will test the quality of each man's work. If what he has built survives, he will receive his reward. If it is burned up, *he will suffer loss*; he himself *will be saved*, but *only as one escaping through the flames*" (1 Cor 3:11-15). If we go through life as Lot seems to be here, riding the fence and wanting to mix the world's ways with God's ways, our faith in Christ will save us, but only by the skin of our teeth. Why? Because though it is faith, not works, which saves, "faith without works is dead" (James 2:17).

Lot's worldliness continued to show as the angels, after leading Lot and his family out of town, told them to flee and don't look back. They were to go to the surrounding hills for safety, but Lot does not want to go there. Lot claimed that to have to live in the mountains would kill him. He apparently had become accustomed to city life. At a moment when Lot should have been thankful for his salvation, he continued to think of his means of comfort and asked to live in Zoar, a small city. The angel surprisingly gave Lot permission, and thus the city of Zoar was saved.

It is interesting to note that, though Zoar was spared, Lot did not continue to live there, but went to the mountains where he was instructed to go at first. Why he left Zoar we are not told, but perhaps he began to wise up and turn to God rather than the world. In any case, this is a good example of how our Father deals with us, His children. Just as today when a child asks his father for something, sometimes the father must say no because it isn't the best thing for his child. Other times, though it isn't the best thing for the child, the father gives it to him anyway, so that the child can learn the lesson on his own. Lot needed to learn a lesson on his own and was, therefore, allowed to go to Zoar where he would then make his own decision to leave, this time not looking back.

The sun was up by the time Lot and his family reached Zoar, so the destruction was in plain view, but they were not to look back. Looking back would not show curiosity, but a longing and a sadness for a past life; a worldly life that one should not desire or long for.

Gen 19:24 Then the LORD rained down burning sulfur on Sodom and Gomorrah--from the LORD out of the heavens. 19:25 Thus He overthrew those cities and the entire plain, including all those living in the cities--and also the vegetation in the land.

Now the LORD (who *was* with Abraham), not the angels, threw down fire from heaven and destroyed the entire plain, including its cities and vegetation. There are many different ideas as to what this "burning sulfur out of the heavens" means. When it comes right down to it, it doesn't matter because the point is, God judged these evil cities. Some believe that this may have been a volcano, since this area today shows much volcanic evidence. Also, sulfur comes from the earth below. Some translations use the word "brimstone," which is usually associated with sulfur and simply means "God's fire." If volcanoes were used by God to destroy Sodom, how then could sulfur come "out of the heavens?" Some suggest that volcanic activity threw burning rock and sulfur into the air and then it fell down upon them out of the sky, much like ash does today. One problem with this volcano theory is that, archaeologically speaking, it took place long before the time of Abraham and, therefore, may have already taken place at the time of the Flood or soon after. Though this volcano theory is doubtful, it is possible. However, we must also remember that God is all powerful and this could have been something "supernatural," which is probably the case.

Another interesting site has recently been uncovered. On the west side of the Dead Sea just north of Masada are some very interesting land shapes that, when viewed carefully, seem to have the shapes of buildings and streets. Quite often rock formations can be shaped as familiar objects, yet the number and consistency of this phenomenon is indeed unusual. Even more astounding is the fact that they have found balls of sulfur in various sizes everywhere amidst these formations. This sulfur is unique to the entire world, with its origin unknown. Thus, if this location is indeed the plain which was destroyed, it must have been a supernatural destruction, which seems to be the context here. For years it has also been thought that Sodom was under the Dead Sea. This may suggest otherwise, but is still not conclusive.

Today, the area of the Dead Sea is a very infertile and desolate plain, fitting the description given here. It is very likely, if not certain, that this area is indeed where Sodom was situated, yet the *exact* location in the plain is unknown. There are mountains on either side which are filled with many caves, where Lot was told to flee (v. 17). We will also see Abraham look down to Sodom (v.28), also giving further credibility to this area. The mention of salt (v. 26) alludes to the saltiest sea in the world, the Dead Sea. It is nearly impossible to sink in this water, due to its mineral content today. Zoar appears to have been located at the southern end of the Dead Sea, and this was one of the "cities of the plain" which was not destroyed.

Gen 19:26 But Lot's wife looked back, and she became a pillar of salt. 19:27 Early the next morning Abraham got up and returned to the place where he had stood before the LORD. 19:28 He looked down toward Sodom and Gomorrah, toward all the land of the plain, and he saw dense smoke rising from the land, like smoke from a furnace. 19:29 So when God destroyed the cities of the plain, he remembered Abraham, and he brought Lot out of the catastrophe that overthrew the cities where Lot had lived.

God warned Lot and his family not to look back, but Lot's wife did so anyway. As a result she was turned into a pillar of salt. Lot's wife simply disobeyed God, which in itself was a grave sin. However, her sin gives us insight into her heart as well. The very fact that she looked back showed her sadness and unwillingness to leave the city. (Remember, the angels even had to drag her away in verse 16). Even though the men in this city almost dragged her own husband out of his house to do detestable things to him, she still longed for this life. This was not a curious look back: "Remember Lot's wife! Whoever tries to keep his life will lose it, and whoever loses his life will preserve it" (Luke 17:32-33). Luke does not mean a physical life, but a spiritual one. Lot's wife was hanging on to the debauchery and sin that this city offered. We would do well to learn from this, because God will again destroy the world with fire just as he did at Sodom: "If He condemned the cities of Sodom and Gomorrah by burning them to ashes, and made them an *example of what is going to happen to the ungodly* and if He rescued Lot, a righteous man, who was distressed by the filthy lives of lawless men (for that righteous man, living among them day after day, was tormented in his righteous soul by the lawless deeds he saw and heard)-- if this is so, then the Lord knows how to *rescue godly men* from trials and to hold the unrighteous for the day of judgment, while continuing their punishment" (2 Pet 2:6-9). Though the world goes about its sinful ways we are not to be of the world, so we too may be saved as Lot was.

Gen 19:30 Lot and his two daughters left Zoar and settled in the mountains, for he was afraid to stay in Zoar. He and his two daughters lived in a cave. 19:31 One day the older daughter said to the younger, "Our father is old, and there is no man around here to lie with us, as is the custom all over the earth. 19:32 Let's get our father to drink wine and then lie with him and preserve our family line through our father." 19:33 That night they got their father to drink wine, and the older daughter went in and lay with him. He was not aware of it when she lay down or when she got up. 19:34 The next day the older daughter said to the younger, "Last night I lay with my father. Let's get him to drink wine again tonight, and

101

you go in and lie with him so we can preserve our family line through our father." 19:35 So they got their father to drink wine that night also, and the younger daughter went and lay with him. Again he was not aware of it when she lay down or when she got up. 19:36 So both of Lot's daughters became pregnant by their father. 19:37 The older daughter had a son, and she named him Moab ; he is the father of the Moabites of today. 19:38 The younger daughter also had a son, and she named him Ben-Ammi ; he is the father of the Ammonites of today.

We are not told exactly why, but Lot left the city to which he had fled to. We only know for sure that Lot was afraid to remain there, most likely because the sins of Zoar were just like those of Sodom and it too was almost destroyed. Lot may have feared that soon God would also destroy this city and maybe this time he would not escape. Perhaps with his wife now gone it was easier for him to focus on more Godly things; things Zoar was not known for. Sometimes it takes this kind of tragedy to slap us out of our sins.

Lot went to the caves of the hillside, taking his two daughters along. The years of living surrounded by sin took its toll on Lot's family. His two daughters (the virgins he tried to offer in place of the angels in Sodom) were still alone and now felt more than ever that they would never find a husband. Having the evil ways of Sodom fresh in their mind, they plotted to get Lot drunk and sleep with him so that they could have children. Lot should have never allowed himself to become drunk, but perhaps his worldliness allowed his depression of living in the hills to overtake his faith in God (v. 19). Though a righteous man by faith (2 Peter 2:6-9), Lot's life application still seemed to be weak.

First the older daughter got Lot drunk beyond consciousness and slept with him; then the younger daughter the next night. We are not told when Lot became aware of this sin, and nothing is ever said of his reaction. Moab and Ben-Ammi were the result. Both the Moabites and the Ammonites were a people of hostility toward God's people, Israel. The infamous Balaak, who hired Balaam to curse Israel, was a Moabite, and they settled near family and lived on the east side of the Dead Sea. However, certain individuals among these nations also served the LORD. Ruth was a Moabite woman and was an ancestor of Christ. Naamah was an Ammonite who became one of Solomon's wives and gave birth to King Rehoboam, and therefore is also in the ancestral line of Christ.

God judged both the Moabites and Ammonites severely as a result of their hostility toward Israel. However, there are some indications that God will restore them in the last days: "Yet I will restore the fortunes of Moab in days to come, declares the LORD. Here ends the judgment on Moab" (Jeremiah 48:47); and "Yet afterward, I will restore the fortunes of the Ammonites, declares the LORD" (Jeremiah 49:6).

Gen 20:1 Now Abraham moved on from there into the region of the Negev and lived between Kadesh and Shur. For a while he stayed in Gerar, 20:2 and there Abraham said of his wife Sarah, "She is my sister." Then Abimelech king of Gerar sent for Sarah and took her. 20:3 But God came to Abimelech in a dream one night and said to him, "You are as good as dead because of the woman you have taken; she is a married woman." 20:4 Now Abimelech had not gone near her, so he said, "Lord, will you destroy an innocent nation? 20:5 Did he not say to me, 'She is my sister,' and didn't she also say, 'He is my brother'? I have done this with a clear conscience and clean hands." 20:6 Then God said to him in the dream, "Yes, I know you did this with a clear conscience, and so I have kept you from sinning against Me. That is why I did not let you touch her. 20:7 Now return the man's wife, for he is a prophet, and he will pray for you and you will live. But if you do not return her, you may be sure that you and all yours will die." 20:8 Early the next morning Abimelech summoned all his officials, and when he told them all that had happened, they were very much afraid.

This is a very puzzling section, as Abraham once again fell prey to a lack of trust in God. One would think he would have been over this by now, but we must remember that Abraham, like us, was a man born into the sinful flesh.

Abraham left home and lived in the Negev for awhile. Gerar was the very prosperous capital city of the Philistines near the Egyptian border. As he did once before (12:13), Abraham said that his wife Sarah was his sister to avoid anything happening to him. Sarah was now 90 years old and still a beautiful woman. This is rather surprising, but we must remember that the LORD was preserving her body to give birth to Isaac. In any case, Abimelech (the name of the office, not a personal name, just as the Pharaoh in Egypt) took Sarah into his palace to prepare her to be part of his harem. However, God inflicted some disease upon Abimelech, perhaps to keep him from sleeping with Sarah (v. 17). God came to Abimelech in a dream, which is how he found out Sarah was not just Abraham's half sister, but his wife as well. Abimelech pleaded for himself and his country, since he was innocent in this matter. God pronounced his innocence and told him to return Sarah to Abraham, a prophet who, ironically, will pray for Abimelech's life and the cure of the disease God had given him.

The next morning Abimelech told all his officials what had happened, and all were filled with fear. This shows a genuine fear of the LORD; however, they were a polytheistic nation and feared many gods.

Gen 20:9 Then Abimelech called Abraham in and said, "What have you done to us? How have I wronged you that you have brought such great guilt upon me and my kingdom? You have done things to me that should not be done." 20:10 And Abimelech asked Abraham, "What was your reason for doing this?" 20:11 Abraham replied, "I said to myself, 'There is surely no fear of God in this place, and they will kill me because of my wife.' 20:12 Besides, she really is my sister, the daughter of my father though not of my mother; and she became my wife. 20:13 And when God had me wander from my father's household, I said to her, 'This is how you can show your love to me: Everywhere we go, say of me, "He is my brother."'" 20:14 Then Abimelech brought sheep and cattle and male and female slaves and gave them to Abraham, and he returned Sarah his wife to

103

him. 20:15 And Abimelech said, "My land is before you; live wherever you like." 20:16 To Sarah he said, "I am giving your brother a thousand shekels of silver. This is to cover the offense against you before all who are with you; you are completely vindicated." 20:17 Then Abraham prayed to God, and God healed Abimelech, his wife and his slave girls so they could have children again, 20:18 for the LORD had closed up every womb in Abimelech's household because of Abraham's wife Sarah.

Even though a prophet, Abraham was rebuked by Abimelech, and rightly so. When asked why he did such a wicked thing, the answer was the same as before in Genesis 12:13, ultimately a lack of faith in God. This must not have been much of a witness to this nation. It was also strange that Abraham would ask his wife to show his love in such a sinful manner. Even though it wasn't a complete lie, it was still a clear deception.

Just as in Egypt, Abraham was given many possessions, perhaps as a bribe and peace offering, so that his God would not punish their nation. God continued to bless Abraham despite his weakness, just as the new covenant of Christ's salvation is for us despite our sinfulness (actually, because of our sinfulness).

Some have been surprised that Abraham accepted these gifts, since earlier he refused to accept anything from the spoils of the kings who conquered Sodom (Gen 14:22-23) because he did not want anyone to say they had made Abraham rich. It is possible that Abraham accepted these gifts, not for his sake, but for the sake of Abimelech paying restitution, as we see in verse 16.

Another interesting note about verse 16 is the difference in translation between the NIV and the KJV which states, "And unto Sarah he said, 'Behold, I have given thy brother a thousand pieces of silver: behold, *he is to thee a covering of the eyes*, unto all that are with thee, and with all other: thus she was reproved.'" It is possible that this was a rebuke to Sarah (as this verse states at the end) that Sarah need not fear other men because Abraham, her brother, was "a covering of the eyes" for her. Since Abraham was a prophet and protected by God, that was all the protection she needed to keep the eyes of men off her. Therefore, let that be a lesson to her. This being the case, both Abraham and Sarah received a righteous rebuke from Abimelech.

Abraham prayed to God, and Abimelech was healed along with his family and slaves. The LORD had closed up the womb of all Abimelech's household, which in those days was a great disgrace. It is unfortunate that we do not place the same value on children today.

It appears that this time Abraham learned his lesson, as we never see him do this again (although his son will).

Gen 21:1 Now the LORD was gracious to Sarah as He had said, and the LORD did for Sarah what He had promised. 21:2 Sarah became pregnant and bore a son to Abraham in his old age, at the very time God had promised him. 21:3 Abraham gave the name Isaac to the son Sarah bore him. 21:4 When his son Isaac was eight days old, Abraham circumcised him, as God commanded him. 21:5 Abraham was a hundred years old when his son Isaac was born to him. 21:6 Sarah said, "God has brought me laughter, and everyone who hears about this will laugh with me." 21:7 And she added, "Who would have said to Abraham that Sarah would nurse children? Yet I have borne him a son in his old age." 21:8 The child grew and was weaned, and on the day Isaac was weaned Abraham held a great feast.

Only with God's grace did Abraham and Sarah bear a child. The promise was fulfilled and Isaac was finally born after 25 years. Abraham never gave up faith concerning this matter but instead, "Without weakening in his faith, he faced the fact that his body was as good as dead--since he was about a hundred years old--and that Sarah's womb was also dead. Yet he did not waver through unbelief regarding the promise of God, but was strengthened in his faith and gave glory to God, being fully persuaded that God had power to do what He had promised." This is why "it was credited to him as righteousness" (Rom 4:19-22).

This event is of utmost importance for the New Testament believers because it shows our salvation comes not by works but by grace. Abraham was considered righteous, yet at this time he had not been circumcised nor were the ten commandments available (Rom 4:9-12; Gal 3:16-18). It was Abraham's faith that "was credited to him as righteousness" (Rom 4:9). It was also through his faith that he became the "father of many nations," (Rom 4:17) and the "father of all those who believe" (4:11). After Sarah died, Abraham continued to have six more children through his wife Keturah (Gen 25:2).

In naming this child Isaac, they would always remember the joy and laughter this promise was to bring. First, the laughter of doubt in Sarah's case, but later the laughter of joy and amazement (v. 6).

In following God's command (Gen 17:12) Isaac was circumcised on the 8th day as was the custom. He grew up and was weaned, usually at about two to three years of age. At this time, Abraham held a great feast for his son to again celebrate God's fulfilled promise.

Gen 21:9 But Sarah saw that the son whom Hagar the Egyptian had borne to Abraham was mocking, 21:10 and she said to Abraham, "Get rid of that slave woman and her son, for that slave woman's son will never share in the inheritance with my son Isaac." 21:11 The matter distressed Abraham greatly because it concerned his son. 21:12 But God said to him, "Do not be so distressed about the boy and your maidservant. Listen to whatever Sarah tells you, because it is through Isaac that your offspring will be reckoned. 21:13 I will make the son of the maidservant into a nation also, because he is your offspring." 21:14 Early the next morning Abraham took some food and a skin of water and gave them to Hagar. He set them on her shoulders and then sent her off with the boy. She went on her way and wandered in the desert of Beersheba. 21:15 When the water in the skin was gone, she put the boy under one of the bushes. 21:16 Then she went off and sat down nearby, about a bowshot away, for she thought, "I cannot watch the boy die." And as she sat there nearby, she began to sob. 21:17 God

heard the boy crying, and the angel of God called to Hagar from heaven and said to her, "What is the matter, Hagar? Do not be afraid; God has heard the boy crying as he lies there. 21:18 Lift the boy up and take him by the hand, for I will make him into a great nation." 21:19 Then God opened her eyes and she saw a well of water. So she went and filled the skin with water and gave the boy a drink. 21:20 God was with the boy as he grew up. He lived in the desert and became an archer 21:21 While he was living in the Desert of Paran, his mother got a wife for him from Egypt.

These next verses seem harsh, yet true. Isaac was now about two or three years old, but Ishmael was about 16 years old (Abraham was 86 when Ishmael was born in Genesis 16:16, 100 years old when Isaac was born in Genesis 21:5, and it is now about two or three years after Isaac's birth). Ishmael, old enough to know better, began to mock Isaac severely, probably due to the obvious attention Isaac received as being the "promised child." We read in the New Testament, "Now you, brothers, like Isaac, are children of promise. At that time the son born in the ordinary way *persecuted* the son born by the power of the Spirit. It is the same now" (Gal 4:28-29). This is certainly no ordinary brotherly quarrel.

This relationship between Isaac and Ishmael goes much deeper than what is first seen. As we will see, Ishmael represents the Law given on Mount Sinai and Isaac represents the covenant promise. In Galatians we see that the son born the ordinary way (our sinful nature and desire to follow the Law) persecutes the son born by the Spirit (the new man of God who clings to Christ's love and forgiveness). This is exactly what goes on today. Often when we do something wrong and sinful, we continue to beat ourselves and feel guilty long after we have been forgiven. The Law continues to work when it should not. Someone once told me that the 10 commandments had no meaning in their life. At first I was shocked, until I realized what was being said. The 10 commandments don't have any use in the Christian life unless they fall away and begin doing something sinful. Then the Law is needed to convict you. However, once you are convicted we throw the Law away so that we can get rid of the guilt, and let Christ's loving forgiveness take hold of our life. After all, is it the Law that causes you not to murder. NO! It is the Gospel and the love of Christ that motivates us to lead a Godly life. But, when we allow the law to remain in our Christian lives when it shouldn't, it persecutes us into an attitude of works righteousness. That is why we read in Romans, "Therefore no one will be declared righteous in His sight by observing the law; rather, through the law we become conscious of sin. But now a righteousness from God, apart from law, has been made known, to which the Law and the Prophets testify. This righteousness from God comes through faith in Jesus Christ to all who believe" (Rom 3:20-22); "But now, by dying to what once bound us, we have been released from the law so that we serve in the new way of the Spirit, and not in the old way of the written code" (Rom 7:6); "Christ is the end of the law so that there may be righteousness for everyone who believes" (Rom 10:4); "So, my brothers, you also died to the law through the body of Christ, that you might belong to another, to Him who was raised from the dead, in order that we might bear fruit to God" (Rom 7:4). Still other verses verify that, "To the Jews I became like a Jew, to win the Jews. To those under the law I became like one under the law (though I myself am not under the law), so as to win those under the law" (1 Cor 9:20); "What, then, was the purpose of the law? It was added because of transgressions **until** the Seed to whom the promise referred had come. The law was put into effect through angels by a mediator" (Gal 3:19); "So the law was put in charge to lead us to Christ that we might be justified by faith. **Now** that faith has come, **we are no longer under the supervision of the law**" (Gal 3:24); "For through the law I died to the law so that I might live for God" (Gal 2:19). These are just a few examples of Scripture where we clearly see that those who live by faith need not hold the ten commandments near their heart. If this person of the faith begins to fall away or sin unrepentantly, only then does the law need to be brought back into their lives. We must not let the "son born naturally" persecute "the son born of the Spirit." For, "It is through Isaac that your offspring will be reckoned. In other words, it is not the natural children who are God's children, but it is the children of the promise who are regarded as Abraham's offspring" (Rom 9:7). Therefore, we, as children of the promise, are Abraham's offspring and we will not be persecuted by the Law any longer.

As a result of this "persecution," spoke of in Galatians Sarah told Abraham to get rid of Hagar and her son. This was partly motivated by jealousy, now that Sarah had her own child, and she was simply being a "protective mother" at this point. However, she adds the fact that Ishmael would never share in the inheritance that Isaac would receive. This is painfully true, as we will discuss soon. This distressed Abraham, because even though Ishmael was not Sarah's son, he was his real son. As always, this was part of God's plan, however, and He told Abraham to listen to Sarah because the promise will be fulfilled through Isaac. We see this elaborated on by Paul who stated, "Nor because they are his descendants are they all Abraham's children. On the contrary, 'It is through Isaac that your offspring will be reckoned.' In other words, it is not the natural children who are God's children, but it is the children of the promise who are regarded as Abraham's offspring" (Rom 9:7-8). Only the children of the promise, which came through Isaac, are Abraham's offspring. However, since Ishmael was of Abraham, not just the promise, God assured Abraham that Ishmael would become a great nation as well. We see in Genesis 25:13-15 that he will have 12 sons and, indeed, become a great nation.

The next morning Abraham sent Hagar and Ishmael away with what seemed to be nothing compared to the riches Abraham was blessed with. Though we are not told, this may have been part of God's instruction to make Abraham, Hagar and Ishmael trust in God and His promised care. On the other hand, it could amplify the fact that Ishmael was to have no part in the covenant promise; the Law would have no part in the Gospel.

Hagar began wandering in the desert of Beersheba where she became lost and ran out of water. She put Ishmael (at least 16 years old) under a bush while she herself went off a short distance so she did not have to see her son suffer. Both were crying at this point (v. 16-17) but God heard the boy crying and came to Hagar. Here we see what Sarah meant when she said that Ishmael would not share in the promise of "her son." Back in 16:7, the angel of the LORD appeared to Hagar when she ran away from Sarah. Here, however, the angel of God comes. This is a very important distinction, because as long as Hagar and Ishmael were under Abraham's roof they were under the covenant God gave Abraham. In 16:7 (and everywhere else this term is used) the word LORD in capital letters is Jehovah. Jehovah is the name used to represent the covenant God. In 21:17, however, we have the "angel of God" or the "angel of Elohim." Elohim is the more impersonal, Creator name given to God. Thus we see that now Hagar has left the roof of Abraham, she and her son are no longer under the covenant given to Abraham, and Ishmael is not to share in Isaac's inheritance.

Hagar, though not under the covenant, was still under the protection of the one and only God, who opened her eyes to see water. They drank and went on their way to the desert of Paran in the Sinai peninsula. This is important because it further symbolizes the difference in the covenant promise of Isaac and that of Ishmael. We read in Galatians, "Abraham had two sons, one by the slave woman and the other by the free woman. His son by the slave woman was born in the ordinary way; but his son by the free woman was born as the result of a promise. These things may be taken figuratively, for the women represent two covenants. One covenant is from Mount Sinai and bears children who are to be slaves: This is Hagar. Now Hagar stands for Mount Sinai in Arabia and corresponds to the present city of Jerusalem, because she is in slavery with her children. But the Jerusalem that is above is free, and she is our mother. For it is written: 'Be glad, O barren woman, who bears no children; break forth and cry aloud, you who have no labor pains; because more are the children of the desolate woman than of her who has a husband.' Now you, brothers, like Isaac, are children of promise" (Gal 4:22-28). As Hagar was a slave woman, she represents the law of Mt. Sinai, where she dwelt, and the earthly Jerusalem. Ishmael, the offspring of the slave woman, is natural or ordinary, just as the law is naturally in our hearts and, therefore, we become slaves to the law (Rom 2:15). Isaac was born by a promise, and he represents freedom from the law. Sarah, likewise, represents the New Jerusalem of heaven (Rev 3:12; 21:2) which all believers are to receive since we are "children of the promise."

Ishmael became an archer, which would have been a useful skill in these areas. Hagar, being an Egyptian, then found an Egyptian woman to be Ishmael's wife. As mentioned, he will become the father of 12 nations, listed in 25:15.

Gen 21:22 At that time Abimelech and Phicol the commander of his forces said to Abraham, "God is with you in everything you do. 21:23 Now swear to me here before God that you will not deal falsely with me or my children or my descendants. Show to me and the country where you are living as an alien the same kindness I have shown to you." 21:24 Abraham said, "I swear it." 21:25 Then Abraham complained to Abimelech about a well of water that Abimelech's servants had seized. 21:26 But Abimelech said, "I don't know who has done this. You did not tell me, and I heard about it only today." 21:27 So Abraham brought sheep and cattle and gave

them to Abimelech, and the two men made a treaty. 21:28 Abraham set apart seven ewe lambs from the flock, 21:29 and Abimelech asked Abraham, "What is the meaning of these seven ewe lambs you have set apart by themselves? 21:30 He replied, "Accept these seven lambs from my hand as a witness that I dug this well." 21:31 So that place was called Beersheba, because the two men swore an oath there. 21:32 After the treaty had been made at Beersheba, Abimelech and Phicol the commander of his forces returned to the land of the Philistines. 21:33 Abraham planted a tamarisk tree in Beersheba, and there he called upon the name of the LORD, the Eternal God. 21:34 And Abraham stayed in the land of the Philistines for a long time.

We now see Abimelech again, more than likely the same one who just rebuked Abraham and Sarah in 20:14. He saw that Abraham had become very wealthy and powerful because of his God (v. 22), so he wanted to make a treaty. Abimelech reminded Abraham how he treated him fairly by allowing him to stay in the land. Now Abimelech wanted the same treatment. Abraham accepted the offer but had a few complaints. Apparently some of Abimelech's servant's took away a well that Abraham had dug without the knowledge of Abimelech. To make this treaty effective, Abraham brought sheep and cattle to Abimelech, yet nothing was said of Abimelech giving anything to Abraham. Along with this gift, Abraham had set aside seven ewe lambs to show proper ownership of the well and to seal the covenant.

They called the well Beersheba, meaning "well of the oath." This well was obviously of great importance for Abraham to go through this trouble. Insight into the reason why is given later, as Abraham will return to live there in Genesis 22:19. Beersheba became a common boundary line that would be heard often in passages such as, "Then all the Israelites from Dan to Beersheba and from the land of Gilead came out as one man and assembled before the LORD in Mizpah" (Judges 20:1). This place is found no less than 34 times in the rest of Scripture and is the site of many historical events. (See Gen 26:23,33; 28:10; 46:1,5; Josh 15:8; 19:2; 1 Sam 3:20; 8:2; 2 Sam 3:10; 17:11; 24:2,7,15; 1 Kings 4:25; 19:3; 2 Kings 12:1; 23:8; 1 Chr 4:8; 21:2; 2 Chr 19:4; 24:1; 30:5; Neh 11:27,30; Amos 5:5; 8:14).

Abimelech and Phicol returned home, while Abraham planted tamarisk trees near the well. He then "calls upon the name of the LORD, the Eternal God." Many more times the LORD will be called upon at this location (see verses listed above).

Gen 22:1 Some time later God tested Abraham. He said to him, "Abraham!" "Here I am," he replied. 22:2 Then God said, "Take your son, your only son, Isaac, whom you love, and go to the region of Moriah. Sacrifice him there as a burnt offering on one of the mountains I will tell you about." 22:3 Early the next morning Abraham got up and saddled his donkey. He took with him two of his servants and his son Isaac. When he had cut enough wood for the burnt offering, he set out for the place God had told him about. 22:4 On the third day Abraham looked up and saw the place in the distance. **22:5 He said to his servants, "Stay here with the donkey while I and the boy go over there. We will worship and then we will come back to you." 22:6 Abraham took the wood for the burnt offering and placed it on his son Isaac, and he himself carried the fire and the knife. As the two of them went on together, 22:7 Isaac spoke up and said to his father Abraham, "Father?" "Yes, my son?" Abraham replied. "The fire and wood are here," Isaac said, "but where is the lamb for the burnt offering?" 22:8 Abraham answered, "God himself will provide the lamb for the burnt offering, my son." And the two of them went on together. 22:9 When they reached the place God had told him about, Abraham built an altar there and arranged the wood on it. He bound his son Isaac and laid him on the altar, on top of the wood. 22:10 Then he reached out his hand and took the knife to slay his son. 22:11 But the angel of the LORD called out to him from heaven, "Abraham! Abraham!" "Here I am," he replied. 22:12 "Do not lay a hand on the boy," he said. "Do not do anything to him. Now I know that you fear God, because you have not withheld from me your son, your only son." 22:13 Abraham looked up and there in a thicket he saw a ram caught by its horns. He went over and took the ram and sacrificed it as a burnt offering instead of his son. 22:14 So Abraham called that place The LORD Will Provide. And to this day it is said, "On the mountain of the LORD it will be provided."**

The phrase "some time later" may actually mean a number of years, as there appears to be a significant jump in time from the end of chapter 21 to the beginning of chapter 23, where it says that Sarah died at 127 years old. Since Isaac was weaned when Sarah was 92 or 93 years old, that leaves about 35 years of time given in the end of chapters 21 through 22. We also see that Isaac was now old enough to carry the wood up the mountain (22:6) and was probably almost twenty years old. He will be 37 when his mother dies.

God decided to test Abraham's love for Him. Abraham was told to go and sacrifice Isaac, his only son. Early the next morning (I am sure he couldn't sleep that night) Abraham saddled the donkey, got the wood for the offering and two servants to accompany him. No time was wasted in thinking about this "test." Abraham obeyed immediately. They departed to the place God had told him about.

Three days later they saw the place in the distance, so Isaac and Abraham left the servants behind. Verse 25 gives us insight into this story. Abraham knew that the LORD was going to rescue Isaac because he said, "we" will worship and "we" will come back. Abraham knew that Isaac was the promised child through whom his descendants would come. Therefore, Abraham was going to sacrifice Isaac and God would then raise him from the dead. Some think this lessened the faith involved in this test. Not at all. In fact, it even shows Abraham's faith stronger. First, he never doubted the promise God gave earlier. Second, he still had to kill his only son, which would be no easy task. Third, Abraham had faith that the LORD could and would raise the dead. What a tremendous example of what faith truly is for us today. The New Testament offers further support for this line of thought, "By faith Abraham, when God tested him, offered Isaac as a sacrifice. He who *had received the promises was about to sacrifice* his one and only son, *even though* God had said to him, 'It is *through Isaac* that your offspring will be reckoned.' Abraham *reasoned that God could raise the dead*, and figuratively speaking, he did receive Isaac back from death" (Heb 11:17-19).

Here we begin to see the many parallels of Isaac and Christ. Indeed Isaac was a "type" of Christ, foreshadowing what was to come. We read, "The promises were spoken to Abraham and to his seed. The Scripture does not say 'and to seeds,' meaning many people, but 'and to your seed,' meaning one person, who is Christ" (Gal 3:16). Let us look at the similarities. Father Abraham was about to show his love to God by offering his "one and only son" (Gen 22:2; Heb 11:17) as a sacrifice but, "This is how God *showed His love among us*: He sent *His one and only Son* into the world that we might live through Him" (1 John 4:9). Isaac carried his own wood on his back (Gen 22:6) and Christ, "Carrying His own cross, He went out to the place of the Skull (which in Aramaic is called Golgotha)" (John 19:17). Genesis 22:6 shows Isaac and his father went on together as did God the Father and God the Son. Isaac willingly went up the hill, and Christ says, "The reason My Father loves Me is that *I lay down My life*--only to take it up again" (John 10:17). Isaac was about to be crucified on Mount Moriah. This is where the Dome of the Rock (Muslim building built in A.D. 691) is today and where the old Temple of Solomon was. It is here that many sacrifices were to be made years later in the Temple (2 Chronicles 3:1), all foreshadowing the Sacrifice to come, Christ our Savior who would die not far from here. In Hebrews we read how "figuratively speaking, he did receive Isaac back from death" (Heb 11:19). Once Abraham set out to go to Mount Moriah, his son was "figuratively" dead until God saved him. Note in Genesis 22:4 it took three days to get to the mountain, just as Christ was dead three days and rose again thereafter. This must also foreshadow the resurrection. Both took long journeys away from home. Isaac spoke up to his father (22:7), just as Jesus spoke up to His Father many times in prayer (Luke 4:42; 6:12; Matt 26:36). Isaac was the promised son as was Jesus the promised Messiah. Isaac was bound (v. 9) as was Jesus (Matt 27:2). Isaac was conceived and born miraculously as was Jesus (Luke 1:35). Isaac was given a name by God before birth (Gen 17:19) as was Christ (Matt 1:21).

On the way up the hill, Isaac asked his father where the sacrifice was. Abraham responded with, "God will provide." What a deep truth lies within this statement. Though the LORD did provide a ram in place of Isaac (22:13), the Lamb that WILL BE provided was yet to come. Christ was our Passover Lamb, which is why when John saw Jesus coming he said, "Look, the Lamb of God, who takes away the sin of the world!" (John 1:29). These are just a few examples of the many times Christ is found in the Old Testament. What a beautiful picture of God's love for us that was provided near that very mountain.

Gen 22:15 The angel of the LORD called to Abraham from heaven a second time 22:16 and said, "I swear by Myself, declares the LORD, that because you have done this and have not withheld your son, your only son, 22:17 I will surely bless you and make your descendants as numerous as

the stars in the sky and as the sand on the seashore. Your descendants will take possession of the cities of their enemies, 22:18 and through your offspring all nations on earth will be blessed, because you have obeyed Me." 22:19 Then Abraham returned to his servants, and they set off together for Beersheba. And Abraham stayed in Beersheba. 22:20 Some time later Abraham was told, "Milcah is also a mother; she has borne sons to your brother Nahor: 22:21 Uz the firstborn, Buz his brother, Kemuel (the father of Aram), 22:22 Kesed, Hazo, Pildash, Jidlaph and Bethuel." 22:23 Bethuel became the father of Rebekah. Milcah bore these eight sons to Abraham's brother Nahor. 22:24 His concubine, whose name was Reumah, also had sons: Tebah, Gaham, Tahash and Maacah.

Abraham heard a voice as the Angel of the LORD called a second time from heaven. This Angel is, again, none other than God Himself, as He swore by Himself. God did this because there is none greater to swear by, and thus confirms this covenant soundly. This is so important that we see it again in Hebrews, where it states, "When God made His promise to Abraham, since there was no one greater for Him to swear by, He swore by himself. . . And so after waiting patiently, Abraham received what was promised. Men swear by someone greater than themselves, and the oath confirms what is said and puts an end to all argument. Because God wanted to make the unchanging nature of His purpose very clear to the heirs of what was promised, He confirmed it with an oath. God did this so that, by two unchangeable things in which it is impossible for God to lie, we who have fled to take hold of the hope offered to us may be greatly encouraged" (Heb 6:13-18). God has never gone back on a promise, and this statement leaves us with complete faith that He never will.

This is the last time we see God speaking to Abraham in Scripture, and it leaves us with the previous promises restated once again. Because Abraham obeyed God, his descendants would be like the number of stars or grains of sand by the sea (Gen 13:16; 15:5). (Only through telescopes have we seen how true this statement was, with the stars indeed being as numerous as grains of sand). They would possess the land of their enemies, as also stated numerous times before (Gen 12:7;13:15; 15:7,18; 17:8), and all nations would be blessed through Abraham (Gen 12:3; 18:18). Just as Abraham did not withhold his only son, God did not withhold His only Son, thereby making this a promise of salvation in that, through Abraham's offspring, all would be blessed. That offspring is none other than Christ Himself. As Jesus said, "Anyone who loves his son or daughter more than Me is not worthy of Me" (Matt 10:37).

The word for descendant in verses 17-18 is *zera,* meaning "seed." This is important because this points to Christ as being that seed of Abraham. "The promises were spoken to Abraham and to his seed. The Scripture does not say "and to seeds," meaning many people, but "and to your seed," meaning one person, who is Christ" (Gal 3:16).

Abraham and Isaac returned to their servants just as Abraham had said they would (verse 5), and they go back to Beersheba where they will live from then on.

We now hear some good news about Abraham's brother, Nahor. Abraham had two brothers named in Scripture, Nahor and Haran. Nahor may still have been living in the town of Nahor and, according to the Biblical account, it may have been 60 years since they last saw each other. Abraham's other brother Haran (Lot's father -Gen 11:26-27) died while they were living in Ur. Nahor's wife was Milcah, one of Haran's daughters (Gen 11:29), and he also had a concubine named Reumah. Milcah had eight sons listed, while Reumah had only four. It is through Bethuel, one of Milcah's sons, that Rebekah will come. This entire genealogical account is given primarily to bring us to Rebekah, who will become Isaac's wife and through whom we trace the line of Christ. Since Abraham had Isaac at such an old age, he would have had to find a wife from among Nahor's grandchildren. Hearing of Nahor's children was a blessing for Abraham, because he must have strongly desired to have his son marry someone from his own family, rather than intermarry among the Amorites and Hittites that lived around them.

As for the rest of the names listed, not much is known. As mentioned, they were probably listed simply to give a complete account and to show that God had provided Rebekah as a wife for Isaac.

Gen 23:1 Sarah lived to be a hundred and twenty-seven years old. 23:2 She died at Kiriath Arba (that is, Hebron) in the land of Canaan, and Abraham went to mourn for Sarah and to weep over her. 23:3 Then Abraham rose from beside his dead wife and spoke to the Hittites. He said, 23:4 "I am an alien and a stranger among you. Sell me some property for a burial site here so I can bury my dead."

Sarah died at 127 years old. She was the only woman in all of Scripture whose age of death is given. We saw earlier how she must have been a beautiful woman for Abraham to fear his death over her beauty. Peter, however, shows us that her beauty was not just skin deep: "For this is the way the holy women of the past who put their hope in God used to make themselves beautiful. They were submissive to their own husbands, like Sarah, who obeyed Abraham and called him her master. You are her daughters if you do what is right and do not give way to fear" (1 Pet 3:5-6). Not only do we see the source of her beauty, but we see that just as Abraham is the father of all who believe (Rom 4:11), Sarah is the mother of all who "do what is right." She died in a town called Kiriath Arba, which is the same as Hebron. It was the city of Arba, settled by Arba, the greatest man among the Anakites (Joshua 14:15; 15:13). Also, Isaac was 37 years old when Sarah died and, not knowing for sure how old he was when Abraham was going to sacrifice him, we do not know how long this was from the time chapter 22 ended.

An interesting word in verse two is "went." Abraham "went" to mourn for Sarah. This may imply that the two of them were away from each other at this point and that Sarah died suddenly. We had previously left Abraham at Beersheba, but Sarah died at Hebron. It could be that they moved to Hebron or that Sarah simply died there.

The fact that Abraham bought land in Hebron to bury Sarah is a testimony to their faith in God's promises. Though this is the only land that Scripture says was ever "purchased" by Abraham, he never saw the promise fulfilled when his descendants would live in this land. Yet he did not doubt that this promise would come true and therefore buried his wife where his family and final home would be. Joseph likewise will share this attitude as his bones will be brought from Egypt into the promised land (Gen 50:25).

Gen 23:5 The Hittites replied to Abraham, 23:6 "Sir, listen to us. You are a mighty prince among us. Bury your dead in the choicest of our tombs. None of us will refuse you his tomb for burying your dead." 23:7 Then Abraham rose and bowed down before the people of the land, the Hittites. 23:8 He said to them, "If you are willing to let me bury my dead, then listen to me and intercede with Ephron son of Zohar on my behalf 23:9 so he will sell me the cave of Machpelah, which belongs to him and is at the end of his field. Ask him to sell it to me for the full price as a burial site among you."

When Abraham asked to buy land from the Hittites they offered him any cave he desired, as he apparently was well respected, or at least feared among the people. Abraham in all humbleness and wisdom, however, refused to have any land "given" to him. He purchased it to assure that it would remain his descendants' forever. Abraham decided to buy the cave at Machpelah from Ephron.

The following verses show that this transaction will be successful; however, other Scriptures leave us with some unanswered questions. In Acts, Stephen says that Abraham bought a piece of land in Shechem from the sons of Hamor for a burial plot: "Then Jacob went down to Egypt, where he and our fathers died. Their bodies were brought back to Shechem and placed in the tomb that Abraham had bought from the sons of Hamor at Shechem for a certain sum of money" (Acts 7:15-16). However, we read in Genesis 50:13 that "They carried him [*Jacob*] to the land of Canaan and buried him in the cave in the field of Machpelah, near Mamre, which Abraham had bought as a burial place from Ephron the Hittite, along with the field." How could Jacob be buried in a plot of Hamor at Shechem and a plot at Ephron? It appears that Jacob bought some land at Shechem, which would make sense, since this was where Jacob lived for many years (Gen 34). We also read, "Joseph's bones, which the Israelites had brought up from Egypt, were buried at **Shechem** in the tract of land that **Jacob bought** for a *hundred pieces of silver* from the **sons of Hamor**, the father of Shechem" (Josh 24:32). Also, "For a *hundred pieces of silver*, he [Jacob] bought from the *sons of Hamor*, the father of Shechem, the plot of ground where he pitched his tent" (Gen 33:19). It appears that Jacob was not buried (Gen 50:13) in the land he bought (Gen 33:19; Josh 24:32), but in the land Abraham bought (Acts 7:15). Henry Morris explains, "Abraham lived another 38 years after Sarah died (Genesis 17:17; 23:1; 25:7). During that period he met and married Keturah and had six more sons. It seems plausible that he might have purchased a second parcel of ground for use by his second family, in the region near Shechem, where he had built his first altar in Canaan (Genesis 12:6,7). When Abraham died, however, he was buried with Sarah in Mamre. Keturah and her sons may not have retained possession of the Shechem property. . .Then about 85 years after Abraham's death, when Jacob came to the Shechem area, knowing that this tract had once belonged to his grandfather, he purchased it back again. As Abraham built an altar there, so Jacob did the same" (Record, p.389). Scripture does not say this; however, it does seem possible, and one would think that Stephen's statement would have been corrected by the Pharisees, who knew these Scriptures well, if his statement was untrue. This explanation still does not answer the question of how Jacob could be buried in Shechem (Acts 7) and in the cave of Machpelah (Gen 50:13)? The answer to this may be in Acts 7 where Stephen says, "Then Jacob went down to Egypt, where he and our fathers died. Their bodies were brought back to Shechem." It says that Jacob went to Egypt where he AND the fathers died. "Their" bodies does not have to include Jacob but some of the other fathers.

Gen 23:10 Ephron the Hittite was sitting among his people and he replied to Abraham in the hearing of all the Hittites who had come to the gate of his city. 23:11 "No, my lord," he said. "Listen to me; I give you the field, and I give you the cave that is in it. I give it to you in the presence of my people. Bury your dead." 23:12 Again Abraham bowed down before the people of the land 23:13 and he said to Ephron in their hearing, "Listen to me, if you will. I will pay the price of the field. Accept it from me so I can bury my dead there." 23:14 Ephron answered Abraham, 23:15 "Listen to me, my lord; the land is worth four hundred shekels of silver, but what is that between me and you? Bury your dead." 23:16 Abraham agreed to Ephron's terms and weighed out for him the price he had named in the hearing of the Hittites: four hundred shekels of silver, according to the weight current among the merchants. 23:17 So Ephron's field in Machpelah near Mamre--both the field and the cave in it, and all the trees within the borders of the field--was deeded 23:18 to Abraham as his property in the presence of all the Hittites who had come to the gate of the city. 23:19 Afterward Abraham buried his wife Sarah in the cave in the field of Machpelah near Mamre (which is at Hebron) in the land of Canaan. 23:20 So the field and the cave in it were deeded to Abraham by the Hittites as a burial site.

Abraham had only asked for the cave, but now Ephron offered his field along with the cave. Some have suggested that without the cave, the field may have been useless. The Hittite laws show any ownership of land brought additional financial responsibilities (similar to taxes). Therefore, Ephron may have wanted to get rid of the field if the cave was gone.

Though the land was offered freely to Abraham, he would only accept it if he could pay for it. It may have only been offered in politeness, anyway. Ephron said the land was worth 400 shekels, which according to the Babylonian records was a high price for land. Nevertheless, Abraham did not argue (as may have been expected), but simply pays the amount stated.

For 38 years this cave would be the burial place for Abraham; even later, for Isaac and Rebekah. This fact declares that the future of this nation was to be in the land of Canaan.

Gen 24:1 Abraham was now old and well advanced in years, and the LORD had blessed him in every way. 24:2 He said to the chief servant in his household, the one in charge of all that he had, "Put your hand under my thigh. 24:3 I want you to swear by the LORD, the God of heaven and the God of earth, that you will not get a wife for my son from the daughters of the Canaanites, among whom I am living, 24:4 but will go to my country and my own relatives and get a wife for my son Isaac." 24:5 The servant asked him, "What if the woman is unwilling to come back with me to this land? Shall I then take your son back to the country you came from?" 24:6 "Make sure that you do not take my son back there," Abraham said. 24:7 "The LORD, the God of heaven, who brought me out of my father's household and my native land and who spoke to me and promised me on oath, saying, 'To your offspring I will give this land'--He will send His angel before you so that you can get a wife for my son from there. 24:8 If the woman is unwilling to come back with you, then you will be released from this oath of mine. Only do not take my son back there." 24:9 So the servant put his hand under the thigh of his master Abraham and swore an oath to him concerning this matter.

Verse one tells us that Abraham was getting old. Looking at 25:20 we see that Isaac was about 40 years old now, and thus Abraham was about 140.

Not long ago in 22:20, Abraham learned that his brother Nahor was still living and well. He even had a granddaughter named Rebekah about the same age as Isaac. Abraham did not know that Rebekah would soon be Isaac's wife, but he did know that he still had family 500 miles away in Mesopotamia. Therefore, he called his servant to make a promise. As was the custom of this day, a promise was sealed by putting your hand under the thigh while swearing to do this or that, much like saying "cross my heart hope to die." The word "thigh" is *yarek* and can mean the male genital organ. The ancient Jewish writers understood this as placing the hand under the genital organ and making an oath. In doing so, it was much like making a covenant like that of circumcision.

In any case, the servant swore to Abraham that he would go find Isaac a wife from Abraham's own clan. Abraham knew the importance of his promised son having a pure wife. This was also partly due to Isaac typifying Christ, as discussed in 22:1-15. If Isaac was a type of Christ, then his wife had to represent the church of Christ who is promised to one husband, Christ, so that we might be presented as a pure virgin to Him (2 Cor 11:2). This will take place at the great wedding banquet of the Lamb in Revelation 19:7-9.

Further, if Isaac was Christ and Rebekah the church, then the servant must have been the Holy Spirit who calls all to Christ. Just as Rebekah was given to Isaac, we too "died to the law through the body of Christ, that you might belong to another, to Him who was raised from the dead, in order that we might bear fruit to God" (Rom 7:4). We will examine other examples as they appear.

The servant asked Abraham if the woman did not want to come back, should Isaac be sent? Abraham made it very clear that Isaac was not to leave Canaan. In fact, during Isaac's whole life, he never left the promised land. Abraham said that since this land was promised to his descendants, he wanted Isaac to stay in Canaan. Just as Isaac remained in the promised land, Christ also lives in our promised land, heaven. Abraham had full faith that his servant would be successful, because he knew that an angel was going ahead, but to relieve the servant he said that if the woman was unwilling to come back, he would be released from this oath. Understanding the servant to represent the Holy Spirit, this also shows that when people reject God's call, it is not God's fault, nor is the Holy Spirit held responsible. If we reject God, we are held responsible and we will be judged for it.

Gen 24:10 Then the servant took ten of his master's camels and left, taking with him all kinds of good things from his master. He set out for Aram Naharaim and made his way to the town of Nahor. 24:11 He had the camels kneel down near the well outside the town; it was toward evening, the time the women go out to draw water. Then he prayed, "O LORD, God of my master Abraham, give me success today, and show kindness to my master Abraham. 24:13 See, I am standing beside this spring, and the daughters of the townspeople are coming out to draw water. 24:14 May it be that when I say to a girl, 'Please let down your jar that I may have a drink,' and she says, 'Drink, and I'll water your camels too'--let her be the one you have chosen for your servant Isaac. By this I will know that You have shown kindness to my master." 24:15 Before he had finished praying, Rebekah came out with her jar on her shoulder. She was the daughter of Bethuel son of Milcah, who was the wife of Abraham's brother Nahor. 24:16 The girl was very beautiful, a virgin; no man had ever lain with her. She went down to the spring, filled her jar and came up again.

Taking ten camels and other gifts, the servant set out for the town of Nahor (probably named after Abraham's brother Nahor). Upon arrival, the servant prayed to God for success. He asked that the woman who was to be Isaac's wife would come and give him a drink of water upon request. However, she was also to go the "extra mile" and offer on her own to water his ten camels. This was not going to be any easy task; to water ten camels could take almost an hour. Not only was the servant's prayer specific, so that he could be sure God was bringing this woman to him, it also showed a personality trait that was desirable for Isaac. Any woman willing to water his camels without being asked would have been a loving, kind, patient and sincere woman.

The servant did not even finish his prayer when he saw Rebekah coming to the well. She is described as a beautiful virgin, just like the church of God (2 Cor 11:2; Rev 14:4).

Gen 24:17 The servant hurried to meet her and said, "Please give me a little water from your jar." 24:18 "Drink, my lord," she said, and quickly lowered the jar to her hands and gave him a drink. 24:19 After she had given him a drink, she said, "I'll draw water for your camels too, until they have finished drinking." 24:20 So she quickly emptied her jar into the trough, ran back to the well to draw more water, and drew enough for all his camels. 24:21 Without saying a word, the man watched her closely to learn whether or not the LORD had made his journey successful. 24:22 When the camels had finished drinking, the man took out a gold nose ring weighing a beka and two gold bracelets weighing ten shekels. 24:23 Then he asked, "Whose daughter are you? Please tell me, is there room in your father's house for us to spend the night?" 24:24 She answered him, "I am the daughter of Bethuel, the son that Milcah bore to Nahor." 24:25 And she added, "We have plenty of straw and fodder, as well as room for you to spend the night." 24:26 Then the man bowed down and worshipped the LORD, 24:27 saying, "Praise be to the LORD, the God of my master Abraham, Who has not abandoned His kindness and faithfulness to my master. As for me, the LORD has led me on the journey to the house of my master's relatives."

When Rebekah came to the well, the servant asked for a drink and she gave it to him. Just as he had requested in prayer, she also voluntarily offered to water his camels. Note that she did not simply offer to give them some water, but all that they wanted. When Rebekah did a job, she did it well.

Meanwhile, the servant watched her carefully, noting her care and genuine love. After she had finished, he paid Rebekah for her services with a gold nose ring and two gold bracelets; showing a rich man's wealth (the KJV says an earring, but this is an inaccurate translation). He then asked whose daughter she was, only to find out that she was Nahor's (Abraham's brother) granddaughter. Again, Rebekah went the extra mile and invited the servant to their home to eat and sleep. Upon seeing this, the servant knew for certain that the LORD had made his journey successful, and without delay he stopped to pray and give thanks.

Gen 24:28 The girl ran and told her mother's household about these things. 24:29 Now Rebekah had a brother named Laban, and he hurried out to the man at the spring. 24:30 As soon as he had seen the nose ring, and the bracelets on his sister's arms, and had heard Rebekah tell what the man said to her, he went out to the man and found him standing by the camels near the spring. 24:31 "Come, you who are blessed by the LORD," he said. "Why are you standing out here? I have prepared the house and a place for the camels." 24:32 So the man went to the house, and the camels were unloaded. Straw and fodder were brought for the camels, and water for him and his men to wash their feet. 24:33 Then food was set before him, but he said, "I will not eat until I have told you what I have to say." "Then tell us," Laban said. 24:34 So he said, "I am Abraham's servant. 24:35 The LORD has blessed my master abundantly, and he has become wealthy. He has given him sheep and cattle, silver and gold, menservants and maidservants, and camels and donkeys. 24:36 My master's wife Sarah has borne him a son in her old age, and he has given him everything he owns. 24:37 And my master made me swear an oath, and said, 'You must not get a wife for my son from the daughters of the Canaanites, in whose land I live, 24:38 but go to my father's family and to my own clan, and get a wife for my son.' 24:39 Then I asked my master, 'What if the woman will not come back with me?' 24:40 He replied, 'The LORD, before whom I have walked, will send his angel with you and make your journey a success, so that you can get a wife for my son from my own clan and from my father's family. 24:41 Then, when you go to my clan, you will be released from my oath even if they refuse to give her to you--you will be released from my oath.' 24:42 "When I came to the spring today, I said, 'O LORD, God of my master Abraham, if you will, please grant success to the journey on which I have come. 24:43 See, I am standing beside this spring; if a maiden comes out to draw water and I say to her, "Please let me drink a little water from your jar," 24:44 and if she says to me, "Drink, and I'll draw water for your camels too," let her be the one the LORD has chosen for my master's son.' 24:45 "Before I finished praying in my heart, Rebekah came out, with her jar on her shoulder. She went down to the spring and drew water, and I said to her, 'Please give me a drink.' 24:46 "She quickly lowered her jar from her shoulder and said, 'Drink, and I'll water your camels too.' So I drank, and she watered the camels also. 24:47 "I asked her, 'Whose daughter are you?' "She said, 'The daughter of Bethuel son of Nahor, whom Milcah bore to him.' "Then I put the ring in her nose and the bracelets on her arms, 24:48 and I bowed down and worshipped the LORD. I praised the LORD, the God of my master Abraham, who had led me on the right road to get the granddaughter of my master's brother for his son. 24:49 Now if you will show kindness and faithfulness to my master, tell me; and if not, tell me, so I may know which way to turn."

Rebekah ran ahead to her mother's house. It is interesting that it is called her "mother's" rather than "father's." This may indicate that her father Bethuel was not well and, therefore, Laban and her mother were running things. This would also explain why Laban speaks up in verse 33-34. In any case, we are here introduced to Laban, another important person in God's long plan of salvation. It is Laban's daughters who will later marry Jacob, Isaac and Rebekah's son. During Jacob's courtship of Laban's future daughters we see that Laban was a selfish and somewhat deceitful man. We also see a possible indication of this here, as well. Only after seeing the gold jewelry did Laban run out to see the man at the spring. Laban then invited the servant back to the house.

Once at the house, the servant did not delay (view the servant as the Spirit here). He had a purpose and that was to call a bride for Isaac (who is a type of Christ). He refused to eat before saying why he came. Laban jumped in and told the servant to speak. The servant then gave a detailed account of who he and his master were. After this, he gave a detailed (and repetitive) account of his oath to Abraham and his prayer to God to identify Isaac's wife. He closed looking for an answer, as if to say, "Choose for yourselves this day whom you will serve" (Josh 24:15). Just as we must answer our call by the Spirit, Rebekah had to answer the call of the servant.

Gen 24:50 Laban and Bethuel answered, "This is from the LORD; we can say nothing to you one way or the other. 24:51 Here is Rebekah; take her and go, and let her become the wife of your master's son, as the LORD has directed." 24:52 When Abraham's servant heard what they said, he bowed down to the ground before the LORD. 24:53 Then the servant brought out gold and silver jewelry and articles of clothing and gave them to Rebekah; he also gave costly gifts to her brother and to her mother. 24:54 Then he and the men who were with him ate and drank and spent the night there. When they got up the next morning, he said, "Send me on my way to my master." Gen 24:55 But her brother and her mother replied, "Let the girl remain with us ten days or so; then you may go." 24:56 But he said to them, "Do not detain me, now that the LORD has granted success to my journey. Send me on my way so I may go to my master." 24:57 Then they said, "Let's call the girl and ask her about it." 24:58 So they called Rebekah and asked her, "Will you go with this man?" "I will go," she said. 24:59 So they sent their sister Rebekah on her way, along with her nurse and Abraham's servant and his men. 24:60 And they blessed Rebekah and said to her, "Our sister, may you increase to thousands upon thousands; may your offspring possess the gates of their enemies." 24:61 Then Rebekah and her maids got ready and mounted their camels and went back with the man. So the servant took Rebekah and left.

Again we see Laban taking an apparently equal role with Bethuel, indicating Bethuel may have been very old and ill. They both admitted that this was from the LORD (how could they not after the servant's testimony?) and gave Rebekah to be married to Isaac, as the LORD directed.

Without delay, the servant bowed before God in prayers of thanks. We would do well to learn from this example of thanksgiving. After the most important prayer, the gifts were brought in. Laban and his mother received gifts but the father was left out, once more suggesting a possible illness on his part. Rebekah, too received jewelry and new clothing. These gifts may also symbolize the precious gifts that will be given to all believers: "Fine linen, bright and clean, was given her to wear. (Fine linen stands for the righteous acts of the saints)" (Rev 19:8).

The next morning they awoke and without delay, asked to depart. Laban and his mother (not father) asked to have Rebekah remain ten days before leaving, but the servant requested no further delay. To settle the matter, Rebekah was asked whether or not she would go. This reminds us of the man who asked to follow Jesus but wanted to take care of his family first (Luke 9:56ff). Jesus said, "If anyone would come after Me, he must deny himself and take up his cross and follow Me" (Mat 16:24).

Rebekah agreed to follow without delay, leaving family behind. She was given a nurse, and they left to go see Isaac.

Gen 24:62 Now Isaac had come from Beer Lahai Roi, for he was living in the Negev. 24:63 He went out to the field one evening to meditate, and as he looked up, he saw camels approaching. 24:64 Rebekah also looked up and saw Isaac. She got down from her camel 24:65 and asked the servant, "Who is that man in the field coming to meet us?" "He is my master," the servant answered. So she took her veil and covered herself. 24:66 Then the servant told Isaac all he had done. 24:67 Isaac brought her into the tent of his mother Sarah, and he married Rebekah. So she became his wife, and he loved her; and Isaac was comforted after his mother's death.

Isaac was going out in the field to pray, as he often must have done, when he looked up to see his father's caravan returning. He immediately went out to meet his bride to be. Rebekah also saw Isaac and got off her camel to meet Isaac. Again we see a wonderful parallel to what it will be like when we are given to Christ. We will "be caught up together with them in the clouds to meet the Lord in the air. And so we will be with the Lord forever" (1 Thess 4:17).

The covering of the face was simply a custom in those days when meeting your betrothed husband.

Gen 25:1 Abraham took another wife, whose name was Keturah. 25:2 She bore him Zimran, Jokshan, Medan, Midian, Ishbak and Shuah. 25:3 Jokshan was the father of Sheba and Dedan; the descendants of Dedan were the Asshurites, the Letushites and the Leummites. 25:4 The sons of Midian were Ephah, Epher, Hanoch, Abida and Eldaah. All these were descendants of Keturah.

After Sarah died and Isaac got married, Abraham took another wife named Keturah. As you recall, it was a miracle for both Abraham and Sarah to have Isaac to begin with, and now Abraham had six other children. Abraham was 140 years old when Isaac married Rebekah and lived 35 years beyond that. Therefore, these children must have been born to Abraham after 140 years of age.

Regarding these sons of Abraham, little is known about Zimran, Medan, Ishbak and Shuah. Jokshan, however, was said to father Sheba and Dedan, who are frequently talked about in Scripture. Which Sheba and Dedan are referred in these later passages is difficult to surmise, because Genesis 10:7 told of a Sheba and Dedan as the grandsons of Cush. Also, Genesis 10:28 told of a Sheba being the grandson of Eber.

Midian, on the other hand, is quite well known because of his descendants, the Midianites. The Midianites were against the Israelites and were often associated with the Amalekites (Judges 6:3), the Moabites (Numbers 25:1; 6-15) and the Ishmaelites (Genesis 37:25-36).

Gen 25:5 Abraham left everything he owned to Isaac. **25:6** But while he was still living, he gave gifts to the sons of his concubines and sent them away from his son Isaac to the land of the east. **25:7** Altogether, Abraham lived a hundred and seventy-five years. **25:8** Then Abraham breathed his last and died at a good old age, an old man and full of years; and he was gathered to his people. **25:9** His sons Isaac and Ishmael buried him in the cave of Machpelah near Mamre, in the field of Ephron son of Zohar the Hittite, **25:10** the field Abraham had bought from the Hittites. There Abraham was buried with his wife Sarah. **25:11** After Abraham's death, God blessed his son Isaac, who then lived near Beer Lahai Roi. **25:12** This is the account of Abraham's son Ishmael, whom Sarah's maidservant, Hagar the Egyptian, bore to Abraham. **25:13** These are the names of the sons of Ishmael, listed in the order of their birth: Nebaioth the firstborn of Ishmael, Kedar, Adbeel, Mibsam, **25:14** Mishma, Dumah, Massa, **25:15** Hadad, Tema, Jetur, Naphish and Kedemah. **25:16** These were the sons of Ishmael, and these are the names of the twelve tribal rulers according to their settlements and camps. **25:17** Altogether, Ishmael lived a hundred and thirty-seven years. He breathed his last and died, and he was gathered to his people. **25:18** His descendants settled in the area from Havilah to Shur, near the border of Egypt, as you go toward Asshur. And they lived in hostility toward all their brothers.

When Abraham was alive he made sure his sons (other than Isaac) were taken care of and sent them east to Arabia. He essentially gave them their freedom, because normally the sons of concubines were slaves. This also made it clear that Isaac was the only bearer of the covenant promise. When Abraham died at 175, however, everything he owned went to Isaac. The law at this time stated that *at least* a double share of the father's belongings went to the firstborn son (Deut 21:15-17). This is also why Esau was so upset when he lost the blessing in 27:34.

Abraham was buried with Sarah in the cave at Machpelah that he purchased from Ephron in 23:16. It also says that Abraham was "gathered to his people." These people can be none other than those who walked in the faith as did Abraham, because as far as Scripture is concerned, Abraham is the one chosen as our example, but by no means was he the only one. After this, God began to pour out his blessings on Isaac, the only line to Christ.

Next we follow the line of Ishmael, who would have been 90 years old when his father Abraham died. Little is known about most of Ishmael's sons, though they seem to have settled in Arabia. Kedar and Nebaioth were linked together in Isaiah 60:7. The name Kedar was also used to describe the entire Arab nation at times (Isa 21:17; Jer 49:28; Ezek 27:21). Nebaioth may have started the Nabateans, who lived near the Edomites. Dumah was mentioned in Isa 21:11 with Seir, also the home of the Edomites. Tema may possibly have been linked to a town called Teyma in Arabia. Twelve nations came from Ishmael, just as God had said to Abraham (Genesis 17:20).

Ishmael lived 137 years and then died and was also "gathered to his people." This suggests that, though his descendants would not walk in the faith, he himself did.

Gen 25:19 This is the account of Abraham's son Isaac. Abraham became the father of Isaac, 25:20 and Isaac was forty years old when he married Rebekah daughter of Bethuel the Aramean from Paddan Aram and sister of Laban the Aramean. 25:21 Isaac prayed to the LORD on behalf of his wife, because she was barren. The LORD answered his prayer, and his wife Rebekah became pregnant. 25:22 The babies jostled each other within her, and she said, "Why is this happening to me?" So she went to inquire of the LORD. 25:23 The LORD said to her, "Two nations are in your womb, and two peoples from within you will be separated; one people will be stronger than the other, and the older will serve the younger." 25:24 When the time came for her to give birth, there were twin boys in her womb. 25:25 The first to come out was red, and his whole body was like a hairy garment; so they named him Esau. 25:26 After this, his brother came out, with his hand grasping Esau's heel; so he was named Jacob. Isaac was sixty years old when Rebekah gave birth to them.

The account (or possibly "written record") of Isaac is very insightful for ages. It took Isaac 40 years to marry and another 20 to have children (Gen 25:20,26). Just as God tested Abraham in his many years of childlessness, Isaac also went many years without this blessing. Isaac did take the matter to God in prayer, which was answered. Once she was pregnant, the babies began fighting within Rebekah, so much so that the nurses could not explain it. Rebekah inquired of the LORD, who explained that she was having twins who were already at each others throats. Sinful nature comes long before one can "think" about his sins: "Surely I was sinful at birth, sinful from the time my mother conceived me" (Ps 51:5). Though Jacob and Esau were already quarreling in the womb, we see later that other babies in Scripture were joyful in the womb: "As soon as the sound of your greeting reached my ears, the baby in my womb leaped for joy" (Luke 1:44).

In Rebekah's case, however, the younger child would rule over the older. Although this was contrary to the custom of the day, it was right in line with what God many times directed (Isaac, Seth, Judah, David and Jacob were all in the Messianic line, but none of them were the oldest son). Years later Paul writes about this event, "Not only that, but Rebekah's children had one and the same father, our father Isaac. Yet, before the twins were born or had done anything good or bad--*in order that God's purpose in election might stand:* not by works but by Him who calls--she was told, 'The older will serve the younger.' . . . What then shall we say? Is God unjust? Not at all!" (Rom 9:10-14).

The fact that this battle went on even in the womb showed God's plan already at work prior to birth. Abortionists should think this over carefully, since life does begin at conception. David wrote, "I praise You because I am fearfully and wonderfully made; Your works are wonderful, I know that full well. My frame was not hidden from You when I was made in the secret place. When I was woven together in the depths of the earth, Your eyes saw my unformed body. All the days ordained for me were written in Your book *before one of them came to be*" (Psa 139:14-16). If only the pro-choice people would realize, "As you do not know the path of the wind, or how the body is formed in a mother's womb, so you cannot understand the work of God, the Maker of all things" (Ecc 11:5).

Finally, at 60 years of age, Isaac became a father. Esau was born with red hair on his entire body, while Jacob was smooth. Already there was quite a contrast between these two boys. Jacob came out grasping Esau's heel, and thus his name means "heal grabber." Although this is often used to explain Jacob's deceptiveness, Hosea used it to describe his strength: "In the womb he grasped his brother's heel; as a man he struggled with God. He struggled with the angel and overcame Him" (Hosea 12:3-4). In any case, it was symbolic of Jacob's struggle with Esau, not only in the early years of their lives, but also throughout history. Esau's descendants, the Edomites (Gen 36:9), would also be against the nation of Israel. In fact, during the Exodus the Israelites were not even allowed to cross through the land of Edom (Num 20:18). As a result, God judged them and they later became subjects of David (2 Sam 8:14; see also, Isa 34:5-6, 11; Jer 49:17-20; Joel 3:19; Amos 1:9-12; Mal 1:4). One good example of this judgment was predicted in Obadiah, which reads, "The house of Esau will be stubble, and they will set it on fire and consume it. There will be no survivors from the house of Esau. The LORD has spoken" (Obadiah 1:18). This was fulfilled through a long turn of events. In 435 B.C. an Arab tribe called the Nabateans captured Petra and drove the Edomites out to the barren Negev. The Edomites were then called the Idumeans (Greek for Edomites- see Mark 3:8). The Idumeans harassed Judah until the Jewish leader, Judas Maccabaeus, defeated them in 185 B.C. by killing over 20,000 of them. Fifty years later another of the ruling Macabees, John Hyrcanus, forced Judaism upon them and made them accept Jewish laws, including circumcision. For a time this worked in their favor, because the Romans who conquered Palestine in 64 B.C. allowed some Idumeans to rise to power. People like Antipater, who was procurator of Judea: His son, Herod the Great, who was king of Judea when he killed the children at Bethlehem; Herod Antipas, who was the one who beheaded John the Baptist and was ruler of Galilee; and, Herod Agrippa I, who was also an Idumean and king of Palestine when James was killed and when Peter was imprisoned. This time of prosperity for the Idumeans was short lived, however, because they later joined a revolt against Rome in 70 A.D. The few who survived this battle were absorbed into other tribes. Thus, as God said, "There will be no survivors."

Gen 25:27 The boys grew up, and Esau became a skillful hunter, a man of the open country, while Jacob was a quiet man, staying among the tents. 25:28 Isaac, who had a taste for wild game, loved Esau, but Rebekah loved Jacob. 25:29 Once when Jacob was cooking some stew, Esau came in from the open country, famished. 25:30 He said to Jacob, "Quick, let me have some of that red stew! I'm famished!" (That is why he was also called

Edom.) 25:31 Jacob replied, "First sell me your birthright." 25:32 "Look, I am about to die," Esau said. "What good is the birthright to me?" 25:33 But Jacob said, "Swear to me first." So he swore an oath to him, selling his birthright to Jacob. 25:34 Then Jacob gave Esau some bread and some lentil stew. He ate and drank, and then got up and left. So Esau despised his birthright.

It has been said that twins have the same personality, but in Jacob and Esau's case, they were nothing alike. Perhaps because Jacob stayed home more, he was loved by Rebekah while Esau, possessing the skills to satisfy Isaac's wild game appetite, was loved more by his father. The exact reasons for these preferences cannot be known; however, the differences between these two boys were not just physical. It is said that Jacob was a "quiet" man. A lot can be said of stillness of the mouth: "The quiet words of the wise are more to be heeded than the shouts of a ruler of fools" (Eccl 9:17). Even so, the word "quiet" is a rather disappointing translation. The Hebrew word used is *tam* and means "gentle," "perfect," or "upright." The exact same word is used of Job: "In the land of Uz there lived a man whose name was Job. This man was *blameless and upright*; he feared God and shunned evil" (Job 1:1; see also Ps 37:37; Prov 29:10; Song 6:9). Thus Jacob seems to have been more mature and Godly than Esau. I would like to think this is why he was loved by Rebekah.

Esau on the other hand was a hunter. The only other hunter mentioned in Scripture was evil Nimrod (Gen 10:9). Esau must have been after the physical cares of the world, as he could only be described as a sportsman. They had no real need of wild game for food because the LORD had already blessed them abundantly and, therefore, Esau hunted more for sport. He must have found great pride in this and thus was a selfish man of the world. We see in Hebrews, "See that no one is sexually immoral, or is godless like Esau" (Heb 12:16). Scripture states that Isaac loved Esau because he had a taste for wild game. This is hardly a reason to love someone. The fact that Rebekah later prepared a meal at home without Isaac knowing the difference shows how carnal and pointless it was to base love on the skill of hunting. Even the patriarchs experienced moments of weakness.

One day Esau came in from an unsuccessful hunt famished while Jacob was cooking stew. The smell aroused Esau, who showed no self control, giving in to the carnal desires of the world. Once more we see how physical pleasures get in the way of our Godly focus. Jacob wouldn't give away any stew until Esau sold his birthright. According to God's promise (25:23), it really wasn't Esau's to begin with, but because of Isaac's carnality at this point, Esau had it. Normally the oldest son received twice what the younger would get (Deut 21:17), and he then became head of the house (Gen 27:29). Jacob longed for the spiritual aspect of this blessing, but Esau cared only for the material blessings that came along with it. This also was evident in Esau's statement that he was about to die and that the birthright would then have no purpose for him. Esau's focus was on the here and now, not realizing that the benefits of a spiritual blessing would go far beyond this lifetime.

It was Esau who was wrong here, as he was the one who despised his birthright and the spiritual things of life. Despite his lack of interest in his birthright now, he later wept because of his loss (material, not spiritual). Again we see in Hebrews, "Afterward, as you know, when he wanted to inherit this blessing, he was rejected. He could bring about no change of mind, though he sought the blessing with tears" (Heb 12:17).

The red stew is also significant because Esau himself had red hair. Because he ate this red stew he became known as Edom (means red). Every time he saw red stew he would have been reminded of the loss of his birthright.

Gen 26:1 Now there was a famine in the land--besides the earlier famine of Abraham's time--and Isaac went to Abimelech king of the Philistines in Gerar. 26:2 The LORD appeared to Isaac and said, "Do not go down to Egypt; live in the land where I tell you to live. 26:3 Stay in this land for a while, and I will be with you and will bless you. For to you and your descendants I will give all these lands and will confirm the oath I swore to your father Abraham. 26:4 I will make your descendants as numerous as the stars in the sky and will give them all these lands, and through your offspring all nations on earth will be blessed, 26:5 because Abraham obeyed me and kept my requirements, my commands, my decrees and my laws."

Earlier (Gen 12:10) there was a famine during Abraham's day. Now Isaac was experiencing a remarkably similar experience in more than one way. Isaac must have been around 80 years old at this time, just as Abraham was near this age during the famine of his time (Gen 12:4).

Isaac decided to go to Gerar near the coast, where there may have been more food, though still not a lot, because it appears he was planning to move further to Egypt, just as his father did. However, God spoke to Isaac (first time according to Scripture) telling him not to go to Egypt but to remain where he was. Just as Abraham was going through a time of testing and purifying of the faith, so Isaac now would be put through the same test. To give comfort and increase faith, the LORD assured Isaac that He would bless him and never leave him. Also, the covenant God gave to Abraham is reaffirmed to Isaac and is now seen for the ninth time in Scripture.

As mentioned earlier, Isaac never left the promised land his whole life, further typifing Christ. This is perhaps why God told him to remain where he was.

Abraham, living before the ten commandments were given, leaves us with a question in verse five. What were God's "laws" at this time? The "commands, decrees and laws" of God that were followed by Abraham were simply the commands God gave Abraham throughout his life (such as sacrificing Isaac and moving here and there). In addition, it was the law written in his heart, as it is in all of our hearts today. We read in Romans about the gentiles who did not have the law themselves: "Since they show that the requirements of the law are written on their hearts, their consciences also bearing witness, and their thoughts now accusing, now even defending them (Rom 2:15).

126

Gen 26:6 So Isaac stayed in Gerar. **26:7** When the men of that place asked him about his wife, he said, "She is my sister," because he was afraid to say, "She is my wife." He thought, "The men of this place might kill me on account of Rebekah, because she is beautiful." **26:8** When Isaac had been there a long time, Abimelech king of the Philistines looked down from a window and saw Isaac caressing his wife Rebekah. **26:9** So Abimelech summoned Isaac and said, "She is really your wife! Why did you say, 'She is my sister'?" Isaac answered him, "Because I thought I might lose my life on account of her." **26:10** Then Abimelech said, "What is this you have done to us? One of the men might well have slept with your wife, and you would have brought guilt upon us." **26:11** So Abimelech gave orders to all the people: "Anyone who molests this man or his wife shall surely be put to death." **26:12** Isaac planted crops in that land and the same year reaped a hundredfold, because the LORD blessed him. **26:13** The man became rich, and his wealth continued to grow until he became very wealthy. **26:14** He had so many flocks and herds and servants that the Philistines envied him. **26:15** So all the wells that his father's servants had dug in the time of his father Abraham, the Philistines stopped up, filling them with earth. **26:16** Then Abimelech said to Isaac, "Move away from us; you have become too powerful for us."

Isaac obeyed God and remained in Gerar. Just as Abraham had done, Isaac told Abimelech that his wife was his sister because he was afraid he would be killed because of her beauty. Again, Abimelech was a title for a king, just as Pharaoh was in Egypt and, therefore, this was not the same Abimelech whom Abraham encountered. God had great timing in reaffirming the Covenant with Isaac a few verses earlier, because it should have strengthened Isaac by showing him that God would protect him and he would have more descendants. This promise did not remain fresh on Isaac's mind, however, as he feared for his life.

Isaac, like Abraham, called his wife his sister (Genesis 12:10 and 20:1-18). It seems that even though Isaac called Rebekah his sister, she was not taken by any other man because, when caught in this lie, Abimelech said one of his men *could have* slept with her. One day, Abimelech looked down and saw Isaac and Rebekah intimately together. He confronted Isaac and rebuked him, just as Abraham had been. Rather than showering him with gifts and sending him on his way, Abimelech made a decree that Isaac and Rebekah were to be left alone. Why Abimelech did this is not known for sure; perhaps because of the treaty the Philistines made with Abraham earlier (Gen 21:22-24) or out of respect for Abraham himself.

Isaac remained there and God blessed him profusely, just as He had promised. As a result, the rest of the Philistines grew envious and began to vandalize his father's wells. Later, Abimelech asked Isaac to leave, since the Philistines were beginning to fear Isaac because of all the blessings God had given him.

Gen 26:17 So Isaac moved away from there and encamped in the Valley of Gerar and settled there. **26:18** Isaac reopened the wells that had been dug in the time of his father Abraham, which the Philistines had stopped up after Abraham died, and he gave them the same names his father had given them. **26:19** Isaac's servants dug in the valley and discovered a well of fresh water there. **26:20** But the herdsmen of Gerar quarreled with Isaac's herdsmen and said, "The water is ours!" So he named the well Esek, because they disputed with him. **26:21** Then they dug another well, but they quarreled over that one also; so he named it Sitnah. **26:22** He moved on from there and dug another well, and no one quarreled over it. He named it Rehoboth, saying, "Now the LORD has given us room and we will flourish in the land." **26:23** From there he went up to Beersheba. **26:24** That night the LORD appeared to him and said, "I am the God of your father Abraham. Do not be afraid, for I am with you; I will bless you and will increase the number of your descendants for the sake of my servant Abraham." **26:25** Isaac built an altar there and called on the name of the LORD. There he pitched his tent, and there his servants dug a well.

Isaac moved further east in the valley of Gerar and reopened the wells his father Abraham had dug. The Philistines had plugged many wells of Abraham as a result of envy (v 15), and others perhaps to keep people from settling in their land. In any case, Isaac renamed them with the same names Abraham had used, perhaps further clarifying his right to them as Abraham's son. After all, Abimelech had given his father the right to own all these wells (Genesis 20:15) and, thus, they were Isaac's inheritance.

Isaac also dug an additional well in the valley of Gerar, but the herdsmen living in the valley argued over it, perhaps out of continued envy or dislike of Isaac. As a result, Isaac gave the well the appropriate name of "Esek," meaning dispute. Rather than argue, Isaac moved on and dug a second well, which also brought quarreling, so he named it "Sitnah," meaning opposition or hatred. For these herdsmen to follow Isaac, seemingly just to torment him, suggests hatred was their motivation for these arguments.

Finally, Isaac moved further on and dug a well where there was no more fighting, so he called it "Rehoboth," meaning room. The LORD had shown him a place where there was room for Isaac to settle.

Isaac then returned to Beersheba, where he had lived as a younger man after his "near death experience" on Mount Moriah (Genesis 22:19). This was the same place Abraham had built an altar to the LORD years earlier (21:30-34). It was here that Abraham had made a covenant with the Philistines regarding the ownership of the wells he had dug and, thus, named the well "Beersheba," meaning "well of the seven" or "well of oath."

The LORD appeared to Isaac that night, and he was reminded of the Covenant promise (tenth time it is seen Gen 26:3-4; 22:17-18; 18:18; 17:1-2; 17:15; 16:10; 15:18; 13:15-17; 12:1-3).

Isaac either built a new altar or rebuilt the one Abraham had earlier built and called on the LORD. This was perhaps done in thanksgiving, because

Isaac not only received the rights to well water but was reassured of his future blessings.

Gen 26:26 Meanwhile, Abimelech had come to him from Gerar, with Ahuzzath his personal adviser and Phicol the commander of his forces. 26:27 Isaac asked them, "Why have you come to me, since you were hostile to me and sent me away?" 26:28 They answered, "We saw clearly that the LORD was with you; so we said, 'There ought to be a sworn agreement between us'--between us and you. Let us make a treaty with you 26:29 that you will do us no harm, just as we did not molest you but always treated you well and sent you away in peace. And now you are blessed by the LORD." 26:30 Isaac then made a feast for them, and they ate and drank. 26:31 Early the next morning the men swore an oath to each other. Then Isaac sent them on their way, and they left him in peace. 26:32 That day Isaac's servants came and told him about the well they had dug. They said, "We've found water!" 26:33 He called it Shibah, and to this day the name of the town has been Beersheba. 26:34 When Esau was forty years old, he married Judith daughter of Beeri the Hittite, and also Basemath daughter of Elon the Hittite. 26:35 They were a source of grief to Isaac and Rebekah.

Abimelech and Phicol came to Isaac, seeing that he continued to flourish despite their constant efforts to chase him away. Abimelech wisely asked for a treaty with Isaac, knowing he could not win a battle against the LORD. Just as another Abimelech (not a common name, but a title) had made an agreement with Abraham about 100 years earlier, now Isaac agreed to this treaty. Abimelech used a bit of worldly wisdom in bringing up the fact that they did not harm Isaac, even after he had lied about his wife. The ironic thing is that even if Abimelech had tried he would have lost, because the LORD was with Isaac and his offspring

Phicol also appears to be a title, as the Abimelech of Abraham's day also came with a "Phicol" (Gen 21:22).

Isaac prepared a feast for these men, as was often done, especially before treaties were made. After the treaty was made, they left in peace. Upon Abimelech's departure, Isaac's servants brought the good news of a well that was dug and contained good water. This was rather appropriate as, it seemed to confirm God's covenant with Isaac, and the well was named "Shibah," meaning oath or seven, similar to Beersheba.

This chapter closes on a sad note when we see that Esau not only married a Hittite woman (a foreigner) but he also practiced polygamy. Both of these ungodly decisions brought grief to Isaac and Rebekah, especially since he was old enough (40) to know better.

Gen 27:1 When Isaac was old and his eyes were so weak that he could no longer see, he called for Esau his older son and said to him, "My son." "Here I am," he answered. 27:2 Isaac said, "I am now an old man and don't know the day of my death. 27:3 Now then, get your weapons-- your quiver and bow--and go out to the open country to hunt some wild

game for me. 27:4 **Prepare me the kind of tasty food I like and bring it to me to eat, so that I may give you my blessing before I die." 27:5 Now Rebekah was listening as Isaac spoke to his son Esau. When Esau left for the open country to hunt game and bring it back, 27:6 Rebekah said to her son Jacob, "Look, I overheard your father say to your brother Esau, 27:7 'Bring me some game and prepare me some tasty food to eat, so that I may give you my blessing in the presence of the LORD before I die.' 27:8 Now, my son, listen carefully and do what I tell you: 27:9 Go out to the flock and bring me two choice young goats, so I can prepare some tasty food for your father, just the way he likes it. 27:10 Then take it to your father to eat, so that he may give you his blessing before he dies."**

When Isaac was "old" his sight was failing and he was near death. It was time to give his son the blessing. Isaac must have been around 135 years old. Jacob and Esau were born when Isaac was 60 (Gen 25:26). Jacob and Esau married at the age of 40, making Isaac at least 100 years old at the wedding (Gen 26:34). At this time, Jacob may have been about 75 years old, making Isaac 135. Jacob was 130 when Joseph was 39 (Gen 47:9; 41:46; 41:53; 45:11), and Joseph was born 18 years after Jacob left his parents (Gen 31:38: 30:25). In any case, all four members of the family were old enough and mature enough to do the Godly thing. However, all four did wrong: Esau despised his birthright, Jacob deceived his father and Esau, Rebekah deceived her husband (for right reasons, though), and Isaac tried to give a blessing to Esau, even though God had told him to do otherwise (Gen 25:23).

Rebekah heard Isaac tell Esau to go out hunting and prepare a meal so that he could receive the blessing. Thus began a rather suspenseful and deceptive plot involving the entire family. Rebekah must have known that her plan would eventually become known, as Esau would soon return; therefore, she must have felt strongly about Isaac receiving the blessing. Some believe this was because Isaac was her favorite; however, this was not the case. Rebekah knew that the Lord had called Jacob to be blessed, and thus what seems deceptive, was actually a show of faith. Similar incidents in which God blessed a lie can be found in Exodus 1:15-20, where the Hebrew midwives lied about the Hebrew women having babies quickly. This was done out of fear and respect for God and His commands. Also, Rahab lied about the spies in Joshua 2:3-6; 6:25. As a result of this obedience and faith, the writer of Hebrews states, "By faith the prostitute Rahab, because she welcomed the spies, was not killed with those who were disobedient" (Heb 11:31). James records, "In the same way, was not even Rahab the prostitute considered righteous for what she did when she gave lodging to the spies and sent them off in a different direction?" (James 2:25). Likewise, Rebekah was doing a righteous act in trying to have Isaac receive the blessing.

Gen 27:11 Jacob said to Rebekah his mother, "But my brother Esau is a hairy man, and I'm a man with smooth skin. 27:12 What if my father touches me? I would appear to be tricking him and would bring down a curse on myself rather than a blessing." 27:13 His mother said to

him, "My son, let the curse fall on me. Just do what I say; go and get them for me." 27:14 So he went and got them and brought them to his mother, and she prepared some tasty food, just the way his father liked it. 27:15 Then Rebekah took the best clothes of Esau her older son, which she had in the house, and put them on her younger son Jacob. 27:16 She also covered his hands and the smooth part of his neck with the goatskins. 27:17 Then she handed to her son Jacob the tasty food and the bread she had made. 27:18 He went to his father and said, "My father." "Yes, my son," he answered. "Who is it?" 27:19 Jacob said to his father, "I am Esau your firstborn. I have done as you told me. Please sit up and eat some of my game so that you may give me your blessing." 27:20 Isaac asked his son, "How did you find it so quickly, my son?" "The LORD your God gave me success," he replied. 27:21 Then Isaac said to Jacob, "Come near so I can touch you, my son, to know whether you really are my son Esau or not." 27:22 Jacob went close to his father Isaac, who touched him and said, "The voice is the voice of Jacob, but the hands are the hands of Esau." 27:23 He did not recognize him, for his hands were hairy like those of his brother Esau; so he blessed him. 27:24 "Are you really my son Esau?" he asked. "I am," he replied. 27:25 Then he said, "My son, bring me some of your game to eat, so that I may give you my blessing." Jacob brought it to him and he ate; and he brought some wine and he drank.

One can almost feel the tension that must have been felt by Rebekah and Isaac. Knowing Esau could return at any time, Rebekah had to rush to prepare a meal and get everything ready. While Jacob visited with his father, he must have had one eye keeping a look out for his brother's return.

Jacob was concerned about this deception, or at least about getting caught. He did not want to be cursed rather than blessed. His mother offered to take full responsibility, and thus relieved Jacob's conscience. Paul wrote, "Consequently, he who rebels against the authority is rebelling against what God has instituted, and those who do so will bring judgment on themselves" (Rom 13:2). Isaac was Jacob's authority; however, Isaac was going against his authority: God. Therefore, Jacob was following Rebekah, who was obeying the true authority of God.

Isaac loved the taste of wild game, mainly because his favorite son Esau was skilled at hunting, and thus his pride made the meat taste even better. Since Rebekah could make a goat taste just like the wild game, it was not simply the wild flavor he enjoyed.

After the meal was prepared, Esau's clothes were put on, and the rough skin was applied to the hands- Jacob was ready to go to his father. The meal was prepared rather quickly, as Isaac was surprised that Esau returned so soon. (so he thinks). Jacob explained that the LORD had brought success in the hunt. This was true, as it was the LORD who was keeping Esau from returning too soon, and it was He who kept Isaac from recognizing Jacob. We often like to take credit for certain situations in our lives, but be assured the Lord is deeply involved. In any case, Rebekah and Jacob had done everything they could to keep Isaac from knowing what was going on. Isaac's sight was too far gone to see Jacob, so he relied on his other senses. He felt the animal skin and was satisfied, but Jacob's voice left Isaac suspicious. Isaac then asked for the meal that his son Esau had, and that too was ready. As Isaac ate, Jacob must have become increasingly nervous, since his brother could return at any moment.

Gen 27:26 Then his father Isaac said to him, "Come here, my son, and kiss me." 27:27 So he went to him and kissed him. When Isaac caught the smell of his clothes, he blessed him and said, "Ah, the smell of my son is like the smell of a field that the LORD has blessed. 27:28 May God give you of heaven's dew and of earth's richness-- an abundance of grain and new wine. 27:29 May nations serve you and peoples bow down to you. Be lord over your brothers, and may the sons of your mother bow down to you. May those who curse you be cursed and those who bless you be blessed." 27:30 After Isaac finished blessing him and Jacob had scarcely left his father's presence, his brother Esau came in from hunting. 27:31 He too prepared some tasty food and brought it to his father. Then he said to him, "My father, sit up and eat some of my game, so that you may give me your blessing." 27:32 His father Isaac asked him, "Who are you?" "I am your son," he answered, "your firstborn, Esau." 27:33 Isaac trembled violently and said, "Who was it, then, that hunted game and brought it to me? I ate it just before you came and I blessed him--and indeed he will be blessed!"

After the meal was over, Isaac called Esau (really Jacob) over so that he could kiss him. The smell of Esau's clothes relieved any doubt he may have had, and he gave the blessing.

The blessing contained mostly material prosperity, and nothing of a messianic blessing was mentioned, unless one includes "those who curse you will be cursed and those who bless you will be blessed." This was very similar to the blessing of Abraham in Genesis 12:3, which reads, "I will bless those who bless you, and whoever curses you I will curse; and all peoples on earth will be blessed through you." Since Jacob was in the line of Christ, anyone who cursed him would indeed be cursed.

Isaac should certainly have known better than to say he would be "lord over your brothers" (v.29). Isaac thought he was talking to Esau, yet the LORD said, "the older will serve the younger" (Gen 25:23).

Immediately after Jacob left, Esau returned. As mentioned, this timing was no coincidence, rather God was involved. Esau prepared a meal and brought it to his father. Upon the deceptive plot being exposed, Isaac "trembled violently." The Hebrew word is *charad* and is a very graphic word to describe great anxiety or fear. This word is extremely important, because it appears that at this moment Isaac received the full force of the law. He was filled with remorse and shame as he began to realize the deceptiveness he was practicing in trying to give a blessing to Esau that was not his to receive. Isaac had put his entire home in jeopardy by disobeying God's command and following his own desires. From here on, Isaac's attitude changed, and that is why nothing was done to change this blessing. Even if something could have been done, no further steps would have been taken, for Hebrews states, "By faith Isaac blessed

Jacob and Esau in regard to their future" (Heb 11:20). Isaac simply told Esau, "indeed he [Jacob] will be blessed."

Gen 27:34 When Esau heard his father's words, he burst out with a loud and bitter cry and said to his father, "Bless me--me too, my father!" 27:35 But he said, "Your brother came deceitfully and took your blessing." 27:36 Esau said, "Isn't he rightly named Jacob ? He has deceived me these two times: He took my birthright, and now he's taken my blessing!" Then he asked, "Haven't you reserved any blessing for me?" 27:37 Isaac answered Esau, "I have made him lord over you and have made all his relatives his servants, and I have sustained him with grain and new wine. So what can I possibly do for you, my son?" 27:38 Esau said to his father, "Do you have only one blessing, my father? Bless me too, my father!" Then Esau wept aloud. 27:39 His father Isaac answered him, "Your dwelling will be away from the earth's richness, away from the dew of heaven above. 27:40 You will live by the sword and you will serve your brother. But when you grow restless, you will throw his yoke from off your neck." 27:41 Esau held a grudge against Jacob because of the blessing his father had given him. He said to himself, "The days of mourning for my father are near; then I will kill my brother Jacob." 27:42 When Rebekah was told what her older son Esau had said, she sent for her younger son Jacob and said to him, "Your brother Esau is consoling himself with the thought of killing you. 27:43 Now then, my son, do what I say: Flee at once to my brother Laban in Haran. 27:44 Stay with him for a while until your brother's fury subsides. 27:45 When your brother is no longer angry with you and forgets what you did to him, I'll send word for you to come back from there. Why should I lose both of you in one day?" 27:46 Then Rebekah said to Isaac, "I'm disgusted with living because of these Hittite women. If Jacob takes a wife from among the women of this land, from Hittite women like these, my life will not be worth living."

Esau began to weep and beg for a blessing; however, none would be given. Isaac responded by explaining that Jacob had deceived him, knowing it was rightly so. Esau, on the other hand, did not see this trickery as righteousness, rather as deception. Later Esau blamed Jacob for deceiving him twice, yet he failed to remember that he gave up his own birthright because he despised it (Gen 25:34). Even Hebrews states, "See that no one is sexually immoral, or is godless like Esau, who for a single meal sold his inheritance rights as the oldest son. Afterward, as you know, when he wanted to inherit this blessing he was rejected. He could bring about no change of mind, though he sought the blessing with tears" (Heb 12:16-17). It was Esau's godlessness that God foresaw, and that was why he did not receive the blessing. This was also why God said, "Jacob I loved, but Esau I hated" (Rom 9:13).

It must have pained Isaac greatly to pronounce what appeared to be a curse to his favorite son, Esau. Esau would live away from the earth's riches. This was true, as he later lived south of the Dead Sea, a barren and rocky land. He was to "live by the sword" and "serve his brother." This was fulfilled during

133

the reign of Saul in 1 Samuel 14:47, where Saul fought against and punished the Edomites. In 2 Samuel 8:14 we see that all the Edomites became "subject to David." Esau's descendants would also "grow restless" and "throw off the yolk from their neck." At times Edom did rebel, but they never got out from under their yolk completely. We read, "So Jehoram went to Zair with all his chariots. The Edomites surrounded him and his chariot commanders, but he rose up and broke through by night; his army, however, fled back home. To this day Edom has been in rebellion against Judah" (2 Ki 8:21-22; see also 2 Ki 21:8-10). (See note on Genesis 25:26 for further historical information on Edom's demise).

Esau was angry and decided he was going to kill Jacob when his father died, which apparently would come soon. Rebekah heard of this plan and sent Jacob to her brother's house in Haran. Jacob was instructed to stay there for "a while." This turned out to be 20 years, and as far as Scripture tells us, this was the last time Rebekah saw her son. She was going to send word to him, but never did, probably because she died before she was able to.

Rebekah closes the chapter by stating her disgust with the Hittite women, perhaps because she saw what moral corruption Esau's Hittite wife (Gen 26:34) had brought, hence the words, "like these" in verse 46. This is the last we hear of Rebekah other than her burial in the cave of Machpelah with Abraham, Sarah and Isaac (Gen 49:30-31).

Gen 28:1 So Isaac called for Jacob and blessed him and commanded him: "Do not marry a Canaanite woman. 28:2 Go at once to Paddan Aram, to the house of your mother's father Bethuel. Take a wife for yourself there, from among the daughters of Laban, your mother's brother. 28:3 May God Almighty bless you and make you fruitful and increase your numbers until you become a community of peoples. 28:4 May he give you and your descendants the blessing given to Abraham, so that you may take possession of the land where you now live as an alien, the land God gave to Abraham." 28:5 Then Isaac sent Jacob on his way, and he went to Paddan Aram, to Laban son of Bethuel the Aramean, the brother of Rebekah, who was the mother of Jacob and Esau. 28:6 Now Esau learned that Isaac had blessed Jacob and had sent him to Paddan Aram to take a wife from there, and that when he blessed him he commanded him, "Do not marry a Canaanite woman," 28:7 and that Jacob had obeyed his father and mother and had gone to Paddan Aram. 28:8 Esau then realized how displeasing the Canaanite women were to his father Isaac; 28:9 so he went to Ishmael and married Mahalath, the sister of Nebaioth and daughter of Ishmael son of Abraham, in addition to the wives he already had.

Isaac, having realized his fault, held no grudge against Jacob. He blessed Jacob and warned him not to take a wife from among the Canaanites. This command was very similar to what Abraham told Isaac's servant in 24:3. Intermarriage was the downfall of many, because these heathen wives brought their idols and evil ways with them, thereby corrupting the Israelite religion. Many warnings were later given about marrying foreigners. We read, "Do not intermarry with them. Do not give your daughters to their sons or take their daughters for your sons" (Deu 7:3); "if you intermarry with them and associate with them, then you may be sure that the LORD your God will no longer drive out these nations before you" (Josh 23:12-13); and "You must not intermarry with them, because they will surely turn your hearts after their gods" (1 Kings 11:2; see also Ezra 9:14). Though the wisest man that ever lived, Solomon himself fell into this trap and lost faith (1 Kings 11:4-14).

Isaac was sent to Paddan Aram to find a wife. As far as the record goes, he never saw his mother again, and it was twenty years before he saw Esau (Gen 31:38-41). Though he left as the "heal grabber" (Jacob), he later returned as "he struggles with God" (Israel).

Esau heard Isaac give Jacob yet another blessing, reaffirming the fact that the blessing would never be his. Esau must have felt empty and hurt because, for the first time, he became aware that he had let his father down. In a rather poor attempt to make amends and please his father, he found another wife from his Uncle Ishmael's family. Mahalath was probably the same as Basemath in 36:3. Though not a Hittite, she was still not under the covenant given to Abraham, so she could just as well have been a foreigner.

Gen 28:10 Jacob left Beersheba and set out for Haran. 28:11 When he reached a certain place, he stopped for the night because the sun had set. Taking one of the stones there, he put it under his head and lay down to sleep. 28:12 He had a dream in which he saw a stairway resting on the earth, with its top reaching to heaven, and the angels of God were ascending and descending on it. 28:13 There above it stood the LORD, and he said: "I am the LORD, the God of your father Abraham and the God of Isaac. I will give you and your descendants the land on which you are lying. 28:14 Your descendants will be like the dust of the earth, and you will spread out to the west and to the east, to the north and to the south. All peoples on earth will be blessed through you and your offspring. 28:15 I am with you and will watch over you wherever you go, and I will bring you back to this land. I will not leave you until I have done what I have promised you."

After leaving Beersheba, Jacob set out toward Laban's house in Haran, nearly 500 miles away. After traveling a few days, he stopped at Bethel (28:19) to spend the night. (Since Bethel is about 75 miles north of Beersheba, it must have taken him a few days to reach it.) While asleep he had a dream with a stairway leading from heaven down to earth. The LORD stood above it while angels went up and down on it. The Hebrew word for "stairway" is *sullam* and is only used this one time in all of Scripture; therefore, a simple ladder or stairway probably is not accurate. Nonetheless, the meaning of what Jacob saw is what is important. The New Testament gives us further insight into what "Jacob's ladder" really was. In John we hear Jesus state, "I tell you the truth, you shall see heaven open, and the angels of God ascending and descending on the Son of Man" (John 1:51). This ladder represented Christ, the only way to heaven: "For there is one God and one Mediator between God and men, the man Christ Jesus" (1 Tim 2:5). We also read, "Jesus answered, 'I am the way and the truth and the life. No one comes to the Father except through Me'" (John 14:6). Ephesians states, "When He ascended on high, He led captives in His train and gave gifts to men. (What does 'He ascended' mean except that He also descended to the lower, earthly regions ? He who descended is the very One who ascended higher than all the heavens, in order to fill the whole universe)" (Eph 4:8-10). Apart from Christ, we have no other access to God or heaven.

Other interesting side notes regarding this dream involve the angels. We see in Luke 16:22 that angels will carry us up to heaven. When the Lord returns He will be "revealed from heaven in blazing fire with His powerful angels" (2 Thess 1:7). Other involvement concerning angels can be seen in 2 Kings 6:17; 2 Chronicles 18:18; Job 1:6; 2:1; Daniel 9:21-23; 10:10-13; Mark 1:13; Luke 22:43; 1 Cor 4:9; Ephesians 3:10; 1 Peter 1:12; Psalm 34:7; 91:11; Luke 15:10; Hebrews 1:14; 12:22; Acts 12:11 and 27:23.

Bethel is where Abraham had earlier built an altar (12:8; 13:3). The name Bethel appears many times in Scripture, second only to Jerusalem. Jacob will later return here in 35:1, where he will build another altar. No doubt, Bethel held a special meaning for the patriarchs, as it was a reminder of God's care and Covenants. Also, according to the record, this was the first time God had in any way spoken to Jacob and, therefore, this alone would make Bethel very memorable for Jacob.

Gen 28:16 When Jacob awoke from his sleep, he thought, "Surely the LORD is in this place, and I was not aware of it." 28:17 He was afraid and said, "How awesome is this place! This is none other than the house of God; this is the gate of heaven." 28:18 Early the next morning Jacob took the stone he had placed under his head and set it up as a pillar and poured oil on top of it. 28:19 He called that place Bethel, though the city used to be called Luz. 28:20 Then Jacob made a vow, saying, "If God will be with me and will watch over me on this journey I am taking and will give me food to eat and clothes to wear 28:21 so that I return safely to my father's house, then the LORD will be my God 28:22 and this stone that I have set up as a pillar will be God's house, and of all that you give me I will give you a tenth."

Jacob's excitement and awe is felt in verse 16 and 17. Jacob took the stone he slept on and used it to build an altar. He then poured oil on top of the rock. The act of pouring oil on the rock served as a means of consecration (Ex 30:25-29).

Jacob named the place Bethel, meaning "house of God." Even the name showed what high respect this place would hold. It is unfortunate that the later descendants of Jacob did not give Bethel the same respect. About 1,000 years after this, idols were set up in Bethel and heathen sacrifices were made here by the Israelites (1 Kings 12:28-33). As a result, Josiah ended up destroying this place (2 Kings 23:15-17), and righteously so.

An interesting vow was made by Jacob when he gave a conditional dedication of himself. The text reads "if" God watches over him "then" the LORD would be his God. There are indications that suggest Jacob had not fully recognized the LORD as his God, rather the God only of his father. When Jacob brought his father the meal to get the blessing, Isaac asked how he was back so soon, upon which Jacob replied, "The LORD, *your* God gave me success" (27:20). Likewise, in 28:13 God introduced Himself as "the God of your father Abraham." Therefore, some say that this was the first time Jacob made a personal commitment to God, even though God had already been committed to him. Jacob later returned in chapter 35.

Another possibility which seem more plausible regarding this conditional dedication comes from the Hebrew. In the original language, verse 20 could be read, "Since God will be with me, then shall Jehovah be my God." This also seems to fit the attitude of the tithe much better, as well. Jacob wasn't testing God here and saying "if the LORD gives me stuff, I will then give Him a tenth;" rather, "because the LORD will provide for me I will give Him a tenth." We read in Deuteronomy, "Do not test the LORD your God as you did at Massah" (Deu 6:16).

The tithe that Jacob gave was probably in sacrifices, since there didn't seem to be anyone to give anything to, outside of God. Even though it was not a requirement to give a tithe until the Mosaic Law came into effect (Lev 27:30; Num 18:21-24), Jacob gave his tenth anyway. Why? Because it was his love for God that motivated his giving. Today, there is no law which states we must give a tenth of our blessings in order to receive salvation, but it is our love for Christ that motivates us to share with others. Paul writes, "Each man should give what he has decided in his heart to give, not reluctantly or under compulsion, for God loves a cheerful giver" (2 Cor 9:7; see Rom 12:8, 1 Cor 16:2).

Gen 29:1 Then Jacob continued on his journey and came to the land of the eastern peoples. 29:2 There he saw a well in the field, with three flocks of sheep lying near it because the flocks were watered from that well. The stone over the mouth of the well was large. 29:3 When all the flocks were gathered there, the shepherds would roll the stone away from the well's mouth and water the sheep. Then they would return the stone to its place over the mouth of the well. 29:4 Jacob asked the shepherds, "My brothers, where are you from?" "We're from Haran," they replied. 29:5 He said to them, "Do you know Laban, Nahor's grandson?" "Yes, we know him," they answered. 29:6 Then Jacob asked them, "Is he well?" "Yes, he is," they said, "and here comes his daughter Rachel with the sheep." 29:7 "Look," he said, "the sun is still high; it is not time for the flocks to be gathered. Water the sheep and take them back to pasture." 29:8 "We can't," they replied, "until all the flocks are gathered and the stone has been rolled away from the mouth of the well. Then we will water the sheep." 29:9 While he was still talking with them, Rachel came with her father's sheep, for she was a shepherdess. 29:10 When Jacob saw Rachel daughter of Laban, his mother's brother, and Laban's sheep, he went over and rolled the stone away from the mouth of the well and watered his uncle's sheep. 29:11 Then Jacob kissed Rachel and began to weep aloud. 29:12 He had told Rachel that he was a relative of her father and a son of Rebekah. So she ran and told her father.

Jacob finally reached Haran after a journey of which nothing more was said. Upon arriving he saw three flocks of sheep next to a well waiting to be watered. God obviously led him to this well, just as God had earlier led the servant to the well of Rebekah to find Isaac a wife. Many other similarities between Jacob's journey and that of the servant can be noted in this chapter.

Apparently, all the sheep were brought together to water at about the same time, perhaps because it normally took more than one person to remove the stone which covered the water.

Jacob asked about Laban, Nahor's grandson, and received an exciting answer. Laban's daughter was a shepherdess and she was on her way to the well. Jacob apparently wanted some privacy in this introduction, because he urged the other shepherds to water their flocks and leave. However, the other shepherds announced that it was not time for the sheep to be watered.

Almost immediately Rachel arrived and Jacob ran over to remove the stone from the well. This showed Jacob's strength, as the stone was very large (v. 2). No doubt Jacob was somewhat excited, not only at the prospect of meeting his Uncle, but also at the sight of Rachel's beauty. Right after the flocks had been watered, Jacob went over and kissed Rachel in greeting, as was common among relatives. Rachel also must have been excited to meet Jacob. Rachel was very aware of who Jacob was, as Laban must have often shared with his family knowledge of his close family and distant ancestors, much like we do today.

Rachel ran to tell Laban about Jacob's arrival, while Jacob stayed behind, perhaps to watch the flock while she was gone.

Gen 29:13 As soon as Laban heard the news about Jacob, his sister's son, he hurried to meet him. He embraced him and kissed him and brought him to his home, and there Jacob told him all these things. 29:14 Then Laban said to him, "You are my own flesh and blood." After Jacob had stayed with him for a whole month, 29:15 Laban said to him, "Just because you are a relative of mine, should you work for me for nothing? Tell me what your wages should be." 29:16 Now Laban had two daughters; the name of the older was Leah, and the name of the younger was Rachel. 29:17 Leah had weak eyes, but Rachel was lovely in form, and beautiful. 29:18 Jacob was in love with Rachel and said, "I'll work for you seven years in return for your younger daughter Rachel." 29:19 Laban said, "It's better that I give her to you than to some other man. Stay here with me." 29:20 So Jacob served seven years to get Rachel, but they seemed like only a few days to him because of his love for her. 29:21 Then Jacob said to Laban, "Give me my wife. My time is completed, and I want to lie with her." 29:22 So Laban brought together all the people of the place and gave a feast. 29:23 But when evening came, he took his daughter Leah and gave her to Jacob, and Jacob lay with her. 29:24 And Laban gave his servant girl Zilpah to his daughter as her maidservant.

Laban soon came out to meet Jacob and greeted him with a kiss. Jacob was brought to Laban's house, where they caught up with all the news of each other's family.

Jacob began helping Laban, and after a month Laban took notice and offered to pay Jacob whatever Jacob stated as wages. (Laban probably expected Jacob to ask for little, which is why he left it up to him.) It is at this point that we are introduced to Leah, Laban's other daughter. Leah's name meant cow and Rachel's, ewe. Both were appropriate names given by a shepherd. Leah had "weak eyes," which probably meant simple, and having nothing attractive about them. However, Rachel not only had beautiful eyes, but a shapely body as well. Thus, Jacob fell in love and used this opportunity to request Rachel in return for seven years of work. This would then pay the bride price given to the father.

Jacob began serving his seven years immediately and they went by fast, as he was in love with Rachel. In view of Jacob's excitement, I am sure it was seven years later to the day when he went to Laban and requested what was now rightfully his. However, Laban deceived the heal grabber himself and gave him Leah without Jacob knowing it. This was perhaps due to the darkness or the veil Leah was wearing (see 24:65). One can only imagine what must have been going through the minds of Rachel and Leah. Whether Rachel was simply obeying her father, or if she was locked up for a while, we do not know. Nor do we have any indication of what type of relationship Rachel and Leah had at this point. One must assume that even Leah was somewhat hurt, knowing that Jacob could only be thinking of Rachel.

In verse 22 we see that Laban prepared a great feast for the day of the wedding. After this wedding feast was given, another celebration lasting seven days would have taken place after the wedding.

As was the custom, especially in wealthier families, a daughter was given a servant to help out. Zilpah is given to Leah, while Rachel received Bilhah (v. 28). Both servant's later became Jacob's wives, and he had children with them as a result of jealousy between Rachel and Leah (Gen 46:18; 30:9-12; 35:26).

Gen 29:25 When morning came, there was Leah! So Jacob said to Laban, "What is this you have done to me? I served you for Rachel, didn't I? Why have you deceived me?" 29:26 Laban replied, "It is not our custom here to give the younger daughter in marriage before the older one. 29:27 Finish this daughter's bridal week; then we will give you the younger one also, in return for another seven years of work." 29:28 And Jacob did so. He finished the week with Leah, and then Laban gave him his daughter Rachel to be his wife. 29:29 Laban gave his servant girl Bilhah to his daughter Rachel as her maidservant. 29:30 Jacob lay with Rachel also, and he loved Rachel more than Leah. And he worked for Laban another seven years. 29:31 When the LORD saw that Leah was not loved, he opened her womb, but Rachel was barren. 29:32 Leah became pregnant and gave birth to a son. She named him Reuben, for she said, "It is because the LORD has seen my misery. Surely my husband will love me now." 29:33 She conceived again, and when she gave birth to a son she said, "Because the

LORD heard that I am not loved, he gave me this one too." So she named him Simeon. 29:34 Again she conceived, and when she gave birth to a son she said, "Now at last my husband will become attached to me, because I have borne him three sons." So he was named Levi. 29:35 She conceived again, and when she gave birth to a son she said, "This time I will praise the LORD." So she named him Judah. Then she stopped having children.

One can't help but wonder if this event reminded Jacob of his deception of Isaac and Esau. Perhaps this memory lessened Jacob's anger.

Laban's reply to Jacob was simply that it was the custom to marry the older daughter first. This was because to be unmarried was to be shamed in those days and, therefore, marrying the older daughter first would serve as a safeguard for one's family. Nevertheless, this was no doubt an excuse to get seven more years of service from Jacob, who was a good worker.

It was agreed that Jacob could marry Rachel in return for another seven years of work. However, Jacob need only finish the wedding week to marry Rachel. After this wedding, Jacob then served his additional seven years while being married to both women.

As always in Scripture, polygamy caused added stress in the marriage. Never did God openly rebuke polygamous marriages, but no doubt they were not in God's plan, as we saw in the order of Creation, one woman and one man created to have children and worship God (Mal 2:15). Nevertheless, God blessed the marriage despite their sinfulness, just as He blesses us today, despite our wrongdoings. It is difficult for us to understand how such things could occur, but it seems that the stigma of being barren or not having a family name to extend meant more than the heartache that would be caused by sharing your husband with another woman.

God saw that Jacob did not love Leah as he did Rachel and, therefore, he closed up Rachel's womb and opened Leah's. It is interesting to note that Rachel was barren just as Sarah (11:30) and Rebekah (25:21) were for a time.

Leah gave birth to Reuben, meaning "He has seen my misery." Soon afterward she gave birth to a second son, Simeon, which means "hearing," showing Leah's thanks to God for hearing her prayers. However, Jacob still did not seem to love Leah, as indicated by the words "at last" in verse 34. Therefore, God gave Leah a third son named Levi, meaning "attachment," showing Leah's hope that Jacob would now become more attached to her. All three of these sons received names showing Leah's focus to be on her own misery and desires. Her fourth son, however, was named Judah, meaning "praise." Leah said, "This time I will praise the LORD!" What beautiful words these were, as it showed that Leah was finding comfort in God before her husband. This showed a mature attitude of surrender and dedication to the LORD. It was also significant that it was through Leah (the less loved) and Judah that Christ's line is traced.

Gen 30:1 When Rachel saw that she was not bearing Jacob any children, she became jealous of her sister. So she said to Jacob, "Give me children, or I'll die!" 30:2 Jacob became angry with her and said, "Am I in

the place of God, who has kept you from having children?" 30:3 Then she said, "Here is Bilhah, my maidservant. Sleep with her so that she can bear children for me and that through her I too can build a family." 30:4 So she gave him her servant Bilhah as a wife. Jacob slept with her, 30:5 and she became pregnant and bore him a son. 30:6 Then Rachel said, "God has vindicated me; he has listened to my plea and given me a son." Because of this she named him Dan. 30:7 Rachel's servant Bilhah conceived again and bore Jacob a second son. 30:8 Then Rachel said, "I have had a great struggle with my sister, and I have won." So she named him Naphtali. 30:9 When Leah saw that she had stopped having children, she took her maidservant Zilpah and gave her to Jacob as a wife. 30:10 Leah's servant Zilpah bore Jacob a son. 30:11 Then Leah said, "What good fortune!" So she named him Gad. 30:12 Leah's servant Zilpah bore Jacob a second son. 30:13 Then Leah said, "How happy I am! The women will call me happy." So she named him Asher.

Rachel now became jealous of Leah, as she saw that Leah was providing children for her husband. However, she apparently could not see that Jacob still loved her anyway. As a result of this internal torment, she went to Jacob and demanded that he give her children or she would die. It is rather ironic that it was the giving of a child that would cause her death (35:16-19).

Jacob took offense at the accusation that he was responsible for her lack of children and pointed out that God was the source of these blessings, or lack thereof. Rachel then responded the same way Sarah did when she could not have children (16:2) and gave her servant, Bilhah, to Jacob so that she would no longer be shamed and keep up with her sister Leah. It is sad to see such worldly cares enter into such a blessed gift as children and marriage.

When Bilhah had a baby, it was Rachel's son by law. She named him Dan, meaning "to vindicate," showing God's removal of Rachel's shame. There is no doubt that God was directly intervening in these matters, but I question whether or not it was to vindicate Rachel, especially in the worldly state she appeared to be in. This is further evidenced in verse eight when Bilhah had a second child. Rachel had been viewing these children as pawns in a competition between herself and Leah and, therefore, she named this son Naphtali, meaning "wrestlings."

This continued "wrestling" between Leah and Rachel did not end with Naphtali. Leah was now realizing she was starting to lag behind in this race so she gave Jacob her servant Zilpah again. This time Gad, meaning "good fortune," was born. The name Gad was later associated with a pagan god of luck, but here Leah simply expressed her joy. It wasn't until later the name was corrupted.

Once more Jacob slept with Zilpah and had Asher, meaning "happy." Happy is certainly the word for it, not joy. Joy comes from being content. If only they had confessed, "I have learned to be content whatever the circumstances. I know what it is to be in need, and I know what it is to have plenty. I have learned the secret of being content in any and every situation,

141

whether well fed or hungry, whether living in plenty or in want. I can do everything through him who gives me strength" (Phil 4:11-13).

Gen 30:14 During wheat harvest, Reuben went out into the fields and found some mandrake plants, which he brought to his mother Leah. Rachel said to Leah, "Please give me some of your son's mandrakes." 30:15 But she said to her, "Wasn't it enough that you took away my husband? Will you take my son's mandrakes too?" "Very well," Rachel said, "he can sleep with you tonight in return for your son's mandrakes." 30:16 So when Jacob came in from the fields that evening, Leah went out to meet him. "You must sleep with me," she said. "I have hired you with my son's mandrakes." So he slept with her that night. 30:17 God listened to Leah, and she became pregnant and bore Jacob a fifth son. 30:18 Then Leah said, "God has rewarded me for giving my maidservant to my husband." So she named him Issachar. 30:19 Leah conceived again and bore Jacob a sixth son. 30:20 Then Leah said, "God has presented me with a precious gift. This time my husband will treat me with honor, because I have borne him six sons." So she named him Zebulun. 30:21 Some time later she gave birth to a daughter and named her Dinah.

Not long afterward, Reuben found some mandrakes in the field and brought them to his mother. Mandrakes were a small, orange, berry-like fruit. They were believed to enhance fertility and were used as an aphrodisiac. Some have called it the "love apple" or the "May apple." Reuben must have been around seven or eight years old, because Jacob had eight sons and it appears that about eight years had passed since he was married. In any case, he was old enough to be playing alone in the field and was aware of the rivalry between his mother and Leah, since he brought his mother a fruit known for fertility.

Rachel saw the mandrakes and begged Leah to let her have them. Leah responded harshly and blamed Rachel for taking away her husband, when in fact it was Jacob who chose Rachel. Apparently Jacob had been spending most of his evenings with Rachel (v.15), so perhaps Leah was feeling a little left out in this area. As a result Leah was willing to trade her mandrakes for the right to sleep with her husband that night. When Jacob came in from working, Leah ran out to meet him (obviously excited) and informed him that he had been hired. How sad that her own husband had to be hired in order to spend time with her. Leah must have been in constant prayer regarding the love of her husband (the ultimate goal of all these children for Rachel and Leah) and the LORD heard her and gave her a fifth son, Jacob. Leah responded by naming this child Issachar, meaning "reward." Though Leah believed this reward came as a result of giving her maidservant to Jacob, it is more probable it was simply God's mercy and answer to prayer. Soon after, Leah had a sixth son and named him Zebulun, meaning "honor." Leah reasoned that six sons would cause Jacob to love her more. It is unfortunate that Leah and Rachel didn't try to just be submissive and make themselves beautiful like Sarah did, rather than quarrel over Jacob all the time (1 Peter 3:5-6).

Jacob now had ten sons. There was no mention of daughters up to verse 21. This does not mean Jacob did not have any daughters, but they may not have been mentioned because they did not fit into the theme of Scripture - Christ's line and the tribes of Israel (other daughters are mentioned in 37:35). Dinah, meaning "Judgment," is mentioned here because she will later be raped by the Shechemites, and this will cause Jacob to be disliked in the land. This event played an important part in bringing Joseph to Egypt (Genesis 34).

Gen 30:22 Then God remembered Rachel; He listened to her and opened her womb. 30:23 She became pregnant and gave birth to a son and said, "God has taken away my disgrace." 30:24 She named him Joseph, and said, "May the LORD add to me another son." 30:25 After Rachel gave birth to Joseph, Jacob said to Laban, "Send me on my way so I can go back to my own homeland. 30:26 Give me my wives and children, for whom I have served you, and I will be on my way. You know how much work I've done for you." 30:27 But Laban said to him, "If I have found favor in your eyes, please stay. I have learned by divination that the LORD has blessed me because of you." 30:28 He added, "Name your wages, and I will pay them."

God remembered Rachel as well. He heard her prayers and opened her womb. It must be noted that the mandrakes had nothing to do with it, because that event had taken place a long time ago. She gave birth to Joseph. The name Joseph, meaning "may he add," indicated that Rachel was already asking for more children. God would add one more child, but it would cost Rachel her life (35:16-20). Jacob now had been with Laban for twenty years (31:38). Since the first seven were served as a single man, that left thirteen years to have his eleven sons and one daughter. It is most probable that this happened with more than one wife being pregnant at a time.

After Rachel had Joseph, Jacob went to Laban asking permission to leave and go back home to see his family. His mother was going to send word but he had not heard anything. Laban, however, does not want Jacob to leave, as the Lord had been blessing his flocks because of Jacob. Laban claimed to have learned this from divination. The King James translates divination as "experience." However, the Hebrew clearly tells us that it was by ungodly means. Not only does this explain Laban's materialistic and selfish behavior, but it also gives good reason for Jacob's readiness to leave. Laban asked Jacob how much he would have to pay in order for him to stay.

Gen 30:29 Jacob said to him, "You know how I have worked for you and how your livestock has fared under my care. 30:30 The little you had before I came has increased greatly, and the LORD has blessed you wherever I have been. But now, when may I do something for my own household?" 30:31 "What shall I give you?" he asked. "Don't give me anything," Jacob replied. "But if you will do this one thing for me, I will go on tending your flocks and watching over them: 30:32 Let me go through all your flocks today and remove from them every speckled or spotted

sheep, every dark-colored lamb and every spotted or speckled goat. They will be my wages. 30:33 And my honesty will testify for me in the future, whenever you check on the wages you have paid me. Any goat in my possession that is not speckled or spotted, or any lamb that is not dark-colored, will be considered stolen." 30:34 "Agreed," said Laban. "Let it be as you have said." 30:35 That same day he removed all the male goats that were streaked or spotted, and all the speckled or spotted female goats (all that had white on them) and all the dark-colored lambs, and he placed them in the care of his sons. 30:36 Then he put a three-day journey between himself and Jacob, while Jacob continued to tend the rest of Laban's flocks.

So far Jacob's labor has benefited only Laban and his household. Jacob was now ready to provide for his own household as he should, since he was now over 90 years old. Jacob did not want to be given anything, perhaps for the same reason Abraham accepted nothing from the King of Sodom (14:22-23). Scripture is clear regarding the unacceptable practice of divination (Lev 19:26; Deut 18:10-14). Jacob made a rather unusual request. He wanted to separate every speckled or spotted sheep and goat, and every dark lamb to be his as wages, not as a gift. Jacob put his sons in charge of his flock and then put a three day journey's distance between them and Laban's flock, which Jacob was watching. Any non-speckled or spotted goats or white lambs in Jacob's flock would be considered Laban's.

It is interesting that Jacob chose the most uncommon of the sheep and goats. This showed great faith in the LORD because, by all appearances, Laban was getting the better end of the deal.

Gen 30:37 Jacob, however, took fresh-cut branches from poplar, almond and plane trees and made white stripes on them by peeling the bark and exposing the white inner wood of the branches. 30:38 Then he placed the peeled branches in all the watering troughs, so that they would be directly in front of the flocks when they came to drink. When the flocks were in heat and came to drink, 30:39 they mated in front of the branches. And they bore young that were streaked or speckled or spotted. 30:40 Jacob set apart the young of the flock by themselves, but made the rest face the streaked and dark-colored animals that belonged to Laban. Thus he made separate flocks for himself and did not put them with Laban's animals. 30:41 Whenever the stronger females were in heat, Jacob would place the branches in the troughs in front of the animals so they would mate near the branches, 30:42 but if the animals were weak, he would not place them there. So the weak animals went to Laban and the strong ones to Jacob. 30:43 In this way the man grew exceedingly prosperous and came to own large flocks, and maidservants and menservants, and camels and donkeys.

Once the separation was complete, Jacob began cutting branches from various trees and stripping the bark off them in stripes. When the flocks were in heat and saw these striped sticks, they mated and had striped or spotted young.

144

Whenever the stronger animals were watering he continued this practice, but when the weaker animals came, he removed the sticks so that they would produce weaker offspring for Laban. Throughout time (6 years - 31:41), Laban's flock grew exceedingly weak, while Jacob's flock grew stronger and stronger.

There is no real good evidence to answer why striped sticks would cause striped offspring. Many scientists have tried to explain how, just as we blush upon seeing something, these sheep also had a physical change upon seeing these branches. However, it is very possible that the LORD told Jacob to do this (31:10-13). After all, it was the LORD who was blessing Jacob, it wasn't Jacob's own cunningness that was causing increase. We would often do well to recognize this ourselves for, "Every good and perfect gift is from above, coming down from the Father of the heavenly lights, who does not change like shifting shadows" (James 1:17). Jacob also realized where these gifts came from: "I am unworthy of all the kindness and faithfulness you have shown your servant. I had only my staff when I crossed this Jordan, but now I have become two groups" (Gen 32:10). Also we read in Genesis 31:9: "So God has taken away your father's livestock and has given them to me." Jacob clearly saw that his blessings were not a result of any deception or trick on his part; rather, they were God's doing.

Another interesting note worth mentioning is the fact that the branches used had "white" strips. Esau earlier sold his birthright for red stew. With Esau meaning "red," his name symbolized what he fell to. Likewise, Laban means "white," and Jacob triumphed over Laban by using Laban's own tactics of deception. (Although in this case we cannot say that Jacob was wrongly deceiving, because the LORD was blessing Jacob's faith). We know that there was much more to this story than we see here, as indicated by Laban changing Jacob's wages ten times (31:41). Laban was the deceiver in this situation, while Jacob was following God's word.

Gen 31:1 Jacob heard that Laban's sons were saying, "Jacob has taken everything our father owned and has gained all this wealth from what belonged to our father." 31:2 And Jacob noticed that Laban's attitude toward him was not what it had been. 31:3 Then the LORD said to Jacob, "Go back to the land of your fathers and to your relatives, and I will be with you." 31:4 So Jacob sent word to Rachel and Leah to come out to the fields where his flocks were. 31:5 He said to them, "I see that your father's attitude toward me is not what it was before, but the God of my father has been with me. 31:6 You know that I've worked for your father with all my strength, 31:7 yet your father has cheated me by changing my wages ten times. However, God has not allowed him to harm me. 31:8 If he said, 'The speckled ones will be your wages,' then all the flocks gave birth to speckled young; and if he said, 'The streaked ones will be your wages,' then all the flocks bore streaked young. 31:9 So God has taken away your father's livestock and has given them to me.

Jacob heard Laban's sons complaining about Jacob, and Laban himself was not as cordial to Jacob as he once was. Their anger stemmed from jealousy over Jacob's belongings. The LORD knew Laban's heart and came to Jacob in a dream and told him to go back home. Jacob immediately got ready to go by first explaining things to his wives, Laban's daughters. He reminded them of how Laban had changed his wages ten times in the last six years. Although not mentioned earlier, we now see that Jacob's flocks had been changed from speckled to plain after Laban saw all the sheep and goats coming out speckled or streaked. Jacob did not take credit for these blessings; rather, he realized that these gifts came from God (v. 9).

Though he probably would have preferred to let Rachel and Leah say good-bye to their father, Jacob knew they must leave quietly, or else Laban would not let them leave, at least not with their belongings (31:42). In order to keep their departure quiet, Jacob even had his wives come out to the field to discuss the matter. God had called, and Jacob obeyed.

Gen 31:10 "In breeding season I once had a dream in which I looked up and saw that the male goats mating with the flock were streaked, speckled or spotted. 31:11 The Angel of God said to me in the dream, 'Jacob.' I answered, 'Here I am.' 31:12 And He said, 'Look up and see that all the male goats mating with the flock are streaked, speckled or spotted, for I have seen all that Laban has been doing to you. 31:13 I am the God of Bethel, where you anointed a pillar and where you made a vow to me. Now leave this land at once and go back to your native land.'" 31:14 Then Rachel and Leah replied, "Do we still have any share in the inheritance of our father's estate? 31:15 Does he not regard us as foreigners? Not only has he sold us, but he has used up what was paid for us. 31:16 Surely all the wealth that God took away from our father belongs to us and our children. So do whatever God has told you." 31:17 Then Jacob put his children and his wives on camels, 31:18 and he drove all his livestock ahead of him, along with all the goods he had accumulated in Paddan Aram, to go to his father Isaac in the land of Canaan. 31:19 When Laban had gone to shear his sheep, Rachel stole her father's household gods. 31:20 Moreover, Jacob deceived Laban the Aramean by not telling him he was running away. 31:21 So he fled with all he had, and crossing the River, he headed for the hill country of Gilead.

Jacob continued to tell his wives what God had previously shown him. These verses indicate that what seemed to be Jacob's cunningness in breeding was actually God's instruction. We also see that the reason Jacob was blessed was because God knew the motives and heart of Laban (v. 12). God identified Himself to Jacob as the God who appeared at Bethel where he saw the ladder extending from earth to heaven (28:10).

Rachel and Leah also sensed their father's worldly ways and lack of love. Not only was he treating them as foreigners rather than daughters, he had also spent the money that was paid to him as the bride-price (v. 15). According to Mesopotamian law, the father was to keep some of the bride-price and invest it for his daughter, just in case she would ever need it. It seemed that even his daughters are mostly concerned about their inheritance and, realizing there was none for them, they were more than ready to leave. This speaks volumes of the relationship between Laban and his daughters.

Jacob put his wives on their camels and began to drive their herds on ahead of him. This must have been a very large caravan, from what we see in the next chapter. (When Jacob prepared to meet Esau he would give away 200 female goats, 20 male goats, 200 ewes, 20 rams, 30 female camels, 40 cows, 10 bulls, 20 female donkeys and 10 male donkeys (32:13-16). This was only a small portion of what Jacob possessed; quite a contrast from when he arrived at Paddan Aram with nothing.) If the three day separation was still between Laban and Jacob (30:36), this means that they had a 60 to 90 mile headstart on Laban. Typically, people traveled about 30 miles in a day without restrictions. However, with cattle it was cut down to 15 or 20 miles per day. At that rate it would take them about ten days to reach Mount Gilead, which was east of the Jordan River and just southeast of the Sea of Galilee.

An interesting note on Rachel is given in verse 19. While Jacob went to shear the sheep, Rachel stole her father's household gods. The Hebrew word for these gods is *teraphim,* meaning small figurines used in divination. It must have been these gods that Laban used in 30:27 to see that the LORD was with Jacob. The question is, why did Rachel take pagan idols? There are two possible explanations. It is very possible that the years of growing up and living near such idolatrous ways corrupted her a bit. Though she knew the LORD through Jacob and prayed to Him for children, she may have still believed in their protective power. There were others in Jacob's caravan who possessed other gods, as we see in 35:2 where Jacob commanded everyone to get rid of their gods. It is strange and confusing for Christians today to understand why Jacob took so long to do this. One would think, even while living near Laban, this would not have been allowed. The second explanation may come from the Nuzu tablets found in 1930. They explain that *teraphim* were often associated with property rights, much like deeds are today. Therefore, Rachel may have taken the idols not for worship or protection, but to insure ownership of her husband's flocks in case Laban tried to take them away. In a sense, she was taking the inheritance that she felt was rightly hers (v. 14).

Gen 31:22 On the third day Laban was told that Jacob had fled. 31:23 Taking his relatives with him, he pursued Jacob for seven days and caught up with him in the hill country of Gilead. 31:24 Then God came to Laban the Aramean in a dream at night and said to him, "Be careful not to say anything to Jacob, either good or bad." 31:25 Jacob had pitched his tent in the hill country of Gilead when Laban overtook him, and Laban and his relatives camped there too. 31:26 Then Laban said to Jacob, "What have you done? You've deceived me, and you've carried off my daughters like captives in war. 31:27 Why did you run off secretly and deceive me? Why didn't you tell me, so I could send you away with joy and singing to the music of tambourines and harps? 31:28 You didn't even let me kiss my grandchildren and my daughters good-by. You have done a foolish thing.

31:29 I have the power to harm you; but last night the God of your father said to me, 'Be careful not to say anything to Jacob, either good or bad.' **31:30** Now you have gone off because you longed to return to your father's house. But why did you steal my gods?"

Jacob and his caravan had a three day jump on Laban, not to mention the three day distance that was between them to begin with. Laban's family all pursued Jacob and caught up with him in only seven days. It was about three hundred miles to the hill country of Gilead, so Laban made fast tracks, indicating that his mind was set on revenge. God, knowing the heart of Laban, came to him in a dream to warn him not to harm Jacob; in fact, not to even say a harsh word.

When the two caravans met, Laban immediately confronted Jacob, accusing him of running off with his daughters (which may be true, but with good reason). Laban outright lied and said that had he known they were going to leave he would have sent them off with music and festivities. The very fact that they traveled so far in such short time and that God had to come to him in a dream shows this to be a lie. Perhaps he was trying to fool God and be as sly as possible, considering his dream. As a final touch he mentioned his disappointment in not being able to kiss his grandchildren or daughters good-bye. Obviously this was not what upset him, especially since we saw how he was treating them (31:15).

Verse 29 gets to the heart of the matter. Laban wrongly admitted that he had power to harm Jacob; with God watching out for Jacob, not even Pharaoh's army could have touched a hair on his head. Laban told of his dream, showing why he has restrained himself, but at the same time exposing his true intentions. Laban understood his desire to go see his family, but he asked why they took his household gods.

Gen 31:31 Jacob answered Laban, "I was afraid, because I thought you would take your daughters away from me by force. 31:32 But if you find anyone who has your gods, he shall not live. In the presence of our relatives, see for yourself whether there is anything of yours here with me; and if so, take it." Now Jacob did not know that Rachel had stolen the gods. 31:33 So Laban went into Jacob's tent and into Leah's tent and into the tent of the two maidservants, but he found nothing. After he came out of Leah's tent, he entered Rachel's tent. 31:34 Now Rachel had taken the household gods and put them inside her camel's saddle and was sitting on them. Laban searched through everything in the tent but found nothing. 31:35 Rachel said to her father, "Don't be angry, my lord, that I cannot stand up in your presence; I'm having my period." So he searched but could not find the household gods.

Jacob answered one question at a time. First, he admitted that he left suddenly because he knew Laban would not have let him leave, at least not with his wives and cattle. He had tried to leave once before, but Laban was very adamant about his staying (30:25 ff.). Second, Jacob stated his innocence regarding the theft of any household gods. Jacob had no idea what Rachel had done and, therefore, felt very confident that Laban would find nothing. Rachel, on the other hand, must have been terrified as Laban searched everyone's tent. Rachel had good reason to fear, because laws of this time stated that the theft of any temple god was a capital crime.

Rachel had put the gods in her saddle, upon which she was sitting. This shows that these were rather small idols. The saddle appeared to have been taken off of the camel and was in her tent where she was sitting on it. She used the excuse of her menstrual period to avoid standing up and getting off her saddle. Either Laban trusted his daughter or the LORD kept him from searching further. It may be that people viewed the saddle as unclean, because Leviticus 15:20 tells us that anything a woman sat on while having her period was considered unclean. Perhaps the LORD was not protecting Rachel, rather Jacob. If Laban had found the gods on Rachel, he would have surely placed blame on Jacob. Maybe God was also teaching a lesson to Laban, showing him the lack of power these worthless idols had.

Gen 31:36 Jacob was angry and took Laban to task. "What is my crime?" he asked Laban. "What sin have I committed that you hunt me down? 31:37 Now that you have searched through all my goods, what have you found that belongs to your household? Put it here in front of your relatives and mine, and let them judge between the two of us. 31:38 "I have been with you for twenty years now. Your sheep and goats have not miscarried, nor have I eaten rams from your flocks. 31:39 I did not bring you animals torn by wild beasts; I bore the loss myself. And you demanded payment from me for whatever was stolen by day or night. 31:40 This was my situation: The heat consumed me in the daytime and the cold at night, and sleep fled from my eyes. 31:41 It was like this for the twenty years I was in your household. I worked for you fourteen years for your two daughters and six years for your flocks, and you changed my wages ten times. 31:42 If the God of my father, the God of Abraham and the Fear of Isaac, had not been with me, you would surely have sent me away empty-handed. But God has seen my hardship and the toil of my hands, and last night he rebuked you."

After Laban was done searching, Jacob let his anger out and began to question Laban about his accusations. Jacob even went so far as to tell Laban to display any stolen goods before the people there and let them judge between the two of them. Obviously, Jacob was very confident that nobody in his caravan had taken anything from Laban. In suggesting that the people judge between them, it made Laban look foolish and, no doubt, he felt a little embarrassed.

Jacob continued his defense, telling how he had faithfully worked the past 20 years for Laban. He went on to explain his care of Laban's flock. Never did any animal miscarry as a result of mistreatment, nor did Jacob ever eat any of Laban's animals (which was a shepherd's right). Also, if an animal was ever killed by wild beasts, the shepherd was to bring the remains of the animal to the owner, showing him that the shepherd defended the sheep, not allowing the wild beast to drag it off. Then the master would bear the loss rather than the shepherd. However, Jacob noted that never did he bring any torn animal to Laban; rather, he bore the loss himself. Despite this faithful service, Laban still demanded Jacob replace anything that was ever stolen, treating Jacob as if he were a thief. Jacob went on to explain the harsh conditions of his work, day and night, for 20 years. (Six of these years he worked for the flock and fourteen of them for Laban's daughters.) Perhaps for Leah's sake, he did not mention that 14 of those years were spent working for his daughters, seven of which were for a daughter he did not even want to marry in the first place. Jacob's wages had been changed ten times. Jacob said all of these things in the presence of everyone there, and thus Laban was put in his place. Jacob concluded by showing the source of his blessings: God! If God had not been with Jacob, surely Laban would have been even more deceitful; instead, the LORD rebuked Laban. This fact alone should have put Laban in shaking boots, because who can question God's judgment?

Laban must have been somewhat shocked as Jacob went on and on displaying his deceitfulness. The Jacob who had been such a good and submissive worker was now letting it all out. Laban could do nothing but listen in silence, probably somewhat embarrassed.

Gen 31:43 Laban answered Jacob, "The women are my daughters, the children are my children, and the flocks are my flocks. All you see is mine. Yet what can I do today about these daughters of mine, or about the children they have borne? 31:44 Come now, let's make a covenant, you and I, and let it serve as a witness between us." 31:45 So Jacob took a stone and set it up as a pillar. 31:46 He said to his relatives, "Gather some stones." So they took stones and piled them in a heap, and they ate there by the heap. 31:47 Laban called it Jegar Sahadutha, and Jacob called it Galeed. 31:48 Laban said, "This heap is a witness between you and me today." That is why it was called Galeed. 31:49 It was also called Mizpah, because he said, "May the LORD keep watch between you and me when we are away from each other. 31:50 If you mistreat my daughters or if you take any wives besides my daughters, even though no one is with us, remember that God is a witness between you and me." 31:51 Laban also said to Jacob, "Here is this heap, and here is this pillar I have set up between you and me. 31:52 This heap is a witness, and this pillar is a witness, that I will not go past this heap to your side to harm you and that you will not go past this heap and pillar to my side to harm me. 31:53 May the God of Abraham and the God of Nahor, the God of their father, judge between us." So Jacob took an oath in the name of the Fear of his father Isaac. 31:54 He offered a sacrifice there in the hill country and invited his relatives to a meal. After they had eaten, they spent the night there. 31:55 Early the next morning Laban kissed his grandchildren and his daughters and blessed them. Then he left and returned home.

In order to save any more embarrassment, Laban tried to change the subject, knowing that his reputation was being tarnished (if he had a good one to begin with). Laban claimed ownership of Jacob's wives, children and flock; even though Jacob had earned them all. The only part with any truth was that his daughters were still his daughters; however, after marriage their roles were to be Jacob's wives before Laban's daughters. Laban was still treating Jacob as a thief and recognizing the 20 years of faithful service Jacob had given him. Though Laban came to take them back, the LORD's intervention spoiled his plans.

What more could Laban do, other then request a covenant between the two families. Though Laban requested it, Jacob and his relatives built the pillar to commemorate it. Laban called it Jegar Sahadutha, which was Aramaic for "testimony, or witness heap." Jacob called the same pillar Galeed, which was Hebrew for "witness heap." An interesting parallel to this pillar can be found in Joshua 22:10-12, 34, where the Reubenites and Gadites gave an altar almost the same name under similar circumstances.

Laban continued to show no trust in Jacob. The pillar was also called Mizpah, meaning "watchtower." (Today, many people use "Mizpah" chains to symbolize a type of blessed separation, but Biblically speaking the word implies a distrustful watching over). Laban said that this pillar was to serve as a reminder that God would watch over the two of them. However, Laban alluded to the fact that it was Jacob who needed to be watched. Laban even gave Jacob added instructions not to abuse his wives or marry anyone other than Laban's daughters, or else the LORD (Jehovah) would see it and judge him. Note that Laban used Jehovah, Jacob's God, not his own gods, further indicating that Jacob was the one to be watched over. This is somewhat ironic, considering Jacob had only wanted to marry Rachel; it was Laban who had forced him to marry Leah, a second wife.

The pillar was also to serve as a boundary between Jacob and Laban. Laban was the only one of the two who had any intention of harming the other, and he knew that God would not allow him to do so, therefore, these were empty words to take the focus off of himself and make Jacob look like he was still partly to blame.

Note also that Laban claimed to have built this heap himself (v. 51) when it was Jacob and his family that had erected it (v. 45-46). Laban simply refused to give Jacob credit for anything, further showing the conditions Jacob had lived in for the past 20 years.

Laban finally concludes his sad display of blind selfishness and greed by invoking the name of *Elohim* (God). The word *Elohim* could be applied to the one and only Creator God or any idol god as well. Therefore, when Laban said the God of Abraham (Jacob's spiritual father) he was referring to the true God of this world. However, when he refered to the God of Nahor (Laban's spiritual father- see Josh 24:2), it was probably the idol god which Laban himself worshipped. Thus, the "God of their fathers" meant both the true God and Laban's god. Indeed, the God of Abraham would judge between them.

Jacob probably could have viewed this worldly treaty as worthless because it was intermingled with a polytheistic oath. However, Jacob took another oath himself in the name of the "Fear of his father Isaac" (also in v. 42). The word "Fear" is capitalized and is another name for God. In the Hebrew it may also mean "kinsman," showing a personal relationship between the patriarch and God Himself. Jacob indeed had a personal walk with the "God of Isaac," as we saw at Bethel (28:13). Remember Jacob's words: "If God will be with me and will watch over me on this journey I am taking and will give me food to eat and clothes to wear so that I return safely to my father's house, then the LORD will be my God" (Gen 28:20). No doubt this oath was still fresh in Jacob's memory (see 31:9, 29, 42).

Jacob also offered a sacrifice to the "Fear of his father Isaac" in thanksgiving and fellowship for the protection God had given him (see Ex 24:5).

Early the next morning Laban kissed his daughters and grandchildren good-bye, without once saying any words of apology or taking any blame on himself. Clearly Laban was unrepentant. This is the last we hear of Laban or his sons.

Gen 32:1 Jacob also went on his way, and the angels of God met him. 32:2 When Jacob saw them, he said, "This is the camp of God!" So he named that place Mahanaim. 32:3 Jacob sent messengers ahead of him to his brother Esau in the land of Seir, the country of Edom.

Jacob left, and angels came and comforted him. It is very possible that Jacob was somewhat nervous about returning home. After all, his mother had told him she would send for him when Esau's anger had subsided (27:45), but he never received that message. Maybe Esau was still upset. Jacob had served a greedy man for the past 20 years and, though he had many cattle, he did not have many servants who would serve well as an army of soldiers.

When Jacob saw the angels, he was reassured of God's promises. Scripture suggests that only Jacob saw the angels and not his servants, thereby reassuring Jacob but doing little to comfort his servants (See 2 Kings 6:16-17 for a similar example). He named the place "camp of God," or the "army of God." Jacob realized that God's army would fight for him if necessary. After all, Laban had been held off in his anger, so why not Esau too? With this assurance he named the place Mahanaim, meaning "two camps or hosts," suggesting plenty of help for Jacob.

The encampment of angels reminds me of a story I heard once about a missionary who had been caught in a country at war. When the war was over years later, a man came to the missionary and told him about the many nights he and his men had tried to kill him. When the missionary asked why they had not, the old soldier told him that they never could get past the guards. This was quite a surprise to the missionary because he was by himself. Apparently, every night there were twelve armed guards surrounding his tent; a Mahanaim it seems.

The appearance of angels was very appropriate at this time for another reason, as well. Just as Jacob saw angels when he was fleeing from his brother Esau and going to Laban (28:12), he now saw angels when he was fleeing from Laban and going to Esau. God was keeping His promise (28:15; 31:3).

Jacob then sent men ahead to find Esau in the land of Seir. Seir was named after a Horite chief who had lived in the area (36:30), but now Esau had taken over and it could be thought of as synonymous with Edom. Though Seir was far south and out of the way on the trip home, Jacob was going there to make amends, wondering if his brother had forgiven him. Jacob knew it was best to deal with this problem rather than continue to run away from it. Also, this showed Jacob's trust in God at that moment, especially after seeing the two encampments of angels (Mahanaim) who would follow him.

Gen 32:4 He instructed them: "This is what you are to say to my master Esau: 'Your servant Jacob says, I have been staying with Laban and have remained there till now. 32:5 I have cattle and donkeys, sheep and goats, menservants and maidservants. Now I am sending this message to my lord, that I may find favor in your eyes.'" 32:6 When the messengers returned to Jacob, they said, "We went to your brother Esau, and now he is coming to meet you, and four hundred men are with him." 32:7 In great fear and distress Jacob divided the people who were with him into two groups, and the flocks and herds and camels as well. 32:8 He thought, "If Esau comes and attacks one group, the group that is left may escape."

The servants were instructed to go to Esau and tell him Jacob had been staying with Laban for the past twenty years. In those years Jacob had acquired many animals and servants but he was now looking to find favor in his brother's eyes.

When the servants returned Jacob was told that Esau was coming to meet him with 400 men. This naturally caused Jacob to be fearful, so he divided his people into two groups. If Esau attacked, he could flee with the second group while the first group fought them off for a time. The LORD must have been testing Jacob, as He wanted Jacob to learn to have faith in him no matter what the odds. Jacob no doubt seemed to be lacking some of that trust, despite the promises he had heard and visions he had seen; not unlike many of us today. When the going gets rough, we often tend to try to help God out with His promises, lacking complete faith in those moments.

What Jacob failed to realize in his fear, however, was that Esau himself may have been a little nervous. The last time he saw Jacob he was receiving a blessing in which it was said that he would "rule over his brother." Esau may have felt that Jacob was now coming to subjugate him, since he had many animals and servants.

Gen 32:9 Then Jacob prayed, "O God of my father Abraham, God of my father Isaac, O LORD, who said to me, 'Go back to your country and your relatives, and I will make you prosper,' 32:10 I am unworthy of all the kindness and faithfulness you have shown your servant. I had only my staff when I crossed this Jordan, but now I have become two groups. 32:11 Save me, I pray, from the hand of my brother Esau, for I am afraid he will come and attack me, and also the mothers with their children. 32:12 But You have said, 'I will surely make you prosper and will make your descendants like the sand of the sea, which cannot be counted.'" 32:13 He spent the night there, and from what he had with him he selected a gift for his brother Esau: 32:14 two hundred female goats and twenty male goats, two hundred ewes and twenty rams, 32:15 thirty female camels with their young, forty cows and ten bulls, and twenty female donkeys and ten male

donkeys. **32:16 He put them in the care of his servants, each herd by itself, and said to his servants, "Go ahead of me, and keep some space between the herds." 32:17 He instructed the one in the lead: "When my brother Esau meets you and asks, 'To whom do you belong, and where are you going, and who owns all these animals in front of you?' 32:18 then you are to say, 'They belong to your servant Jacob. They are a gift sent to my lord Esau, and he is coming behind us.'" 32:19 He also instructed the second, the third and all the others who followed the herds: "You are to say the same thing to Esau when you meet him. 32:20 And be sure to say, 'Your servant Jacob is coming behind us.'" For he thought, "I will pacify him with these gifts I am sending on ahead; later, when I see him, perhaps he will receive me." 32:21 So Jacob's gifts went on ahead of him, but he himself spent the night in the camp.**

After Jacob felt that he had done everything he could, he rightly turned to God in prayer. We, too, should always remember to take everything to God in prayer, both prayers of thanks and of need. Jacob's prayer was interesting, as he seemed to be reminding God of His promise but was probably trying to reassure himself about God's promises. He brought up the fact that it was God who told him to leave Laban and that He had promised to protect Jacob and make his descendants many. Therefore, he begged for deliverance, not only for his sake but, also for the women and children with him. Jacob did pray in humility, however, because recognizing that though he went to Laban with nothing, he was leaving with enough possessions to make two groups. In his prayer Jacob recognized God as *Elohim*, the powerful Creator, and *Jehovah*, the more personal God of the promise and covenant. Indeed, God's promise to prosper and have many descendants (28:14) was being fulfilled. I believe that after this prayer Jacob was strengthened; and though not for sure, it is possible that the LORD had instructed him to send Esau gifts. One thing is for sure: if Jacob did not feel safe then, he soon would. We see in 33:12-15 that Jacob refused to accept extra help for protection because he knew that God was with him (Mahanaim-the two hosts) and He would be the only army needed.

Perhaps encouraged by his prayer, Jacob spent the night in that spot and prepared the gifts for Esau. He separated a total of 580 animals into five groups, with each group of animals to be sent separately. This way, Esau would receive five gifts at five different times.

Each servant was to "be sure to" present the gift to Esau as being from "Your servant, Jacob." This would certainly relieve any suspicion that Esau might have about Jacob trying to subjugate him, since Jacob was calling himself the "servant." If that didn't relieve Esau's mind, Jacob had hope that the gifts would. Surely these gifts were a good gesture of peace that Esau would not be able to overlook.

Jacob spent the rest of the night at his camp while the servants went on ahead of him to take these gifts to his brother Esau.

Gen 32:22 That night Jacob got up and took his two wives, his two maidservants and his eleven sons and crossed the ford of the Jabbok. 32:23

After he had sent them across the stream, he sent over all his possessions. 32:24 So Jacob was left alone, and a man wrestled with him till daybreak. 32:25 When the man saw that he could not overpower him, he touched the socket of Jacob's hip so that his hip was wrenched as he wrestled with the man. 32:26 Then the man said, "Let me go, for it is daybreak." But Jacob replied, "I will not let you go unless you bless me." 32:27 The man asked him, "What is your name?" "Jacob," he answered. 32:28 Then the man said, "Your name will no longer be Jacob, but Israel, because you have struggled with God and with men and have overcome." 32:29 Jacob said, "Please tell me your name." But he replied, "Why do you ask my name?" Then he blessed him there.

While it was still dark, Jacob took his family and all his possessions across the Jabbok, a stream which flowed into the Jordan from the east and entered roughly half-way between the Sea of Galilee and the Dead Sea. By crossing the river, Jacob clearly showed his intentions were not to retreat, but rather to trust in the LORD as he faced Esau. This also allowed Jacob to be alone and probably to pray to God, just as he had at Bethel (28:10).

Appropriately, Jabbok means "wrestler." The text reads, "God wrestled (*yeabeq*) with Jacob (*yaaqob*) by the Jabbok (*yabboq*). This occured at a time when Jacob was about to enter into the promised land and, since he had wrestled with Esau and Laban, it was now time to wrestle with God, the source of his blessings.

It was while Jacob was alone that Christ came in the form of a man and wrestled with Jacob until daybreak. Jacob did not give up so the Man touched his hip by the socket, causing some type of pain and a permanent limp. Jacob still would not let go until the Man blessed him. This is a rather strange account, which we will not fully be able to grasp. Hosea gives us further insight and understanding of this passage: In the womb he grasped his brother's heel; as a man he struggled *with God*. He struggled with *the Angel* and overcame Him; *he wept and begged for His favor*. He found Him at Bethel and talked with Him there-- the LORD God Almighty, the LORD is His name of renown!" (Hosea 12:3-5). One is tempted to call this a dream, or symbolic of some greater lesson to be learned. Indeed, there is a lesson to be learned, but it was no dream; it was real. Jacob really wrestled with an angel, and that Angel was Christ. It was not uncommon in those days for Christ to appear as a man, as we have already seen (18:1-2). Hosea said Jacob struggled with God. Jacob said he saw God *face to face* (v. 30). We may not understand how this could happen, but we must believe it. Just as Jacob "wrestled" with Esau in the womb in order to receive the blessing, so now he "wrestled" with God to receive a blessing again. The fact that Jacob's hip was wrenched clearly tells us that this was a physical struggle, but no doubt it also represented an emotional and spiritual struggle going on within Jacob's heart. Jacob must have been fervently praying for God's guidance and blessing upon his life, while at the same time struggling with his own flesh which brought fear, lust, and anger. We, too, wrestle with our sinful flesh but can only overcome through the blood of Christ; clinging to the cross to which all of our sins were nailed. We must, as Jacob, go to God face to face in prayer. Jesus encouraged us to "always pray and not give up. . . and will not God bring about justice for His chosen ones, who cry out to Him day and night? Will He keep putting them off?" (Luke 18:1,7). Jacob never gave up. He kept holding on to God until his prayers were answered.

How could Jacob actually overcome this Man? Only because the Man allowed it, and perhaps to make sure Jacob would never forget it He gave him a permanent limp.

While Jacob was still holding on, the Angel asked his name, not to *find out* Jacob's name but to *show meaning* in his name by making him say it out-loud and to think about it. The Angel then told Jacob his new name was to be Israel, meaning "he struggles with God." From now on this name would not only be used to describe all of the twelve tribes, but it also symbolized strength, perseverance and faith in God. Just as Abram received a new name (Abraham-17:5) from God to show that he was God's special servant, Jacob became Israel and also God's special servant. Also, Abraham was given this new name to indicate that he was going to be the father of many nations. Likewise, Jacob became Israel not only to show personal change but also that he was the father of the twelve tribes of Israel; hence many nations. God would appear to Jacob again in 35:10 to remind him of his new name.

Jacob in return asked the Angel His name, but the Angel asked why he needed to ask. Clearly, Jacob knew who this Man was. Jacob was then blessed. (Technically, I think he received his blessing once his new name was given, indicating a new spiritual nature.)

Gen 32:30 So Jacob called the place Peniel, saying, "It is because I saw God face to face, and yet my life was spared." 32:31 The sun rose above him as he passed Peniel, and he was limping because of his hip. 32:32 Therefore to this day the Israelites do not eat the tendon attached to the socket of the hip, because the socket of Jacob's hip was touched near the tendon.

As a result of all these events, Jacob called that place Peniel, meaning "face of God." This name was later changed to Penuel and would be remembered as such until the time the nations of Israel and Judah divided (1 Kings 12:25).

According to Scripture, no one is allowed to see God's face and still live (Exodus 33:20), yet Jacob said he saw God "face to face." People have only been able to see God's back (Exodus 33:23), His feet (Exodus 24:10), or His form. We read in Numbers, "With Him I speak face to face, clearly and not in riddles; he sees the **form** of the LORD" (Num 12:8). Therefore, Jacob saw Christ in the "form" of a man, yet face to face with this "Man."

The sun began to rise above Jacob as he passed by Peniel, and no doubt this scene was etched in Jacob's mind, as the bright sun from then on would always remind him of the face of God. We read about God's face in Revelation where it says, "His face was like the sun shining in all its brilliance" (Rev 1:16; see also Rev 10:1; Ex 34:29; 1 Pet 1:19; 2 Thess 2:8; Acts 26:13).

Jacob went away limping. Because of this, the Jews did not eat the tendon attached to the hip socket because that is where Jacob was "touched by God." This was probably the sciatic muscle. No place in Scripture records God telling them to restrain from eating this muscle, but the Israelites did it not only to remember this event, but to also indicate its importance.

Gen 33:1 Jacob looked up and there was Esau, coming with his four hundred men; so he divided the children among Leah, Rachel and the two maidservants. 33:2 He put the maidservants and their children in front, Leah and her children next, and Rachel and Joseph in the rear. 33:3 He himself went on ahead and bowed down to the ground seven times as he approached his brother. 33:4 But Esau ran to meet Jacob and embraced him; he threw his arms around his neck and kissed him. And they wept. 33:5 Then Esau looked up and saw the women and children. "Who are these with you?" he asked. Jacob answered, "They are the children God has graciously given your servant." 33:6 Then the maidservants and their children approached and bowed down. 33:7 Next, Leah and her children came and bowed down. Last of all came Joseph and Rachel, and they too bowed down.

By looking at 47:9; 41:46; 45:11; 29:27; 31:38, one can see that both Jacob and Esau were in their nineties and both should have been quite mature by now.   Esau was now in view with his 400 men. To prepare, Jacob arranged his family in what seemed to be the order of importance in Jacob's eyes. In the rear was his favorite wife (Rachel) and son (Joseph). In front of them were Leah and her children, then the two maidservants and their children. Perhaps Jacob reasoned that if there was fighting, his beloved Rachel would have the best chance of escaping.

Jacob himself went out in front of them all to meet Esau. As Jacob approached he bowed down seven times. This was an act of respect done before kings, which was recorded in the Tell el-Amarna tablets in Egypt dating to the 14th century B.C. Therefore, Esau was very likely the king or ruler in this region.

Jacob's fears had proven unnecessary, as Esau ran up to greet him with hugs, kisses, and tears. Esau immediately asked who the women and children were only to find out they were all Jacob's. The record does not say, but perhaps Jacob's practice of polygamy was a surprise to Esau, since Jacob was always the religious one. In any case, Jacob introduced them and they all bowed down before Esau in the same order they had been arranged.

Gen 33:8 Esau asked, "What do you mean by all these droves I met?" "To find favor in your eyes, my lord," he said. 33:9 But Esau said, "I already have plenty, my brother. Keep what you have for yourself." 33:10 "No, please!" said Jacob. "If I have found favor in your eyes, accept this gift from me. For to see your face is like seeing the face of God, now that you have received me favorably. 33:11 Please accept the present that was brought to you, for God has been gracious to me and I have all I need."

And because Jacob insisted, Esau accepted it. **33:12** Then Esau said, "Let us be on our way; I'll accompany you." **33:13** But Jacob said to him, "My lord knows that the children are tender and that I must care for the ewes and cows that are nursing their young. If they are driven hard just one day, all the animals will die. **33:14** So let my lord go on ahead of his servant, while I move along slowly at the pace of the droves before me and that of the children, until I come to my lord in Seir." **33:15** Esau said, "Then let me leave some of my men with you." "But why do that?" Jacob asked. "Just let me find favor in the eyes of my lord." **33:16** So that day Esau started on his way back to Seir. **33:17** Jacob, however, went to Succoth, where he built a place for himself and made shelters for his livestock. That is why the place is called Succoth.

Esau's next question dealt with the rather extravagant gifts Jacob had sent. Jacob responded by telling Esau they were to find favor in the eyes of his "lord." Note that Jacob still seemed unsure of Esau's intent, or at least he was being extremely respectful, because in verse five Jacob called himself Esau's "servant" and here his "lord." Esau, on the other hand, simply responded by saying, "I already have plenty, my *brother*." Esau's response showed genuine love and compassion for his "brother."

An interesting point is seen in the original language regarding Esau having "plenty" (v. 9) and Jacob having "all he needs." The Hebrew would better read Esau as saying, "I have much," and Jacob saying, "I have everything." Even though Esau probably had more material blessings at this point, Jacob indeed had everything with God's blessing.

Jacob insisted that Esau keep these gifts, as it would not have been respectable to take them back. Besides, Esau's acceptance of these gifts was a sign of reconciliation with no hard feelings. Jacob was seeking Esau's favor, and therefore, the acceptance of this gift was more for Jacob than it was for Esau. As Jacob had said, Esau not holding a grudge was like seeing the face of God (and Jacob could actually relate to that- 32:30).

Esau then invited Jacob to travel with him to Seir, but Jacob respectfully declined, saying that his cattle needed rest and would also travel too slowly. Instead, they would later meet again at Seir (even though Jacob was really planning to go to Succoth). Jacob probably realized that it was important to stay separated from Esau in order not to interfere with God's future plans for the children of Israel. When Esau offered to leave extra men for Jacob's protection, they too are refused, as he has not only found favor in Esau's eyes, but in the LORD's as well. Therefore, Jacob had all the protection he needed.

While Esau left to go to Seir, Jacob went to Succoth (meaning "booths," perhaps the same place in Joshua 13:27 and Judges 8:15-16) which was east of the Jordan and north of the Jabbok. It was probably a fertile valley between those rivers and, therefore, Jacob decided to stay there a while and let everyone rest before going back to his father's house. This stay would not be permanent, but it wouldn't be just a few days either, as indicated by Jacob's building shelters or booths for himself and his livestock. It is also interesting that, though Jacob was going to return to see his father, no mention was made of either Isaac or Rebekah in the rest of Genesis, other than their deaths (35:27-29; 49:31). Although Isaac was around 153 when Jacob returned, he would live to be 180 years old. This shows family relations are not the focus of Scripture, rather God's faithfulness to His promises.

Gen 33:18 After Jacob came from Paddan Aram, he arrived safely at the city of Shechem in Canaan and camped within sight of the city. 33:19 For a hundred pieces of silver, he bought from the sons of Hamor, the father of Shechem, the plot of ground where he pitched his tent. 33:20 There he set up an altar and called it El Elohe Israel.

After Jacob left Paddan Aram (plain of Aram, and another name for Aram Naharaim, as in 24:10) he arrived safely at Shechem. Twenty years before Jacob had said a prayer about returning safely (28:21; 31:3) and here it was answered.

Shechem was an important city in Canaan, resting on Mount Gerizim. It would later be part of the territory belonging to Ephraim. It was there that God had first appeared to Abram when he entered the promised land (12:6-7). Though we are not told here, Jacob also dug a well here as we see in John 4:5-6. Shechem, unfortunately, would be Jacob's first true dwelling in the promised land. At that time it was inhabited by the Hivites under the rule of Hamor. Hamor had a son named Shechem, who was perhaps named after the city itself. Living this close to a heathen Canaanite city could only bring about trouble. We are not told why Jacob did not continue on to Bethel. But as the record shows, trouble would come in chapter 34, as Jacob's daughter would be raped by Shechem. It is not until chapter 35 that we see Jacob finally left the area and moved on to Bethel, where he had his dream of heaven opened (28:10). This was the place to which God had promised to bring him back (28:18).

Instead of settling in Bethel, Jacob purchased land in Shechem from Hamor to live for a few years. This same land was where his son, Joseph, would be buried over 400 years later when his bones were brought out of Egypt at the Exodus (Joshua 24:32).

Jacob also built an altar with the name *El Elohe* Israel, meaning "mighty is the God of Israel." This shows us that Jacob (Israel) now recognized the God of his father Isaac as his God, too. Twenty years before, Jacob had said, "If God will be with me and will watch over me on this journey I am taking and will give me food to eat and clothes to wear so that I return safely to my father's house, then the *LORD will be my* God" (Gen 28:20-21). Verse 20 is the first time we see Jacob referring to himself using his new name of Israel. It is significant that this took place first in the promised land, the home of all Israel.

Gen 34:1 Now Dinah, the daughter Leah had borne to Jacob, went out to visit the women of the land. 34:2 When Shechem son of Hamor the Hivite, the ruler of that area, saw her, he took her and violated her. 34:3 His heart was drawn to Dinah daughter of Jacob, and he loved the girl and spoke tenderly to her. 34:4 And Shechem said to his father Hamor, "Get me this girl as my wife." 34:5 When Jacob heard that his daughter Dinah

had been defiled, his sons were in the fields with his livestock; so he kept quiet about it until they came home. **34:6** Then Shechem's father Hamor went out to talk with Jacob. **34:7** Now Jacob's sons had come in from the fields as soon as they heard what had happened. They were filled with grief and fury, because Shechem had done a disgraceful thing in Israel by lying with Jacob's daughter--a thing that should not be done. **34:8** But Hamor said to them, "My son Shechem has his heart set on your daughter. Please give her to him as his wife. **34:9** Intermarry with us; give us your daughters and take our daughters for yourselves. **34:10** You can settle among us; the land is open to you. Live in it, trade in it, and acquire property in it."

We ended chapter 33 with God, and we will begin chapter 35 with God; however, chapter 34 is without mention of him.

It is likely that Dinah had few, if any, girlfriends her age and, therefore, she was driven to the nearby town of Shechem to socialize. At this time Dinah must have been in her early teens, and with so many brothers and perhaps no sisters, she desired to be with other girls her age.

While in Shechem, the son of Hamor (Shechem) saw Dinah and found that she was beautiful so he raped her. Nothing is said of Dinah's participation or rejection of this, but we do know that she was kept in Shechem's house (v. 26). Shechem fell in love with her, so he asked his father to get her to be his wife legally.

When Jacob heard what had happened to Dinah he was very upset, but did nothing until his sons came in from the field. Somehow they heard about this disgrace (Jacob may have sent a servant out to get them) and they immediately came in from the fields. Obviously they were upset that their sister had been defiled, but they were also angry that it was a disgrace to Israel. This recognition of Israel as a whole shows these boys had a deeper understanding of the future promise than we often give them credit for.

Around the same time that Jacob's sons came from the field, Hamor also arrived to talk with Jacob. No apology or recognition of fault was ever given by Hamor or his son. Nor do we see Hamor ever rebuking his son; rather, he seemed to approve of the whole situation. This clearly shows the vileness and lack of true spirituality in Shechem. Hamor's goal was to get Shechem his wife by convincing Jacob's family to intermarry with them. If Hamor could get Jacob to do that, Israel would eventually be absorbed into the Hivite culture (v. 16) and the town of Shechem would benefit through Jacob's blessings (v. 21). Being absorbed into that culture would have meant disaster for God's people.

Gen 34:11 Then Shechem said to Dinah's father and brothers, "Let me find favor in your eyes, and I will give you whatever you ask. **34:12** Make the price for the bride and the gift I am to bring as great as you like, and I'll pay whatever you ask me. Only give me the girl as my wife." **34:13** Because their sister Dinah had been defiled, Jacob's sons replied deceitfully as they spoke to Shechem and his father Hamor. **34:14** They said to them, "We can't do such a thing; we can't give our sister to a man who is not circumcised. That would be a disgrace to us. **34:15** We will give our consent to you on one condition only: that you become like us by circumcising all your males. 34:16 Then we will give you our daughters and take your daughters for ourselves. We'll settle among you and become one people with you. 34:17 But if you will not agree to be circumcised, we'll take our sister and go."

Shechem could not hold his tongue or his excitement and jumped right to the point. He wanted Dinah and would pay whatever bride-price was necessary. Jacob's sons took this as an insult, because Shechem was treating their sister as a prostitute who could be purchased (v. 31). In their anger, Jacob's sons devised a plot to avenge Israel's disgrace. (The word "deceitfully" in verse 13 lets the reader know that this is all an act to achieve a greater end.) They told Shechem that in order to intermarry and settle among them, the Shechemites must be circumcised to fit into their religious beliefs. If they would not become circumcised, they would go into town and get their sister back (v. 26).

Jacob's sons were using a very sacred covenant sign for evil means (v. 25). However, Jacob had done nothing to protect his daughter or prevent intermarriage with ungodly foreigners, which meant sure destruction for Israel. Jacob himself did not know what his sons were plotting, as he said nothing, but he would later rebuke them when he found out why they did this (v. 30).

Gen 34:18 Their proposal seemed good to Hamor and his son Shechem. 34:19 The young man, who was the most honored of all his father's household, lost no time in doing what they said, because he was delighted with Jacob's daughter. 34:20 So Hamor and his son Shechem went to the gate of their city to speak to their fellow townsmen. 34:21 "These men are friendly toward us," they said. "Let them live in our land and trade in it; the land has plenty of room for them. We can marry their daughters and they can marry ours. 34:22 But the men will consent to live with us as one people only on the condition that our males be circumcised, as they themselves are. 34:23 Won't their livestock, their property and all their other animals become ours? So let us give our consent to them, and they will settle among us." 34:24 All the men who went out of the city gate agreed with Hamor and his son Shechem, and every male in the city was circumcised.

Circumcision seemed good to Hamor and his son. Hamor saw the opportunity for wealth, while Shechem was blinded by love. However, what would the rest of the town think? Shechem was "most honored" among the townsmen and, no doubt, played a key role in convincing the rest of the town to follow him in this venture.

Hamor and Shechem went to the city gate where most business was done. They reminded everyone that the Israelites had been friendly and there was plenty of room for them to stay. Besides, all the townsmen could intermarry with them. At this point everyone must have been very agreeable. Now the catch was given. In order to do this all the males had to be circumcised. No

161

doubt this caused many a male to cringe, but Hamor quickly went on to add other benefits, primarily financial (v. 23). Now that they were promised money and women, all the men at the gate agreed to be circumcised.

Gen 34:25 Three days later, while all of them were still in pain, two of Jacob's sons, Simeon and Levi, Dinah's brothers, took their swords and attacked the unsuspecting city, killing every male. 34:26 They put Hamor and his son Shechem to the sword and took Dinah from Shechem's house and left. 34:27 The sons of Jacob came upon the dead bodies and looted the city where their sister had been defiled. 34:28 They seized their flocks and herds and donkeys and everything else of theirs in the city and out in the fields. 34:29 They carried off all their wealth and all their women and children, taking as plunder everything in the houses.

We now see which of Jacob's sons had devised this plot. Only Simeon and Levi went into town with their swords. We are not told if the other brothers were aware of this plan or not. Other than Reuben and Judah, the others may have been too young for battle. If Reuben and Judah were aware, they most likely declined to participate because both seem nonviolent (37:21,26). They perhaps knew God's principle to "not take revenge, my friends, but leave room for God's wrath, for it is written: 'It is mine to avenge; I will repay,' says the Lord" (Rom 12:19).

It was three days after the proposal to be circumcised that Simeon and Levi went to finish what they started. All of the Shechemites were still in great pain and, therefore, could not fight back. Every male in the town was killed, including Hamor and Shechem, and Dinah was taken back home. The entire city was looted and all the animals, women, children and wealth of the city became Israel's.

Gen 34:30 Then Jacob said to Simeon and Levi, "You have brought trouble on me by making me a stench to the Canaanites and Perizzites, the people living in this land. We are few in number, and if they join forces against me and attack me, I and my household will be destroyed." 34:31 But they replied, "Should he have treated our sister like a prostitute?"

There was no keeping it a secret any longer. Jacob now knew what his sons had done and he rebuked Simeon and Levi because they made Israel a stench in the land. Again Jacob showed a lack of faith (which is why he was still called Jacob and not Israel here) and feared for his life if the neighboring Canaanite towns took revenge. The Perizzites may have been people who lived nearby, outside of actual towns. However, God would take care of this by causing these towns to fear Israel (35:5).

Later, as a result of Simeon and Levi's anger and rash behavior at Shechem, both of their descendants were cursed to be scattered (49:7). The tribe of Simeon would be absorbed by Judah (Josh 19:1,9) and the tribe of Levi would be split into 48 towns to be priests (Nu 35:2-7; Josh 14:4; 21:41). It is also significant to mention that both Simeon and Levi were the son's of Leah, not Rachel.

Simeon and Levi simply asked whether or not they should have sat back and done nothing (as did Jacob) while their sister was being treated as a prostitute (v. 12). This question seemed to silence Jacob, as indeed he should have done something, if only to speak up and condemn Shechem for raping his daughter. And as mentioned, Jacob should never have even considered allowing intermarriage because of the threat to Israel's existence. However, Jacob's silence did not make Simeon and Levi's actions right.

The event at Shechem played an important role in getting Israel to Egypt. Not only did this cause Jacob to return to his father's home in Bethel (which he should have done a long time ago), but it would also cause Joseph to be sold into Egypt. Jacob's sons would later be tending sheep near Shechem where Joseph was sent to check up on them (perhaps because Jacob was worried that someone might try to harm them as a result of their destruction of Shechem). Joseph was then captured and sold as a slave to Egypt, but would later bring the rest of Jacob's family (Israelites) to Egypt and deliver them from a famine.

Gen 35:1 Then God said to Jacob, "Go up to Bethel and settle there, and build an altar there to God, who appeared to you when you were fleeing from your brother Esau." 35:2 So Jacob said to his household and to all who were with him, "Get rid of the foreign gods you have with you, and purify yourselves and change your clothes. 35:3 Then come, let us go up to Bethel, where I will build an altar to God, who answered me in the day of my distress and who has been with me wherever I have gone." 35:4 So they gave Jacob all the foreign gods they had and the rings in their ears, and Jacob buried them under the oak at Shechem.

God told Jacob to leave Shechem and settle in Bethel. God had already told Jacob to return to his "native land" (31:13), but here He was more specific in telling Jacob to stay in Bethel. One would have thought Jacob would have returned to Bethel immediately after leaving Laban, but for unknown reasons he settled near Shechem. This Divine message could not have come at a better time, since Jacob was not well respected after what Simeon and Levi had just done at Shechem. Besides, Jacob needed a spiritual boost by returning to the Bethel, "the house of God." It was there that Jacob had spent the night over 20 years earlier and had his dream of heaven opened (28:12-15).

It is interesting that Bethel was only about 15 miles south of Shechem, and Jacob apparently had never returned there. Even more confusing, it was about half way between Shechem and Hebron, the home of his father. While living in Shechem, Jacob must have traveled to visit Isaac because Deborah, Rebekah's nurse, was now living with them (35:8). This not only meant that Rebekah had died, but that Jacob must have been home in order to bring Deborah back with him. Therefore, Jacob would have had to go out of his way not to go through Bethel. Yet the record seems to suggest that Jacob had not yet returned to Bethel. Why? It is possible that Jacob did journey here and the record just does not mention it. This time God was telling him to "settle" there.

Another possibility is that he felt unworthy to enter "God's house" while he felt so sinful. He may have felt a need to purify himself before going there, which leads us to verse two.

Now that God had "invited" Jacob to live in Bethel, Jacob was forced to purify his household by commanding them to do something he should have had them do a long time ago. All of his family and servants were to get rid of their foreign gods and purify themselves. No doubt much of the loot taken from Shechem consisted of foreign idols. Also, Rachel may still have had Laban's idols in her possession (31:19). In any case, it was only appropriate to purify his household and get rid of all idols before entering Bethel, "God's house." This is a good lesson for us today when entering a house of worship. Often we attend worship services with our hearts in the wrong places. We may be angry, bored, or just going through the motions, but God would have us daily prepare our hearts for prayer, communion and fellowship with Him. Next time we go to church, let us begin preparing our hearts and minds before we enter the church door.

Part of the purification for Jacob's household involved changing their clothing. This, too, symbolized a righteous and pure heart. All Christians will receive new clothes before entering God's house in heaven: "Let us rejoice and be glad and give Him glory! For the wedding of the Lamb has come, and His bride has made herself ready. Fine linen, bright and clean, was given her to wear." (Fine linen represents the righteous acts of the saints.) (Rev 19:7-8)

All of the idols and remnants of their old life were then buried underneath an oak tree at Shechem. This symbolized their, "putting off of the sinful nature" (Col 2:11). They would leave this lifestyle behind and begin a new dedication and commitment to the God of Jacob, who had watched over them this entire time, just as Jacob had asked Him to (28:21). It is also possible that this oak tree was the same tree Abraham had stayed near in Genesis 12:6 (though probably not the same tree; see also Joshua 24:26).

Gen 35:5 Then they set out, and the terror of God fell upon the towns all around them so that no one pursued them. 35:6 Jacob and all the people with him came to Luz (that is, Bethel) in the land of Canaan. 35:7 There he built an altar, and he called the place El Bethel, because it was there that God revealed himself to him when he was fleeing from his brother. 35:8 Now Deborah, Rebekah's nurse, died and was buried under the oak below Bethel. So it was named Allon Bacuth.

Jacob had earlier feared that the surrounding people would come and attack him to avenge the town of Shechem, but God stepped in and caused the exact opposite to occur. Now the surrounding peoples fear Jacob; no doubt this happened to ensure Jacob's safety.

When Jacob arrived at Luz (Bethel) he built an altar just as God had told him to (v. 1). This time he changed the name slightly to El Bethel, meaning the "God of the house of God." This altar acknowledged that Bethel belonged to God in a special way.

164

Next we read that Deborah, Rebekah's nurse, died and was buried under the oak tree below Bethel. Because of her death, the oak tree was named Allon Bacuth, meaning "oak of weeping." This must have been a true time of weeping for Jacob, as he had known Deborah all his life. When Rebekah (Jacob's mother) had left her family to marry Isaac (24:59), Deborah came along with her to be a nurse and may have even helped deliver Jacob and Esau. The question is, why was she now with Jacob and not Rebekah? Deborah did not go to Laban's with Jacob; therefore, she must have joined him sometime when they were living in Shechem. Perhaps she came to live with him after one of his trips to see his father (only 50 miles from Shechem) because Rebekah had already died. Jacob never saw his mother once he fled from Esau.

Gen 35:9 After Jacob returned from Paddan Aram, God appeared to him again and blessed him. 35:10 God said to him, "Your name is Jacob, but you will no longer be called Jacob; your name will be Israel. " So he named him Israel. 35:11 And God said to him, "I am God Almighty ; be fruitful and increase in number. A nation and a community of nations will come from you, and kings will come from your body. 35:12 The land I gave to Abraham and Isaac I also give to you, and I will give this land to your descendants after you." 35:13 Then God went up from him at the place where he had talked with him. 35:14 Jacob set up a stone pillar at the place where God had talked with him, and he poured out a drink offering on it; he also poured oil on it. 35:15 Jacob called the place where God had talked with him Bethel.

While at Bethel, God once again appeared to Jacob, identifying Himself as "God Almighty," which in Hebrew is *El Shaddai.* God had already revealed Himself as such to Abraham (17:1) and to Isaac (28:3), but this was the first time for Jacob. *El Shaddai* comes from the word *shad*, meaning breast. Therefore, God is the source of nourishment and comfort for His people.

God blessed Jacob again and reminded him that he was no longer to be called Jacob, but Israel. We mentioned earlier that Jacob may not have felt "good enough" for God's calling, which was one possible reason it seemed to have taken Jacob so long to return to Bethel. The fact that Jacob continued to be called Jacob supports this theory. God here reminded Jacob that he had put off his sinful nature and was walking under a covenant with the *El Shaddai*. The name Israel "wrestles with God" would be a constant reminder of his unending commitment and dedication to God, as if God was saying, "As a prisoner for the Lord, then, I urge you to live a life worthy of the calling you have received" (Eph 4:1). Jacob could have benefited from Paul's letter to the Romans where he wrote, "And if I do what I do not want to do, I agree that the law is good. As it is, it is no longer I myself who do it, but it is sin living in me. I know that nothing good lives in me, that is, in my sinful nature. For I have the desire to do what is good, but I cannot carry it out. . . .For in my inner being I delight in God's law; but I see another law at work in the members of my body, waging war against the law of my mind and making me a prisoner of the law of sin at work within my members. What a wretched man I am! Who will rescue me from this body of death? Thanks be to God--through Jesus Christ our Lord!" (Rom 7:16-25).

Once more we see the covenant God made with Abraham and Isaac being given to Jacob (Gen 13:16; 15:5; 12:7; 13:15; 15:7,18; 17:1-8; 12:3; 18:18; 28:3). Also, we see the command to "be fruitful and multiply" repeated once more, just as at Creation and after the Flood (1:28; 9: 1,7).

God then "went up" from that place. Perhaps Jacob saw something similar to his earlier dream where heaven was opened and a ladder came down to earth. See note on 28:12.

Jacob again felt compelled to make a drink-offering and anoint the stone pillar he had built for God Almighty. The drink offerings were acts of devotion and purification. They were never commanded under the Levitical law and, therefore, we see a clear picture of dedication on Jacob's part in anointing the pillar.

Gen 35:16 Then they moved on from Bethel. While they were still some distance from Ephrath, Rachel began to give birth and had great difficulty. 35:17 And as she was having great difficulty in childbirth, the midwife said to her, "Don't be afraid, for you have another son." 35:18 As she breathed her last--for she was dying--she named her son Ben-Oni. But his father named him Benjamin. 35:19 So Rachel died and was buried on the way to Ephrath (that is, Bethlehem). 35:20 Over her tomb Jacob set up a pillar, and to this day that pillar marks Rachel's tomb. 35:21 Israel moved on again and pitched his tent beyond Migdal Eder. 35:22 While Israel was living in that region, Reuben went in and slept with his father's concubine Bilhah, and Israel heard of it. Jacob had twelve sons:

Jacob then left Bethel, and while they were still traveling Rachel began giving birth. About 15 years ago Rachel had given birth to Joseph, meaning "may He extend," showing Rachel's desire to have more children (30:24). That time had come, but it cost Rachel her life. Rachel must have been well over 100 years old by now and, therefore, the birth was too hard for her. Because of this difficult birth, Rachel's last breath was used to name the child Ben-Oni, meaning "son of my trouble." This was Jacob's twelfth and final son, but he could not give him this name, perhaps because the guilt that would go with it, would hang over his head for the rest of his life. Therefore, Israel (Jacob) wisely renamed him Benjamin, meaning "son of my right hand." Rachel only gave Jacob two sons, but they would clearly be his favorites (37:3; 42:38).

Israel was going to Ephrath which was Bethlehem (Ru 1:2). This birth while traveling to Bethlehem should remind us of a birth that would take place in Bethlehem many years later; the promised Messiah who would be born years later (Micah 5:2).

Israel made a pillar to mark Rachel's tomb. This tomb would be seen years later, even after the days of Moses (1 Sam 10:2). Today there is a traditional sight which is called Rachel's tomb near Bethlehem; however, it is probably not authentic.

From Bethlehem, Israel continued to Migdal Eder, which means "tower of the flock." This was probably a watchtower very near Jerusalem, built to discourage thieves from stealing sheep (see 2 Chron 26:10). We see the same name used to figuratively describe the flock as God's people in Micah 4:8, which reads, "As for you, O watchtower of the flock, O stronghold of the Daughter of Zion, the former dominion will be restored to you; kingship will come to the Daughter of Jerusalem."

While living near Midgal Eder, Israel's oldest son, Reuben slept with his father's concubine. Reuben must have been about 30 years old at this time, but with all the moving and really no Godly relatives to speak of, finding a wife must have been very difficult. Therefore, he apparently began to get quite friendly with Bilhah, Rachel's maid. Though she must have been much older than Reuben, both were in need of companionship and they fell into sin. As a result of this incest, Reuben would lose his legal status as firstborn: "The sons of Reuben the firstborn of Israel (he was the firstborn, but when he defiled his father's marriage bed, his rights as firstborn were given to the sons of Joseph, son of Israel; so he could not be listed in the genealogical record in accordance with his birthright" (I Chron 5:1). Along with the legal status, Reuben also lost his exalted position: "Reuben, you are my firstborn, my might, the first sign of my strength, excelling in honor, excelling in power. Turbulent as the waters, you will no longer excel, for you went up onto your father's bed, onto my couch and defiled it" (Gen 49:3-4).

We will look at the twelve sons of Israel in the next section.

Gen 35:23 The sons of Leah: Reuben the firstborn of Jacob, Simeon, Levi, Judah, Issachar and Zebulun. 35:24 The sons of Rachel: Joseph and Benjamin. 35:25 The sons of Rachel's maidservant Bilhah: Dan and Naphtali. 35:26 The sons of Leah's maidservant Zilpah: Gad and Asher. These were the sons of Jacob, who were born to him in Paddan Aram. 35:27 Jacob came home to his father Isaac in Mamre, near Kiriath Arba (that is, Hebron), where Abraham and Isaac had stayed. 35:28 Isaac lived a hundred and eighty years. 35:29 Then he breathed his last and died and was gathered to his people, old and full of years. And his sons Esau and Jacob buried him.

The names of Jacob's children are given again because these were the twelve tribes of Israel. Jacob finally was home with his father Isaac in Mamre (Hebron), the same place Abraham had stayed.

Since Isaac was nearly blind at the time Jacob had left, I am sure he must have been completely so by this time and probably very feeble, as implied by "old and full of years." At 180 years old, Isaac died. Since he was about 135 years old when Jacob left, that meant Jacob was gone about 25 years. Also, since Isaac was 60 years old when his sons were born (25:26), that meant Jacob and Esau were 120 years old at his death. Though his death is mentioned here, it is probably not chronologically correct, because it seems that Isaac was still living when Joseph was sold as a slave and taken to Egypt. (Joseph was born 18 years after Jacob left his father - 31:38, 30:25, and Isaac died at 180 years of age -

35:29- when Esau and Jacob were about 120 years old. Joseph was only 17 when he was sold.) Isaac was then buried in the cave at Machpelah where Rebekah, Abraham and Sarah were buried (49:31).

Jacob and Esau were still united as a family, since they both were there to bury their father. Though they did not live in the same place, all the things of the past had been forgiven.

Gen 36:1 This is the account of Esau (that is, Edom). 36:2 Esau took his wives from the women of Canaan: Adah daughter of Elon the Hittite, and Oholibamah daughter of Anah and granddaughter of Zibeon the Hivite-- 36:3 also Basemath daughter of Ishmael and sister of Nebaioth. 36:4 Adah bore Eliphaz to Esau, Basemath bore Reuel, 36:5 and Oholibamah bore Jeush, Jalam and Korah. These were the sons of Esau, who were born to him in Canaan. 36:6 Esau took his wives and sons and daughters and all the members of his household, as well as his livestock and all his other animals and all the goods he had acquired in Canaan, and moved to a land some distance from his brother Jacob. 36:7 Their possessions were too great for them to remain together; the land where they were staying could not support them both because of their livestock. 36:8 So Esau (that is, Edom) settled in the hill country of Seir.

A list of Esau's descendants is listed throughout chapter 36, which is the beginning of "The account of Esau." As mentioned at the beginning of this commentary, Genesis can be divided nicely into ten "written accounts" or records that had been compiled. This is the beginning of the ninth record.

Leave it to Esau to give us what appears to be a contradiction upon first glance. Verse two says that Esau married more than one wife: *Adah, daughter of Elon the Hittite*; **Basemath, daughter of Ishmael and sister of Nebaioth**; Oholibamah, daughter of Anah. However, we read earlier, "When Esau was forty years old, he married *Judith daughter of Beeri the Hittite*, and also **Basemath daughter of Elon** the Hittite" (Gen 26:34), and "he went to Ishmael and married Mahalath, the sister of Nebaioth" (28:9). From this we see the following:

1. Basemath seems to be daughter of Ishmael (v.3) and daughter of Elon (26:34).
2. Both Adah and Basemath seem to be daughters of Elon the Hittite.
3. Basemath and Mahalath were sisters of Nebaioth.
4. There are five names listed: Basemath, Oholibamah, Adah, Mahalath, Judith.

These apparent discrepancies can be explained by realizing that, more often than not, people had more than one name. It is very probable that when Esau first married, these women had a family name, and soon after they received another name. It seems that Esau had already been married for 80 years (26:34) and these names were just now being recorded. Note the following solutions:

168

1. Judith was probably the same as Oholibamah and thus Anah and Beeri were the same.
2. Basemath, daughter of Elon was the same as Adah.
3. Basemath, daughter of Ishmael was the same as Mahalath.
4. Esau may have married more than three wives.

Esau had five sons who would become the Edomites. Because Jacob and Esau both had so many material blessings, they had to move a good distance apart. Esau moved south into the mountainous regions on the southeast side of the Dead Sea. This area used to be called Seir. The Edomites took over the Horite regions (Deut 2:12, 22) both by force and assimilation by intermarriage. Thus Seir and Edom would become known as one and the same. However, the rest of Seir's descendants are listed in verses 20-28. It is also interesting to note that there was much sandstone that is reddish in color in the area of Seir. With Edom (meaning "red," 25:30) this was very appropriate.

Gen 36:9 This is the account of Esau the father of the Edomites in the hill country of Seir. 36:10 These are the names of Esau's sons: Eliphaz, the son of Esau's wife Adah, and Reuel, the son of Esau's wife Basemath. 36:11 The sons of Eliphaz: Teman, Omar, Zepho, Gatam and Kenaz. 36:12 Esau's son Eliphaz also had a concubine named Timna, who bore him Amalek. These were grandsons of Esau's wife Adah. 36:13 The sons of Reuel: Nahath, Zerah, Shammah and Mizzah. These were grandsons of Esau's wife Basemath. 36:14 The sons of Esau's wife Oholibamah daughter of Anah and granddaughter of Zibeon, whom she bore to Esau: Jeush, Jalam and Korah. 36:15 These were the chiefs among Esau's descendants: The sons of Eliphaz the firstborn of Esau: Chiefs Teman, Omar, Zepho, Kenaz, 36:16 Korah, Gatam and Amalek. These were the chiefs descended from Eliphaz in Edom; they were grandsons of Adah. 36:17 The sons of Esau's son Reuel: Chiefs Nahath, Zerah, Shammah and Mizzah. These were the chiefs descended from Reuel in Edom; they were grandsons of Esau's wife Basemath. 36:18 The sons of Esau's wife Oholibamah: Chiefs Jeush, Jalam and Korah. These were the chiefs descended from Esau's wife Oholibamah daughter of Anah. 36:19 These were the sons of Esau (that is, Edom), and these were their chiefs.

We now have listed the sons and grandsons of Esau, all of whom became "chiefs," showing importance. Out of the 11 grandsons mentioned, seven came from Eliphaz and four from Reuel. In addition to the grandsons, three sons were named from Oholibamah, making 14 leaders all together.

Note also in verse 12 that the wife of Eliphaz is not mentioned yet his concubine is. This is probably because of her notable offspring, Amalek. The Amalekites would live further west than the rest of the Edomites and became dire enemies of the Israelites. They would be the first people to deny entrance into the promised land when the Israelites requested safe passage (Exodus 17:8).

The fact that Eliphaz was an Edomite is interesting. We see that Job's friend was named Eliphaz the Temanite (Job 2:11) and that Job himself lived in the land of Uz (Job 1:1). This leads us to believe that Job lived in Edom, because of the following: 1) the common names of Eliphaz, 2) the mention of Uz in Genesis 36:28 as one of Esau's descendants, and 3) the mention of Temanites in Genesis 36:31 also ruling Edom.

Gen 36:20 These were the sons of Seir the Horite, who were living in the region: Lotan, Shobal, Zibeon, Anah, 36:21 Dishon, Ezer and Dishan. These sons of Seir in Edom were Horite chiefs. 36:22 The sons of Lotan: Hori and Homam. Timna was Lotan's sister. 36:23 The sons of Shobal: Alvan, Manahath, Ebal, Shepho and Onam. 36:24 The sons of Zibeon: Aiah and Anah. This is the Anah who discovered the hot springs in the desert while he was grazing the donkeys of his father Zibeon. 36:25 The children of Anah: Dishon and Oholibamah daughter of Anah. 36:26 The sons of Dishon : Hemdan, Eshban, Ithran and Keran. 36:27 The sons of Ezer: Bilhan, Zaavan and Akan. 36:28 The sons of Dishan: Uz and Aran. 36:29 These were the Horite chiefs: Lotan, Shobal, Zibeon, Anah, 36:30 Dishon, Ezer and Dishan. These were the Horite chiefs, according to their divisions, in the land of Seir.

Here we see the descendants of Seir listed because they eventually became assimilated into the Edomites through intermarriage. Seir's sons must have lived at the same time as Isaac because Esau married Anah's daughter, Oholibamah (v. 25). Though 19 sons are listed, Oholibamah was the only daughter named, probably because of this connection with Esau.

One daughter of Seir himself is also mentioned in verse 23. Timna was called "Lotan's sister" and since Lotan was a son of Seir, obviously Timna was his daughter. Also, since she was called "sister" rather than daughter, this leads us to suspect Timna was the daughter of only one of many wives of Seir.

Zibeon had two sons (v. 24). Of those two, Anah is said to have discovered hot springs in the desert. An alternate translation is seen in the KJV which says that Anah had found "mules in the wilderness, as he fed the asses of Zibeon his father." The Hebrew word is *yem* and has an unclear meaning (only used this one time in all of Scripture.) It can mean either hot water or mules so one can only take it in context and there is not much to go on. Most Jewish writers believe it to mean mules, but it is still left open to interpretation. Whatever it is, it was noteworthy enough to include in this genealogy, and Anah was well known for this discovery. It seems that a hot spring would not have been a discovery of great fame.

One must also be careful not to confuse the two Anahs. Verse 25 clearly shows that the Anah who bore Oholibamah was a different person. One was the son of Seir (v. 20) and the other a son of Zibeon (v. 24).

A similar account of Seir's descendants that is somewhat abbreviated is found in 1 Chronicles 1:38-42. Again, these were tribal chiefs and men of renown.

Gen 36:31 These were the kings who reigned in Edom before any Israelite king reigned : 36:32 Bela son of Beor became king of Edom. His

city was named Dinhabah. 36:33 When Bela died, Jobab son of Zerah from Bozrah succeeded him as king. 36:34 When Jobab died, Husham from the land of the Temanites succeeded him as king. 36:35 When Husham died, Hadad son of Bedad, who defeated Midian in the country of Moab, succeeded him as king. His city was named Avith. 36:36 When Hadad died, Samlah from Masrekah succeeded him as king. 36:37 When Samlah died, Shaul from Rehoboth on the river succeeded him as king. 36:38 When Shaul died, Baal-Hanan son of Acbor succeeded him as king. 36:39 When Baal-Hanan son of Acbor died, Hadad succeeded him as king. His city was named Pau, and his wife's name was Mehetabel daughter of Matred, the daughter of Me-Zahab.

These names are a list of kings in Edom who reigned long after Esau was dead, continuing up to the time of Moses. Even though Israel had no king at this time, Edom did. In fact, the surrounding kings are what made Israel (many years later) desire a king. Moses never experienced a time when Israel was ruled by kings, although he knew they would one day have them (Deut 17:14-20). It was probably a good thing, because Israel had 19 kings and none of them were Godly. Judah ended up having 20 kings, and only 8 of them followed the Lord. It was this kind of leadership that caused the Israelites' destruction and Babylonian captivity.

The names in the above list are not known elsewhere in the Scriptures. It is interesting that it is mentioned that each of the eight kings died (except the last one, Hadad, who may still have been alive when this account was written). It is most probable that these kings died by war or assassination.

Gen 36:40 These were the chiefs descended from Esau, by name, according to their clans and regions: Timna, Alvah, Jetheth, 36:41 Oholibamah, Elah, Pinon, 36:42 Kenaz, Teman, Mibzar, 36:43 Magdiel and Iram. These were the chiefs of Edom, according to their settlements in the land they occupied. This was Esau the father of the Edomites.

These last verses list eleven of the most important chiefs of Edom. They seem to be listed in a geographical order (v. 40). We see these names listed again in 1 Chronicles 1:35-54, so obviously they were important enough for the author of Chronicles to mention them again, perhaps to make a clear distinction between the chosen people of Israel and the nation of Edom. However, eventually the descendants of Edom would be wiped away from the earth, because during the Exodus the Israelites were not even allowed to cross through the land of Edom (Num 20:18). As a result, God judged them (2 Sam 8:14; Isa 34:5-6, 11; Jer 49:17-20; Joel 3:19; Amos 1:9-12; Mal 1:4). One good example of this judgment was predicted in Obadiah, which reads, "The house of Esau will be stubble, and they will set it on fire and consume it. There will be no survivors from the house of Esau. The LORD has spoken" (Obadiah 1:18; see notes on 25:19).

Gen 37:1 Jacob lived in the land where his father had stayed, the land of Canaan. 37:2 This is the account of Jacob. Joseph, a young man of seventeen, was tending the flocks with his brothers, the sons of Bilhah and the sons of Zilpah, his father's wives, and he brought their father a bad report about them. 37:3 Now Israel loved Joseph more than any of his other sons, because he had been born to him in his old age; and he made a richly ornamented robe for him. 37:4 When his brothers saw that their father loved him more than any of them, they hated him and could not speak a kind word to him.

The events in chapter 37 actually took place prior to Isaac's death (See notes on 35:35) when Jacob was living in Hebron (35:27; 37:14). Joseph was only 17 (v. 2) and was around 15 when his mother died (35:19) just before reaching Hebron.

The fact that Jacob stayed in the land of Canaan was important because, though they were foreigners now, this was the promised land. Esau, on the other hand, had left Canaan; it had no part in his future, since he was not under the covenant.

Verse two now begins the final "account of" section in Genesis, as mentioned in our introduction. This section was written mainly to record the life of Joseph, who would save the covenant family by bringing them into Egypt and, therefore, set the stage for God's exodus.

Joseph was tending the flocks with Dan and Naphtali (Bilhah's sons), Gad and Asher (Zilpah's sons -35:25-26). It is most likely that these boys were closest to Joseph's age, as Benjamin was too young to be shepherding at this time and Judah, Levi, Simeon and Reuben would have been much older. Joseph was Israel's favorite son (v. 3) and the rest of the family knew it. Just as younger brothers often tend to do, Joseph tattled on his brothers for something they had done. A combination of his being favorite and a tattler did not make Joseph a well liked brother.

Israel had made a "richly ornamented" coat for Joseph. Sometimes it is referred to as the "coat of many colors." However, the Hebrew for colors is *passim,* and it is uncertain what its meaning really is. Many believe that it simply means long sleeves. In 2 Samuel 13:18 it is described as something that the virgin daughters of the king wore. In any case, it is likely that it indicated Joseph had some authority and was a type of foreman among his brothers (probably not expected to do heavy work); just one more thing to turn his brothers against him.

Gen 37:5 Joseph had a dream, and when he told it to his brothers, they hated him all the more. 37:6 He said to them, "Listen to this dream I had: 37:7 We were binding sheaves of grain out in the field when suddenly my sheaf rose and stood upright, while your sheaves gathered around mine and bowed down to it." 37:8 His brothers said to him, "Do you intend to reign over us? Will you actually rule us?" And they hated him all the more because of his dream and what he had said. 37:9 Then he had another dream, and he told it to his brothers. "Listen," he said, "I had another

dream, and this time the sun and moon and eleven stars were bowing down to me." 37:10 When he told his father as well as his brothers, his father rebuked him and said, "What is this dream you had? Will your mother and I and your brothers actually come and bow down to the ground before you?" 37:11 His brothers were jealous of him, but his father kept the matter in mind.

On two separate nights Joseph had dreams which he probably should have kept to himself. However, Joseph's apparent boastfulness was not one of his finer qualities. Not only was Joseph the favorite, a tattler and proud, but now he was having these dreams which seemed to suggest his family would one day bow down before him (v. 8).

The first dream consisted of sheaves of grain out in the field. His brother's sheaves had risen up and bowed down before Joseph's. The brothers properly interpreted this dream (though did not believe it) that they would be ruled by Joseph. In Deuteronomy Joseph is called the "prince" of his brothers (Deut 33:16).

The second dream showed the sun, moon and eleven stars bowing down before Joseph. After Joseph told his brothers and father (because his father was in this dream), Jacob rebuked him. This rebuke may have seemed a result of his disbelief of the dream; however, Jacob kept the matter in his mind. Therefore, the rebuke may have been given to instruct and keep Joseph's pride from getting the best of him in the future. But it was too late; his brothers had already had enough of Joseph.

The dream itself was understood by the family, though in our day it would seem less clear. However, we see a similar event recorded by John, "A great and wondrous sign appeared in heaven: a woman clothed with the sun, with the moon under her feet and a crown of twelve stars on her head" (Rev 12:1). Taken in context, we see that here as well the twelve stars represent the 12 tribes of Israel. Since Joseph had 11 brothers, all future tribes of Israel, only eleven stars bowed down before him in his dream. The sun and the moon represented Jacob (Israel) and either Rachel or Leah (Rachel had already died, so probably Leah is meant). The dream would later come true in 42:6; 43:26; and 44:14.

Gen 37:12 Now his brothers had gone to graze their father's flocks near Shechem, 37:13 and Israel said to Joseph, "As you know, your brothers are grazing the flocks near Shechem. Come, I am going to send you to them." "Very well," he replied. 37:14 So he said to him, "Go and see if all is well with your brothers and with the flocks, and bring word back to me." Then he sent him off from the Valley of Hebron. When Joseph arrived at Shechem, 37:15 a man found him wandering around in the fields and asked him, "What are you looking for?" 37:16 He replied, "I'm looking for my brothers. Can you tell me where they are grazing their flocks?" 37:17 "They have moved on from here," the man answered. "I heard them say, 'Let's go to Dothan.'" So Joseph went after his brothers and found them near Dothan.

Joseph's brothers had taken their flocks to Shechem, the place that Simeon and Levi had earlier destroyed, causing them to be hated in that area (34:30). Though they still owned land there (33:19, John 4:5), it was perhaps because of this that Jacob was nervous and decided to send Joseph to check on them and make sure "all is well." Shechem was nearly 50 miles from Hebron, so it took Joseph a few days to travel there.

When Joseph arrived at Shechem, his brothers could not be found. A man noticed Joseph looking for something so he asked if he could be of help. When Joseph asked for his brothers' whereabouts, the man told him he overheard that they were going to Dothan. No doubt the people of Shechem kept a close eye on the Israelite brothers while they were there. Dothan was about 15 miles north of Shechem and was a well established city at that time. The name Dothan is believed to mean "two cisterns." Joseph would be put into one of these cisterns, which was dried out (v. 22).

Gen 37:18 But they saw him in the distance, and before he reached them, they plotted to kill him. 37:19 "Here comes that dreamer!" they said to each other. 37:20 "Come now, let's kill him and throw him into one of these cisterns and say that a ferocious animal devoured him. Then we'll see what comes of his dreams." 37:21 When Reuben heard this, he tried to rescue him from their hands. "Let's not take his life," he said. 37:22 "Don't shed any blood. Throw him into this cistern here in the desert, but don't lay a hand on him." Reuben said this to rescue him from them and take him back to his father.

Even while Joseph was at a distance and could not even say a word to provoke them, the brothers plotted to kill him. It appears that they were still upset over Joseph's dream. It is hard for us to understand such lack of love between brothers, but coming from a polygamous home there probably was not the bond between them that could have been had they all had the same mother.

Reuben was not only the oldest but also the wisest in this situation. Although Reuben had not made the best choices in the past (35:22), he certainly showed more maturity now. Since Reuben was the oldest and was losing his birthright to Joseph (1 Chron 5:1), he had more cause to hate him than anyone else. But, rather than blame Joseph, Reuben tried to help him by getting the brothers to throw him into a pit, thinking he could return later and rescue Joseph. It is likely that Reuben even told Joseph what he was planning, because he would later spare Reuben because of this. When Joseph was in Egypt he would hold Simeon, the second oldest, prisoner (although they didn't know it was Joseph) rather than Reuben (42:22-24).

Simeon and Levi both had plenty of practice with deceit and murder at Shechem (Genesis 34). Though they may have been able to justify in their own minds the murders at Shechem, Joseph had done nothing. As Timothy would say, " their consciences have been seared as with a hot iron" (1 Tim 4:2).

Gen 37:23 So when Joseph came to his brothers, they stripped him of his robe--the richly ornamented robe he was wearing-- 37:24 and they

took him and threw him into the cistern. Now the cistern was empty; there was no water in it. 37:25 As they sat down to eat their meal, they looked up and saw a caravan of Ishmaelites coming from Gilead. Their camels were loaded with spices, balm and myrrh, and they were on their way to take them down to Egypt. 37:26 Judah said to his brothers, "What will we gain if we kill our brother and cover up his blood? 37:27 Come, let's sell him to the Ishmaelites and not lay our hands on him; after all, he is our brother, our own flesh and blood." His brothers agreed. 37:28 So when the Midianite merchants came by, his brothers pulled Joseph up out of the cistern and sold him for twenty shekels of silver to the Ishmaelites, who took him to Egypt.

The first thing the brothers did was strip Joseph of the hated robe and then threw him into the dry cistern. While the brothers were eating they looked up and saw a caravan of Ishmaelites. Judah also seemed to be apprehensive about killing Joseph, although he still disliked him enough to get rid of him. He proposed to sell Joseph to the Ishmaelites so they did not have to shed any blood; in addition they would get some money out of the deal.

In verse 28 the Ishmaelites were also called Midianites. In verse 36 the NIV footnote tells us they were also called Medanites. All three were interrelated, since Midian, Medan and Ishmael were all sons of Abraham (25:2). We see in Judges 8:22-26 that the same names were also interchanged. It is probable that the caravan consisted of members of each tribe.

The caravan was coming from Gilead, which was southeast of the Sea of Galilee. They were going down to Egypt to sell balm, which was a type of oil or gum taken from the stems of certain trees and used for healing (Jer 51:8). Apparently Gilead was known for its balm, because Jeremiah wrote, "Is there no balm in Gilead? Is there no physician there? Why then is there no healing for the wound of my people?" (Jer 8:22), and "Go up to Gilead and get balm, O Virgin Daughter of Egypt. But you multiply remedies in vain; there is no healing for you" (Jer 46:11).

They were also going to sell Myrrh or labdanum, an aromatic substance taken from the leaves of the cistus rose. It was used in beauty treatments (Est 2:12), for perfume (Ps 45:8, Pr 7:17, SS 3:6, 5:13), mixed with wine to kill pain (Mark 15:23), a gift for kings (Matt 2:11), and for Jesus' burial (John 19:39-40).

Though the text does not say so here, while the brothers bartered Joseph's life away he was crying out for help and pleading with his brothers not to sell him (42:21). The brothers did not care, however, and sold him for 20 shekels of silver. This was the price to dedicate a young boy to the Lord (Lev 27:5). This is significant, as Joseph was indeed being sold to accomplish God's plan of bringing all of Israel into Egypt. A slave would have been sold for at least 30 pieces of silver (Exodus 21:32), so the Midianites made a good purchase.

Gen 37:29 When Reuben returned to the cistern and saw that Joseph was not there, he tore his clothes. 37:30 He went back to his brothers and said, "The boy isn't there! Where can I turn now?" 37:31

Then they got Joseph's robe, slaughtered a goat and dipped the robe in the blood. 37:32 They took the ornamented robe back to their father and said, "We found this. Examine it to see whether it is your son's robe." 37:33 He recognized it and said, "It is my son's robe! Some ferocious animal has devoured him. Joseph has surely been torn to pieces." 37:34 Then Jacob tore his clothes, put on sackcloth and mourned for his son many days. 37:35 All his sons and daughters came to comfort him, but he refused to be comforted. "No," he said, "in mourning will I go down to the grave to my son." So his father wept for him. 37:36 Meanwhile, the Midianites sold Joseph in Egypt to Potiphar, one of Pharaoh's officials, the captain of the guard.

We do not know where Reuben was when Joseph was sold, but when he returned he became filled with sorrow. The tearing of his clothes was a sign of mourning.

When he returned to his brothers he was no doubt afraid; what would they tell Jacob? They decided to take Joseph's robe and dip it in the blood of a slaughtered goat. They then took the robe back to Jacob, who filled in the blanks for them. The brothers lied in saying that they had "found" the robe; the silent lie was not confessing the truth. After this, Jacob decided for himself that a wild animal had killed Joseph. Jacob then tore his clothes and put on the rough sackcloth used for mourning.

All of Jacob's sons and daughters came to comfort him, though he could not be comforted. This is the first mention of any daughters other than Dinah, but they will be mentioned again in 46:7,15. Note the name "Jacob" is used rather than "Israel," because Jacob was clinging to his son and not finding comfort in God's promises. So great was Jacob's grief that he said he would mourn until the day he went to the grave. The word used for "grave" is *Sheol*, which is simply the place of departed spirits and is seen 65 times in the Old Testament (see Job 3:13-19).

While Jacob mourned, the Midianites sold Joseph to Potiphar in Egypt. Potiphar was the captain of the guard for Pharaoh. This meant that he was the head of the prison and perhaps the executioner of those sentenced to die. It is also interesting that Potiphar was called an official. The Hebrew is *saris,* which means a eunuch. This may explain why Potiphar's wife so avidly pursued Joseph.

Gen 38:1 At that time, Judah left his brothers and went down to stay with a man of Adullam named Hirah. 38:2 There Judah met the daughter of a Canaanite man named Shua. He married her and lay with her; 38:3 she became pregnant and gave birth to a son, who was named Er. 38:4 She conceived again and gave birth to a son and named him Onan. 38:5 She gave birth to still another son and named him Shelah. It was at Kezib that she gave birth to him.

Chapter 38 is the only record of what was going on with the rest of the Israelites for the 20 years Joseph was in Egypt (other than the time they went to

Egypt for food). The record of Judah is traced because it was through him that the Messiah would come (Mat 1:3; Rev 5:5).

Whether the selling of Joseph had anything to do with Judah moving to Adallam or not, we do not know. Perhaps his frustration with his brothers drove him away (37:26). Adallam was southwest of Jerusalem (2 Chron 11:5-7), and while there he met a Canaanite woman. Judah should have known better than to marry outside his spiritual family, but his physical lusts apparently got the better of him.

It wasn't long and they had their first child, so Judah named him Er, meaning "watcher." Soon after they had a second son whom the mother named Onan, meaning "strong." (The names Er and Onan have also been found in records of Mesopotamia around this time). Then they moved to Kezib where a third son was born and the mother named him Shelah, the meaning of which is not known. The fact that the last two sons were named by his wife may suggest that she wore the pants in the family. Kezib may have been the same as Aczib in Joshua 15:44, which was about three miles west of Adallam. In fact, we see that the descendants of Shelah were called "men of Cozeba" in 1 Chron 4:21-22.

Gen 38:6 Judah got a wife for Er, his firstborn, and her name was Tamar. 38:7 But Er, Judah's firstborn, was wicked in the Lord's sight; so the LORD put him to death. 38:8 Then Judah said to Onan, "Lie with your brother's wife and fulfill your duty to her as a brother-in-law to produce offspring for your brother." 38:9 But Onan knew that the offspring would not be his; so whenever he lay with his brother's wife, he spilled his semen on the ground to keep from producing offspring for his brother. 38:10 What he did was wicked in the Lord's sight; so he put him to death also.

Judah may have tried to find a woman with good morals for his son because he was now seeing the importance of a good wife. Tamar was selected as the wife for Er, perhaps in hopes of bringing Er to repentance and faith. However, Er was wicked in God's sight and unsuitable for Tamar, so He killed him. It was through Tamar that the next person would come for the Messianic line.

In those days they had a practice called the "levirate marriage," coming from the Latin *levir*, meaning "brother-in-law." It stated that if your brother left a widow, the next oldest in the line of that family was to marry that widow, and thus bear offspring for the brother who had died. That way his name would be carried on. The practice was outlined in Deuteronomy 25:5-6 and was still practiced in the New Testament era (Matt 22:24). Sometimes if the brother was not available, the closest living relative was then called a "kinsman-redeemer," as seen in Ruth 4:5-6. It was because of this practice that Judah told his second oldest son, Onan, to lie with Tamar and "fulfill his duty."

Onan was obviously a selfish man. He knew that any child that he and Tamar had would not be his, but rather his brother's; therefore, he would always spill his seed on the ground so that no offspring would be produced for his brother. In addition, since Onan was the oldest now, he would inherit the double portion of his father's possessions. However, if he had a son for Er, then that son could legally receive the double portion. This betrayal was wicked in God's eyes so Onan was put to death. However, it did not seem to be the fact that Onan "spilled his seed" that angered God; it was his rebellion against producing offspring for his brother. As a result of this practice, however, the term "onanism" has become known as a means of birth control. This also may lead us to believe that perhaps Er was killed because he refused to consummate the marriage that his father had set up.

Gen 38:11 Judah then said to his daughter-in-law Tamar, "Live as a widow in your father's house until my son Shelah grows up." For he thought, "He may die too, just like his brothers." So Tamar went to live in her father's house. 38:12 After a long time Judah's wife, the daughter of Shua, died. When Judah had recovered from his grief, he went up to Timnah, to the men who were shearing his sheep, and his friend Hirah the Adullamite went with him.

After two of his sons died, Judah was afraid to give Shelah to Tamar. Apparently Shelah was still very young; therefore, Judah lied and told Tamar to wait at her fathers home until Shelah was old enough to marry. However, Judah never had any intention of giving his last son to this woman. Meanwhile, though Tamar would live under her own father's roof, she technically belonged to Judah's family.

Shelah will never marry Tamar. We are not told who he later married, though we know he did because in Numbers 26:20 we see his descendants called the Shelanites.

Perhaps as a judgment upon Judah for his deception, God had his wife pass away. Judah must have been very young (late 30's), which suggests his wife's death was anything but natural.

Once Judah finished grieving, he and his friend Hirah went to Timnah in the hill country of Judah (Josh 15:48,57), where his flock was being sheared. Sheep shearing was often viewed as an occasion to celebrate; it is possible, therefore, that Judah and Hirah went not only to take care of the sheep but to have a good time, as well.

Gen 38:13 When Tamar was told, "Your father-in-law is on his way to Timnah to shear his sheep," 38:14 she took off her widow's clothes, covered herself with a veil to disguise herself, and then sat down at the entrance to Enaim, which is on the road to Timnah. For she saw that, though Shelah had now grown up, she had not been given to him as his wife. 38:15 When Judah saw her, he thought she was a prostitute, for she had covered her face. 38:16 Not realizing that she was his daughter-in-law, he went over to her by the roadside and said, "Come now, let me sleep with you." "And what will you give me to sleep with you?" she asked. 38:17 "I'll send you a young goat from my flock," he said. "Will you give me something as a pledge until you send it?" she asked. 38:18 He said, "What pledge should I give you?" "Your seal and its cord, and the staff in your hand," she answered. So he gave them to her and slept with her, and she

became pregnant by him. 38:19 After she left, she took off her veil and put on her widow's clothes again.

When Tamar heard that her father-in-law, Judah, went to Timnah, she quickly changed out of her widow's clothing and got into a prostitutes attire. She now knew that Judah had no intention of giving Shelah to her, so she sat near the roadside (as was common for prostitutes -Jer. 3:2) at the entrance to Enaim on the way to Timnah.

When Judah arrived and saw her, he thought she was a temple prostitute because of her veil, which prevented her from being recognized. It is well known that in many of these pagan cities, all the women living there were required to act as prostitutes and dedicate themselves to various gods. It is most likely that Tamar was pretending to consecrate herself to Asarte, the sister-spouse of the god Baal. These prostitutes were often called "*qedeshah,*" meaning "one set apart." In verses 21-22 we see that Tamar was referred to as a *qedeshah* in the Hebrew.

He then asked to purchase her "services" with a goat from his flock. Since he did not have it with him, Tamar requested that his staff, seal and cord be left as a pledge. The seal was often used to leave an impression on the clay seal of documents. Each person had their own seal, and letters could thus be recognized by it. The cord was probably the string that went around the neck or arm and held the seal.

Judah then slept with Tamar without knowing her true identity, and she became pregnant. After he left, Tamar went back to her home and put her widow's clothes back on. Little did either know that Tamar was bearing the ancestor of Christ.

Gen 38:20 Meanwhile Judah sent the young goat by his friend the Adullamite in order to get his pledge back from the woman, but he did not find her. 38:21 He asked the men who lived there, "Where is the shrine prostitute who was beside the road at Enaim?" "There hasn't been any shrine prostitute here," they said. 38:22 So he went back to Judah and said, "I didn't find her. Besides, the men who lived there said, 'There hasn't been any shrine prostitute here.'" 38:23 Then Judah said, "Let her keep what she has, or we will become a laughingstock. After all, I did send her this young goat, but you didn't find her." 38:24 About three months later Judah was told, "Your daughter-in-law Tamar is guilty of prostitution, and as a result she is now pregnant." Judah said, "Bring her out and have her burned to death!" 38:25 As she was being brought out, she sent a message to her father-in-law. "I am pregnant by the man who owns these," she said. And she added, "See if you recognize whose seal and cord and staff these are." 38:26 Judah recognized them and said, "She is more righteous than I, since I wouldn't give her to my son Shelah." And he did not sleep with her again.

When Judah returned to his flock he had his friend, Hirah, take the goat back to the woman to pay her fee. Whether Judah was ashamed of his sin we do not know, but perhaps sending his trusted friend (who may have been with him and knew about it anyway) rather than a servant, may indicate that he didn't want anyone to know about it (see v. 23).

In any case, Hirah was unable to locate this woman, even after asking the locals. Apparently there were no shrine prostitutes around that town. When Judah heard this he felt that he had kept his end of the bargain and, therefore, did not need to go out of his way to search for her or his cheap, easily replaced seal, cord and staff. Besides, if too many people found out about this he would have become a laughing-stock. This also suggests that Judah was trying to keep his endeavor quiet.

About three months later, news reached Judah that Tamar had been guilty of prostitution and was pregnant. Without hesitation Judah ordered that she be brought to him and burned. Finally, Judah had what he wanted, an honest way out of his predicament of giving his son Shelah to Tamar in marriage. The practice of burning or stoning for punishment of prostitution was still used after the Exodus (Lev 21:9; Deut 22:20-24). Judah had every right to make this judgment in a normal case, even in an idol-filled land like Canaan. According to the Code of Hammurabi, the Canaanite laws said that any woman caught in adultery was to be put to death; however, the same did not apply for the man. This double standard may have come about because in adultery it was the man's name who was shamed by having someone else's name attached to a member of his family.

When Tamar was brought out, she sent a message to Judah, telling him that the father of her baby was the one who owned the seal, staff and cord that she presented. It is interesting that Tamar did not simply come out and blame Judah; rather, she asked Judah who these things might belong to. In so doing, Judah was forced to face his sin, confess and repent. It is good that Judah realized "she was more righteous" than he was. Though Tamar was spared from death and would now live under Judah's roof, she would have to live alone. It was no longer right for Shelah to be given to Tamar, nor was it right for Judah to sleep with her anymore. Therefore, Judah would accept this son as his heir but would not accept Tamar as his wife.

Gen 38:27 When the time came for her to give birth, there were twin boys in her womb. 38:28 As she was giving birth, one of them put out his hand; so the midwife took a scarlet thread and tied it on his wrist and said, "This one came out first." 38:29 But when he drew back his hand, his brother came out, and she said, "So this is how you have broken out!" And he was named Perez. 38:30 Then his brother, who had the scarlet thread on his wrist, came out and he was given the name Zerah.

When Tamar gave birth, she had twins. This story is very similar to Jacob and Esau, who fought within the womb and right up through delivery (25:24-26). When giving birth, Zerah stuck his hand out first, so the midwife put a scarlet thread around it so they would know which child was the first born. However, Zerah pulled his hand back in and Perez came out first. Zerah means "rising" and Perez means "breaking through." Both sons would have large families in the tribe of Judah, but it was Perez who would lead us to David (Ruth 4:18-22) and, therefore, to Christ (Matt 1:1-6).

Even though Tamar seemed to have been deceptive in this situation, she would also have her name listed in the genealogy of Christ (Matt 1:3). It is interesting to note that only four women were named in the genealogy of Christ, and all four were non-Jews. Tamar was a Canaanite; Rahab was from Jericho and probably also a Canaanite; Ruth was a Moabite; and Bathsheba was probably a Hittite. All four women also had skeletons in their closets. We just discussed how Tamar posed as a prostitute; Rahab was a prostitute until she joined the Israelites and married Salmon; Ruth persuaded Boaz to marry her by first spending the night with him while he was drunk; and Bathsheba committed adultery with King David before she later married him. Out of these four, Rahab seems to have been the most morally corrupt (at one point in her life), yet she alone is mentioned in the great faith chapter of Hebrews (Heb 11:31). What a testimony for us today! There is no sin too great for Christ to forgive, and there is no sinner too sinful for Christ to love.

Gen 39:1 Now Joseph had been taken down to Egypt. Potiphar, an Egyptian who was one of Pharaoh's officials, the captain of the guard, bought him from the Ishmaelites who had taken him there. 39:2 The LORD was with Joseph and he prospered, and he lived in the house of his Egyptian master. 39:3 When his master saw that the LORD was with him and that the LORD gave him success in everything he did, 39:4 Joseph found favor in his eyes and became his attendant. Potiphar put him in charge of his household, and he entrusted to his care everything he owned. 39:5 From the time he put him in charge of his household and of all that he owned, the LORD blessed the household of the Egyptian because of Joseph. The blessing of the LORD was on everything Potiphar had, both in the house and in the field. 39:6 So he left in Joseph's care everything he had; with Joseph in charge, he did not concern himself with anything except the food he ate. Now Joseph was well-built and handsome,

Chapter 39 goes back to trace the events that were taking place in Egypt. We can not be certain at what time in history this was taking place; however, clues indicate it was around 1720 BC. The most complete account of rulers ever found in Egypt was written by an Egyptian priest named Manetho in the third century B.C.. Manetho named 31 dynasties, but the debate begins as to how many of these rulers reigned simultaneously in Upper and Lower Egypt. The first ruler was Menes, who is believed to have reigned any time from 5500 B.C. to 2000 B.C., depending on the Egyptologist. The consensus of most secular Egyptologists seems to be somewhere around 3100 B.C.; however, modern scholars have noted that this date could be drastically reduced. In any case, the majority believed that these events took place during the Hyksos dynasty. They were foreign invaders of Egypt around 1720 B.C. and were expelled from Egypt shortly after Joseph died, since the new ruler "did not know about Joseph" (Exodus 1:8).

Evidence that supports the idea that the Hyksos were ruling Egypt at this time is the fact that Potiphar is explained to be an "Egyptian" three times (v. 1, 2, 5). One would think that being in Egypt this would go without saying. However, with foreigners ruling, such as the Hyksos, true Egyptian rulers would have been few.

It turns out that Joseph had been sold to a captain of the guard named Potiphar, one of Pharaoh's officials. The LORD warmed Potiphar's heart toward Joseph. Just as Laban had seen the LORD bless Jacob, so Potiphar saw the LORD bless everything Joseph did; therefore, he was made a personal attendant. As attendant, Joseph was in charge of everything Potiphar owned and was a highly trusted friend.

Potiphar was also being blessed as a result of Joseph's blessings. It was just as God had earlier said to Abraham, "I will bless those who bless you, and whoever curses you I will curse; and all peoples on earth will be blessed through you" (Gen 12:3). A similar event also took place when Laban was blessed because of Jacob's presence (30:27).

Potiphar was also called an "official" of Pharaoh. The Hebrew word, *saris*, means eunuch, which fits well with the customary practices of these ancient lands. For example, in pagan countries like Sumeria, all important officers working in the king's court were castrated. This way the officers were more fully dedicated to the king, and it also kept any of them from sleeping with the queen, thereby reducing any chance of one taking over the throne.

We see the point stressed that the LORD was with Joseph (v. 3, 21, 23), showing God's intervention in this entire event. Even Stephen stresses this fact (Acts 7:9) to show that God had a plan for Israel's salvation long before their slavery and captivity.

The only thing Potiphar concerned himself with was eating. This may have been because Joseph obviously could not do that for him; however, there would have been other things Joseph could not do for Potiphar, as well. Therefore, it is most likely that this was because of religious reasons. Often times there were prescribed rituals for Egyptian food preparation and consumption. These were things that Potiphar would need to do himself.

Verse six closes by saying that Joseph was handsome. This will play a large role in his being thrown into prison in the following verses.

Gen 39:7 and after a while his master's wife took notice of Joseph and said, "Come to bed with me!" 39:8 But he refused. "With me in charge," he told her, "my master does not concern himself with anything in the house; everything he owns he has entrusted to my care. 39:9 No one is greater in this house than I am. My master has withheld nothing from me except you, because you are his wife. How then could I do such a wicked thing and sin against God?" 39:10 And though she spoke to Joseph day after day, he refused to go to bed with her or even be with her. 39:11 One day he went into the house to attend to his duties, and none of the household servants was inside. 39:12 She caught him by his cloak and said, "Come to bed with me!" But he left his cloak in her hand and ran out of the house. 39:13 When she saw that he had left his cloak in her hand and had run out

of the house, 39:14 she called her household servants. "Look," she said to them, "this Hebrew has been brought to us to make sport of us! He came in here to sleep with me, but I screamed. 39:15 When he heard me scream for help, he left his cloak beside me and ran out of the house."

One day Potiphar's wife took notice of Joseph's handsome appearance. The Hebrew word also shows a deep physical desire. She boldly asked Joseph to go to bed with her. However, Joseph respectfully turned her down, explaining how it would be not only a betrayal of her husband's trust but a sin, as well (v. 9). Even if Joseph's master would never know, God would: "The eyes of the LORD are everywhere, keeping watch on the wicked and the good" (Prov 15:3). Besides, any sin is a sin against God (Psalm 51:4).

This harassment went on day after day and Joseph even tried to avoid being around her because of it. One day while attending his normal duties, however, she grabbed Joseph by the cloak and demanded that he sleep with her since the servants were gone. If there was ever a time that they could have gotten away with it, that was it. Joseph again refused, however, keeping his values because of his faithful duty and love for the LORD. As he turned and ran, his cloak was left behind. Potiphar's wife had now had enough rejection and decided that if Joseph was too good for her, she was now going to destroy him. Looking down and seeing the cloak in her hand, she screamed for the servants to come inside the house and began to make up a story by simply switching roles with Joseph. She claimed that Joseph had tried to rape her and was making sport of her. She made it sound as if he was a danger not only to her, but to all the servants. She even blamed this on the fact that Joseph was a Hebrew foreigner (apparently she was also Egyptian).

Gen 39:16 She kept his cloak beside her until his master came home. 39:17 Then she told him this story: "That Hebrew slave you brought us came to me to make sport of me. 39:18 But as soon as I screamed for help, he left his cloak beside me and ran out of the house." 39:19 When his master heard the story his wife told him, saying, "This is how your slave treated me," he burned with anger. 39:20 Joseph's master took him and put him in prison, the place where the king's prisoners were confined. But while Joseph was there in the prison, 39:21 the LORD was with him; He showed him kindness and granted him favor in the eyes of the prison warden. 39:22 So the warden put Joseph in charge of all those held in the prison, and he was made responsible for all that was done there. 39:23 The warden paid no attention to anything under Joseph's care, because the LORD was with Joseph and gave him success in whatever he did.

When Potiphar returned he met a woman scorned. She continued to tell this "story" and almost seemed to put some of the blame on Potiphar because it was he who had brought in a Hebrew slave.

After hearing this "story," Potiphar "burned with anger" (v. 19). It is interesting to note that it did not specify who Potiphar was angry with. Though at first glance it seems obvious that it must have been Joseph, that may not have

183

been the case. Anyone living with such a selfish and worldly woman would have known her true character and, therefore, it is possible he may have questioned her truthfulness. It would have been legally justifiable to have had Joseph killed, especially since Potiphar was the "captain of the guard" (v. 1) who probably often acted as executioner. Normally, any slave caught in adultery would certainly have been put to death. Instead, Potiphar only put him in the prison that he himself was in charge of (40:3), and even that was with political prisoners rather than with the true criminals. With Potiphar showing such great trust and faith in Joseph, he no doubt found this difficult to believe and may have had enough doubt to question his wife's story. The only thing Potiphar could do to save face was act upon this accusation. Also, since the LORD was with Joseph, it is not unlikely that Potiphar continued to hold Joseph in high regard. However, do not be fooled into thinking this was an easy prison sentence for Joseph, because we read in Psalm 105:18-19, "They bruised his feet with shackles, his neck was put in irons, till what he foretold came to pass, till the word of the LORD proved him true."

Another noble note for Joseph is that, as far as the record goes, he never tried to defend himself. It may be that Joseph willingly submitted to God's plan, though it was unknown to him. Similarly, Jesus willingly gave His life (Is 53:7; 1 Pet 2:19-23).

In any case, while Joseph was in prison the LORD caused the warden to show him favor, and he was once again put in charge, this time over all the other prisoners. If Potiphar had truly believed his wife and held a grudge, it is doubtful that he would have allowed this to happen in his own prison (40:3). Therefore, Potiphar may have been forced to put Joseph in jail for appearance, so as to not be a laughing stock because of his unfaithful wife.

As always, things flourished under the care of God's servant. Likewise, today Christian employees seem to make the best workers, not only because God blesses them, but because while working they realize that it is for the Lord (See 1 Sam 10:7; Prov 16:3).

Gen 40:1 Some time later, the cupbearer and the baker of the king of Egypt offended their master, the king of Egypt. 40:2 Pharaoh was angry with his two officials, the chief cupbearer and the chief baker, 40:3 and put them in custody in the house of the captain of the guard, in the same prison where Joseph was confined. 40:4 The captain of the guard assigned them to Joseph, and he attended them. After they had been in custody for some time,

Joseph may have been in prison for years before the king's cupbearer and baker were put in jail. Since he was 17 when he was sold as a slave by his brothers (37:2) and thirty when he was put in charge of Egypt's famine preparation (41:46), he was either a servant of Potiphar or in prison for a total of 13 years. The cupbearer's job was to take care of the vineyards and wine for the king, as well as to make sure it was of good quality and safe. Likewise, the baker was in charge of keeping the king's food safe. Both men were called "officials," but again this meant they were eunuchs. We are not told why they were arrested, but it is most probable that the king was nearly poisoned or had at least heard about an assassination attempt.

Joseph was assigned to these two men and surely became very familiar with them, as they were also in prison for "some time" while the investigation to find the guilty party was continuing.

Gen 40:5 each of the two men--the cupbearer and the baker of the king of Egypt, who were being held in prison--had a dream the same night, and each dream had a meaning of its own. 40:6 When Joseph came to them the next morning, he saw that they were dejected. 40:7 So he asked Pharaoh's officials who were in custody with him in his master's house, "Why are your faces so sad today?" 40:8 "We both had dreams," they answered, "but there is no one to interpret them." Then Joseph said to them, "Do not interpretations belong to God? Tell me your dreams." 40:9 So the chief cupbearer told Joseph his dream. He said to him, "In my dream I saw a vine in front of me, 40:10 and on the vine were three branches. As soon as it budded, it blossomed, and its clusters ripened into grapes. 40:11 Pharaoh's cup was in my hand, and I took the grapes, squeezed them into Pharaoh's cup and put the cup in his hand." 40:12 "This is what it means," Joseph said to him. "The three branches are three days. 40:13 Within three days Pharaoh will lift up your head and restore you to your position, and you will put Pharaoh's cup in his hand, just as you used to do when you were his cupbearer. 40:14 But when all goes well with you, remember me and show me kindness; mention me to Pharaoh and get me out of this prison. 40:15 For I was forcibly carried off from the land of the Hebrews, and even here I have done nothing to deserve being put in a dungeon."

While in prison, both the cupbearer and the baker had dreams on the same night. Since Joseph was familiar with them, when he saw them the next day he could tell that something was bothering them (v. 6). When Joseph questioned their sadness, they told him they had had dreams but there was no one available to interpret them. In the ancient near east, dreams were considered to be an important means of predicting the future and, therefore, not understanding a dream would have been rather stressful. Apparently, dreams were interpreted often, but not in prison, of course.

Joseph responded by telling them that interpretations belonged to God and asked them to tell him their dreams. In so doing, Joseph was presenting himself as God's instrument in this revelation. However, Joseph clearly realized he was only the instrument, not the source (41:16,25,28; Dan 2:28). The cupbearer told Joseph his dream first, probably because he knew his innocence and did not have a guilty conscience.

The cupbearer's dream consisted of a vine with three branches that had budded and blossomed with grapes. The cupbearer saw himself squeeze the grapes into Pharaoh's cup and then present it to him. Joseph interpreted the dream, showing that in three days the cupbearer would have his old job back, as indicated by, "he will lift up your head." The same terminology can be found in

185

Psalms, which says, "But You are a shield around me, O LORD; You bestow glory on me and lift up my head" (Ps 3:3; see also 27:6).

Knowing that the cupbearer would again be working for the Pharaoh, Joseph asked him to remember him when he was freed by telling Pharaoh about him. He had hoped that perhaps a common bond had developed, since both were innocent and had been wrongly accused of a crime. However, Joseph apparently didn't make a big impression, because the cupbearer would forget about him for two years (v. 23). Nevertheless, eventually, he would play an important role in bringing Pharaoh's attention to Joseph (41:1,9-14).

Gen 40:16 When the chief baker saw that Joseph had given a favorable interpretation, he said to Joseph, "I too had a dream: On my head were three baskets of bread. 40:17 In the top basket were all kinds of baked goods for Pharaoh, but the birds were eating them out of the basket on my head." 40:18 "This is what it means," Joseph said. "The three baskets are three days. 40:19 Within three days Pharaoh will lift off your head and hang you on a tree. And the birds will eat away your flesh." 40:20 Now the third day was Pharaoh's birthday, and he gave a feast for all his officials. He lifted up the heads of the chief cupbearer and the chief baker in the presence of his officials: 40:21 He restored the chief cupbearer to his position, so that he once again put the cup into Pharaoh's hand, 40:22 but he hanged the chief baker, just as Joseph had said to them in his interpretation. 40:23 The chief cupbearer, however, did not remember Joseph; he forgot him.

Here we have an indication that the chief baker was guilty, even before his dream was interpreted. The baker saw that the cupbearer's dream had been favorable and, therefore, he felt maybe his would be good as well. Apparently, he was feeling guilty about something and felt that his dream would reveal what his conscience was already telling him.

Three was a significant number in both dreams because both would be fulfilled in three days. In one of the baskets (days) was food for Pharaoh; however, the birds were eating it. Assuming that the baker was in prison because he had perhaps tried to poison the Pharaoh, he may have thought (prior to seeing the cupbearer's dream interpretation) the dream could be telling him that since he had failed to protect Pharaoh's food, his crime would be exposed. In a sense, that is exactly what was interpreted by Joseph. However, the birds would eat the baker's flesh, not Pharaoh's food. Since birds were considered sacred, there probably were many around.

Three day's after the dreams was Pharaoh's birthday. It was customary for him to celebrate by giving a feast to his officials (eunuchs), and on that day everything that Joseph had predicted came true. The cupbearer was restored and the baker was hung. The criminal investigation had ended and the guilty party was executed. However, the innocent cupbearer forgot about Joseph in his excitement and would not remember him for another two years (41:1). It seems unusual that the cupbearer would forget such an important, life altering event, but I believe the LORD did not keep it in his mind because He knew Joseph needed a little more time. God had a plan, and Joseph would be very involved in that plan, which would also include dreams once again.

It might be noted that some commentators believe that the cupbearer was released because of the tradition in some countries for kings to grant amnesty to a prisoner on an important day (see Mat 27:16). However, it is unlikely that Pharaoh would have released a guilty man and brought him into his own house again, especially one in charge of Pharaoh's wine.

It is also interesting to see the changes in Joseph's personality over the years. At seventeen he was a proud and cocky youth who was ready to rule over his family just as his dream had foretold (Genesis 37). However, the LORD had training plans for him, just as he would later with Moses. Not until Joseph reached thirty years of age did he become the leader he once tried to be on his own. However, then he would be a humble and gracious leader who gave credit only to God. No doubt, Joseph of all people realized that, "Pride goes before destruction, a haughty spirit before a fall" (Prov 16:18). Thirty was an important age in Biblical times. In the Levitical priesthood, one had to be thirty years old before beginning service (Num 4:46-47). David did not become king until thirty years of age (2 Sam 5:4), nor did Christ begin His public ministry until He was thirty (Luke 3:23).

Gen 41:1 When two full years had passed, Pharaoh had a dream: He was standing by the Nile, 41:2 when out of the river there came up seven cows, sleek and fat, and they grazed among the reeds. 41:3 After them, seven other cows, ugly and gaunt, came up out of the Nile and stood beside those on the riverbank. 41:4 And the cows that were ugly and gaunt ate up the seven sleek, fat cows. Then Pharaoh woke up. 41:5 He fell asleep again and had a second dream: Seven heads of grain, healthy and good, were growing on a single stalk. 41:6 After them, seven other heads of grain sprouted--thin and scorched by the east wind. 41:7 The thin heads of grain swallowed up the seven healthy, full heads. Then Pharaoh woke up; it had been a dream.

Joseph spent another two years in prison before the LORD gave Pharaoh this dream. While standing by the Nile, Pharaoh saw seven fat, healthy cows grazing. Soon after watching them, seven other skinny cows came out of the Nile and ate the seven fat cows. No doubt, this dream caught Pharaoh's attention. In Egypt, the cow was a sacred animal that was made into the god Isis, the goddess of fertility. In the Egyptian "Book of the Dead," the most prominent and important document of Egyptology shows the god of vegetation was Osiris, a great bull accompanied by seven cows. Therefore, Pharaoh knew there was special significance to this dream. He must have been shocked to see the first set of fat cows "chewed up," as the Hebrew states, by the lean cows. This is even more strange when we realize that cows are vegetarians.

An added assurance that this was no simple dream was seen when Pharaoh had a second dream with many parallels to the first. This time seven poor heads of grain grew up and "swallowed" the seven healthy ones next to them. Though a strange dream, the similarities between the two were puzzling for Pharaoh.

Gen 41:8 In the morning his mind was troubled, so he sent for all the magicians and wise men of Egypt. Pharaoh told them his dreams, but no one could interpret them for him. 41:9 Then the chief cupbearer said to Pharaoh, "Today I am reminded of my shortcomings. 41:10 Pharaoh was once angry with his servants, and he imprisoned me and the chief baker in the house of the captain of the guard. 41:11 Each of us had a dream the same night, and each dream had a meaning of its own. 41:12 Now a young Hebrew was there with us, a servant of the captain of the guard. We told him our dreams, and he interpreted them for us, giving each man the interpretation of his dream. 41:13 And things turned out exactly as he interpreted them to us: I was restored to my position, and the other man was hanged."

The next morning Pharaoh was troubled (just like the baker and cupbearer, 40:6) because of his dream, so he sent for the magicians and wise men. The magicians were very skilled in dream interpretations and trickery. We will see about four centuries later that they were able to do some remarkable things during the time of Moses (Ex 7:11-12; 8:7). It is most probable that demonic spirits had given them these insights. However, we must remember that no one can predict the future except God (Eccl 7:14; 8:7). The spirits indeed have limited control of future events, as God allows and, therefore, can predict only those things they are allowed to control. We see in Acts 16:16 that there was "a slave girl who had a spirit by which she predicted the future. She earned a great deal of money for her owners by fortune-telling." Likewise today, though many are frauds, many fortune tellers may indeed be possessed by unwanted spirits that give them limited abilities in this area. But one thing is for sure, they are not from God and, therefore, are evil. We read, "If what a prophet proclaims in the name of the LORD does not take place or come true, that is a message the LORD has not spoken" (Deu 18:22). Also, this type of practice is forbidden: "Let no one be found among you who sacrifices his son or daughter in the fire, who practices divination or sorcery, interprets omens, engages in witchcraft, or casts spells, or who is a medium or spiritist or who consults the dead. Anyone who does these things is detestable to the LORD" (Deu 18:10-12). In any case, the spirits in these magicians were not allowed to see the interpretation of this dream because God had someone else in mind.

There are a few things to explain regarding Pharaoh's dream. Because cattle would often go out into the Nile to escape insects, they were probably seen standing in the water and then came out. Also, the east wind that had scorched the grain was called the Palestinian sirocco, or the khamsin in Egypt. This wind came in from the desert in late spring (Hosea 13:15; see also Ezek 17:10).

Finally, the cupbearer was reminded of Joseph, who had interpreted his dream two years earlier. The cupbearer had reminded Pharaoh of when he had been in prison under the captain of the guard (Potiphar 39:1). While there, this Hebrew man interpreted both he and the baker's dreams 100% accurately.

Joseph, therefore, remained in prison until, "what he foretold came to pass, till the word of the LORD proved him true" (Psa 105:19).

Gen 41:14 So Pharaoh sent for Joseph, and he was quickly brought from the dungeon. When he had shaved and changed his clothes, he came before Pharaoh. 41:15 Pharaoh said to Joseph, "I had a dream, and no one can interpret it. But I have heard it said of you that when you hear a dream you can interpret it." 41:16 "I cannot do it," Joseph replied to Pharaoh, "but God will give Pharaoh the answer he desires."

Pharaoh had renewed hope upon hearing the cupbearer's testimony and immediately sent for Joseph to be brought out of the dungeon. According to the well known historian, Herodotus, the Egyptians were known for their cleanliness. Men were always clean shaven, unless they were in mourning. Therefore, Joseph was shaved and made clean before being presented to Pharaoh. This was in contrast to the Palestinian tradition of wearing beards (2 Sam 10:5; Jer 41:5).

When Pharaoh told Joseph the reason he had been brought out of prison, Joseph quickly and humbly denied any power of his own to interpret dreams: "God will give" the interpretation. Nor did he attack the other wisemen because of their inability to interpret Pharaoh's dream. If ever there was a time when Joseph could have tried to build himself up, now would have been it, because his freedom depended upon it. Nevertheless, Joseph gave all credit to God and humbled himself. What a change from the Joseph we knew back in Canaan! Though he used to strive to gain leadership by drawing attention to his own deeds, now he gained the trust of Pharaoh by denying his own abilities. Joseph knew that as Christians we are not "competent in ourselves to claim anything for ourselves, but our competence comes from God" (2 Cor 3:5). Daniel gave a similar testimony hundreds of years later (Dan 2:27-30).

Gen 41:17 Then Pharaoh said to Joseph, "In my dream I was standing on the bank of the Nile, 41:18 when out of the river there came up seven cows, fat and sleek, and they grazed among the reeds. 41:19 After them, seven other cows came up--scrawny and very ugly and lean. I had never seen such ugly cows in all the land of Egypt. 41:20 The lean, ugly cows ate up the seven fat cows that came up first. 41:21 But even after they ate them, no one could tell that they had done so; they looked just as ugly as before. Then I woke up. 41:22 "In my dreams I also saw seven heads of grain, full and good, growing on a single stalk. 41:23 After them, seven other heads sprouted--withered and thin and scorched by the east wind. 41:24 The thin heads of grain swallowed up the seven good heads. I told this to the magicians, but none could explain it to me." 41:25 Then Joseph said to Pharaoh, "The dreams of Pharaoh are one and the same. God has revealed to Pharaoh what he is about to do. 41:26 The seven good cows are seven years, and the seven good heads of grain are seven years; it is one and the same dream. 41:27 The seven lean, ugly cows that came up afterward are seven years, and so are the seven worthless heads of grain scorched by the east wind: They are seven years of famine. 41:28 "It is just as I said to

Pharaoh: God has shown Pharaoh what he is about to do. 41:29 Seven years of great abundance are coming throughout the land of Egypt, 41:30 but seven years of famine will follow them. Then all the abundance in Egypt will be forgotten, and the famine will ravage the land. 41:31 The abundance in the land will not be remembered, because the famine that follows it will be so severe. 41:32 The reason the dream was given to Pharaoh in two forms is that the matter has been firmly decided by God, and God will do it soon."

Pharaoh repeated his dreams to Joseph, and we get a few additional insights, as well. This time we see that Pharaoh had never seen such ugly cows as the ones he saw in his dream. Also, after they ate they looked no better off.

Joseph made it clear that the interpretation was not from him, but from God (at least four times, v. 16, 25, 28, 32). That is how he was the only one able to interpret the dreams.

Joseph began to explain the meaning of the sevens being seven years, similar to the threes in the dreams of the cupbearer and baker being days. The healthy grain and cows represented seven good years of crop production that God would bring about. The poor grain and cows represented seven poor years of crops that God would also bring about. Famines such as these would have been extremely rare in Egypt because the Nile river overflowed yearly and they were used to the abundance of food. Stephen gave credibility to this historical event in Acts 7:11.

The reason Pharaoh had two dreams meaning the same thing was to assure him that this was true. It was no accident that Pharaoh had dreamed this. Other instances where this double assurance was given can be found in Amos 7:1-9; 8:1-3. Joseph himself received a double dream having one and the same meaning; in fact, one also involved grain (Gen 37:5-9).

An interesting note of word usage is that anytime Joseph spoke to the Egyptians he used the word *Elohim* for God. This was the name of the powerful Creator God that the Egyptians could know. However, anytime a narrative note about God's dealing with Joseph is mentioned, the word Jehovah is used. This was the covenant name for God and was only used by those who would receive the promises earlier given (Gen 39:2-5, 21, 23).

Gen 41:33 "And now let Pharaoh look for a discerning and wise man and put him in charge of the land of Egypt. 41:34 Let Pharaoh appoint commissioners over the land to take a fifth of the harvest of Egypt during the seven years of abundance. 41:35 They should collect all the food of these good years that are coming and store up the grain under the authority of Pharaoh, to be kept in the cities for food. 41:36 This food should be held in reserve for the country, to be used during the seven years of famine that will come upon Egypt, so that the country may not be ruined by the famine."

The first advice Joseph gave to Pharaoh was to find an honest and wise man to put in charge of Egypt. Along with him would be appointed commissioners who would take a 20% portion of the harvest for the next seven years as a form of taxes. Although it is known that Egypt and other countries at this time did practice a 10% tax, or tithe, a 20% tax was indeed uncommon.

The fact that Joseph did not recommend himself for the job, as he could have easily done, shows how humble and mature Joseph's years have made him. Joseph could have confessed, as did Paul: "Am I now trying to win the approval of men, or of God? Or am I trying to please men? If I were still trying to please men, I would not be a servant of Christ" (Gal 1:10).

Whatever was collected was to be stored in that city for food later on when the famine hit. The grain would then be under the authority of Pharaoh, to be handled as he saw fit (v. 55). This way Egypt would not be ruined; in fact, it would flourish.

The famine in Egypt not only showed God's control over His creation, but also His omnipotent plan to bring Israel into Egypt and to later deliver them out of slavery. It was the slavery and exodus that served to strengthen Israel as a nation. In order for this to happen, God first had to make Egypt the world power. The famine that God would bring about would accomplish this very purpose, because soon all the land and people would become the property of Egypt as they sell themselves and their land for food (47:13-26). Once Egypt became this power, the stage was set for Israel to be brought into Egypt. Therefore, Joseph was not given the dream simply to free him from prison and make him powerful, but also to use him as a means of making Pharaoh very powerful; hence, verse 36.

We also read concerning God's plan with Joseph and Israel: "He sent a man before them-- Joseph, sold as a slave. They bruised his feet with shackles, his neck was put in irons, till what he foretold came to pass, till the word of the LORD proved him true. The king sent and released him, the ruler of peoples set him free. He made him master of his household, ruler over all he possessed, to instruct his princes as he pleased and teach his elders wisdom. Then Israel entered Egypt" (Psalm 105:17-21; See also Acts 7:10).

Gen 41:37 The plan seemed good to Pharaoh and to all his officials. 41:38 So Pharaoh asked them, "Can we find anyone like this man, one in whom is the spirit of God?" 41:39 Then Pharaoh said to Joseph, "Since God has made all this known to you, there is no one so discerning and wise as you. 41:40 You shall be in charge of my palace, and all my people are to submit to your orders. Only with respect to the throne will I be greater than you." 41:41 So Pharaoh said to Joseph, "I hereby put you in charge of the whole land of Egypt." 41:42 Then Pharaoh took his signet ring from his finger and put it on Joseph's finger. He dressed him in robes of fine linen and put a gold chain around his neck. 41:43 He had him ride in a chariot as his second-in-command, and men shouted before him, "Make way !" Thus he put him in charge of the whole land of Egypt. 41:44 Then Pharaoh said to Joseph, "I am Pharaoh, but without your word no one will lift hand or foot in all Egypt."

Pharaoh and his officials (eunuchs) were pleased with Joseph's counsel. It took no time for Pharaoh to realize that Joseph was the man for the job. Pharaoh recognized that the Spirit of God was with Joseph because, not only was he wise, but he was given the ability to interpret dreams that no one else in all of Egypt could.

Joseph, therefore, became second in power in Egypt, second only to Pharaoh. This was remarkable, considering Pharaoh only knew Joseph for a few hours. The reason again was because "God has made this known to you." It was the outward appearance and actions of a Christian that drew Pharaoh to Joseph. However, we must not forget that God was with Joseph and was fulfilling a plan that was foretold years before (37:1-11).

To officially give Joseph this power, he was given Pharaoh's signet ring, a ring used to put a personalized seal or "signature" on important documents (see Est 3:10). In addition, he received a gold chain and fine linen robes; both were outward signs of authority (see Est 6:11; Dan 5:7,16, 29).

To make this announcement public, Pharaoh also put Joseph in a chariot and had him ride through the land while men shouted "make way." The words "make way" in the Hebrew can also mean to "bow the knee." The phrase "as his second-in-command" (v. 43) indicates Pharaoh also rode in the chariot, but Joseph was slightly less decorated and was probably stationed behind Pharaoh.

The fact that no one could lift hand or foot in all Egypt without Joseph's permission was not to be taken literally; however, it did show his absolute authority throughout the land.

Joseph's life has been likened to that of Christs' by many commentators. Since Scripture does not make this connection, we must be careful in allegorizing where it is not warranted. Nonetheless, we see that Joseph was exalted only after humbling himself as a servant. Likewise, "The Son of Man did not come to be served, but to serve, and to give His life as a ransom for many." Also we read, "He made Himself nothing, taking the very nature of a servant, being made in human likeness. And being found in appearance as a man, He humbled Himself and became obedient to death-- even death on a cross! Therefore, God exalted Him to the highest place and gave Him the name that is above every name, that at the name of Jesus every knee should bow, in heaven and on earth and under the earth" (Phil 2:7-10).

Gen 41:45 Pharaoh gave Joseph the name Zaphenath-Paneah and gave him Asenath daughter of Potiphera, priest of On, to be his wife. And Joseph went throughout the land of Egypt. 41:46 Joseph was thirty years old when he entered the service of Pharaoh king of Egypt. And Joseph went out from Pharaoh's presence and traveled throughout Egypt. 41:47 During the seven years of abundance the land produced plentifully. 41:48 Joseph collected all the food produced in those seven years of abundance in Egypt and stored it in the cities. In each city he put the food grown in the fields surrounding it. 41:49 Joseph stored up huge quantities of grain, like the sand of the sea; it was so much that he stopped keeping records because it was beyond measure.

In order to ensure the proper respect of the people, Pharaoh gave Joseph an Egyptian name, Zaphenath-Paneah, the meaning of which is not known for certain. He was also given an Egyptian wife, daughter of the priest of On. Her name was Asenath, which means "belonging to Neith." Since Neith was an Egyptian goddess, we see that her background was certainly not a Christian one. Even the father's name, Potiphera, means "he whom Ra has given" (Ra was the Egyptian sun god). Potiphera's name was perfect for a priest in On, which was ten miles northeast of what is now Cairo. The Greeks called On Heliopolis (city of the sun), and it was appropriately named because it was the center of worship for Ra, the sun god.

Joseph was 30 years old when he became second in command of Egypt. Since he was 17 years old when he was forced out of Canaan (37:2), he had been away from home for 13 years, all of which had been spent as servant or prisoner.

Joseph began traveling through Egypt and overseeing the storehouses of grain during the seven years of abundance. Each city had its own granary and could see what was being done with their "taxes," leaving no room for complaint. So much grain was being stored up that it was like the sand of the sea. They couldn't even keep records of it any longer. These statements give us an indication of what blessings the Lord was pouring out upon Egypt at this time. So much grain was being stored up, yet this was only 20% of all that was grown (41:34). This leads us to believe that the 20% tax did not put anyone in financial stress. It would seem that farmers would have had plenty to begin storing grain for themselves as well, if any were wise enough to do so.

Gen 41:50 Before the years of famine came, two sons were born to Joseph by Asenath daughter of Potiphera, priest of On. 41:51 Joseph named his firstborn Manasseh and said, "It is because God has made me forget all my trouble and all my father's household." 41:52 The second son he named Ephraim and said, "It is because God has made me fruitful in the land of my suffering." 41:53 The seven years of abundance in Egypt came to an end, 41:54 and the seven years of famine began, just as Joseph had said. There was famine in all the other lands, but in the whole land of Egypt there was food. 41:55 When all Egypt began to feel the famine, the people cried to Pharaoh for food. Then Pharaoh told all the Egyptians, "Go to Joseph and do what he tells you." 41:56 When the famine had spread over the whole country, Joseph opened the storehouses and sold grain to the Egyptians, for the famine was severe throughout Egypt. 41:57 And all the countries came to Egypt to buy grain from Joseph, because the famine was severe in all the world.

In the first seven years of Joseph's marriage, he had two sons by Asenath (she was the only wife he would have). The first was Manasseh, meaning "forgetting." This showed that Joseph had forgotten his troubles that the LORD had taken care of. Joseph now saw that his "troubles" had taken place for a purpose, as he would later tell his brothers: "You intended to harm me, but God intended it for good to accomplish what is now being done, the saving of many lives" (Gen 50:20). Joseph, no doubt, could confess as did Paul, "I consider that our present sufferings are not worth comparing with the glory that will be revealed in us" (Rom 8:18).

Both Manasseh and Ephraim would become great tribes among those of Israel. In fact, sometimes the term Ephraim is used to mean all of Israel.

Joseph's second son was named Ephraim, meaning "doubly fruitful." This was clearly a name given to praise God, from whom his blessings flowed.

The seven years of famine then began right on time, as God had predicted. Joseph had now been in Egypt 20 years. Because God had allowed Pharaoh to have his dream and Joseph to interpret it, Egypt had food while the rest of the land (probably only the Middle East) was suffering.

Eventually, however, those who did not store up for themselves began to feel the famine even in Egypt, so they cried out to Pharaoh, who passed the job on to Joseph. Joseph then opened the storehouses of grain and began selling it back to the Egyptians and anyone who came from distant lands. Many think it was wrong of Joseph to sell the grain when he could have given it away. However, just as welfare often does today, hand-outs often lead to waste and laziness. It is also most likely that other provisions were made for those who did not have money to buy food, so that no one starved. There were, no doubt, many jobs needed to distribute food, etc., so others could have worked in exchange for food.

Though the Egyptians seemed to have been dependent upon the government, one would hope they realized that it was God who allowed the government to be prepared. Likewise, we would do well to recognize that it is God who provides for all of our needs (Phil 4:19). The Lord giveth and the Lord can take away.

Gen 42:1 When Jacob learned that there was grain in Egypt, he said to his sons, "Why do you just keep looking at each other?" 42:2 He continued, "I have heard that there is grain in Egypt. Go down there and buy some for us, so that we may live and not die." 42:3 Then ten of Joseph's brothers went down to buy grain from Egypt. 42:4 But Jacob did not send Benjamin, Joseph's brother, with the others, because he was afraid that harm might come to him. 42:5 So Israel's sons were among those who went to buy grain, for the famine was in the land of Canaan also. 42:6 Now Joseph was the governor of the land, the one who sold grain to all its people. So when Joseph's brothers arrived, they bowed down to him with their faces to the ground. 42:7 As soon as Joseph saw his brothers, he recognized them, but he pretended to be a stranger and spoke harshly to them. "Where do you come from?" he asked. "From the land of Canaan," they replied, "to buy food." 42:8 Although Joseph recognized his brothers, they did not recognize him. 42:9 Then he remembered his dreams about them and said to them, "You are spies! You have come to see where our land is unprotected."

While those in Egypt were being inconvenienced, the rest of the Middle East was in dire straits. When Jacob heard of the grain available in Egypt, he sent ten of his sons to buy grain. Apparently they had been "looking at each other" as if there was nothing that could be done.

Only ten of the brothers went to Egypt. Benjamin stayed home because Jacob was taking all precautions to keep anything from happening to him. After Joseph had died (he thought, anyway - 37:33) Benjamin was his last son from his favorite wife Rachel who had died (35:19). Years later, Stephen would record their traveling to Egypt in Acts 7:12.

Once the brothers of Joseph arrived in Egypt, they bowed down before Joseph, not realizing who he was. This fulfilled Joseph's dream (37:1-11). Some have wondered how he could not have been recognized. It is not difficult to understand when we realize that Jacob was sold into Egypt at 17 and he was now about 37 or 38 years old. Also, he was dressed in his Egyptian attire, clean shaven (41:14), speaking Egyptian while using an interpreter (v. 23), and was ruler of the land. His brothers were certainly not looking to see Joseph alive after 20 years had passed, let alone as ruler of Egypt.

Joseph, on the other hand, may have been watching for his brothers and he recognized them. Rather than let them know who he was, he pretended to be a stranger and spoke harshly to them. It may have been that when they bowed to the ground in verse six they remained on the ground through verse nine, because Joseph then remembered his dream (37:1-11) and continued to play his role of the harsh Egyptian by accusing them of being spies. This game had a dual purpose. First of all, when Joseph left his brothers they were very selfish, violent and jealous. In order to find out if his brothers had matured as he had, he had to test them; especially since Benjamin was not with them. Had they killed him? By questioning them he was able to find out that Benjamin was at home and that his father was alive (43:7), but were they telling the truth? Joseph knew that Benjamin would have been Jacob's favorite now, and the fact that he wasn't there confirmed this thought. The only way to tell if his brothers had changed was to see how they treated Benjamin and, thus, Joseph could not yet reveal himself.

Gen 42:10 "No, my lord," they answered. "Your servants have come to buy food. 42:11 We are all the sons of one man. Your servants are honest men, not spies." 42:12 "No!" he said to them. "You have come to see where our land is unprotected." 42:13 But they replied, "Your servants were twelve brothers, the sons of one man, who lives in the land of Canaan. The youngest is now with our father, and one is no more." 42:14 Joseph said to them, "It is just as I told you: You are spies! 42:15 And this is how you will be tested: As surely as Pharaoh lives, you will not leave this place unless your youngest brother comes here. 42:16 Send one of your number to get your brother; the rest of you will be kept in prison, so that your words may be tested to see if you are telling the truth. If you are not, then as surely as Pharaoh lives, you are spies!" 42:17 And he put them all in custody for three days.

Again his brothers fulfilled part of Joseph's earlier dream by submitting themselves and calling him "lord" (37:8).

After being accused of being spies, the brothers answered quickly and honestly. Although Joseph must have wondered how truthful they were being when they said that they were "honest men" (v. 11), considering his past relationship with them.

It seems Jacob had written Joseph off as dead, because they said that one of their brothers was "no more." Either this or they simply couldn't explain what had happened to the other brother without incriminating themselves.

Joseph stated that they must send one brother back to get the youngest (Benjamin, who was now about 23 years old) in order to prove they were not spies. Actually, Joseph was trying to get them to prove they were now truly honest. This was the only way that all the brothers would be able to go back home. However, for the time being, he put all ten of them in prison for three days, probably so that he could figure out what he was going to do. Besides, it would also be good for his brothers to experience a little of what they made Joseph go through. It is not improbable that Joseph had already run through some type of plan long before the brothers even arrived. Knowing the entire land was dealing with the famine, his brothers would surely have come eventually. Therefore, Joseph may have had time to think about what he would do.

The term "as surely as Pharaoh lives" showed this to be the most solemn of oaths. We see this type of oath using the names of rulers or gods often (Amos 8:14; Ps 16:4). More appropriately, it was also used in connection with the LORD Himself over 34 times. (Judges 8:19; 1 Sam 14:39, 45; 19:6; 25:26; Ruth 3:13; 1 Kings 1:29 are a few examples.)

Gen 42:18 On the third day, Joseph said to them, "Do this and you will live, for I fear God: 42:19 If you are honest men, let one of your brothers stay here in prison, while the rest of you go and take grain back for your starving households. 42:20 But you must bring your youngest brother to me, so that your words may be verified and that you may not die." This they proceeded to do. 42:21 They said to one another, "Surely we are being punished because of our brother. We saw how distressed he was when he pleaded with us for his life, but we would not listen; that's why this distress has come upon us." 42:22 Reuben replied, "Didn't I tell you not to sin against the boy? But you wouldn't listen! Now we must give an accounting for his blood." 42:23 They did not realize that Joseph could understand them, since he was using an interpreter. 42:24 He turned away from them and began to weep, but then turned back and spoke to them again. He had Simeon taken from them and bound before their eyes.

After Joseph's brothers had been in prison for three days, he went to them and said that all but one of them may go back home to take grain to their father, but they must return with the youngest (Benjamin). If they did not they would never see their brother again, and they would be considered spies if they ever returned. The reason Joseph gave them for changing his mind and only keeping one brother in prison rather than nine (v. 16) was that he feared God. This was not an unheard of possibility that an Egyptian would fear God; they feared many gods. We saw Abimelech fear the true God (20:3-5; 21:22; 26:9-10), and Laban as well (31:24).

After Joseph's pronouncement the brothers began talking among themselves, not realizing that Joseph could understand them. Together they admitted that this trouble was coming upon them because of what they had done to their "brother" (Joseph). They remembered how he had pleaded for his life, but they had not listened. Now they were pleading for their lives, yet this Egyptian would not listen or believe them. They were "reaping what they sowed" (Gal 6:7). Just as Joseph had undergone a necessary period of spiritual growth, his brothers were also in need of confession and humbly turning to God for help. If the brothers were going to be heads of the tribes of Israel, they had to be spiritually mature as well.

If Joseph did not already know, Reuben's reply must have been sweet music to his ears. Reuben had tried to tell the other brothers not to hurt Joseph (37:21-22), but they would not listen to him either. Therefore, Reuben was now suffering because of their sins.

At this point, Joseph had to turn away and weep because he was touched by Reuben's honesty. No doubt he would love to have given Reuben a warm welcome and a big hug, but he could not give away his identity yet because he didn't know if the other brothers had changed. The only way to know for sure was to see how they treated Benjamin, the other favorite son of Jacob. If they were jealous of anyone, it would be Benjamin.

Another cause for Joseph's weeping may have been hearing that his brothers were actually repenting and confessing their sin. Their violent act of jealousy had remained in their minds for 20 years.

It would seem most likely that Joseph would have kept the oldest since he would have been held most responsible, but perhaps because he had heard how Reuben had tried to save him Joseph kept Simeon in prison instead. From Simeon's past record, he needed this humbling experience more than any of them, and Joseph may have known this. It may be that even the other brothers and Jacob realized this, as well, because none of them seemed to be in any great hurry to return to Egypt and save him. Had they not run out of food, Simeon may well have spent the rest of his life in prison (43:1-2).

Gen 42:25 Joseph gave orders to fill their bags with grain, to put each man's silver back in his sack, and to give them provisions for their journey. After this was done for them, 42:26 they loaded their grain on their donkeys and left. 42:27 At the place where they stopped for the night one of them opened his sack to get feed for his donkey, and he saw his silver in the mouth of his sack. 42:28 "My silver has been returned," he said to his brothers. "Here it is in my sack." Their hearts sank and they turned to each other trembling and said, "What is this that God has done to us?" 42:29 When they came to their father Jacob in the land of Canaan, they told him all that had happened to them. They said, 42:30 "The man who is lord over the land spoke harshly to us and treated us as though we were spying on the land. 42:31 But we said to him, 'We are honest men; we are not spies. 42:32 We were twelve brothers, sons of one father. One is no

more, and the youngest is now with our father in Canaan.' 42:33 Then the man who is lord over the land said to us, 'This is how I will know whether you are honest men: Leave one of your brothers here with me, and take food for your starving households and go. 42:34 But bring your youngest brother to me so I will know that you are not spies but honest men. Then I will give your brother back to you, and you can trade in the land.'" 42:35 As they were emptying their sacks, there in each man's sack was his pouch of silver! When they and their father saw the money pouches, they were frightened. 42:36 Their father Jacob said to them, "You have deprived me of my children. Joseph is no more and Simeon is no more, and now you want to take Benjamin. Everything is against me!"

The brothers who were going home were each taking a sack of grain. However, Joseph gave orders to put the silver that was used to pay for it back in each one's sack without them knowing about it. After this was done, they were given provisions for their journey, they loaded their donkeys and left.

Assuming that Joseph was stationed near Memphis, one of the oldest cities of Egypt about 10 miles south of Cairo, the brothers would have had about a 250 mile trip back to Hebron. At that distance, it would probably have taken about three weeks to get home. Somewhere along the line, they stopped and one of them opened his sack to get grain for his donkey. To his surprise he saw his silver had been returned. This was not a joyous sight because, knowing this Egyptian ruler was harsh, he would no doubt use this to say they were thieves and imprison them all.

They were continuing to believe that this was a punishment because of what they had done (42:21), since they thought it was God who had done this. Their hearts sank, as there was nothing that could be done to solve this increasingly large problem. If they returned, they would surely be accused of stealing; if they didn't return, Simeon would never be seen again and they would starve.

When they arrived back home, they told their father Jacob all that had happened. Surprisingly, Jacob seemed to take the news fairly well up to this point. However, as soon as the rest of the brothers began emptying their sacks, they all found their money had been returned. Now both Jacob and his sons were frightened. At this point Jacob was overwhelmed with the situation. His favorite son, Joseph, was no more, Simeon was now gone, and they wanted Benjamin, too? Now if he sent them back, they would all be taken away because they would be considered thieves. Everything that could go wrong seemed to be happening (see Job 3:25). Jacob blamed his sons for this trouble and, ironically, it was all their fault. Had they not sold Joseph, none of this would have happened.

Rather than trust in God, Jacob was overcome with sorrow. But, as in everything, he should have realized that "in all things God works for the good of those who love Him, who have been called according to His purpose" (Rom 8:28).

Gen 42:37 Then Reuben said to his father, "You may put both of my sons to death if I do not bring him back to you. Entrust him to my care, and I will bring him back." 42:38 But Jacob said, "My son will not go down there with you; his brother is dead and he is the only one left. If harm comes to him on the journey you are taking, you will bring my gray head down to the grave in sorrow."

As usual, Reuben was the one who tried to step forward and make things right. He offered to go back himself, and if he did not return Benjamin safely Jacob could hold him responsible by taking the lives of his two sons (Thanks dad . . .huh?). Though his motives were right, Reuben's solution was lacking in wisdom. What joy could Jacob have if Reuben did not return. Not only would he have lost Benjamin, but now he would lose two grandchildren? It is most likely that Reuben was simply showing how dedicated he was in putting his full effort into protecting Benjamin, even if it meant losing his own life.

Jacob still refused to let Benjamin go. It was better to lose Simeon than his beloved Benjamin. He continued to show his lack of trust in the LORD and his unhealthy clinging on to a favored son. We close the chapter with a shameful Jacob, promising he would die if anything happened to Benjamin. (Note he is not being called Israel, the name which belongs to the man of great faith).

We would do well to learn from this example. There is nothing on this earth worth rejecting our faith and trust in God. Jacob should have realized there is nothing on this earth that can be taken to heaven with us; or is there? Yes there is! Our children! That is why it is so important to raise our children in a Godly home, teaching them about Christ and His salvation through His death and resurrection. Because we train our children out of love for them and for Christ, we will see them again in heaven. Death is not a sad occasion, it is a joyous one for those who believe in Jesus. Knowing this, we will be the Godly examples Christ would have us be.

Gen 43:1 Now the famine was still severe in the land. 43:2 So when they had eaten all the grain they had brought from Egypt, their father said to them, "Go back and buy us a little more food." 43:3 But Judah said to him, "The man warned us solemnly, 'You will not see my face again unless your brother is with you.' 43:4 If you will send our brother along with us, we will go down and buy food for you. 43:5 But if you will not send him, we will not go down, because the man said to us, 'You will not see my face again unless your brother is with you.'" 43:6 Israel asked, "Why did you bring this trouble on me by telling the man you had another brother?" 43:7 They replied, "The man questioned us closely about ourselves and our family. 'Is your father still living?' he asked us. 'Do you have another brother?' We simply answered his questions. How were we to know he would say, 'Bring your brother down here'?" 43:8 Then Judah said to Israel his father, "Send the boy along with me and we will go at once, so that we and you and our children may live and not die. 43:9 I myself will guarantee his safety; you can hold me personally responsible for him. If I do not bring him back to you and set him here before you, I will bear the

blame before you all my life. **43:10 As it is, if we had not delayed, we could have gone and returned twice."**

It must have been about four to six months since the brothers had returned from Egypt (v. 10) and already everything had been eaten. Jacob knew that the only way to survive was to go back to Egypt and get "a little more food." He may have thought the famine would have to end soon, but little did he know there were still five more years to come (45:6).

This time Judah stepped forward and respectfully told Jacob that the only way they would go back to Egypt was if Benjamin went along; otherwise, he would never see their faces again, as they would not be able to return. In the past Reuben had been the one who seemed to take charge, but now this changes. For whatever reason, Judah now seemed to be the spokesman for his brothers (43:8-10; 44:14-34; 46:28). This also seems to be evident in his blessing, as he will become one of the most blessed of the twelve tribes (49:8-10), especially in that Christ would descend from him (Matt 1:2, 17; Luke 3:23, 33).

At this point Jacob realized he must trust in God; hence, the change from "Jacob" to "Israel" in verse six. This is the first time "Israel" had been used since 37:13.

Israel again seemed to blame his sons for this misfortune. Why did they have to get so personal with this ruler in Egypt? The sons told Israel that the man had questioned them thoroughly. There was no reason for them to suspect that being honest about their answers would cause this kind of trouble. From the questions Joseph had asked, it was obvious that he was trying to find out about his family, especially his father, whom he had not seen in over 20 years.

Judah then humbly stated that he would take full responsibility for Benjamin's safety. If anything happened, Judah himself would take the blame. This was a much better approach than when Reuben had offered to take the blame by giving up his sons if anything had happened (42:37).

Gen 43:11 Then their father Israel said to them, "If it must be, then do this: Put some of the best products of the land in your bags and take them down to the man as a gift--a little balm and a little honey, some spices and myrrh, some pistachio nuts and almonds. 43:12 Take double the amount of silver with you, for you must return the silver that was put back into the mouths of your sacks. Perhaps it was a mistake. 43:13 Take your brother also and go back to the man at once. 43:14 And may God Almighty grant you mercy before the man so that he will let your other brother and Benjamin come back with you. As for me, if I am bereaved, I am bereaved."

Israel, still trusting the LORD, told his sons to go, realizing that this "must be." No doubt he was beginning to realize his selfishness and that he was endangering his entire family, all because of one favored son. He, therefore, instructed them to take the best products of the land and give them to the "man" in Egypt as a gift. This was a common practice, as gifts were given to a superior (1 Sam 16:20; 17:18; 2 Kings 5:15).

The gifts included balm, myrrh, and spices. We saw these earlier, because these were the exact items the Ishmaelites were taking to Egypt when they bought Joseph from his brothers (see notes on 37:25). All three items were not native to Egypt and, therefore, cherished. Also included were almonds and pistachio nuts, not native to Egypt. Pistachio nuts are mentioned only here in all of Scripture, and they were grown only in Asia Minor, Syria and Palestine. The honey mentioned was probably different from what we think of as honey. Often times date or grape juice was boiled down to make a thick syrup. This was also a treat not produced in Egypt. Thus all the gifts would have been considered very special and would have indeed been welcomed. Since the famine was so severe, these items should have been perceived as being even more generous a gift.

Along with these gifts, Israel told them to return the money that was put in their sacks on the first trip, along with new money to buy additional grain. Here an interesting parallel can be made with Joseph's being betrayed. Since there were ten brothers, each carrying two bags of money, there were 20 bags of silver (silver and money both *keseph* in Hebrew). This may have reminded them of the 20 pieces of silver they received for selling Joseph that was divided up among them (37:28).

Finally, the last thing they took was Benjamin. With this instruction Israel added, "May God Almighty grant you mercy before the man so that he will let your other brother and Benjamin come back." Israel was indeed leaving things up to God. The word for God Almighty is *El Shaddai* and so far has been used only three times prior to this, once with Abraham (17:1), once with Isaac (28:3), and once with Jacob (35:11). The word occurs 31 times in the book of Job alone and only 17 times in the rest of Scripture. It appears to be a word showing God's great power and had a special meaning for the patriarchs. El Shaddai may mean "God, the Mountain One," either showing His power or His symbolic home on Zion. We read, "And so all Israel will be saved, as it is written: 'The Deliverer will come from Zion; He will turn godlessness away from Jacob'" (Rom 11:26), and "This is what the LORD says: 'I will return to Zion and dwell in Jerusalem'" (Zec 8:3; see also Rev 14:1; 1 Pet 2:6; Heb 12:22; Rom 9:33; Ps 121:1; John 12:15; Matt 21:5).

Israel closed by stating, "If I am bereaved, I am bereaved." This shows that he was content to leave this matter in God's hands. Jacob, too, had been growing in his faith while going through these trials; hence his true name, Israel. His expression of faith was mirrored in Job's statement, "Naked I came from my mother's womb, and naked I will depart. The LORD gave and the LORD has taken away; may the name of the LORD be praised" (Job 1:21). We also see Esther express similar words of surrender: "I and my maids will fast as you do. When this is done, I will go to the king, even though it is against the law. And if I perish, I perish" (Est 4:16). Israel, Job, and Esther were all people of great faith who knew that the wisest thing to do was to surrender one's life to the LORD and He would provide.

Gen 43:15 So the men took the gifts and double the amount of silver, and Benjamin also. They hurried down to Egypt and presented

themselves to Joseph. **43:16 When Joseph saw Benjamin with them, he said
to the steward of his house, "Take these men to my house, slaughter an
animal and prepare dinner; they are to eat with me at noon." 43:17 The
man did as Joseph told him and took the men to Joseph's house. 43:18 Now
the men were frightened when they were taken to his house. They thought,
"We were brought here because of the silver that was put back into our
sacks the first time. He wants to attack us and overpower us and seize us as
slaves and take our donkeys." 43:19 So they went up to Joseph's steward
and spoke to him at the entrance to the house. 43:20 "Please, sir," they
said, "we came down here the first time to buy food. 43:21 But at the place
where we stopped for the night we opened our sacks and each of us found
his silver--the exact weight--in the mouth of his sack. So we have brought it
back with us. 43:22 We have also brought additional silver with us to buy
food. We don't know who put our silver in our sacks." 43:23 "It's all
right," he said. "Don't be afraid. Your God, the God of your father, has
given you treasure in your sacks; I received your silver." Then he brought
Simeon out to them.**

Israel's sons now took the gifts, money, and Benjamin to Egypt. When
Joseph saw Benjamin, he had his servants prepare a feast for them. This must
have seemed strange to the steward, but he did it without question. Joseph's
brothers were frightened and confused when they were taken to the house of
such a powerful man; especially when he had been so harsh with them already.
The only reason they could think of for being taken to his house was the silver
that had been put back in their sacks on the first trip. Since they had brought
Benjamin, as Joseph had asked, that was the only thing they could be accused of
doing wrong. Thinking they would be captured and taken as slaves to be
punished, they went to the steward and told him they had returned the money that
was put in their sacks. However, the steward said he had received their money
and their account was okay. As to the money found in their sacks, God must
have provided for them. With the Egyptians being polytheistic, it is not
surprising that the steward would say such a thing. Also, it is possible that he
was familiar with *Elohim* through Joseph, who still worshipped God Almighty.
Simeon was then brought out to them. No doubt after being in prison
so long, he must have wondered if his father had decided to leave him there.
This must have been a great reunion for them all.

**Gen 43:24 The steward took the men into Joseph's house, gave
them water to wash their feet and provided fodder for their donkeys. 43:25
They prepared their gifts for Joseph's arrival at noon, because they had
heard that they were to eat there. 43:26 When Joseph came home, they
presented to him the gifts they had brought into the house, and they bowed
down before him to the ground. 43:27 He asked them how they were, and
then he said, "How is your aged father you told me about? Is he still
living?" 43:28 They replied, "Your servant our father is still alive and
well." And they bowed low to pay him honor. 43:29 As he looked about
and saw his brother Benjamin, his own mother's son, he asked, "Is this your**

youngest brother, the one you told me about?" And he said, "God be gracious to you, my son." 43:30 Deeply moved at the sight of his brother, Joseph hurried out and looked for a place to weep. He went into his private room and wept there. 43:31 After he had washed his face, he came out and, controlling himself, said, "Serve the food."

Still somewhat confused, the brothers were brought into Joseph's house where their feet were washed and their donkeys fed. So far the whole scene had been typical of Eastern hospitality. When Abraham had met the three men (angels) in 18:2, we saw that the feet of the guests were washed (18:4) and a meal was prepared (18:5-8).

Making every effort to be sure that they pleased this ruler, they prepared the gifts so they would be seen immediately. When Joseph arrived, the brothers bowed down out of respect for his authority. Joseph immediately asked about their (his) father. Again, they bowed to give Joseph honor and respect for his interest in their family. All this time they continued to fulfill the dream Joseph had had over 20 years before (37:7-9).

When Joseph saw Benjamin he asked if this was the youngest which they had told him about. He then said, "God be gracious to you, my son." The phrase "my son" was no doubt used to keep up the facade of being a mature foreign ruler. Nevertheless, this type of blessing was not uncommon among believers (Num 6:25; Ps 67:1). The sight of Benjamin, however, struck Joseph's emotions so deeply that he had to leave the room to weep. Joseph had a close bond with Benjamin because he was his full brother from his mother, Rachel. He cried so much that he even had to wash his face before returning. Joseph seemed to be a very sensitive and emotional man. Not only was he the quiet one while he was home with his father, but the Scriptures record him crying five times: 42:24; 43:30; 45:2, 14; 46:29 (and possibly 42:21). However, under the circumstances I do not believe this was excessive.

Gen 43:32 They served him by himself, the brothers by themselves, and the Egyptians who ate with him by themselves, because Egyptians could not eat with Hebrews, for that is detestable to Egyptians. 43:33 The men had been seated before him in the order of their ages, from the firstborn to the youngest; and they looked at each other in astonishment. 43:34 When portions were served to them from Joseph's table, Benjamin's portion was five times as much as anyone else's. So they feasted and drank freely with him.

Joseph ate at one table, the brothers at another, and the stewards at still another table. This was done because Egyptians did not eat with foreigners, probably for religious reasons (Ex 8:26). We also see that Egyptians did not associate with shepherds (46:34). Even ancient writers such as Herodotus recorded this tradition of the Egyptians.

The brothers were seated in order of their ages from oldest to youngest. They were astonished at this because the odds of this happening were one in 40 million (39,917,000 ways to seat them). They may have thought Joseph had learned this from divination, because they still had no idea who he really was.

When the meal came, Benjamin received five times as much as anyone else. Joseph had purposely done this to see how the others would react. If their attitudes were the same as they had been when Joseph was younger, they would clearly have acted jealous and shown resentment. It is interesting that when this ordeal was over, Joseph would continue to lavish Benjamin by giving him five times as much clothing (45:22). As they say, the youngest is always the spoiled one.

Gen 44:1 Now Joseph gave these instructions to the steward of his house: "Fill the men's sacks with as much food as they can carry, and put each man's silver in the mouth of his sack. 44:2 Then put my cup, the silver one, in the mouth of the youngest one's sack, along with the silver for his grain." And he did as Joseph said. 44:3 As morning dawned, the men were sent on their way with their donkeys. 44:4 They had not gone far from the city when Joseph said to his steward, "Go after those men at once, and when you catch up with them, say to them, 'Why have you repaid good with evil? 44:5 Isn't this the cup my master drinks from and also uses for divination? This is a wicked thing you have done.'" 44:6 When he caught up with them, he repeated these words to them.

Joseph must have been very pleased to see that his brothers had not treated Benjamin scornfully for being favored at dinner. Nevertheless, Joseph had one more test before he could be sure that his brothers had changed.

When the meal was over and the brothers were ready to return home, Joseph had their sacks filled and their money returned again. In addition, Joseph's own silver cup was put in Benjamin's sack. The next morning, Joseph's brothers began their trip home. They must have been elated to be leaving with Benjamin and Simeon.

They had not gone far when Joseph sent his steward after them. He was to accuse them of stealing Joseph's silver cup, the one he used for divination. In reality, Joseph would have never used any sort of divination, as it was against God's Word (Deut 18:10; Lev 19:26). This was simply part of the act he was playing. The word for this cup is "*gabia,*" and it can mean three different things: bowls on the candlesticks (Ex 25:31-34; 37:17-20); as pots for wine (Jeremiah 35:5); or a cup or bowl, as described here. The fact that the word *gabia* is used shows that this was a special cup indeed. The steward probably would have known that Joseph did not use divination, because he so often gave credit to God for his abilities. Nevertheless, with the steward living in a polytheistic society, he may have thought that Joseph used divination but that it came from his God. However, it is doubtful that Joseph would have been this subtle about his worship of the LORD.

Gen 44:7 But they said to him, "Why does my lord say such things? Far be it from your servants to do anything like that! 44:8 We even brought back to you from the land of Canaan the silver we found inside the

mouths of our sacks. So why would we steal silver or gold from your master's house? 44:9 If any of your servants is found to have it, he will die; and the rest of us will become my lord's slaves." 44:10 "Very well, then," he said, "let it be as you say. Whoever is found to have it will become my slave; the rest of you will be free from blame." 44:11 Each of them quickly lowered his sack to the ground and opened it. 44:12 Then the steward proceeded to search, beginning with the oldest and ending with the youngest. And the cup was found in Benjamin's sack. 44:13 At this, they tore their clothes. Then they all loaded their donkeys and returned to the city.

The brothers' joy, no doubt, turned to despair when they saw the steward coming. They honestly denied stealing anything from Egypt and began defending themselves by trying to prove they were honest men. After all, they could have kept the money that was put in their sacks on their first journey, but they had brought it back to return it. Why then, would they steal any silver from Joseph? They were so sure of their innocence that they said if anyone had the cup, that person could be punished by death while the rest would become slaves. We saw a similar statement made earlier by Jacob when Laban had accused him of stealing his household gods that were used for divination (31:32).

The steward agreed to these terms, but changed them slightly by saying that only the person who had stolen the cup would become a slave and the rest would go free. Note the steward said "whoever *is* found," showing that he knew very well it would be found.

Each brother emptied his sack and, therefore, must have seen the money that had been put in their sacks again. However, no mention was made of it by anyone. Benjamin was the last (to build suspense) to be searched, but when he was the cup was there. When the rest of the brothers saw this, they ALL tore their clothes in sorrow. Had this been 20 years earlier, no doubt they would have gone home happy, having rid themselves of a spoiled pest of a brother. However, they showed a true spiritual maturity by having genuine grief and returning to Egypt, even though they were considered free of blame (v. 10).

Gen 44:14 Joseph was still in the house when Judah and his brothers came in, and they threw themselves to the ground before him. 44:15 Joseph said to them, "What is this you have done? Don't you know that a man like me can find things out by divination?" 44:16 "What can we say to my lord?" Judah replied. "What can we say? How can we prove our innocence? God has uncovered your servants' guilt. We are now my lord's slaves--we ourselves and the one who was found to have the cup." 44:17 But Joseph said, "Far be it from me to do such a thing! Only the man who was found to have the cup will become my slave. The rest of you, go back to your father in peace." 44:18 Then Judah went up to him and said: "Please, my lord, let your servant speak a word to my lord. Do not be angry with your servant, though you are equal to Pharaoh himself. 44:19 My lord asked his servants, 'Do you have a father or a brother?' 44:20 And we answered, 'We have an aged father, and there is a young son born to him in

205

his old age. His brother is dead, and he is the only one of his mother's sons left, and his father loves him.' 44:21 "Then you said to your servants, 'Bring him down to me so I can see him for myself.' 44:22 And we said to my lord, 'The boy cannot leave his father; if he leaves him, his father will die.' 44:23 But you told your servants, 'Unless your youngest brother comes down with you, you will not see my face again.' 44:24 When we went back to your servant my father, we told him what my lord had said.

Apparently, the brothers had not gone far from town, because Joseph was still in his house when they returned. Immediately they fell face-down on the ground to beg for mercy. As Joseph continued to play his role of the harsh Egyptian, he asked how they thought they could get away with such a thing, especially since he could find things out through divination.
Though the brothers knew they were innocent in this matter, they believed this trouble was coming upon them because of earlier sins that God was now judging. Therefore, considering the evidence before them, there was nothing more to do but surrender. Joseph, however, stated that only the guilty man (Benjamin) would stay to be a slave.
Judah, who seemed to always be the spokesman for the brothers, now got up to make his plea. He began by recognizing Joseph's power even though it was somewhat wrong since he was only the second most powerful man in Egypt, not equal to Pharaoh. Judah continued by summarizing why Benjamin had come on this trip to begin with. Had Joseph not asked for him to come, Benjamin would have stayed home because his father cherished the boy. In so doing, Judah was not pleading simply for Benjamin's life, but for his father's, as well. Since Benjamin appeared to have been married and had children (46:12) he must have already been in his twenties.

Gen 44:25 "Then our father said, 'Go back and buy a little more food.' 44:26 But we said, 'We cannot go down. Only if our youngest brother is with us will we go. We cannot see the man's face unless our youngest brother is with us.' 44:27 "Your servant my father said to us, 'You know that my wife bore me two sons. 44:28 One of them went away from me, and I said, "He has surely been torn to pieces." And I have not seen him since. 44:29 If you take this one from me too and harm comes to him, you will bring my gray head down to the grave in misery.' 44:30 "So now, if the boy is not with us when I go back to your servant my father and if my father, whose life is closely bound up with the boy's life, 44:31 sees that the boy isn't there, he will die. Your servants will bring the gray head of our father down to the grave in sorrow. 44:32 Your servant guaranteed the boy's safety to my father. I said, 'If I do not bring him back to you, I will bear the blame before you, my father, all my life!' 44:33 "Now then, please let your servant remain here as my lord's slave in place of the boy, and let the boy return with his brothers. 44:34 How can I go back to my father if the boy is not with me? No! Do not let me see the misery that would come upon my father."

As Judah continued to make his plea, he showed how his father's life depended upon Benjamin's safe return. The text shows this by saying Jacob's life was "closely bound up with the boy's." It is interesting that in the Hebrew, the same expression is used for the friendship of Jonathan who was, "one in spirit with David" (1 Sam 18:1). If Benjamin was taken captive, an innocent man would also die. Judah could not bear the thought of returning without Benjamin because of his love for his father. Once before they returned without a favored son, and his father had never gotten over it (37:34-35). Judah could not see his father pained like this again.

Now comes the most remarkable sacrifice seen in this whole event. Judah had promised his father that he would be responsible for Benjamin's safe return. Though Judah could have returned to his father and taken the blame back home, he instead told Joseph he would rather have Benjamin return and he himself stay as a slave in his place, so that his father would not die.

Most people, while reading through Genesis, think Joseph should have been the one in the line of Christ. After all, he seemed to be the most honest and wise of all the brothers. However, it is perhaps this act of self sacrifice that caused Judah to be chosen to be in the line of the Messiah. It was, after all, very Christ-like to offer himself (though innocent) in place of the guilty, not because he had to but because he wanted to, out of love.

Nevertheless, we must also remember that every person in the line of Christ was a sinner, just like you and I. Because of this, we can often find comfort in the fact that, though we are sinners, we are saints through the blood of Christ (Eph 2:13; 3:18; 1 Pet 1:19). Moses was a murderer, yet it is said that, "Moses was a very humble man, more humble than anyone else on the face of the earth" (Num 12:3). Abraham was a polygamist and even offered his own wife as his sister, yet he is called the "man of faith" (Gal 3:9). Rahab was once a prostitute, yet she became an ancestor of Christ (Mat 1:5) and a faithful and righteous woman (Heb 11:31; James 2:25). Likewise, God has special plans for each one of us. We all have our mansion waiting (John 14:2) where we will be clothed in fine linen, representing our righteousness through faith in Christ (Rev 19:8).

Gen 45:1 Then Joseph could no longer control himself before all his attendants, and he cried out, "Have everyone leave my presence!" So there was no one with Joseph when he made himself known to his brothers. 45:2 And he wept so loudly that the Egyptians heard him, and Pharaoh's household heard about it. 45:3 Joseph said to his brothers, "I am Joseph! Is my father still living?" But his brothers were not able to answer him, because they were terrified at his presence.

After seeing such a change in his brothers, Joseph could no longer keep his emotions under control, even around is attendants. He cried out for all of his servants to leave because it would not have been appropriate for them to see him that way. However, even though they left his presence, he wept so loudly that they heard him anyway.

207

Apparently the servants then ran and told Pharaoh the good news about Joseph's family (v. 2, 16). No doubt the servants had been wondering why Joseph was acting so strangely around these foreigners, and now they had their answer.

Once Joseph revealed himself to his brothers, the first thing he wanted to know was if his father was still living. Although he had asked this question a day earlier (43:27), he must have still had a little doubt as to their honesty. Perhaps they were using their father as an excuse to get home safely. This time he was asking the question as a brother under different circumstances. In any case, his brothers were too frightened to answer. After seeing how harshly they had been treated by this Egyptian, and now to find out it was Joseph, they questioned whether or not Joseph had forgiven them. If he hadn't, they were still in trouble.

This entire confrontation and reunion should remind us of the great reunion to come in heaven. Jesus was also betrayed by His own brothers but will one day be reunited with them all: "And I will pour out on the house of David and the inhabitants of Jerusalem a spirit of grace and supplication. They will look on Me, the one they have pierced, and they will mourn for Him as one mourns for an only child, and grieve bitterly for Him as one grieves for a firstborn son" (Zech 12:10).

Gen 45:4 Then Joseph said to his brothers, "Come close to me." When they had done so, he said, "I am your brother Joseph, the one you sold into Egypt! 45:5 And now, do not be distressed and do not be angry with yourselves for selling me here, because it was to save lives that God sent me ahead of you. 45:6 For two years now there has been famine in the land, and for the next five years there will not be plowing and reaping. 45:7 But God sent me ahead of you to preserve for you a remnant on earth and to save your lives by a great deliverance. 45:8 So then, it was not you who sent me here, but God. He made me father to Pharaoh, lord of his entire household and ruler of all Egypt."

To reassure his brothers it was actually him and that he was not going to hurt them, Joseph called them closer and said "I am your brother Joseph, the one you sold into Egypt." In so doing, he again expressed his relationship with them. Without a pause, he continued to tell them that even though they had sold him, not to be distressed because God (not the brothers) had sent him to Egypt to accomplish good. This historical event is mentioned in Acts 7:13.

Joseph had long since forgiven his brothers because he knew well that his situation was "according to the plan of Him who works out everything in conformity with the purpose of His will" (Eph 1:11). It was God who had allowed these things to happen, as mentioned again in verses 7-9. Even Stephen would recognize this a century later when he stated, "Because the patriarchs were jealous of Joseph, they sold him as a slave into Egypt. But God was with him" (Acts 7:9).

Again, Joseph's life seems to foreshadow Christs'. In Acts we see that the events leading to Christ's crucifixion were also in God's plan: "This man was handed over to you by God's set purpose and foreknowledge; and you, with the help of wicked men, put him to death by nailing him to the cross" (Acts 2:23) and, "They did what Your power and will had decided beforehand should happen" (Acts 4:28).

Joseph, who was now 39 years old (41:46, 53), explained that there had been two years of famine and five were yet to come (41:30). It was because of this famine that God had sent Joseph to Egypt, to save lives and deliver his own family out of it. Therefore, his brothers should no longer have felt guilty or angry with themselves, since God had worked this out for the good of all. Not only did God spare the lives of Israel's sons, He even had a plan for them, as well, to be the twelve tribes of Israel. Also in regard to Joseph, he was made "father to Pharaoh." This was a title of honor given to many high officials in Egypt, showing once again the historical accuracy of this event.

Gen 45:9 "Now hurry back to my father and say to him, 'This is what your son Joseph says: God has made me lord of all Egypt. Come down to me; don't delay. 45:10 You shall live in the region of Goshen and be near me--you, your children and grandchildren, your flocks and herds, and all you have. 45:11 I will provide for you there, because five years of famine are still to come. Otherwise you and your household and all who belong to you will become destitute.' 45:12 You can see for yourselves, and so can my brother Benjamin, that it is really I who am speaking to you. 45:13 Tell my father about all the honor accorded me in Egypt and about everything you have seen. And bring my father down here quickly." 45:14 Then he threw his arms around his brother Benjamin and wept, and Benjamin embraced him, weeping. 45:15 And he kissed all his brothers and wept over them. Afterward his brothers talked with him.

After his brothers had been comforted about Joseph's intentions, they were told to hurry back to Jacob (Israel). They were to tell him Joseph was lord of Egypt and he was to move down there. Joseph was no doubt excited to see his father, as he again asked them to hurry (v. 13).

Joseph had decided that they would live in the land of Goshen, a fertile area in northeast Egypt along the Nile delta. Its size was about 900 square miles and would fit the needs of a shepherd.

Joseph was no longer using an interpreter (42:23), and all of them should now have been fully convinced that this was Joseph. If Israel had any doubts about Joseph being alive, his beloved and trusted Benjamin should have been able to assure him that the other brothers were telling the truth. It was very important that Israel move to Egypt because of the five years of famine yet to come. If they could not survive on their own the past two years, they certainly would not make it for five more years in Canaan.

When his instructions were over, Joseph once again began to weep as he hugged his brother Benjamin. Lest there be any doubt that Joseph still loved his other brothers, even though they were only half-brothers, he also kissed and "wept over them." For the first time in 22 years, Joseph and his brothers were able to sit down and talk as brothers without fear or question. What a joyous reunion this must have been!

Gen 45:16 When the news reached Pharaoh's palace that Joseph's brothers had come, Pharaoh and all his officials were pleased. 45:17 Pharaoh said to Joseph, "Tell your brothers, 'Do this: Load your animals and return to the land of Canaan, 45:18 and bring your father and your families back to me. I will give you the best of the land of Egypt and you can enjoy the fat of the land.' 45:19 You are also directed to tell them, 'Do this: Take some carts from Egypt for your children and your wives, and get your father and come. 45:20 Never mind about your belongings, because the best of all Egypt will be yours.'" 45:21 So the sons of Israel did this. Joseph gave them carts, as Pharaoh had commanded, and he also gave them provisions for their journey. 45:22 To each of them he gave new clothing, but to Benjamin he gave three hundred shekels of silver and five sets of clothes. 45:23 And this is what he sent to his father: ten donkeys loaded with the best things of Egypt, and ten female donkeys loaded with grain and bread and other provisions for his journey. 45:24 Then he sent his brothers away, and as they were leaving he said to them, "Don't quarrel on the way!"

When Pharaoh had heard the news (apparently from Joseph's servants v. 2), he was pleased about Joseph's good fortune. Pharaoh indeed respected and cared for Joseph, who had not only been a trusted official but a trusted friend. Because of this, Pharaoh wanted his brothers to return home and bring their father back to Egypt where they could have the "fat of the land." To ensure speed and safety, Pharaoh also gave them carts to bring their major belongings and to make the trip easier for the women, children, and Israel. To save more time, any items like utensils or bowls were to be left behind, because Pharaoh himself would provide replacements.

Finally, the brothers were on their way home and this time without any fear or wonderment. Pharaoh had given them the means to return quickly, but Joseph, being in charge of the grain, loaded their carts with provisions for the trip. In addition, Joseph gave them all new clothing as a gift. However, to Benjamin he gave seven and a half pounds of silver and five sets of clothing. Perhaps this was a gift to honor Benjamin, not because of status as a favorite brother, but as one who had been innocent in this whole matter. Besides, Benjamin had also gone through much undeserved torment when they found the planted silver cup in his grain sack.

To his father, Joseph sent ten donkeys loaded with the finest things of Egypt. An additional ten female donkeys were loaded with grain and provisions for the return journey to Egypt. Since his father was old, Joseph wanted to make the trip as comfortable for him as possible.

When the brothers were leaving, Joseph gave one last instruction not to quarrel among themselves. The word used for "quarrel" is *ragaz* and means to "be troubled." Joseph may have thought that his brothers would argue about who was to blame for selling Joseph in the first place. Even though it was the

LORD who had allowed these situations to take place, they still had to tell Israel that Joseph was alive. How would they now tell their father the secret they had kept inside for 22 years. This thought alone would cause them to be more than just a little troubled and, therefore, Joseph tried to assure them that it would all be okay.

Gen 45:25 So they went up out of Egypt and came to their father Jacob in the land of Canaan. 45:26 They told him, "Joseph is still alive! In fact, he is ruler of all Egypt." Jacob was stunned; he did not believe them. 45:27 But when they told him everything Joseph had said to them, and when he saw the carts Joseph had sent to carry him back, the spirit of their father Jacob revived. 45:28 And Israel said, "I'm convinced! My son Joseph is still alive. I will go and see him before I die."

Apparently there were no significant events on the trip home since nothing is mentioned until they arrived back in Canaan. They immediately told Jacob that Joseph is not only alive but is ruler in Egypt. Not surprisingly, Jacob was stunned and didn't believe them. Actually, the Hebrew word, *puwg*, describes the extent of Jacob's reaction. It implies that he became faint and almost ceased. However, seeing all the carts and donkeys loaded with provisions, as well as the new clothes and hearing about all the events (no doubt the selling of Joseph into Egypt as well), Jacob believed.

Not only did he now believe but his spirit was revived. It is again very significant that in verses 25, 26, and 27 the name Jacob is used because of his disbelief and lack of faith. However, once his spirit is revived he is called Israel (v. 28) once again. The chapter then closes with Israel committing to leave Canaan and go see Joseph before he himself dies. Israel was now about 130 years old (47:9) but he would still live for another 17 years (47:28) to see his son Joseph and his grandchildren through him.

Gen 46:1 So Israel set out with all that was his, and when he reached Beersheba, he offered sacrifices to the God of his father Isaac. 46:2 And God spoke to Israel in a vision at night and said, "Jacob! Jacob!" "Here I am," he replied. 46:3 "I am God, the God of your father," he said. "Do not be afraid to go down to Egypt, for I will make you into a great nation there. 46:4 I will go down to Egypt with you, and I will surely bring you back again. And Joseph's own hand will close your eyes."

Israel set out for Egypt, but on the way he stopped at Beersheba to offer sacrifices to God. That night Israel received a comforting vision. So far in Israel's life, every move he made was directed by God. When he fled from Esau to go to Haran, God appeared to him at Bethel (28:13-15). When he left Laban to go back to Canaan, God came to him in a dream (31:3). When he left Shechem to go to Hebron, God again appeared to him (35:1, 9-12). Therefore, Israel may have been looking for Divine approval of this move, as well. Indeed, he would receive it, as this was the plan since time began.

The fact that he offered sacrifices to the "God of his father" does not mean that Israel had not accepted God as his God; rather the place the sacrifices were being made had a connection with his father. There should have already been an altar built in Beersheba, because Israel's father (Isaac) had built one years ago (Gen 26:24-25). Israel had also lived there with Isaac for some time and, therefore, it was a familiar place (28:10). Beersheba was also the last stop before leaving Canaan. Before he left the promised land, he wanted to be sure this was the right thing to do, and Israel no doubt went to God in prayer for guidance, even though his heart longed to see Joseph.

That night God appeared in a vision for the 8th and final time, as recorded in Scripture (28:13; 31:3; 31:11; 32:1; 32:30; 35:1; 35:9; 46:2). It is also noteworthy that in the vision God called Israel by his first name of "Jacob," even though he had earlier said, "Your name is Jacob, but you will no longer be called Jacob; your name will be Israel" (Gen 35:10). For whatever reason, in these last five chapters of Genesis the names Jacob and Israel seem to be used interchangeably, regardless of faith level (46:8, 27; 47:27-28; 49:1, 2, 28, 33). In any case, God assured Jacob this was His plan and that he would be safe. In fact, Joseph would be there when he died. Basically, the covenant promise was restated again that God would make Israel into a great nation (Gen 12:2).

God also promised that He would go with Jacob to Egypt and would also bring him out of Egypt again (God had promised to be with Jacob in his travels before in 28:15; see also 48:21; 15:16). We are not told whether or not Jacob knew this would be after his death. However, considering that God had said He would make Israel a great nation in Egypt (Exodus 1:7 fulfills), it is likely that he realized this. Either way, Jacob would remember this promise, because he instructed his sons to bring his body out of Egypt when he died (49:29). Joseph would carry out this oath, and Jacob would be buried in the cave at Machpelah with Abraham, Sarah and Isaac. His funeral would also be attended by many dignitaries of Egypt (50:4-8).

Some find it strange that God had brought the nations of Israel into Egypt to be enslaved. This was all part of God's plan, however, to humble His chosen nation. Also, it preserved them by not allowing them to be assimilated into another culture. While in Canaan, the Canaanites had no problem with intermarrying among other cultures. However, the Egyptians felt themselves to be superior to foreigners and would not have intermarried freely. Therefore, while God was refining Israel he was also preserving them.

Gen 46:5 Then Jacob left Beersheba, and Israel's sons took their father Jacob and their children and their wives in the carts that Pharaoh had sent to transport him. 46:6 They also took with them their livestock and the possessions they had acquired in Canaan, and Jacob and all his offspring went to Egypt. 46:7 He took with him to Egypt his sons and grandsons and his daughters and granddaughters--all his offspring.

Now assured that he was following God's direction, Jacob left the promised land, taking with him his sons, their families and their possessions.

Verse seven also points out some additional information. It says that Jacob took his daughters with him. The only daughter mentioned in Scripture is Dinah (30:21) yet here we see a plural word, indicating that he had other daughters that were not mentioned. Likewise Serah, daughter of Asher, is the only granddaughter named (verse 17), yet Jacob did have others.

Gen 46:8 These are the names of the sons of Israel (Jacob and his descendants) who went to Egypt: Reuben the firstborn of Jacob. 46:9 The sons of Reuben: Hanoch, Pallu, Hezron and Carmi. 46:10 The sons of Simeon: Jemuel, Jamin, Ohad, Jakin, Zohar and Shaul the son of a Canaanite woman. 46:11 The sons of Levi: Gershon, Kohath and Merari. 46:12 The sons of Judah: Er, Onan, Shelah, Perez and Zerah (but Er and Onan had died in the land of Canaan). The sons of Perez: Hezron and Hamul. 46:13 The sons of Issachar: Tola, Puah, Jashub and Shimron. 46:14 The sons of Zebulun: Sered, Elon and Jahleel. 46:15 These were the sons Leah bore to Jacob in Paddan Aram, besides his daughter Dinah. These sons and daughters of his were thirty-three in all.

The following verses can be confusing until we realize that this is not a passenger list. Some of the names listed were already in Egypt (v. 19), some had not yet been born (compare 42:37 with 46:9), and some were already dead (compare 38:7-10 with 46:12).

Verses 8-15 list 3 of Jacob's sons and grandsons through his wife, Leah. In addition, the two sons of Perez are mentioned, making 34 total names. Er and Onan are included, even though they had died while living in Canaan (38:8-9); thus, only 29 entered Egypt. Though verse 15 says 33 in all, there are 34 names listed because of the sons of Perez. To get from 34 names to the 33 going to Egypt, some have suggested the possiblility that Ohad, in verse ten, should be omitted because his name does not appear in the parallel texts of Numbers 26:12-13 or 1 Chronicles 4:24. The Hebrew word of "Ohad" is very similar to "Zohar," and it is possible the two were confused in later manuscripts. However, it is unlikely that Ohad would be included as it is in Exodus 6:15 if that were so. Verse 15, however, states that with Dinah and his other daughters there was a total of 33. Therefore, there may be a total of four daughters or granddaughters of Leah not listed (29 listed names of *those living* plus 4 unknown daughters or granddaughters equals 33).

In this list we also see the two sons of Perez, Hezron and Hamul. It seems unlikely that they could have been born in Canaan, since Perez was born after Joseph had been sold into Egypt. Also, Perez would have been born after his brother Shelah was old enough to marry (Gen 38:14, 29). Perez is the one in the line of Christ and his son Hezron would continue this lineage.

Kohath is mentioned as one of the sons of Levi. He would be Moses' ancestor.

This list can be seen again in Exodus 1:1.

Gen 46:16 The sons of Gad: Zephon, Haggi, Shuni, Ezbon, Eri, Arodi and Areli. 46:17 The sons of Asher: Imnah, Ishvah, Ishvi and Beriah.

Their sister was Serah. The sons of Beriah: Heber and Malkiel. 46:18 These were the children born to Jacob by Zilpah, whom Laban had given to his daughter Leah--sixteen in all.

These verses list 16 of Jacob's sons and grandsons through Zilpah, Leah's maidservant.

Gen 46:19 The sons of Jacob's wife Rachel: Joseph and Benjamin. 46:20 In Egypt, Manasseh and Ephraim were born to Joseph by Asenath daughter of Potiphera, priest of On. 46:21 The sons of Benjamin: Bela, Beker, Ashbel, Gera, Naaman, Ehi, Rosh, Muppim, Huppim and Ard. 46:22 These were the sons of Rachel who were born to Jacob--fourteen in all.

Here we see 14 of Jacob's descendants coming from his wife Rachel.

Gen 46:23 The son of Dan: Hushim. 46:24 The sons of Naphtali: Jahziel, Guni, Jezer and Shillem. 46:25 These were the sons born to Jacob by Bilhah, whom Laban had given to his daughter Rachel--seven in all.

Seven more sons and grandsons of Jacob are seen here from Rachel's maidservant, Bilhah.

Gen 46:26 All those who went to Egypt with Jacob--those who were his direct descendants, not counting his sons' wives--numbered sixty-six persons. 46:27 With the two sons who had been born to Joseph in Egypt, the members of Jacob's family, which went to Egypt, were seventy in all.

Now we see that the total number of Jacob's own seed who entered Egypt from Canaan was 66 people. If you count the sons of Joseph who were already in Egypt, there were 70 Israelites who would begin the nation in Egypt. The 66 plus Joseph, Manasseh, Ephraim and Jacob himself (verse 26 says "with" Joseph), equaled 70.

Again we see how seventy seems to hold special significance in Scripture. In Deuteronomy we read, "When the Most High gave the nations their inheritance, when He divided *all mankind,* He set up boundaries for the peoples according to the number of the sons of Israel" (Deut 32:8). This may suggest that these 70 were representative of the 70 nations that came from Noah (See notes on Gen 10:32).

Another problem for some comes from Stephen's speech when he said, "After this, Joseph sent for his father Jacob and his whole family, seventy-five in all" (Acts 7:14). Why did Stephen record 75 rather than 70? Most commentators explain this by showing that Stephen used the Septuagint translation, which lists five of Joseph's descendants coming from his sons Ephraim (two sons and one grandson) and Manasseh (one son and one grandson) in the Genesis 46 account.

Gen 46:28 Now Jacob sent Judah ahead of him to Joseph to get directions to Goshen. When they arrived in the region of Goshen, **46:29** Joseph had his chariot made ready and went to Goshen to meet his father Israel. As soon as Joseph appeared before him, he threw his arms around his father and wept for a long time. **46:30** Israel said to Joseph, "Now I am ready to die, since I have seen for myself that you are still alive." **46:31** Then Joseph said to his brothers and to his father's household, "I will go up and speak to Pharaoh and will say to him, 'My brothers and my father's household, who were living in the land of Canaan, have come to me. **46:32** The men are shepherds; they tend livestock, and they have brought along their flocks and herds and everything they own.' **46:33** When Pharaoh calls you in and asks, 'What is your occupation?' **46:34** you should answer, 'Your servants have tended livestock from our boyhood on, just as our fathers did.' Then you will be allowed to settle in the region of Goshen, for all shepherds are detestable to the Egyptians."

Judah was sent ahead to get directions to Goshen, since he seemed to still be the spokesman among the brothers. After Joseph gave Judah the directions, he went out to Goshen himself to meet his father, whom he had not seen in 22 years (Joseph was now 39 years old). As soon as Joseph saw him he gave him a hug and wept (again) for a while. Israel then made the comment that he could now die in peace, having seen his son's face again just as God had promised (46:4).

Joseph then told his brothers what to say to Pharaoh when they were brought to him. Joseph had already planned that Goshen was the most suitable place for them, but apparently he had not yet received the final okay from Pharaoh. Goshen was adjacent to Canaan and though fertile, was unsettled by the Egyptians. Pharaoh knew that Joseph's family was coming (45:17-20) but he did not know their occupations.

Both Biblical and secular historical records show that, for whatever reason, the Egyptians hated shepherds. Perhaps for the same reasons they viewed eating with foreigners as detestable (43:32). Therefore, Joseph knew that when his brothers mentioned their occupations Pharaoh would naturally pick Goshen as the place for them to settle. In addition, though it is not mentioned, it is likely that Joseph may have suggested they settle in Goshen during his prior arrival and discussion with Pharaoh (v. 31).

Gen 47:1 Joseph went and told Pharaoh, "My father and brothers, with their flocks and herds and everything they own, have come from the land of Canaan and are now in Goshen." **47:2** He chose five of his brothers and presented them before Pharaoh. **47:3** Pharaoh asked the brothers, "What is your occupation?" "Your servants are shepherds," they replied to Pharaoh, "just as our fathers were." **47:4** They also said to him, "We have come to live here awhile, because the famine is severe in Canaan and your servants' flocks have no pasture. So now, please let your servants settle in Goshen." **47:5** Pharaoh said to Joseph, "Your father and your brothers have come to you, **47:6** and the land of Egypt is before you; settle your father and your brothers in the best part of the land. Let them live in Goshen. And if you know of any among them with special ability, put them in charge of my own livestock."

Joseph went to see Pharaoh. After he had spoke to Pharaoh he chose five of his brothers to come before Pharaoh, as well. We do not know which five brothers these were, nor do we know why they were picked out of the eleven.

The conversation went almost exactly as Joseph had planned (46:31-34), except his brothers added a few things. First, they mentioned that they were there to live only for "awhile." They knew God had promised the land of Canaan would be theirs someday and, therefore, had no intention of living in Egypt forever.

Second, it appeared that the brothers in this conversation requested to live in Goshen, though it is not recorded that Joseph had told them to do so (but he probably did instruct them to say this). Therefore, it is most likely that here we are given more information from the conversations that went on between Joseph and his family in 46: 31-34.

Pharaoh responded to this request favorably, as he had earlier offered the best of Egypt to Joseph's brothers (45:18). However, this was before he knew their occupations. Now finding out that they were shepherds, Pharaoh did not take back his word but simply honored their request. He still kept his promise when he said Egypt was before them, but honored their request by saying, "Let them live in Goshen." In fact, Pharaoh even offered one of them a job. Anyone having good skills in their field (no pun intended) could be put in charge of Pharaoh's own livestock. Apparently, even though shepherds were detestable to the Egyptians, it did not stop them from having animals of their own.

Gen 47:7 Then Joseph brought his father Jacob in and presented him before Pharaoh. After Jacob blessed Pharaoh, 47:8 Pharaoh asked him, "How old are you?" 47:9 And Jacob said to Pharaoh, "The years of my pilgrimage are a hundred and thirty. My years have been few and difficult, and they do not equal the years of the pilgrimage of my fathers." 47:10 Then Jacob blessed Pharaoh and went out from his presence.

After everything had been settled with Goshen, Joseph brought his father to meet Pharaoh. No doubt Pharaoh had heard about Israel from Joseph. He must have known what a spiritual man Jacob was because he knew that God had been with him, just as God was with Joseph. Therefore, this was more of an honor for Pharaoh to meet the man that God talked to than it was for Jacob to meet a powerful and wealthy ruler. This is further evidenced in the fact that Jacob blessed Pharaoh. As we saw with Melchizedek, the lesser was blessed by the greater man: "And without doubt the lesser person is blessed by the greater" (Heb 7:7).

In wonderment and awe of such a spiritual man, Pharaoh asked Israel's age and found out that he was 130 years old. These had been difficult years for Jacob and they had taken their toll on his body. Jacob mentioned that 130 were but a few years to live compared to his fathers. Though already greatly reduced from that of the pre-Flood world, the longevity had not yet deteriorated to the point we have today. Jacob's father Isaac had lived 180 years (35:28) and Abraham 175 (25:7); therefore, for Israel, his days had indeed been few. Although, even at 130 he would still have 17 more years before his death.

It is also interesting that Jacob called his life and the life of his forefathers a pilgrimage. Through all this time they had never had a permanent home to settle in and, therefore, they were religious sojourners following God and his instructions (even in coming to Egypt). We see their attitude explained in the New Testament, where it states, "All these people were still living by faith when they died. They did not receive the things promised; they only saw them and welcomed them from a distance. And they admitted that they were aliens and strangers on earth" (Hebrews 11:13; note the KJV states they were strangers and pilgrims. See also Deut 26:5).

Once more Jacob blessed Pharaoh, not to show his superiority over Pharaoh, but to truly bless the man who had treated God's people so generously.

Gen 47:11 So Joseph settled his father and his brothers in Egypt and gave them property in the best part of the land, the district of Rameses, as Pharaoh directed. 47:12 Joseph also provided his father and his brothers and all his father's household with food, according to the number of their children.

Even though Goshen was relatively unsettled, it was still considered the best part of the land near Rameses. After all, Pharaoh did say the land was before them. Rameses, along with Pithom, would later become a storehouse city, as seen in Exodus 1:11 (See also Ex 12:37; Nu 33:3-5). It may have been right along the Nile, since the book of Numbers states, "We remember *the fish* we ate in Egypt at no cost--also the cucumbers, melons, leeks, onions and garlic" (Num 11:5). Also, the book of Psalms states that they were "in the land of Egypt, in the region of Zoan" (Psa 78:12). Zoan was an outlet of the Nile river near the sea, and it lay in the northeast corner of Egypt. Since most of the Egyptian population lived in the south and west, it was a perfect place for shepherds to be by themselves.

However, in this time of famine Joseph still needed to provide food for them, and he did so wisely, by the number in each of their families. This showed that Joseph even had to ration the food for his own family during the next five years of famine.

Gen 47:13 There was no food, however, in the whole region because the famine was severe; both Egypt and Canaan wasted away because of the famine. 47:14 Joseph collected all the money that was to be found in Egypt and Canaan in payment for the grain they were buying, and he brought it to Pharaoh's palace. 47:15 When the money of the people of Egypt and Canaan was gone, all Egypt came to Joseph and said, "Give us food. Why should we die before your eyes? Our money is used up." 47:16 "Then bring your livestock," said Joseph. "I will sell you food in exchange

for your livestock, since your money is gone." 47:17 So they brought their livestock to Joseph, and he gave them food in exchange for their horses, their sheep and goats, their cattle and donkeys. And he brought them through that year with food in exchange for all their livestock. 47:18 When that year was over, they came to him the following year and said, "We cannot hide from our lord the fact that since our money is gone and our livestock belongs to you, there is nothing left for our lord except our bodies and our land. 47:19 Why should we perish before your eyes--we and our land as well? Buy us and our land in exchange for food, and we with our land will be in bondage to Pharaoh. Give us seed so that we may live and not die, and that the land may not become desolate." 47:20 So Joseph bought all the land in Egypt for Pharaoh. The Egyptians, one and all, sold their fields, because the famine was too severe for them. The land became Pharaoh's, 47:21 and Joseph reduced the people to servitude, from one end of Egypt to the other.

The famine had become so severe that all of Egypt and Canaan were "wasting away." The people had spent all their money buying grain, and now there was no more money to spend. Therefore, the people came to Joseph looking for free food. However, knowing this was not the best thing for anyone (even poor, starving individuals), he requested their cattle as payment for food. If the people had to pay for the food, they would certainly continue to help out in the rationing. Also, it is most likely that this was the best thing for both sides. Without enough food, the people would not have been able to even take care of their own cattle without the help of the government. No doubt, Joseph's brothers became very busy, since they were now in charge of Pharaoh's livestock (47:6).

The cattle only lasted for one year and then the people came to Joseph again. This time, however, *the people* made an offer to Joseph by choosing to give their land and their services in exchange for food. In accepting this proposal, the entire land, people and cattle of Egypt became Pharaoh's. As earlier mentioned, this was all part of God's plan to make Egypt the powerful country it needed to be in order for the Israelites to become enslaved.

A footnote for verse 21 leaves open a very possible interpretation, that the people were moved into the cities. This would have made it much easier to distribute and regulate the food dispersion, while at the same time using the people's labor to help out.

Some view Joseph's administration in these last years as harsh. However, we must remember that even though the people lost their freedom and possessions, they were not being ruled by a tyrant. Without the help of the government and its administration, all of the food would have been gone by now. Sometimes the best things aren't the easiest. Joseph continued to administer wisely and honestly to keep the masses from starvation. Welfare, though on the outside might seem humane, leads to dependency and often laziness. That would have been the worst thing for the Egyptian people at this point. Consider some of the following passages: "How long will you lie there, you sluggard? When will you get up from your sleep? A little sleep, a little slumber, a little folding of the hands to rest--and poverty will come on you like a bandit and scarcity like an armed man" (Prov 6:9-11); "The sluggard is wiser in his own eyes than seven men who answer discreetly" (Prov 26:16); "We do not want you to become lazy, but to imitate those who through faith and patience inherit what has been promised" (Heb 6:12). See also Prov 10:4; 13:4; 15:19; 20:4; Ezek 10:18.

Gen 47:22 However, he did not buy the land of the priests, because they received a regular allotment from Pharaoh and had food enough from the allotment Pharaoh gave them. That is why they did not sell their land. 47:23 Joseph said to the people, "Now that I have bought you and your land today for Pharaoh, here is seed for you so you can plant the ground. 47:24 But when the crop comes in, give a fifth of it to Pharaoh. The other four-fifths you may keep as seed for the fields and as food for yourselves and your households and your children." 47:25 "You have saved our lives," they said. "May we find favor in the eyes of our lord; we will be in bondage to Pharaoh." 47:26 So Joseph established it as a law concerning land in Egypt--still in force today--that a fifth of the produce belongs to Pharaoh. It was only the land of the priests that did not become Pharaoh's. 47:27 Now the Israelites settled in Egypt in the region of Goshen. They acquired property there and were fruitful and increased greatly in number.

The only land in all of Egypt that did not belong to Pharaoh was that of the priests. They apparently had a substantial amount of land, since they were able to provide enough food for themselves from it. Also, the fact that Pharaoh was the one who had given this land to them shows that Egypt did have a common religion supported by the government.

Since the people had no money to buy food, Joseph made a new law which stated that the government would provide seed for them to plant, and one-fifth of all that was grown would become Pharaoh's. (The same tax as during the years of abundance- 41:34) The other 80% would be theirs to keep for their wages. This was really quite generous, since there was no rent to be paid on the land. Comparing this to today's standards, a 20% tax doesn't sound bad at all. Another benefit of this program was that the people would now be working, rather than simply looking for handouts as the welfare system tends to cause. Joseph was acting wisely and in the best interest of the people. The program worked out so well that it became a practice "unto this day."

While the Israelites lived in Goshen they "increased greatly in number." This suggests that the annual growth rate was high. This was also fulfilling the promise made to Jacob: "And God said to him, 'I am God Almighty; be fruitful and increase in number. A nation and a community of nations will come from you, and kings will come from your body. The land I gave to Abraham and Isaac I also give to you, and I will give this land to your descendants after you'" (Gen 35:11-12). Looking at this increase more closely, we see that from Jacob and his four wives they had brought a minimum of 70 people into Egypt already. This number was probably closer to 100 if you include the wives of the sons and grandsons listed in chapter 46. If this was so, there was about a 6% increase in nearly 50 years. We see that in Numbers 1:46 there would be over 600,00 men over the age of 20 who left Egypt. That means that one could expect at least 2 million people involved in the Exodus when women and children were included. An increase from 100 to 2 million in only 215 years would represent only a 5% increase in population. When we realize that the Israelites were in Egypt for 430 years, that means the Exodus could have involved well over 3 million people. Indeed, God's promises were being fulfilled.

Gen 47:28 Jacob lived in Egypt seventeen years, and the years of his life were a hundred and forty-seven. 47:29 When the time drew near for Israel to die, he called for his son Joseph and said to him, "If I have found favor in your eyes, put your hand under my thigh and promise that you will show me kindness and faithfulness. Do not bury me in Egypt, 47:30 but when I rest with my fathers, carry me out of Egypt and bury me where they are buried." "I will do as you say," he said. 47:31 "Swear to me," he said. Then Joseph swore to him, and Israel worshipped as he leaned on the top of his staff.

Jacob would continue to live in Egypt until he died at 147, only 17 years after entering that land. When the time came that Israel began realizing his death was near, he called for Joseph to come receive his blessing. Before Israel would bless Joseph, however, he made him swear that his body would be buried in the promised land of Canaan. Even though at this point it was a foreign land away from his family, he knew by faith that this is where his descendants would end up. We see in Hebrews the attitude of both Joseph and Jacob in regard to God's promises: "By faith Jacob, when he was dying, blessed each of Joseph's sons, and worshipped as he leaned on the top of his staff. By faith Joseph, when his end was near, spoke about the exodus of the Israelites from Egypt and gave instructions about his bones" (Heb 11:21-22). Jacob could only worship as he was near his death. No doubt he was praising God for the years of guidance, love, and promises fulfilled.

Jacob would soon be buried "with his fathers" in the cave of Machpelah (50:12-13; see also 23:19; 25:9).

See notes on 24:2 regarding the act of putting ones hand under the "thigh" while making an oath.

Gen 48:1 Some time later Joseph was told, "Your father is ill." So he took his two sons Manasseh and Ephraim along with him. 48:2 When Jacob was told, "Your son Joseph has come to you," Israel rallied his strength and sat up on the bed. 48:3 Jacob said to Joseph, "God Almighty appeared to me at Luz in the land of Canaan, and there he blessed me 48:4 and said to me, 'I am going to make you fruitful and will increase your numbers. I will make you a community of peoples, and I will give this land as an everlasting possession to your descendants after you.' 48:5 Now then, your two sons born to you in Egypt before I came to you here will be reckoned as mine; Ephraim and Manasseh will be mine, just as Reuben and Simeon are mine. 48:6 Any children born to you after them will be yours; in the territory they inherit they will be reckoned under the names of their brothers. 48:7 As I was returning from Paddan, to my sorrow Rachel died

in the land of Canaan while we were still on the way, a little distance from Ephrath. So I buried her there beside the road to Ephrath" (that is, Bethlehem).

Some time later Joseph heard that his father was about to die, so Joseph grabbed his sons and went to see Israel. When Joseph arrived, Jacob had to gather his strength to sit up in bed. Then Jacob began to reminisce about the days past and how "God Almighty" had appeared to him at Luz (same as Bethel). Actually, God had appeared to Jacob twice at Bethel (28:10-19; 35:6-13), but it was the second time at which God gave Jacob these promises.

Jacob now adopted Joseph's sons, making them his and, therefore, eligible for Jacob's blessing. Note that Jacob named Ephraim (the youngest) first. Normally the older sons were named first, just as he named Reuben before Simeon in verse five. However, Jacob already had in mind to bless Ephraim with the greater blessing (v. 20), no doubt due to prophetic insight. Now Joseph's first two sons would be equal with Jacob's first two sons. In fact, Joseph's sons would actually receive a greater blessing, because Reuben would lose his firstborn status as a result of lying with his father's concubine: Reuben "was the firstborn, but when he defiled his father's marriage bed, his rights as firstborn were given to the sons of Joseph son of Israel; so he could not be listed in the genealogical record in accordance with his birthright, and though Judah was the strongest of his brothers and a ruler came from him, the rights of the firstborn belonged to Joseph" (1 Chr 5:1-2; see also Gen 49:3-4). Since Joseph's two sons would receive the blessing and each one would become a separate tribe, Joseph received a double portion of the blessing, which usually went to the firstborn (Joseph received this instead of Rueben).

Any sons born to Joseph after Ephraim and Manasseh, however, would be considered Joseph's own, although the Scriptures do not record that Joseph had any more children. If Joseph did have any more sons, however, they would simply be included in the territory of their brothers, Ephraim and Manasseh.

We see then that Reuben's blessing went to Joseph, but Joseph's blessing was divided among his two sons (there would never be a "tribe of Joseph"). To keep only 12 tribes of Israel, rather than having 13, we see that Jacob's third son, Levi, would not receive any territory. We read in Joshua, "the sons of Joseph had become two tribes--Manasseh and Ephraim. The Levites received no share of the land but only towns to live in, with pasturelands for their flocks and herds" (Josh 14:4).

Finally, Jacob recalled when his favorite wife, Rachel had died (35:16-19) near Bethlehem. Ephrath was simply an older name for Bethlehem (see Ruth 1:2; Micah 5:2). Some believe that since this comment was made in connection with the taking of Ephraim and Manasseh as his own sons, Jacob may have been adopting them as son's that Rachel may have borne had she lived. However, there is no indication of this anywhere else in Scripture.

Gen 48:8 When Israel saw the sons of Joseph, he asked, "Who are these?" 48:9 "They are the sons God has given me here," Joseph said to his father. Then Israel said, "Bring them to me so I may bless them." 48:10

Now Israel's eyes were failing because of old age, and he could hardly see. So Joseph brought his sons close to him, and his father kissed them and embraced them. 48:11 Israel said to Joseph, "I never expected to see your face again, and now God has allowed me to see your children too." 48:12 Then Joseph removed them from Israel's knees and bowed down with his face to the ground. 48:13 And Joseph took both of them, Ephraim on his right toward Israel's left hand and Manasseh on his left toward Israel's right hand, and brought them close to him. 48:14 But Israel reached out his right hand and put it on Ephraim's head, though he was the younger, and crossing his arms, he put his left hand on Manasseh's head, even though Manasseh was the firstborn. 48:15 Then he blessed Joseph and said, "May the God before whom my fathers Abraham and Isaac walked, the God who has been my shepherd all my life to this day, 48:16 the Angel who has delivered me from all harm --may He bless these boys. May they be called by my name and the names of my fathers Abraham and Isaac, and may they increase greatly upon the earth."

When Israel's weak eyes could only see figures rather than clear faces, he asked Joseph who was with him. They were Joseph's sons, Ephraim and Manasseh, who by this time were both in their twenties, since Joseph had married at 30 and was now about 56. Israel requested that they be brought to him so that he could bless them; after all, they were now his own sons (v. 5). This situation may have reminded Jacob of when his father Isaac could not see and how he had tricked him out of his blessing. Also, Jacob would now give the blessing to the youngest son, just as Isaac had done; however, not by being deceived, but rather by faith.

Among the many things Israel was thankful for was the chance to see Joseph alive again. But not only did God bless him with this opportunity, but he now was able to see even his sons. Apparently, Ephraim and Manasseh had bowed down, because Joseph then took them away from his father's knees so that he himself could bow down before his father. (Even though he was ruler of Egypt he had great respect for his father.) At the same time Joseph brought his sons back to Israel so that the oldest (Manasseh) would be on Israel's right side to receive the greater blessing of the first born. It may have been that Joseph had removed them to put them back in this proper order. Meanwhile, while Joseph was still bowed down, Israel crossed his right hand over so that it was on Ephraim's head. Israel then began blessing Joseph. It doesn't appear that Joseph realized that Israel's arms were crossed until he lifted his head up from receiving his blessing (v. 17).

Joseph's blessing was being received indirectly through his sons, and it began with a statement showing who this blessing really was coming from; the Triune God. Here God is called by three names, showing the Trinity. First, God the Father as the one with whom his fathers had walked before. Second, the Shepherd who guided, being the Holy Spirit (Ps 23:1; Is 44:28). Third, the "Angel," who was Christ. Israel realized that God the father was the *Elohim* God of creation whom he and his fathers had reverently feared. This same *Elohim* was also the *Jehovah* God who had given them the everlasting covenant of grace (24:40) before whom they "walked" (17:1). Israel also recognized that the Spirit had been his Shepherd all his life, leading him to the proper pastures and making sure all his needs had been met (24:7). And finally, Israel recalled God the Son as the Angel (16:7-11; 18:33; 22:15; 32:29). The Angel is also He who "delivered" or "redeemed" Israel. The Hebrew word is *gaal* (best translated as redeemed), used for the first time here, and it is very significant that it is in connection with the Angel, who is the preincarnate Christ. Israel was asking the Triune God to bless these boys.

Part of the blessing that Israel was asking for these boys was that his name be transferred to them. Not that they would be called by this name, but rather that what the name of Israel stood for would be put upon Joseph's sons. Abraham, Isaac and Jacob had all been known for their great faith and personal walk with God. Israel was now asking that this same faith and conviction be given to these boys through the Triune God, especially the Holy Spirit. With these characteristics, it would only follow that God would make them increase greatly upon the earth.

Gen 48:17 When Joseph saw his father placing his right hand on Ephraim's head he was displeased; so he took hold of his father's hand to move it from Ephraim's head to Manasseh's head. 48:18 Joseph said to him, "No, my father, this one is the firstborn; put your right hand on his head." 48:19 But his father refused and said, "I know, my son, I know. He too will become a people, and he too will become great. Nevertheless, his younger brother will be greater than he, and his descendants will become a group of nations." 48:20 He blessed them that day and said, "In your name will Israel pronounce this blessing: 'May God make you like Ephraim and Manasseh.'" So he put Ephraim ahead of Manasseh. 48:21 Then Israel said to Joseph, "I am about to die, but God will be with you and take you back to the land of your fathers. 48:22 And to you, as one who is over your brothers, I give the ridge of land I took from the Amorites with my sword and my bow."

Joseph looked up and saw his father's arms were crossed so that his youngest son, Ephraim, was getting the greatest blessing. Being displeased, Joseph went to move his father's hand, but Israel quickly assured Joseph that this was God's plan. Indeed Manasseh would be a great nation, but Ephraim would be even greater. Ephraim would become the dominant tribe in Israel during the divided monarchy from 930-722 B.C. (1 Kings 12:19, 25). In fact, the name Ephraim would sometimes be used to refer to the entire northern kingdom of Israel (Is 7:2-9; Hos 9:13; 12:1, 8). This may be why it was said that he would be a "group of nations."

It is interesting to see how many times God had chosen the younger brother to be blessed. First it was Isaac instead of Ishmael. Then it was Jacob rather than Esau and Joseph rather than Reuben. Now it would be Ephraim instead of Manasseh. God was not concerned with age as much as the heart of these men.

Israel knew he was about to die, just as Joseph would know when his time was near (50:24). Israel also assured Joseph that he would again return to the promised land. This would be sooner than he realized, as he would go back to bury Israel there in 50:7. We do not know for sure where this ridge of land that Israel had conquered was. The Hebrew word for this phrase is *shekem*, the same as that of the place Shechem and, therefore, may refer to the land that Simeon and Levi had taken from the Shechemites in 34:25-29. However, in 33:19 we see that Jacob *purchased* land on which to pitch his tent from the sons of Hamor at Shechem. This does not necessarily exclude the part of Shechem which was taken by force by Simeon and Levi. In any case, there is no other reference to this land anywhere in Scripture, unless it was referred to in the New Testament where it says, "So he came to a town in Samaria called Sychar, near the plot of ground Jacob had given to his son Joseph" (John 4:5). If this was Shechem it would certainly be appropriate, since Joseph would later be buried there with his father (Josh 24:32).

Gen 49:1 Then Jacob called for his sons and said: "Gather around so I can tell you what will happen to you in days to come. 49:2 Assemble and listen, sons of Jacob; listen to your father Israel. 49:3 Reuben, you are my firstborn, my might, the first sign of my strength, excelling in honor, excelling in power. 49:4 Turbulent as the waters, you will no longer excel, for you went up onto your father's bed, onto my couch and defiled it.

Apparently when Jacob had called for Joseph to come (48:1) his brothers were called as well, since all of them seem to be present. This chapter is very important in that God's chosen people were now going to be blessed. Because of the 100% accuracy of these blessings, we know that Jacob was given this information prophetically and, therefore, these were technically not Israel's words, but God's.

Reuben was the firstborn and thus the first to be blessed, or perhaps in this situation, cursed, because Reuben had slept with his father's concubine (35:22), causing him to lose his birthright (1 Chron 5:1). Therefore, even though Reuben was once the first sign of Israel's future strength, being the first son, he would no longer excel as a leader. In later history, the tribe of Reuben would never produce any leaders for any nations. When going into the promised land, it was the tribe of Reuben who asked to receive land on the east side of the Jordan before crossing into the promised land. Reuben's tribe was also marked with indecisiveness, as they would fail to respond with help when needed in battle (Judges 5:15-16). This tribe would also be "turbulent," as they would also participate in the building of an unauthorized place of worship (Josh 22:10-34). Over all, Reuben's tribe would hardly ever be mentioned in Israel's history.

Gen 49:5 "Simeon and Levi are brothers-- their swords are weapons of violence. 49:6 Let me not enter their council, let me not join their assembly, for they have killed men in their anger and hamstrung oxen as they pleased. 49:7 Cursed be their anger, so fierce, and their fury, so cruel! I will scatter them in Jacob and disperse them in Israel.

Simeon and Levi were not just brothers physically, but they were also brothers of the same spirit. Both were close to one another and had been quick to anger. They had earlier joined together in the evil plot to kill the men of Shechem (Gen 34) and hamstring their oxen (cutting the back of the leg rendering them useless). Neither Israel himself, nor the name of Israel, should have any association with this kind of behavior, and thus neither one would become a tribe in Israel. Simeon and Levi were to be scattered and this "bad chemistry" that formed when the two were together would now be broken. In scattering them abroad, it was not only for the good of Israel, but for the good of Simeon and Levi as well, since they could no longer join together in evil. (Ephraim and Manasseh replaced Simeon and Levi).

This prophecy was fulfilled when most of Simeon's descendants were assimilated into the tribe of Judah (Joshua 19:1; 2 Chron 15:9). Others from Simeon were taken captive by the Edomites and Amalekites not even in the promised land (I Chron 4:39-43). When examining the population of Simeon we see that he would decline from 59,000 to 22,000 from the first to the second census.

Levi's descendants were scattered in a different way. They received no land inheritance as a tribe (Josh 14:4) but were appointed to live in 48 towns and the surrounding areas to serve as priests of those towns (Josh 21:1-3, 41; Num 35:2, 7). The job of being a priest was a difficult one with the daily sacrifices and the accountability made to God. It seems the Levites would prove more worthy than the Simeonites, since they would take a stand against idolatry and violence (Ex 32:26-28).

Gen 49:8 "Judah, your brothers will praise you; your hand will be on the neck of your enemies; your father's sons will bow down to you. 49:9 You are a lion's cub, O Judah; you return from the prey, my son. Like a lion he crouches and lies down, like a lioness--who dares to rouse him? 49:10 The scepter will not depart from Judah, nor the ruler's staff from between his feet, until he comes to whom it belongs and the obedience of the nations is his. 49:11 He will tether his donkey to a vine, his colt to the choicest branch; he will wash his garments in wine, his robes in the blood of grapes. 49:12 His eyes will be darker than wine, his teeth whiter than milk.

Judah was quite the contrast compared to Simeon and Levi. Judah's name even means "praise," and thus it is said that his brothers would "praise" him and bow down before him in respect. This was fulfilled, as Judah would become the leader among the tribes of Israel, but not until after the time of King David.

Judah was called a lion's cub. The analogy comparing Judah to a lion is used to point us to the Lion to come. Judah was in the line of Christ, of whom it was said, "See, the Lion of the tribe of Judah, the Root of David, has triumphed" (Rev 5:5). Along the same lines, we also see that Judah was told that the scepter and staff (symbols of kingly power and leadership) would not depart from his tribe until the One comes to whom this power belonged. We see a similar passage in Ezekiel which states, "It will not be restored until He comes *to whom it rightfully belongs*; to Him I will give it (Ezek 21:27). This person is none other than Christ the King. The Hebrew word for "he" in verse ten is "*shiyloh*." This word is closely related to *shalom,* meaning "peace," and refers to the One who will bring peace and rule the nations, the Messiah, the Christ, the Son of God. We read in Isaiah, "For to us a child is born, to us a son is given, and the government will be on His shoulders. And He will be called Wonderful Counselor, Mighty God, Everlasting Father, Prince of Peace" (Isa 9:6). Also in Micah: "But you, Bethlehem Ephrathah, though you are small among the clans of Judah, out of you will come for me One who will be ruler over Israel, whose origins are from of old, from ancient times. Therefore Israel will be abandoned until the time when she who is in labor gives birth and the rest of his brothers return to join the Israelites. He will stand and shepherd His flock in the strength of the LORD, in the majesty of the name of the LORD His God. And they will live securely, for then His greatness will reach to the ends of the earth. *And He will be their peace*" (Micah 5:2-5).

More evidence of this important prophecy is that once Judah became the leader of the tribes of Israel under King David, his scepter, or power, never left until Christ came. (Prior to David, Moses was from the tribe of Levi, Joshua from Ephraim, Gideon from Manasseh, Samson from Dan, Samuel from Ephraim and Saul from Benjamin). Even though the northern and southern kingdoms of Israel had divided and were taken into captivity, there was always someone from the tribe of Judah with that scepter. For example, while in Babylon, Daniel (from the nation of Judah) became third ruler in the land. Once Judah was delivered from this captivity, it was mostly men from the tribes of Judah, Benjamin and the Levite priests who ruled. Judah became synonymous with the people of Israel because the other 10 tribes had mostly been scattered by the Assyrians. (Assyria scattered the northern kingdom of Israel, and then about 170 years later Babylon took captive the southern kingdom of Judah.) Once back in Jerusalem, Judah remained powerful until Christ was crucified and rose from the dead. Then, in 70 A.D., the Romans came and took over the city and scattered the Jewish people. Since that time, all the genealogical records have been lost and the people of Israel have been scattered, knowing only that they are Jews but not knowing of which tribe. That is exactly what Jacob said: the scepter would not leave Judah until the Messiah came. Since this power was taken away in 70 A.D. that means that the Messiah had to have come prior to that time and, therefore, those Jews who are looking for the Messiah to come would do well to realize that He has come and He is risen!

Judah being represented as a lion also showed its leadership and strength. Just as no one dares disturb a resting lion in his den, no one would dare disturb the tribe of Judah.

Judah would also be blessed with productive land. Grape vines were a symbol of strength and pride in those times. Vines meant not only power but economic greatness as well. The fact that Judah would be able to tie his donkeys to the vines showed that there would be an abundance of wine and power. Normally a donkey would pull a vine out of the ground, but this would be no matter with such abundance. So many blessings would come to the tribe of

Judah that even their clothes could be washed in wine, showing it to be just as plentiful as water. Another possibility is that this foreshadowed Christ, as well: "Why are Your garments red, like those of one treading the winepress? I have trodden the winepress alone; from the nations no one was with Me. I trampled them in My anger and trod them down in My wrath; their blood spattered My garments, and I stained all My clothing. For the day of vengeance was in My heart, and the year of My redemption has come" (Isa 63:2-4).

Gen 49:13 "Zebulun will live by the seashore and become a haven for ships; his border will extend toward Sidon. 49:14 Issachar is a rawboned donkey lying down between two saddlebags. 49:15 When he sees how good is his resting place and how pleasant is his land, he will bend his shoulder to the burden and submit to forced labor."

Zebulun and Issachar were both sons of Leah, of whom we know very little. All that was said of Zebulun is that he would live by the sea and his territory would extend toward Sidon. When the promised land was divided, Zebulun was given land toward the sea, but its exact borders are unknown. It is generally believed that Zebulun was between the Sea of Galilee and the Mediterranean Sea, since we read in Deuteronomy 33:19 that "they will feast on the abundance of the seas, on the treasures hidden in the sand." We also know that much of Christ's ministry centered around this area (Matt 4:15-16).

Regarding Issachar, he was described as being strong but peaceful and lazy. Because he did nothing to protect his productive land, foreigners would invade and make him a slave.

Gen 49:16 "Dan will provide justice for his people as one of the tribes of Israel. 49:17 Dan will be a serpent by the roadside, a viper along the path, that bites the horse's heels so that its rider tumbles backward. 49:18 "I look for your deliverance, O LORD. 49:19 "Gad will be attacked by a band of raiders, but he will attack them at their heels. 49:20 "Asher's food will be rich; he will provide delicacies fit for a king. 49:21 "Naphtali is a doe set free that bears beautiful fawns.

Dan, Gad, Asher and Naphtali were all Jacob's sons through the maidservants of Rachel and Leah. Even though they were not children from his true wives, they were his sons and would, therefore, receive a blessing.

Dan was described as a serpent for two possible reasons. Some believe that it showed his strength despite his small appearance. Dan was the smallest of the tribes of Israel and lived along the coastline. Though small, they were sly enough to protect the northern boundaries of Israel. One example was Samson. Though only one man he was able to defeat the Philistines single-handedly (Judges 14-16).

Another explanation for being called the serpent (and most probable) is that this described Dan's wickedness. It would be the tribe of Dan that would introduce a regular practice of idolatry in Israel (Judges 18:30-31). The two golden calves were also set up by Jeroboam in Dan (1 Kings 12:28-30). It may be due to this continuous rebellion against God that the tribe of Dan was not included in Revelation 7:4-8. For they were warned, "Make sure there is no man or woman, clan or tribe among you today whose heart turns away from the LORD our God to go and worship the gods of those nations; make sure there is no root among you that produces such bitter poison. When such a person hears the words of this oath, he invokes a blessing on himself and therefore thinks, 'I will be safe, even though I persist in going my own way.' This will bring disaster on the watered land as well as the dry. The LORD will never be willing to forgive him; His wrath and zeal will burn against that man. All the curses written in this book will fall upon him, and the LORD will blot out his name from under heaven. The LORD will single him out from all the tribes of Israel for disaster, according to all the curses of the covenant written in this Book of the Law" (Deu 29:18-21).

Also significant is that in the middle of these prophetic words, Jacob cries out, "I look for Your deliverance O LORD." The word used for deliverance is *yeshuah* and is used here for the first time in Scripture. It means, appropriately, "salvation" or "Jesus." It is no accident that while talking about a serpent that goes after one's heal, Jacob brings up Christ. We saw way back in chapter three that God said, "I will put enmity between you and the woman, and between your offspring and hers; he will crush your head, and you will strike His heel" (Gen 3:15). Knowing Dan's upcoming idolatrous practices, Jacob could do nothing more than cry out for Christ's deliverance.

Gad will be located east of the Jordan river, bordering the Ammonites and the Moabites to the south and, therefore, would be very open to attacks (2 Kings 3:4; Josh 13:24-27). However, Gad (whose name means "troop") would be able to fight off their enemies and pursue them at their heels (see 1 Chron 5:18; 12:8).

Asher would receive land along the northern seacoast which was very fertile (Josh 19:24-30). However, perhaps due to this easy life, they would become a rather insignificant tribe.

Naphtali was a more isolated tribe in the hill country north of the Sea of Galilee (Josh 19:32-38). They would be more independent, and perhaps that is why they are said to be "set free." The phrase "that bears beautiful fawns" can also mean "utter beautiful words." "Words" may be a better translation, as we see that one of Naphtali's descendants is Barak who helped defeat the Canaanites (Judges 4:6, 15). Both Barak and Deborah would write a beautiful victory song about this battle in Judges 5:1-31.

Gen 49:22 "Joseph is a fruitful vine, a fruitful vine near a spring, whose branches climb over a wall. 49:23 With bitterness archers attacked him; they shot at him with hostility. 49:24 But his bow remained steady, his strong arms stayed limber, because of the hand of the Mighty One of Jacob, because of the Shepherd, the Rock of Israel, 49:25 because of your father's God, who helps you, because of the Almighty, who blesses you with blessings of the heavens above, blessings of the deep that lies below, blessings of the breast and womb. 49:26 Your father's blessings are greater than the blessings of the ancient mountains, than the bounty of the age-old

hills. Let all these rest on the head of Joseph, on the brow of the prince among his brothers.

Joseph would have tribes only through his sons Ephraim and Manasseh. They would be blessed abundantly so that they would flourish just as a well watered vine. Just as vines climb over walls into other territory, so would Ephraim's tribe expand its territories (Josh 17:14-18). Interestingly, the word "fruitful" was a play on the name Ephraim, which meant "twice fruitful." Though the younger brother, Ephraim would be greater than his older brother Manasseh (48:19-20). We read in Hosea, "Ephraim boasts, 'I am very rich; I have become wealthy. With all my wealth they will not find in me any iniquity or sin'" (Hosea 12:8).

In addition, it is said that even though nations would rise against them, the tribes of Joseph's sons would stand firm, not on their own strength, but on the strength of God. Ephraim would be very successful in battle (Josh 17:18) through God's help. Here God was called the, "Mighty One of Jacob," showing that Jacob's God was also Joseph's God, the one and only true God (see verse 25, as well). We see in Isaiah where God said, "I will make your oppressors eat their own flesh; they will be drunk on their own blood, as with wine. Then all mankind will know that I, the LORD, am your Savior, your Redeemer, *the Mighty One of Jacob*" (Isa 49:26). Earlier God was alluded to as the Shepherd in 48:15 (see notes there). Finally, God was also called the Rock of Israel. This same term was used here first but would be used many times to describe Israel's success (Deut 32:4, 15, 18, 30, 31; 2 Sam 23:3; Is 30:29; Ps 18:2, 31, 46; 19:14; 27:5; 28:1 etc.).

Ephraim would be blessed with the rain from above and the waters below. The breast and womb also indicated that they would be blessed by productive land and productive families as well.

Jacob realized that, even though Abraham and Isaac had been greatly blessed by God, he himself had been blessed even more because of his many sons who were becoming the Israelite nations (v. 26). All of these blessings, however, would rest on the head (superiority) of Joseph, who is here called the "prince among his brothers." Joseph had been separated for distinction. We see this fulfilled as many of the important leaders of Israel came from the tribes of Manasseh and Ephraim. Deborah, Joshua and Samuel were all from the tribe of Ephraim, while Gideon and Jephthah were from the tribe of Manasseh. Both tribes would be very strong and productive. When the kingdom of Israel divided, however, the northern kingdom became known as Israel, or Ephraim, and the southern kingdom as Judah. Therefore, we see that the two divisions of Israel became known by the names of the two most prominent children of Jacob, Joseph and Judah.

It is also important to note that, though Ephraim was blessed physically, it was Judah who was blessed spiritually and physically. We read of Ephraim, "When Ephraim spoke, men trembled; he was exalted in Israel. But he became guilty of Baal worship and died" (Hosea 13:1). That is why the northern kingdom of Israel, or Ephraim, was later scattered by the Assyrians and the tribe of Judah was only taken captive for a short time (70 years- Jer 25:11; Dan 9:2) by the Babylonians. God had spiritual plans for Judah, through whom the Messiah would come.

Gen 49:27 "Benjamin is a ravenous wolf; in the morning he devours the prey, in the evening he divides the plunder." 49:28 All these are the twelve tribes of Israel, and this is what their father said to them when he blessed them, giving each the blessing appropriate to him.

Benjamin, even though he was the favored son of Jacob, received a blessing of questionable worth. Again, this shows that Jacob was not spouting words that he would have liked to see fulfilled; rather, these were prophetic words coming from God.

Benjamin would be a ravenous wolf. This tribe was indeed successful in battle, but sometimes at the cost of being cruel and vicious. In fact, one incident almost cost the tribe of Benjamin its identity as a tribe of Israel (Judges 19-21; especially 20). We see other examples of this violent behavior from Ehud (Judges 3:12-30) and from Saul (I Sam 11-15).

With Benjamin the blessings of the twelve tribes of Israel were completed and now these brothers would have this "food for thought" to reflect on for years to come as these prophecies were fulfilled one by one. Each blessing was appropriate for the behavior and the tendencies of each tribe. Some of these words seemed to be more warnings than blessings, giving each brother an opportunity to examine their lives and hearts.

Gen 49:29 Then he gave them these instructions: "I am about to be gathered to my people. Bury me with my fathers in the cave in the field of Ephron the Hittite, 49:30 the cave in the field of Machpelah, near Mamre in Canaan, which Abraham bought as a burial place from Ephron the Hittite, along with the field. 49:31 There Abraham and his wife Sarah were buried, there Isaac and his wife Rebekah were buried, and there I buried Leah. 49:32 The field and the cave in it were bought from the Hittites." 49:33 When Jacob had finished giving instructions to his sons, he drew his feet up into the bed, breathed his last and was gathered to his people.

When the blessings were over, Jacob concluded by requesting that he be buried with his fathers (Abraham and Isaac) in the cave at Machpelah. Rebekah and Leah were buried there, as well; thus, Jacob would not be buried with his beloved Rachel (see 35:16-20). This request again gives testimony of the faith that these patriarchs had in the promises of God. They knew that one day the land of Canaan would be theirs forever. As mentioned earlier, since this land has never truly become Israel's, there will no doubt be a future fulfillment of this promise when the new heaven and the new earth will be created (2 Peter 3:13; Rev 21:1). For further explanation dealing with the cave at Machpelah, see notes on Genesis 23:9.

At this request, Jacob breathed his last and his soul departed to be gathered with his people (all the faithful believers of God and His promises).

The next chapter will show his burial going into great detail regarding his funeral. In fact, it will be the most descriptive of all the burials in Scripture.

Gen 50:1 Joseph threw himself upon his father and wept over him and kissed him. 50:2 Then Joseph directed the physicians in his service to embalm his father Israel. So the physicians embalmed him, 50:3 taking a full forty days, for that was the time required for embalming. And the Egyptians mourned for him seventy days. 50:4 When the days of mourning had passed, Joseph said to Pharaoh's court, "If I have found favor in your eyes, speak to Pharaoh for me. Tell him, 50:5 'My father made me swear an oath and said, "I am about to die; bury me in the tomb I dug for myself in the land of Canaan." Now let me go up and bury my father; then I will return.'" 50:6 Pharaoh said, "Go up and bury your father, as he made you swear to do."

When Joseph saw his father had died, he threw himself over his father and wept. No doubt Joseph knew his father had gone to a better, joyful place, but for those of us left behind death is often a sad occasion. However, we would do well to remember these words: "Brothers, we do not want you to be ignorant about those who fall asleep, or to grieve like the rest of men, who have no hope. We believe that Jesus died and rose again and so we believe that God will bring with Jesus those who have fallen asleep in Him" (1 Th 4:13).

Earlier God had promised Jacob that Joseph would be the one who would close his eyes after he died (Gen 46:4), and we now see that promise fulfilled.

It was common for Egyptians to be embalmed and mummified, especially the wealthier people. Since Joseph was still the second most powerful man in Egypt, not to mention the fact that Jacob was highly esteemed by Pharaoh (see notes on 47:7), it is most probable that Jacob was what we call mummified. The embalming process took about 40 days and the mourning an additional 30 days. It was apparently customary in Egypt to have a 70 day mourning period, but this was recognized even more at the death of important individuals. Therefore, we again see how God had made both Joseph and Jacob highly esteemed in Egypt.

When the 70 days of mourning were over, Joseph went to the officers of Pharaoh's court and, out of respect, first asked them for their blessing to bury his father in the land of Canaan. Joseph had to be sure not to insult the Egyptian people by having his father buried outside of Egypt.

Joseph went about this request carefully, pointing out that he would indeed return after burying his father. This was important, because the Israelites had become an important part of the Egyptian economy. Joseph also appealed to the Egyptian sense of an afterlife by stating that his father had made him swear an oath. To the Egyptians it would have been very important to make sure this oath was carried out to ensure a safe and happy journey into the afterlife.

Pharaoh did not even have to think about Joseph's request, and he immediately gave permission for this funeral to be held outside of Egypt. In fact, not only did Pharaoh give permission, he also made it an official funeral for one who was highly honored, as we see in the following verses.

Gen 50:7 So Joseph went up to bury his father. All Pharaoh's officials accompanied him--the dignitaries of his court and all the dignitaries of Egypt-- 50:8 besides all the members of Joseph's household and his brothers and those belonging to his father's household. Only their children and their flocks and herds were left in Goshen. 50:9 Chariots and horsemen also went up with him. It was a very large company. 50:10 When they reached the threshing floor of Atad, near the Jordan, they lamented loudly and bitterly; and there Joseph observed a seven-day period of mourning for his father. 50:11 When the Canaanites who lived there saw the mourning at the threshing floor of Atad, they said, "The Egyptians are holding a solemn ceremony of mourning." That is why that place near the Jordan is called Abel Mizraim. 50:12 So Jacob's sons did as he had commanded them: 50:13 They carried him to the land of Canaan and buried him in the cave in the field of Machpelah, near Mamre, which Abraham had bought as a burial place from Ephron the Hittite, along with the field. 50:14 After burying his father, Joseph returned to Egypt, together with his brothers and all the others who had gone with him to bury his father.

The funeral procession then began. Not only did Jacob's family go along but also all of Pharaoh's officials and dignitaries. The only Israelite people left behind were the young children and their flocks. This would indeed show that Joseph had every intention of returning to Egypt when the funeral was over.

This great caravan went all the way to the "threshing floor of Atad" on the east side of the Jordan. Here they all mourned for seven days. It was such an impressive sight that all the Canaanites who lived in this region heard and knew about this great event. In fact, they even renamed that place "Abel Mizraim," meaning "mourning of the Egyptians."

It seems that after the seven days of mourning were over, only Jacob's sons crossed the Jordan and continued to the cave at Machpelah to bury their father. When they were finished they all went back to Egypt, where they would remain for just over 400 years. It is very possible that they realized this would be their home for some time, as they reflected on the earlier promises given to Abraham when God had said, "Know for certain that your descendants will be strangers in a country not their own, and they will be enslaved and mistreated four hundred years. But I will punish the nation they serve as slaves, and afterward they will come out with great possessions. You, however, will go to your fathers in peace and be buried at a good old age. In the fourth generation your descendants will come back here, for the sin of the Ammorites has not yet reached its full measure" (Gen 15:13-16).

Gen 50:15 When Joseph's brothers saw that their father was dead, they said, "What if Joseph holds a grudge against us and pays us back for

all the wrongs we did to him?" 50:16 So they sent word to Joseph, saying, "Your father left these instructions before he died: 50:17 'This is what you are to say to Joseph: I ask you to forgive your brothers the sins and the wrongs they committed in treating you so badly.' Now please forgive the sins of the servants of the God of your father." When their message came to him, Joseph wept. 50:18 His brothers then came and threw themselves down before him. "We are your slaves," they said. 50:19 But Joseph said to them, "Don't be afraid. Am I in the place of God? 50:20 You intended to harm me, but God intended it for good to accomplish what is now being done, the saving of many lives. 50:21 So then, don't be afraid. I will provide for you and your children." And he reassured them and spoke kindly to them.

Even though Joseph had earlier assured his brothers that the past events had been forgiven and, in fact, were not really their fault (Gen 45:4-11), they now feared that Joseph would try to take revenge for them selling him into Egypt. They thought now that their father was gone, Joseph would not need to worry about "sending his father to the grave" by getting revenge. Apparently, they did not understand the significance and accuracy of the blessings Jacob had earlier given them.

In any case, the ten brothers sent word to Joseph saying that Jacob had urged Joseph to forgive them for what they had done. This was obviously a made-up story, since Jacob knew that Joseph had already been at ease with the entire situation. In this message, the brothers for the first time (as far as Scripture claims), confessed to Joseph their sin and guilt and were now looking for forgiveness.

When Joseph heard this message he wept, not only because of this confession, but probably also because his brothers were still showing lack of faith and trust not only in God, but in Joseph. What had they been thinking of him all these years? Had they not seen his love for them?

Soon after, the brothers threw themselves before Joseph, offering to be slaves in restitution. This was a final fulfillment of Joseph's dream when he was younger (Gen 37:7-9). It was honorable that the brothers were now sincerely willing to pay for their crime, but sad that this had not come out sooner.

Joseph, however, reminded his brothers that this was all part of God's plan and, therefore, they need not be afraid. Joseph held no grudge and loved them and their families deeply.

Gen 50:22 Joseph stayed in Egypt, along with all his father's family. He lived a hundred and ten years 50:23 and saw the third generation of Ephraim's children. Also the children of Makir son of Manasseh were placed at birth on Joseph's knees. 50:24 Then Joseph said to his brothers, "I am about to die. But God will surely come to your aid and take you up out of this land to the land he promised on oath to Abraham, Isaac and Jacob." 50:25 And Joseph made the sons of Israel swear an oath and said, "God will surely come to your aid, and then you must carry my bones up from this place." 50:26 So Joseph died at the age

of a hundred and ten. And after they embalmed him, he was placed in a coffin in Egypt.

Joseph lived in Egypt the rest of his life, dying at 110 years of age. Since he was only 56 when Jacob died (Gen 41:46, 53; 45:6; 47:28), he lived another 54 years. We have now seen the life-span decrease from Abraham (175) to Isaac (180), to Jacob (147) to Joseph (110). This decline is attributed to the difference in the post-Flood environment. For an explanation, see the book Doubts About Creation? Not After This!

Joseph lived long enough to see the third generation of his son Ephraim's children and, therefore, could see that God's promise of many descendants was being fulfilled (48:19-20). He also saw the children (Gilead - Numbers 26:29) of his grandson Makir. Manasseh had two children, Makir and Asriel (Numb 26:29-31) but only Makir's children are said to have been see by Joseph. The names Makir and Manasseh would later be used interchangeably (Judges 5:14).

When Joseph saw his death was near, he called his brothers, who were still living, to see him. In a similar conversation we saw with Jacob, Joseph asked his brothers to make sure that his body would be buried in the promised land when the LORD delivered them out of Egypt. This oath would not be fulfilled for another 400 years, but it would come about (Exod 13:19, Josh 24:32). In any case, this promise was asked out of faith, as we read, "By faith Joseph, when his end was near, spoke about the exodus of the Israelites from Egypt and gave instructions about his bones" (Heb 11:22).

When Joseph died he, like his father, was embalmed and probably mummified before being placed in a coffin where his body would remain until God delivered his descendants out of Egypt. It is interesting that Joseph died at 110, because according to Egyptian records this was an ideal life-span and, therefore, Joseph's life may have been viewed as a Divine blessing.

With Joseph's death, we are left with the appropriate time and setting for the Exodus. Though nothing is said about the next 400 years other than the Israelites were enslaved, God continued to bring forth His plans by providing the next important individual to accomplish God's purpose - Moses. It is at this point that the book of Exodus will pick up.

Genesis closes leaving us with a firm foundation of history, both Biblical and secular. With this root of understanding, church doctrine and Christian living are made clear so that our hope and faith in Christ may not only stand, but also flourish. May the peace of God, which indeed surpasses ALL understanding, keep your hearts and your minds in Christ Jesus, as you, the salt of the earth, make others thirst for Him.

APPENDIX

EVENT	YEARS AFTER CREATION
Creation-	0
Birth of Seth-	130
Death of Adam-	930
Enoch taken to heaven-	987
Birth of Noah-	1056
Birth of Japeth-	1556
Death of Methuselah-	1656
FLOOD-	1656
Birth of Arphaxad-	1660
Babel dispersion-	1825
Birth of Abraham-	1950
Noah dies-	2006
Abraham goes to Canaan-	2025
Birth of Ishmael-	2035
Birth of Isaac-	2050
Sarah dies-	2087
Isaac & Rebekah marry-	2090
Birth of Jacob & Esau-	2110
Abraham dies-	2125
Esau marries-	2150
Shem dies-	2160
Jacob flees from Esau-	2186
Eber dies-	2189
Jacob marries Rachel & Leah-	2193
Birth of Reuben-	2193
Birth of Judah-	2196
Birth of Joseph-	2200
Jacob returns to Canaan-	2206
Levi & Simeon destroy Shechem-	2211
Birth of Benjamin (Rachel dies)-	2211
Joseph sold by brothers-	2217
Joseph is 2nd power in Egypt-	2230
Birth of Perez-	2237
Israel goes to Egypt-	2240
Jacob dies-	2257
Joseph dies-	2310

The following time line will show you proof positive how Scripture gives dates. There can be no question that the Flood took place 1656 years after Creation. The dates in [ ] show the total time passed since Creation. The dates underneath each [ ] show how much time passes between each date above and below it, along with the Scripture verse to support it. One question that could arise is why there are two years counted for the Flood instead of only one? The answer is in how dates were counted. For example, if Noah's Flood began in February of 1998 and ended in February of 1999, the total time is one year but counting by years it took place during part of 1998 and part of 1999. Therefore, one year after the Flood would be the year 2000. Even though only two years have passed since the Flood began, three years are counted: 1998, 1999, and 2000.

1)	[0] 130	Creation Gen 5:3	13)	[1660] 35	Arphaxad is Born Gen 11:12
2)	[130] 105	Seth Born Gen 5:6	14)	[1695] 30	Sala is Born Gen 11:14
3)	[235] 90	Enosh Born Gen 5:9	15)	[1725] 34	Heber is Born Gen 11:16
4)	[325] 70	Kenan Born Gen 5:12	16)	[1759] 30	Peleg is Born Gen 11:18
5)	[395] 65	Mahalalel Born Gen 5:15	17)	[1789] 32	Reu is Born Gen 11:20
6)	[460] 162	Jared Born Gen 5:18	18)	[1821] 30	Serug is Born Gen 11:22
7)	[622] 65	Enoch Born Gen 5:21	19)	[1851] 29	Nahor is Born Gen 11:24
8)	[687] 187	Methusaleh Born Gen 5:25	20)	[1880] 70	Terah is Born Gen 11:26
9)	[874] 182	Lamech Born Gen 5:28	21)	[1950] 100	Abram is Born Gen 21:5
10)	[1056] 600	Noah Born Gen 7:11	22)	[2050] 60	Isaac is Born Gen 25:26
11)	[1656] 2	Flood Starts Gen 11:10	23)	[2110] 130	Jacob is Born Gen 47:9 Egypt
12)	[1658] 2	Flood is Over Gen 11:10	24)	[2240] 71	Joseph is 39 Gen 41:46, 45:6 Gen 50:26
			25)	[2311]	Joseph dies at 110, 71 years after Jacob entered Egypt.

—A—

Abimelech, 102, 103, 104, 108, 109, 126, 127, 128, 129, 197
Acts, 34, 46, 56, 58, 60, 67, 75, 87, 114, 136, 156, 182, 188, 190, 191, 195, 208, 214
Adam, 3, 4, 7, 9, 15, 16, 17, 18, 19, 20, 23, 24, 25, 27, 28, 29, 30, 31, 32, 33, 34, 35, 36, 37, 39, 46, 55, 58, 60, 61, 62, 72, 80, 85, 235, 236
Amos, 66, 109, 124, 171, 190, 196
Angel, 7, 16, 20, 22, 23, 29, 38, 39, 77, 93, 94, 96, 97, 98, 99, 100, 101, 102, 107, 112, 135, 136, 152, 156, 203, 222
Ararat, 50, 53, 54, 70
Archaeology, 3
Ark, 50

—B—

Baal, 171, 179, 229
Babylon, 65, 66, 70, 71, 81, 226
Baptism, 43, 48, 87, 91
Beersheba, 105, 107, 109, 112, 113, 128, 129, 135, 211, 212
Benjamin, 166, 167, 172, 194, 195, 196, 197, 198, 199, 200, 201, 202, 203, 204, 205, 206, 207, 209, 210, 214, 226, 230, 235
Bethel, 76, 77, 79, 135, 136, 146, 151, 155, 159, 163, 164, 165, 166, 211, 221
Bethlehem, 10, 16, 124, 166, 167, 221, 226
Big Bang, 14
Birthright, 124, 125, 126, 130, 133, 145, 167, 174, 221, 224
Blood, 10, 12, 18, 19, 27, 28, 29, 31, 45, 56, 84, 86, 87, 91, 138, 155, 174, 175, 176, 196, 207, 225, 227, 229

—C—

Cain, 29, 30, 31, 32, 33, 46
Christ, 50

—D—

Chronicles, 35, 51, 64, 66, 73, 111, 136, 167, 170, 171, 174, 177, 213, 224, 225, 228
Circumcision, 58, 90, 91, 116, 124
Colossians, 6, 27, 39, 91, 164
Corinthians, 8, 9, 16, 22, 24, 34, 38, 39, 41, 54, 99, 106, 116, 117, 136, 137, 189
Curse, 4, 14, 16, 17, 21, 25, 26, 27, 28, 29, 30, 31, 34, 37, 54, 55, 61, 62, 75, 76, 102, 130, 132, 133, 182

Dan, 70, 82, 109, 141, 167, 172, 185, 189, 192, 214, 226, 227, 229
Day, 6, 7, 8, 9, 10, 11, 12, 13, 14, 15, 16, 18, 20, 23, 24, 25, 29, 33, 38, 40, 41, 42, 43, 44, 46, 47, 48, 49, 50, 51, 52, 53, 54, 55, 59, 60, 66, 68, 69, 70, 72, 73, 85, 87, 88, 92, 95, 101, 105, 109, 110, 116, 119, 123, 125, 126, 127, 129, 133, 139, 144, 147, 148, 149, 155, 156, 158, 163, 166, 171, 173, 176, 182, 183, 185, 186, 187, 196, 208, 219, 222, 223, 227, 230, 231, 232
Dead Sea, 80, 81, 82, 100, 102, 133, 155, 169
Deborah, 163, 164, 165, 228, 229
Deuteronomy, 5, 36, 82, 122, 125, 137, 169, 171, 173, 177, 180, 204, 214, 217, 227, 229
Dinah, 142, 159, 160, 161, 162, 176, 213
Dinosaurs, 11, 17, 44, 70
Divination, 143, 144, 147, 188, 204, 205, 206
Divorce, 3, 4, 19, 21
Dream, 85, 102, 103, 135, 136, 145, 146, 147, 148, 155, 159, 163, 166, 172, 173, 174, 185, 186, 187, 188, 189, 190, 191, 194, 195, 203, 211, 233

—E—

Ecclesiastes, 11, 14, 125, 188
Eden, 16, 17, 20, 28, 29, 31, 79
Egyptology, 187
Electromagnetic, 28, 73

Elijah, 36, 46
Enoch, 32, 35, 36, 43, 235, 236
Ephesians, 19, 22, 26, 41, 43, 94, 135, 165, 207, 208
Ephraim, 159, 193, 194, 214, 220, 221, 222, 223, 225, 226, 229, 233
Ephrath, 166, 221
Esau, 3, 122, 123, 124, 125, 126, 129, 130, 131, 132, 133, 134, 135, 140, 145, 147, 152, 153, 154, 155, 157, 158, 163, 165, 167, 168, 169, 170, 171, 172, 180, 211, 223, 235
Evolution, 20, 25
Exodus, 14, 15, 29, 33, 45, 46, 50, 51, 58, 85, 87, 91, 97, 124, 130, 136, 152, 156, 159, 169, 171, 175, 180, 181, 188, 203, 204, 212, 213, 217, 220, 225, 234
Ezekiel, 8, 21, 29, 60, 63, 122, 188, 219, 226

—F—

Famine, 77, 126, 163, 184, 189, 190, 191, 193, 194, 196, 199, 200, 201, 208, 209, 215, 217, 218
Firmament, 7, 8, 10, 11, 15, 32, 46, 47, 48, 73
Freud, Sigmund, 39

—G—

Galatians, 19, 27, 55, 76, 80, 85, 86, 105, 106, 107, 108, 111, 112, 191, 197, 207
Genesis, 50, 69
Gentile, 69
Gerizim, 159
Giants, 39, 40, 81, 82
Gilead, 109, 146, 147, 148, 175, 234
Greek, 5, 38, 66, 70, 73, 124
    kataklusmos, 45

—H—

Hagar, 88, 89, 105, 107, 108, 122
Ham, 37, 38, 40, 43, 47, 60, 61, 62, 63, 64, 65, 66, 67, 73, 78, 81
Hamor, 114, 159, 160, 161, 162, 224
Haran, 74, 75, 76, 112, 133, 134, 135, 137, 211

Hebrew, 3, 5, 7, 15, 17, 18, 33, 38, 50, 61, 67, 69, 70, 75, 82, 83, 125, 130, 132, 135, 137, 143, 147, 151, 158, 165, 170, 172, 176, 179, 182, 183, 187, 188, 192, 201, 207, 211, 213, 223, 224, 226
    asaph, 12
    bara, 5, 11, 12
    El Shaddai, 90, 165, 201
    elohiym, 5, 38
    gabia, 204
    nephesh, 11, 12, 16, 56
    qedeshah, 179
    rachaph, 5
    ragaz, 210
    shalom, 226
    shamayim, 8
    towledah, 3
    yequwm, 50
    yeshuah, 228
Hebrews, 6, 11, 27, 28, 29, 30, 37, 43, 45, 56, 58, 76, 77, 83, 111, 112, 125, 130, 132, 133, 181, 201, 207, 216, 219, 220, 234
Hebron, 80, 81, 113, 115, 163, 167, 172, 173, 174, 198, 211
Homosexuality, 21, 41, 97
Hosea, 13, 89, 124, 155, 188, 223, 229
Hyksos, 181, 182

—I—

Ice age, 69
Idumeans, 124
Ishmael, 3, 89, 90, 91, 92, 106, 107, 108, 122, 134, 168, 169, 175, 223, 235

—J—

James, 40, 86, 99, 124, 130, 143, 145, 207
Japheth, 37, 38, 40, 43, 47, 60, 62, 63, 64, 67, 73
Jehovah, 15, 108, 137, 151, 154, 190, 222
Jeremiah, 41, 66, 102, 175, 204
Jerusalem, 14, 65, 66, 77, 83, 108, 136, 167, 177, 208, 226
Jesus, 50
    Christ, 4, 5, 6, 8, 16, 19, 21, 22, 23, 24, 25, 26, 27, 28, 30, 31, 34, 35,

36, 37, 38, 41, 42, 43, 44, 45, 52, 55, 56, 59, 62, 63, 67, 68, 76, 77, 80, 83, 84, 85, 86, 91, 99, 102, 106, 107, 111, 112, 113, 116, 117, 119, 121, 122, 126, 132, 135, 137, 155, 156, 166, 179, 181, 187, 191, 199, 200, 207, 213, 222, 223, 225, 226, 227, 228

Lamb, 6, 28, 29, 55, 111, 116, 164

Son, 6, 12, 22, 40, 58, 83, 111, 112, 135, 192, 223, 226

Spirit, 5, 6, 11, 12, 23, 38, 40, 42, 43, 50, 91, 106, 107, 116, 117, 119, 222, 223

Trinity, 5, 6, 72, 222

Word, 5, 6, 12, 21, 22, 28, 40, 41, 44, 56, 85

Job, 6, 7, 11, 38, 43, 48, 68, 69, 89, 125, 136, 169, 176, 198, 201

John, 5, 6, 12, 17, 19, 21, 22, 23, 24, 26, 29, 30, 31, 37, 42, 44, 70, 77, 85, 111, 124, 135, 159, 173, 174, 175, 201, 207, 224

Josephus, 8, 38, 63, 64, 65, 68

Joshua, 51, 62, 66, 75, 88, 109, 113, 114, 119, 130, 134, 151, 158, 159, 162, 164, 177, 178, 221, 224, 225, 226, 228, 229, 234

Jude, 4, 36

Judges, 62, 66, 82, 109, 121, 158, 175, 196, 224, 227, 228, 230, 234

Jung, Carl, 39

—K—

Kings, 8, 36, 46, 62, 69, 87, 88, 98, 109, 134, 136, 152, 156, 196, 200, 223, 227, 228

—L—

Laban, 118, 119, 120, 123, 133, 134, 137, 138, 139, 143, 144, 145, 146, 147, 148, 149, 150, 151, 152, 153, 154, 155, 163, 182, 197, 205, 211, 214

Lamech, 32, 33, 36, 37, 58, 236

Leah, 138, 139, 140, 141, 142, 145, 146, 148, 151, 157, 159, 163, 167, 173, 213, 214, 227, 230, 235

Leviticus, 12, 29, 56, 72, 97, 137, 144, 175, 180, 204

Lot, 40, 74, 75, 76, 79, 80, 81, 82, 84, 95, 96, 97, 98, 99, 100, 101, 102

Luke, 3, 10, 21, 23, 27, 35, 39, 40, 41, 43, 45, 68, 73, 101, 111, 120, 123, 136, 156, 187, 200

Luther, 17, 30

—M—

Machpelah, 114, 115, 122, 134, 168, 212, 220, 230, 232

Malachi, 13, 19, 30, 124, 140, 171

Manasseh, 193, 194, 214, 220, 221, 222, 223, 225, 226, 229, 233, 234

Matthew, 3, 4, 8, 10, 16, 19, 21, 22, 30, 31, 33, 34, 35, 36, 39, 41, 42, 45, 46, 54, 59, 75, 76, 97, 111, 112, 120, 175, 177, 181, 187, 200, 201, 207, 227

Matthew,, 75, 76

Melchizedek, 58, 83, 84, 216

Messiah, 33, 35, 59, 68, 91, 111, 166, 177, 207, 226, 230

Moon, 4, 6, 8, 9, 10, 173

Morris, 32, 50, 62, 63, 64, 67, 73, 90, 114

Morris, Henry, 50

Moses, 3, 15, 34, 36, 45, 46, 70, 85, 87, 91, 166, 171, 187, 188, 207, 226, 234

—N—

Nehemiah, 66, 109

Nile, 187, 188, 189, 190, 209, 217

Nisan, 51, 52

Noah, 51, 68

Numbers, 21, 46, 51, 70, 82, 124, 137, 156, 162, 171, 187, 203, 207, 217, 225
40, 11, 46, 48, 49, 50, 51, 53, 82, 87, 95, 116, 119, 123, 129, 130, 133, 144, 147, 149, 171, 175, 184, 185, 186, 188, 191, 203, 223, 231
70, 35, 70, 74, 78, 124, 214, 219, 226, 229, 231

—P—

Pangea
days of Peleg?, 68

Passover, 50, 51, 52, 97, 111
Peleg, 68, 69, 73, 74, 236
Perez, 180, 213, 235
Peter, 23, 26, 28, 31, 32, 43, 44, 45, 48, 49, 54, 59, 76, 80, 95, 97, 101, 113, 156, 184, 201, 207
Philippians, 34, 59, 141, 192, 194
Potiphar, 176, 181, 182, 183, 184, 188
Proverbs, 5, 41, 125, 183, 184, 187, 219
Psalms, 6, 8, 27, 29, 39, 49, 72, 83, 85, 123, 125, 175, 186, 189, 196, 201, 203, 217, 222, 229

—R—

Rainbow, 59, 60
Rameses, 217
Reuben, 139, 140, 141, 142, 162, 166, 167, 172, 174, 175, 176, 196, 197, 199, 200, 213, 220, 221, 223, 224, 235
Revelation, 4, 6, 7, 10, 14, 16, 17, 20, 21, 24, 28, 29, 36, 42, 43, 54, 55, 59, 60, 71, 80, 86, 108, 116, 117, 120, 156, 164, 173, 177, 201, 207, 225, 228, 230
Romans, 14, 18, 20, 21, 24, 26, 27, 30, 34, 40, 42, 43, 54, 55, 56, 58, 59, 75, 76, 80, 81, 84, 86, 91, 97, 98, 105, 106, 107, 108, 113, 116, 123, 126, 131, 133, 137, 162, 166, 194, 198, 201

—S—

Samuel, 40, 46, 109, 124, 166, 171, 184, 187, 189, 196, 200, 207, 229, 230
Seir, 81, 122, 152, 158, 168, 169, 170
Seth, 30, 32, 33, 34, 35, 36, 37, 123, 235, 236

Shechem, 76, 77, 114, 159, 160, 161, 162, 163, 164, 165, 173, 174, 211, 224, 225, 235
Shem, 3, 36, 37, 38, 40, 43, 47, 60, 62, 63, 67, 68, 69, 70, 73, 83, 235, 236
Simeon, 77, 139, 140, 162, 163, 167, 172, 174, 196, 197, 198, 199, 202, 204, 213, 220, 221, 224, 225, 235
Sinai, 46, 106, 108
Sodom, 40, 41, 66, 79, 80, 81, 82, 83, 84, 93, 94, 95, 96, 97, 99, 100, 101, 102, 104, 144
Stars, 7, 8, 9, 10, 20, 22, 28, 38, 71, 85, 86, 111, 112, 126, 173
Stephen, 14, 75, 114, 182, 190, 195, 208, 214
Sun, 6, 8, 9, 10, 14, 54, 69, 86, 87, 98, 99, 135, 137, 156, 173, 193

—T—

Tamar, 81, 177, 178, 179, 180, 181
Terah, 3, 73, 74, 75, 235, 236
Thermodynamics, 28
Thessalonians, 31, 41, 43, 121, 136, 156
Timothy, 24, 25, 26, 27, 58, 97, 135, 174
Titus, 27
Tower of Babel, 68, 69
    possible cause plate tectonics, 69
Tree of Life, 4, 14, 16, 28, 29

—U—

Ussher, 35

—V—

Von Fange, Erich, 68, 69

—Z—

Zecheriah, 12, 208

Bibliography

Morris, Henry M.., The Genesis Record, Baker Book House: Grand Rapids, 1993.

Von Fange, Erich A., Noah to Abram: The Turbulent years, Living Word Services, Syracuse, 1994.

World Book Encyclopedia, Vol. 18, p. 207, 1968.

Josephus: Complete Works, Kregal Publications, Grand Rapids, Michigan, 'Antiquities of the Jews'.